The Cinematic Bodies of Eastern Europe and Russia

Between Pain and Pleasure

Edited by Ewa Mazierska, Matilda Mroz and Elżbieta Ostrowska

EDINBURGH
University Press

Edinburgh University Press is one of the leading university presses in the UK. We publish academic books and journals in our selected subject areas across the humanities and social sciences, combining cutting-edge scholarship with high editorial and production values to produce academic works of lasting importance. For more information visit our website: edinburghuniversitypress.com

© editorial matter and organisation Ewa Mazierska, Matilda Mroz and Elżbieta Ostrowska, 2016
© the chapters their several authors, 2016

Edinburgh University Press Ltd
The Tun – Holyrood Road
12 (2f) Jackson's Entry
Edinburgh EH8 8PJ

Typeset in 11/13 Monotype Ehrhardt by
Servis Filmsetting Ltd, Stockport, Cheshire

A CIP record for this book is available from the British Library

ISBN 978 1 4744 0514 0 (hardback)
ISBN 978 1 4744 0515 7 (webready PDF)
ISBN 978 1 4744 0516 4 (epub)

The right of the contributors to be identified as authors of this work has been asserted in accordance with the Copyright, Designs and Patents Act 1988 and the Copyright and Related Rights Regulations 2003 (SI No. 2498).

Contents

List of Figures   v
Notes on the Contributors   vi

Introduction: Shaping the Cinematic Bodies of Eastern
Europe and Russia   1
Ewa Mazierska, Matilda Mroz and Elżbieta Ostrowska

Part I   Wounds and Traumas

1. 'What Does Poland Want from Me?' Male Hysteria in Andrzej
   Wajda's War Trilogy   31
   Elżbieta Ostrowska
2. Alcoholism and the Doctor in Béla Tarr's *Sátántangó*   53
   Calum Watt
3. Playing Dead: Pictorial Figurations of Melancholia in
   Contemporary Hungarian Cinema   67
   Hajnal Király
4. The Body Breached: Post-Soviet Masculinity on Screen   89
   Helena Goscilo

Part II   Transgressions and Pleasures

5. Borowczyk as Pornographer   113
   Ewa Mazierska
6. Queering Masculinity in Yugoslav Socialist Realist Films   132
   Nebojša Jovanović
7. Geographies of Carnality: Slippery Sexuality in Wiktor
   Grodecki's Gay Hustler Trilogy   146
   Bruce Williams

8 A Mass Doubling of Heroes: Post-human Objects of Queer
   Desire in Vladimir Sorokin and Ilya Khrzhanovsky's *4*   166
   Alexandar Mihailovic

Part III Carnal Histories
9 The Touch of History: A Phenomenological Approach to 1960s
   Czech Cinema   187
   David Sorfa
10 Corporeal Exploration in György Pálfi's *Taxidermia*   207
   Małgorzata Bugaj
11 Aerial Bodies in Polish Cinema   222
   Dorota Ostrowska
12 The 'Chemistry' of Art(ifice) and Life: Embodied Paintings in East
   European Cinema   239
   Ágnes Pethő

Index   257

Figures

1.1	Hysterical act of killing in *Ashes and Diamonds*	37
1.2	Male wounded body in *Ashes and Diamonds*	45
2.1	The doctor looks out of the window (*Sátántangó*)	56
2.2	Out of drink (*Sátántangó*)	61
3.1	The father lying on the bed in a pose evoking Hans Holbein's *Dead Christ* (*The Turin Horse*)	72
3.2	Reference to Mantegna's painting in Fliegauf's *Delta*	75
4.1	DVD cover of *Hammer and Sickle*, the newly-minted Evdokim	97
4.2	Sasha and Katia in bodily communication (*The Sword Bearer*)	102
5.1	Łukasz and Ewa in *The Story of Sin*	125
5.2	Humanity and bestiality in *The Beast*	129
6.1	*Monk Brne's Pupil*: Monk Tetka at his most feminine	142
7.1	A new young porno star in Wiktor Grodecki's *Body without Soul*	158
7.2	Young hustlers in Wiktor Grodecki's *Mandragora*	161
8.1	Marina's caress of the dolls, seen from a rocking mirror (*4*)	178
8.2	Hanging dolls (*4*)	178
9.1	*Marketa Lazarová*: The hawk through the branches	196
9.2	*Kočár do Vídně*: The vulnerable body	199
10.1	Györgi Pálfi's *Taxidermia*	209
10.2	Györgi Pálfi's *Taxidermia*	219
12.1	Györgi Pálfi: *Taxidermia*	243
12.2	Andrei Zvyagintsev: *The Return*	246

Notes on the Contributors

Małgorzata Bugaj currently teaches courses on European cinema, avant-garde film and film theory at the University of Edinburgh and the University of Stirling. In 2014 she completed her Ph.D. thesis *Visceral Material: Cinematic Bodies on Screen* (University of Edinburgh). Her academic interests revolve around Eastern European film and cinematic presentations of the body and senses, as well as avant-garde and expanded cinema.

Helena Goscilo, Professor of Slavic at The Ohio State University, focuses her research primarily on culture and gender in Russia, as well as on visual genres. She has also written on Polish film and opera, plus Russian folklore. Her book-length publications in the last five years include *Cinepaternity: Fathers and Sons in Soviet and Post-Soviet Film* (co-ed., 2010), *Reflections and Refractions: The Mirror in Russian Culture* (*Studies in 20th and 21st Century Literature* 2010/2011), *Celebrity and Glamour in Contemporary Russia: Shocking Chic* (co-ed., 2011), *Putin as Celebrity and Cultural Icon* (ed., 2012), *Embracing Arms: Cultural Representations of Slavic and Balkan Women in War* (co-ed., 2012), *Baba Yaga: The Wild Witch of the East in Russian Fairy Tales* (co-ed., 2013) and *Fade from Red: The Cold War Ex-Enemy in Russian and American Film 1990–2005* (co-written, 2014). Among her current projects are a volume entitled *Russian Aviation, Space Flight, and Visual Culture* (co-ed., Routledge 2016) and the monograph *Graphic Ideology: The Soviet Poster from Stalin to Yeltsin*.

Nebojša Jovanović holds a Ph.D. from Central European University in Budapest. His work on gender and sexuality in Yugoslav cinema of the socialist era has been published in edited volumes such as *Retracing Images: Visual Culture after Yugoslavia* (ed. Daniel Šuber and Slobodan Karamanić, 2012), and *Partisans in Yugoslavia: Literature, Film and Visual Culture* (ed. Miranda

Jakiša and Nikica Gilić, Transcript Verlag, 2015). He is an assistant editor of the Routledge journal *Studies in Eastern European Cinema*.

Hajnal Király is a researcher at the Centre for Literary and Cultural Studies, Eötvös Lóránd University of Budapest. She is a member of a research project on 'Cultural Images of Space in Contemporary Hungarian and Romanian Film and Literature', and is also collaborating with Ágnes Pethő on a project on intermediality in Central and East European Cinemas. Her present research interests focus on interferences between intermediality and the concepts of the 'figural' and 'figuration'. She has published a book in Hungarian on adaptation theory and several articles on cinematic intermediality in English in volumes edited by Ágnes Pethő, Lars Elleström and Anne Gjelsvik (with Jürgen Bruhn and Eirik Fritsvold Hansen), respectively.

Ewa Mazierska is Professor of Film Studies at the School of Humanities and Social Sciences, University of Central Lancashire. She has published over twenty monographs and edited collections on European cinema, the representation of work in film, gender and popular music. These include *From Self-Fulfillment to Survival of the Fittest: Work in European Cinema from the 1960s to the Present* (2015), *Work in Cinema: Labor and Human Condition* (2013), *European Cinema and Intertextuality: History, Memory, Politics* (2011) and, with Elżbieta Ostrowska, *Women in Polish Cinema* (2006). Mazierska's work has been translated into nearly twenty languages, including French, Italian, Chinese, Korean, Portuguese, Estonian and Serbian. She is principal editor of the Routledge journal *Studies in Eastern European Cinema*.

Alexandar Mihailovic is Professor Emeritus of Russian and Comparative Literature at Hofstra University. His recent writing on LGBTQ and gender studies includes 'Wings of a Dove: The Shifting Language for Same-Sex Desire in Putin and Medvedev's Russia' (David A. Powell and Judith Kaufman, eds), *The Meanings of Sexual Identity in the 21st Century* (2014) and '"The Order of the Vanquished Dragon": The Performance of Archaistic Homophobia by the Union of Orthodox Banner Bearers in Putin's Russia' (in Patricia Simpson and Helga Druxes, eds, *Digital Media Strategies of the Far Right in Europe and the United States* (2015)). He is the author of *Corporeal Words: Mikhail Bakhtin's Theology of Discourse* (1997), and editor of *Tchaikovsky and His Contemporaries: A Centenary Symposium* (1999). He has written reviews for the online journal *Kinokultura: New Russian Cinema*, and has published articles on nineteenth- and twentieth-century Russian and Ukrainian literature and cultural relations during the Cold War. He is currently finishing a monograph entitled *The Mit'ki and the Art of Postmodern Protest in Russia*, and is a Visiting Professor of Literature at Bennington College.

Matilda Mroz is Lecturer in Film Studies at the University of Sussex. She held a British Academy Postdoctoral Research Fellowship at the University of Cambridge (2008–11), where her research focused on Polish cinema, and where she also completed her Ph.D. in film theory (2004–7). She is the author of *Temporality and Film Analysis* (Edinburgh University Press, 2012), which explores duration through the films of Antonioni, Tarkovsky and Kieslowski, and the co-author of *Remembering Katyn* (2012). Her current research explores contemporary engagements with Polish–Jewish relations in Polish visual culture.

Dorota Ostrowska is a senior lecturer in film and modern media at Birkbeck College, University of London. She publishes in the areas of European film and television studies (French and Polish), film festival studies, and the history of film and media production. Her publications include *Reading the French New Wave: Critics, Writers and Art Cinema in France* (2008), *European Cinemas in the TV Age* (with Graham Roberts) (2007), and *Popular Cinemas in Central Europe: Film Cultures and Histories* (with Zsuzsanna Varga and Francesco Pitassio) (2016). She is working on a monograph on the cultural history of the Cannes film festival and is interested in the crossover between the history of national cinemas and international film festivals.

Elżbieta Ostrowska teaches film at the University of Alberta, Canada. Her publications include *Women in Polish Cinema*, co-authored with Ewa Mazierska (2006), *The Cinema of Roman Polanski: Dark Spaces of the World*, co-edited with John Orr (2006), *The Cinema of Andrzej Wajda: The Art of Irony and Defiance*, co-edited with John Orr (2003), *Przestrzeń filmowa* (2000), and *Gender in Film and the Media: East–West Dialogues*, co-edited with Elżbieta Oleksy and Michael Stevenson (2000). Her articles have appeared in *Slavic Review*, *Studies in European Cinema*, and *Holocaust and Genocide Studies*.

Ágnes Pethő is Professor at the Sapientia Hungarian University of Transylvania in Cluj-Napoca (Romania), where she is currently head of the Department of Film, Photography and Media, as well as the executive editor of the journal *Acta Universitatis Sapientiae: Film and Media Studies*. She is the author of *Cinema and Intermediality. The Passion for the In-Between* (2011), and the editor of the volumes *Film in the Post-Media Age* (2012) and *The Cinema of Sensations* (2015). She has also published several essays on the relationship of painting, photography and film and the aesthetic of the *tableau vivant* in cinema (including in the 2014 Winter issue of *Screen* and in the volume on *Photofilmic Images in Contemporary Art and Visual Culture* edited by Alexander Streitberger and Brianne Caitlin Cohen, published in 2015).

David Sorfa is a Senior Lecturer in Film Studies at the University of Edinburgh and is managing editor of the journal *Film-Philosophy*. He co-edited *The Cinema of Michael Haneke: Europe Utopia* (2012) and has written extensively on Jan Švankmajer and Czech cinema as well as on a broad range of other film subjects. He has particular interests in film-philosophy, phenomenology, the work of Jacques Derrida and film adaptation. He has recently published a reappraisal of the Czech screenwriter Ester Krumbachová, as well as contributing a video essay, 'There Is Nothing Outside the Real: Preston Sturges on André Bazin', to the journal *[in]Transition*.

Calum Watt completed a Ph.D. on the relation between Maurice Blanchot and cinema in 2015 at King's College London, where he also works as a teaching assistant. The thesis examines Blanchot's writings on the image and fascination, how they might be used to theorise contemporary European cinema (including the work of Béla Tarr), and the uses of Blanchot made by filmmakers and writers on film. He is currently preparing a monograph based on the thesis.

Bruce Williams holds a Ph.D. from the University of California at Los Angeles and is Professor and Graduate Director in the Department of Languages and Cultures, and Co-coordinator of the program in International Cinema at the William Paterson University of New Jersey. He has published extensively in the areas of cinema history, film theory, Latin American and European cinemas, and language and cinema. His current research interests include Albanian cinema, radical film reception, celebrity studies, and the sociolinguistics of the cinema.

INTRODUCTION

Shaping the Cinematic Bodies of Eastern Europe and Russia

Ewa Mazierska, Matilda Mroz and Elżbieta Ostrowska

This collection offers a series of perspectives on the bodies of Eastern European and Russian cinema, a terrain of growing scholarly interest, but one which remains under-researched, for reasons that are both general and region-specific. Our aim is not to provide a monolithic vision of how the body has been configured across this vast geographical area; it is not possible to formulate a single argument concerning the Eastern European and Russian body. Rather, the chapters put forward a series of 'openings on the body', to use Shildrick and Price's terminology, in the cinemas of the region (1999: 1). The kaleidoscopic vision that emerges from these perspectives is of the body, whether individual, collective, symbolic or specific, as a nexus of often-competing forces, affects and ideologies, and as multiple and fluid. We hope that, by making corporeality our focus, we will yield new insights into the material and screen cultures of the countries under consideration: former Czechoslovakia and the Czech Republic, Hungary, Poland, Russia and former Yugoslavia. With the possible exception of Russia, the cinematic outputs of these countries are marginalised in studies of both 'European' and 'world' cinema. As Portuges and Hames point out, this is a relatively recent development: between the 1950s and 1970s, these film industries were more widely known and studied; the subsequent decline of interest has meant that 'a generation of critics and audiences have grown up for whom the cinemas of Eastern Europe are very much unknown territory' (2013: 3). With our focus on this region, we thus aim to foster a more inclusive vision of material and film culture.

The question of what this 'region' itself should consist of, or what it should be called, is not a straightforward one, however. The term 'Eastern Europe' has been accused of being Orientalist, and of conjuring negative memories of Russian and Soviet colonialism. Consequently, terms such as 'East Central Europe' and 'Central Europe' have been proposed instead to describe the region made up of the Czech Republic, Hungary, Poland and Slovakia (Hames 2004; Iordanova 2003; Mazierska 2010a). One can also note a particular ambition in the post-communist countries, many of which might prefer to see themselves as belonging to 'Europe' in general, to be seen as participating in the centuries-long tradition of Western or European art. A reflection of this is the extensive use of quotations from Western high art in Russian and Hungarian post-communist films, which both Hajnal Király and Ágnes Pethő discuss in this volume. Nevertheless, we subscribe here to the concept of 'Eastern Europe', on the grounds that it designates a region with a shared history and culture, including screen culture, which remains distinct even after the fall of the Berlin Wall. By including material concerning Russian cinema we wish to explore, through the prism of the cinematic body, the ways in which Russia and the Eastern European countries have been shaped by similar ideologies and systems of government. Many of the chapters in this volume emphasise how bodily discourses, oscillating between complicity and subversiveness, shaped the individuals living under state socialism, as well as a collective vision of the self. At the same time, we seek to recognise the often substantial differences between individual national policies and experiences, and hope that the collection will bring out as much the divergences as the associations across national boundaries.

The terminology used to describe the political and ideological systems of government in the Eastern European and Russian region in the twentieth century is likewise varied. The terms used by the authors in this volume include 'socialism', 'communism', 'real socialism', 'state socialism', and their 'post-' incarnations, 'post-communism' and 'post-socialism'. Our own preference is for 'state socialism'. This is because in their original sense, which can be found in the writings of early utopian socialists, such as Charles Fourier, and in the classic works of socialism, namely by Marx and Engels, the terms 'socialism' and 'communism' carry different meanings from those they acquired in the post-war realities of countries such as Poland, Hungary or the Soviet Union. In particular, 'communism', as seen by Marx, was meant to be both democratic and free from alienation thanks to the abolishment of the division of labour (Marx and Engels 1947: 22). The system that prevailed in post-war Eastern Europe would most likely be labelled by Marx as 'crude communism', because under it surplus value was not collected by individual capitalists, but by a community or its representatives. The author of *Capital* pointed to the similarity of this system to (ordinary) capitalism:

> [For crude communism] the community is simply a community of *labor* and equality of *wages*, which are paid out by the communal capital, the community as universal capitalist. Both sides of the relation are raised to an *unimaginary* universality – labor as the condition in which everyone

is placed and capital as the acknowledged universality and power of the community ... The first positive abolition of private property – crude communism – is therefore only a manifestation of the vileness of private property trying to establish itself as the positive community. (Marx 1977: 95)

The advantage of 'state socialism' over other terms such as 'socialism' lies in its pointing to the role of the state as a 'universal capitalist'. From this perspective other terms can be seen as misleading; nevertheless, we have retained them in this volume owing to their wide use in the discourse on Eastern Europe and Russia and a tacit assumption that their meanings are metaphorical, not literal.

The methodological approaches of the authors in this collection straddle Western and Eastern European scholarship. The prevalence of Western European and American literature in the bibliographies of the majority of the chapters presented here is inevitable, given that the literature on the cinematic body is dominated by studies focusing on Western cinema conducted by authors based in the West. Nevertheless, the authors in this volume also point to the contributions of Eastern European and Russian writers, such as Mikhail Bakhtin, Jan Patočka, Vladimir Sorokin and Alexander Etkind to the theories and histories of the body, as well as those of some Western authors who influenced cinema made by Eastern Europeans or who are particularly useful in the Eastern context, such as Wilhelm Reich. Furthermore, most of the chapters collected here extensively use vernacular cultural theory and analyse the local critical reception of the films under discussion, which helps to adjust Western theory to specific Eastern European historical and political contexts.

In what follows, we aim to provide, in necessarily brief terms, three overlapping contexts for this volume: the first concerned with the configurations of the body in Western thought, the second involving an examination of bodily discourses during and after state socialism, and the third outlining how the first two contexts intersect in scholarly writing on cinema.

BODIES IN WESTERN THOUGHT

For centuries, the body was neglected or dismissed in dominant Western philosophy and the humanities. Western culture continuously rejected the importance of the materiality of the body in constructing the self. The responsibility for this disregard is sometimes traced back as far as Plato, though Cartesian philosophy tends to be posited as the greatest culprit. Since the seventeenth century, Cartesian thought has been predicated on a dualism that asserts the mutual exclusivity of the physical and mental, of mind and body, which composes subjectivity (Grosz 1994: vii). In this equation, the mind or the soul is regarded as immortal and superior to the body in which it is trapped. While the mind is seen as complex, noble and the ultimate source of our humanity, the body is regarded as simple and animal-like, and thus unworthy of scholarly attention (Shilling 2005: 6–7). As Niall Richardson writes, in this view 'the body is not "us" – it is simply the base material' (Richardson 2012: 13).

In the twentieth century, however, this critical neglect of the body changed. On the one hand, largely following the discoveries of Freud, the traditional certainties about the mind began to be questioned. Figuratively speaking, the mind lost much of its old rationality, and began to look like the body – 'soft', irrational and mortal. Although Freud remained committed to a form of Cartesian dualism, in which chemical processes are correlated with, but not caused by, psychological processes, his writing on the ego and the sexual drives nevertheless undermines some of the assumptions governing dualism (Grosz 1999: 67). Theories of the body in the twentieth century, on the other hand, gained in complexity. Particularly since the work of Michel Foucault (1979) on sexuality and the prison system, the body came to be regarded as belonging to society and culture, rather than nature. To underscore the complex and social character of the body, Shilling describes the body as a 'multi-dimensional medium for the constitution of society' and identifies as many as eight types of bodies, including 'classical bodies', 'contemporary bodies', 'sporting bodies', 'musical bodies' and 'technological bodies' (Shilling 2005: 1). What these terms imply is not that there are different types of material substance (different kinds of flesh) behind each type of body, but rather that the body can be located in different cultural contexts and be an object of different discursive regimes.

Research on the body quickly gained currency with the advent of the consumer society, which, broadly speaking, coincided with the development of neoliberalism, poststructuralism and postmodernism in the early 1980s (Shilling 2005: 2; Turner 1996: 2–6). During the period in which this 'somatic turn' took place, Western governments gradually withdrew from welfare provision, shifting the responsibility for the well-being of citizens onto citizens themselves (Harvey 2005: 36–63). Problems such as poverty, illness and obesity largely stopped being seen as social problems, for which society as a whole was responsible, and started to be regarded as problems and failures of the individuals concerned. In this context the body became a marker of social status, a form of 'cultural capital'. Pierre Bourdieu, who introduced this term, observes:

> Most of the properties of cultural capital can be deduced from the fact that, in its fundamental sense, it is linked to the body and presupposes embodiment. The accumulation of cultural capital in the embodied state, i.e., in the form of what is called culture, cultivation, *Bildung*,

presupposes a process of embodiment, incorporation, which, insofar as it implies a labor of inculcation and assimilation, costs time, time which must be invested personally by the investor. Like the acquisition of a muscular physique or a suntan, it cannot be done at second hand. (Bourdieu 1986: 244)

In this fragment the author rejects the body–mind split, arguing that culture is located not outside the body, but inside it. Our bodies testify to the labour invested in them, as much physical as intellectual. By the same token, the 'soul' is not hidden under the skin but is laid bare on its surface. This fact, inevitably, disadvantages those with low capital, because not only do they have little chance to achieve their intellectual potential, but they also have little chance of making their bodies 'attractive'. For Bourdieu, and Harvey, the body is thus a class issue. Capitalism makes us corporally unequal and, at the same time, hypocritically pronounces this inequality to be an individual rather than a social problem.

Another factor influencing the 'somatic turn' was the development of feminism from the 1960s onwards (Turner 1996: 4). Feminist theory has contested the 'incorporeal abstraction' that has been at the heart of traditional Western thought, yet approaches to the body in feminist thinking are by no means unified (Shildrick and Price 1999: 1). One can identify a broad range of approaches to the body in feminist writing, from positing the specificity of the female body as a central problem for feminism, to movements away from issues of the corporeal and material. In the latter strand of thought, influenced largely by poststructuralism and postmodernism, the givenness of the natural body is challenged and a 'textual corporeality' dominates meaning-production (Shildrick and Price 1999: 1). For example, Germaine Greer begins the part entitled 'Body' in her famous book *The Female Eunuch* with an observation that 'many simple forms of life are more strikingly differentiated sexually than humans are. What we do notice, however, is that the differentiations between the human sexes are stressed and exaggerated, and before justifying the process we must ask why' (Greer 1993: 30). Greer's point is that exaggerating sexual difference serves patriarchy. Accordingly, Greer argues for playing down the specificity of the female body while drawing attention to the body as a social construct: an object shaped by ideologies. Since patriarchal oppression has tended to justify itself by connecting women more closely to the corporeal, confining them to the biological requirements of reproduction, it is no surprise that feminist thought has sometimes been suspicious of the body and has attempted to define itself in 'non- or extra-corporeal terms' (Grosz 1994: 14). At the same time, feminist theory has frequently grappled with the need to address the mind/body split as not only gendered, but also as associated with racial and class discourse, in which an 'unthinking physicality' is historically linked not just to women, but also, for example, to working-class people, indigenous people and slaves, in a general devaluing of (particular) bodies (Shildrick and Price 1999: 2).

The body also became a central point of critique in queer theory, which aimed to explore the relationships between identity, sexuality and culture and challenge heteronormative approaches to the corporeal by, in part, positing the body as a fluid and mobile materiality (Ruffolo 2012: 290). The work of Judith Butler on performativity and play, and her explorations of how assumptions about gender and sexuality determine our understanding of biological sex as the origin of gender identity, has been hugely influential in the field (Butler 1990; Turner 2000: 109). More recent work in queer theory has, however, questioned the insistence on performativity as the only adequate way of structuring perception on the world. Nigianni and Storr, for example, argue that such a way of thinking reveals a certain 'short-sightedness in relation to body and materiality' and a refusal to see a positive 'beyond' of language and discourse that is embedded in the specific corporeal experience of different bodies (Nigianni and Storr 2009: 3). According to Parisi, who develops this argument, the emphasis on the body as constituted by performativity threatens to reduce the complexity of the corporeal to a concept of the body as a 'mere container of socio-cultural significations' (Parisi 2009: 78).

As Dorota Ostrowska's chapter in this volume reminds us, technology has always reconfigured our perception and bodily experiences. The development of particular technologies such as virtual reality and social media in recent decades continues to complicate our relationships with, and the status of, the body, allowing us to adopt identities at odds with our materiality. As Susie Orbach maintains:

> In cyberspace anyone with access to a computer terminal and the web can be an artist, creating identities, personalities, and bodies that have existed until now only in one's mind's eye . . . The web democraticises and extends imagination, making it possible for people to enact their dreams within new communities of interest, however obscure, idiosyncratic or fleeting. (Orbach 2010: 79)

The contours of the body have become increasingly problematised in the writing on the cyborg, as exemplified so influentially by Donna Haraway's essay 'A Cyborg Manifesto' (1991), and the discourses of post-humanism, which interrogate the intersections between the material and the digital, and matter and the virtual.

The approaches to the body sketched above have been taken up by film theory in ways that further diversify our conceptions of corporeality, and particularly the manifold ways in which cinema produces the body, configured as female, 'Oriental', exotic, queer, star, animal, and so on, as filmic spectacle. As Teresa de Lauretis notes in relation to feminist film theory, feminism has been so invested in practices of cinema partly because the representation of woman as image, 'and the concurrent representation of the female body as the *locus* of sexuality, site of visual pleasure, or lure of the gaze', is so culturally pervasive that it can constitute a starting point for an understanding of the ideological constructions of sexual difference (1984: 37). Laura Mulvey's polemic delineating the scopophilic male gaze (1989), Doane's exploration of the feminine masquerade (1982), Studlar's attempts to theorise aspects of female spectatorship (1988) – all these now-canonical texts of feminist film theory depend upon particular configurations of the male and female body that continue to be utilised and challenged in contemporary writing, while new light is shed on multiple modes of embodiment. Mulvey and Anna Backman Rogers' 2015 *Feminisms: Diversity, Difference and Multiplicity in Contemporary Film Cultures*, where discussion of the female body is embedded in writing on illness and ageing, intelligence and agency, ethnicity, queerness, affect and the digital, is a case in point. It is notable, however, that there is no discussion of Eastern European or Russian contributions to the 'film cultures' of the title: this is symptomatic of the continued marginalisation of Eastern European and Russian voices in this broader discussion, as noted above.

Explorations of the ways in which cinema might impact upon viewing bodies have formed a key strand of film theory since the 1990s, as seen, for example, in Linda Williams' seminal text on the 'body genres' of pornography, melodrama and horror and their 'seemingly gratuitous' and excessive corporeal effects (1991: 3). The body also emerged as a focal point for phenomenological explorations of the multi-sensory possibilities of film viewing, most notably in the work of Vivian Sobchack, and has since produced a rich literature concerning embodiment and the haptic. Much of this contemporary theory draws on an earlier tradition of writing on film as a sensory experience, in the works of, for example, Jean Epstein, Sergei Eisenstein and Béla Balázs, as a way of opposing the semiotic discourses and apparatus theory of the 1960s (Mroz 2012: 25).[1] The latter frameworks tended to elide the importance of the body in film viewing; Jean-Louis Baudry, for example, posited a cinema viewer whose eye was 'no longer fettered to a body' (1992: 307). Psychoanalytic writing on film has also come under fire for distorting cinematic experience through a definition of cinema as deceptive, illusionary and based on an alienation of vision from the body (Mroz 2012: 26; Sobchack 1992: xv).

In her 1960s essays, especially 'Against interpretation' and 'One culture and the new sensibility', Susan Sontag argued for abandoning the (then) dominant modes of interpreting cinema, namely Marxism and Freudian theory: 'What is important now is to recover our senses. We must learn to see more, to hear more, to feel more . . . In place of a hermeneutics we need an erotics of art'

(Sontag 1994: 14). However, it was arguably the publication of Sobchack's *The Address of the Eye* in 1992, as well as her later work in *Carnal Thoughts* (2004), which constituted the most significant step in the break from the semiotic discourses that had dominated the field for several decades. Sobchack's phenomenological accounts of the film experience posited the viewer's body as an active participant in an intimate relationship with the film. When we see a film, Sobchack writes, we 'do not leave [our] capacity to touch or to smell or to taste at the door' (2004: 65). Seeing is informed by other modes of perception and the other senses: it is synesthetic, always within a '*sighted body*' rather than merely in 'transcendental eyes' (Sobchack 1992: 133).

Engaging with the work of Sobchack, and negotiating between phenomenology and the writing of Gilles Deleuze, Laura U. Marks also produced ground-breaking work in this area, which might be construed as in part responding to Sontag's call for an erotics of art. According to Marks, film images can be 'erotic in that they construct an intersubjective relationship between beholder and image ... the viewer relinquishes her own sense of separateness from the image – not to know it, but to give herself up to her desire for it' (2000: 183). In Marks's writing, certain types of film and video art, which she labels 'intercultural cinema', particularly 'appeal to nonvisual knowledge, embodied knowledge, and experiences of the senses, inviting the viewer to respond to the image in an intimate, embodied way, and thus facilitate the experience of other sensory impressions as well' (Marks 2000: 2). Marks is, however, careful to note that a focus on the haptic should not erase the intellectual processes of film viewing, but rather, a 'tactile epistemology' should give 'as much significance to the physical presence of an other as to the mental operations of symbolisation' (2000: 190). Many of the authors in this collection have been influenced by these discussions of cinematic corporeality, and we will return to them shortly.

BODY POLITICS UNDER AND AFTER STATE SOCIALISM

The official doctrines of the USSR and post-war Eastern Europe were based on 'historical materialism', conceptualised by Marx and Engels, who devoted much of their writings to the suffering of bodies under the capitalist system, especially in the passages devoted to the alienation of labour (Marx 1977). It might come as a surprise, then, that the body was nevertheless neglected in the cultural studies conducted in this region. In her introduction to the volume *Post-Communism and the Body Politic*, Ellen Berry goes so far as to pronounce the 'erasure of the body, sexuality, and gender relations as topics of public discourse' in the countries where state socialism ruled (Berry 1995: 3). This neglect can be explained by several factors. One was the focus on communal living, and on many bodies becoming unified in one system, at the expense of individuality, which regards the body as the most private possession, especially when engaged in sexual activity. As Amir Weiner argues, the Soviet ideal was to transform 'society from an antagonistically divided entity into a conflict-free, harmonious body' (1999: 1114). However, the emergence of the ideal communist collective body was only possible through, to use Foucauldian terminology, the disciplining and punishing of individual bodies. Purified and uniformly shaped, the ideal communist body oscillated towards the classical body that Mary Russo describes as 'transcendent and monumental, closed, static, self-contained, symmetrical, and sleek' (1994: 8). Harmonious and strong bodies of peasants and workers populate socialist realist imagery as if embodying the communist carnal sublime.

Another factor explaining the critical neglect of the body in the region during the socialist era was the gap between the state socialist rhetoric and the everyday reality of living under these regimes. The conditions of work in state socialist factories, especially in the early period of socialism, had much in common with the 'satanic mills' in the early years of the industrial revolution in England (Dąbrowska, quoted in Brzostek 2002: 37). The different needs of male and female bodies were neglected to encourage and justify the employment of women in occupations that had deleterious effects on them, such as some forms of work in factories that led to high incidents of miscarriage. In an economy privileging the extraction of raw materials and troubled by shortages of consumer goods, the care for one's body that drove Western consumerism was presented as a trivial pursuit or even as a betrayal of communist ideals. Equally, the sexual needs of bodies were regarded as at best of secondary importance to the spiritual need to build and develop socialism.

The neglect of particular aspects of individual, material bodies in everyday life was paralleled with an unwillingness to recognise the importance of the body in much Russian and Eastern European philosophy and cultural studies. The seminal case is the troubled career of Mikhail Bakhtin, who, together with Michel Foucault, is perhaps the most important twentieth-century author concerned with the body as a social and cultural construct. It is worth mentioning here that while Foucault draws attention to the body as an object of discipline imposed largely by the state and its institutions, such as the prison system, Bakhtin's main object of interest is the 'unruly body': the body which refuses disciplining. He theorises a grotesque visceral and excessive body that functions within the realm of strictly delineated carnival time as a force disrupting official culture. These unruly bodies contest the communist variant of the classical body that is perfectly sealed off and contained within its own limits. Any indication of transgressing these bodily limits, as for example in a non-reproductive sexual act or excessive eating, undermines the ideal and its ideological premises (Bakhtin 1965: 26). One wonders whether these specific interests reflect on the fact that the supposedly free West (at least as it is generally perceived) is full of restrictions and the totalitarian East (again, as the dominant narrative pronounces) allowed for more freedom than appears to be the case. Either way, bodily discourse in the Eastern Bloc appears more polyphonic than is usually admitted.

Cinema under state socialism both reflected and opposed socialist attitudes towards the body, and one can find a whole spectrum of positions on the corporeal in the film histories of the region. At one end of the spectrum one could posit the films of socialist realism, which often condemned the supposedly frivolous approach to the body, dominant in Western societies and seeming to infiltrate, like a cancer, into the healthy tissue of socialist society. Literally embodying this approach is the stock female bourgeois character who frequently appears in socialist realist films, and who spends her time trying to acquire silk stockings or a bathroom with running water. As Nebojša Jovanović's chapter in this volume demonstrates, however, even the relatively prescribed films of socialist realism can reveal some rather unexpected approaches to the body. At the other end of the spectrum lie the films of directors such as Walerian Borowczyk (explored in this volume by Ewa Mazierska) and Dušan Makavejev, which reveal particularly bold attitudes to the body: directors whose work can be seen as an attempt to not only display bodies, but also to theorise them.[2] Admittedly, both Borowczyk and Makavejev were mobile transnational filmmakers, working in many different countries, including several Western ones, which perhaps can partly explain their innovative approach to this topic. Likewise, other transnational Eastern European directors like Roman Polanski and Agnieszka Holland demonstrate a corporeal sensitivity. Their films often feature 'abject bodies' that result from various forms of socio-political oppressiveness produced by specific historical experiences of the Holocaust and exile (Mazierska 2007: 50–90; see also Marciniak 2000, Goscilo 2006b, Ostrowska 2014).

The collapse of state socialism and the shift towards neoliberalism offered society, politics and culture the opportunity to make up for the neglect of the body by re-examining 'communist bodies' and their transformations into 'post-communist bodies'. When examining bodily discourse in Eastern Europe and the former Soviet Union, it is then tempting to establish 1989 as the liminal point. Indeed, social and cultural criticism often draws such a fault line and links the era of state socialism with constructing disembodied subjects, where the focus on work and politics 'leads to a desexualisation and the almost material obliteration of the body', seen as just a 'receptacle and carrier of the communist idea' (Hanáková 2011: 152). The post-communist period, on the other hand, in its capitalist and liberal variant, is associated with commodified bodies. For example, in her discussion of how post-communist advertising strategies use female bodies, Elza Ibroscheva highlights the rapid change of sexual politics after the collapse of communism:

it is clear that Eastern European women, almost overnight, have adopted a new, highly sexualized identity – one that allows them to occupy both the position of consumer, but more importantly, to occupy the position of the 'consumed', widely and readily offering their sexualized bodies as an expression of a newly found freedom to define their identities in sexual ways. (Ibroscheva 2013: 445)

The change in body politics that occurred in Russia and Eastern Europe after the collapse of state socialism largely fits Jean-Jacques Courtine's account of the transformation of modern bodily discourses from the 1960s onwards, where women and oppressed minorities in the West struggled to reclaim power over their own bodies, in what he terms an informal 'body liberation front' (2006: 166). Drawing on the terminology of Deleuze and Guattari, Courtine notices a shift in the relationship between the body and subjectivity, from 'subjects without bodies' to 'bodies without subjects' which, nevertheless, continued to be 'carried along by the flow of desire or held in the tight grip of power' (2006: 166). While recognising the scale and force of the communist collapse, we must thus be wary of positing a strict or sudden division between the two eras. As Richard Sakwa has pointed out, quoting Václav Havel, 'the fall of the communist empire is an event on the same scale of historical importance as the fall of the Roman empire'; yet one must also recognise that post-communism is 'a multi-faceted, heterogeneous phenomenon shot through with paradoxes while at the same time revealing the underlying paradigmatic shifts' (Sakwa 1999: 1, 7). Implicitly, Sakwa assumes as many continuities as discontinuities between these two epochs that cannot be modelled into a simple bipolar opposition.

The collapse of state socialism by no means led to an uncomplicated 'liberation' of previously repressed bodily experiences. For example, as Griffiths has noted, the queer subcultures that cautiously emerged in the region after 1989 became a target for public dissent rather than being celebrated for rejecting the repressive body politics of the communist empire (2008: 130). When the cinemas of the region began to tackle previously suppressed sociocultural issues, the struggles of the nascent queer community were either ignored or caricatured, though some lone cinematic voices emerged to provide a platform for exploring heteronormativity and homosexual experience (Griffiths 2008: 130). One such director was Wiktor Grodecki, explored in this volume by Bruce Williams. The fall of the Berlin Wall also led to some rather unexpected encounters between feminist activism and the post-socialist countries. Many scholars have pointed out that the Western feminist agenda, sometimes figured as the product of an 'aberrant Western mindset', often met with distrust and resistance in these countries in the early 1990s, even among those who might be expected to support it (Mazierska and Ostrowska

2006: 2; see also Hanáková 2011: 146, Drakulić 1993). Furthermore, the post-communist transitions, with their anxieties about the dismantling of familiar forms of masculinity, inspired an anti-feminist backlash across the region (Graff 2007; Imre 2009: 130).

Undeniably, the disintegration of the Eastern bloc set in motion a series of changes in the geopolitical sphere, from the break-up of Yugoslavia and the ethnic conflicts in the region in the 1990s, to the accession of many of the countries of the region to the European Union in 2004. At the same time, a fundamental transformation was taking place in film production: the nationalised film industries and their political censorship gave way to globalised industries that allowed (or forced) filmmakers to seek funding from other countries while necessitating a kind of economic censorship (see Mazierska and Goddard 2014: 5–11; Imre 2012; Portuges and Hames 2013; Iordanova 2003). A particular kind of bodily discourse has emerged as these two types of mobility have coincided, that is, as the film industries have become more transnational, seeking co-productions and funding by European organisations such as Eurimages, and as the opening of the borders within the European Union has encouraged mass migration across the region. One can find a plethora of post-communist, transnational films in which national identity is questioned, borders are blurred, and bodies become subject to processes of flight, migration, commercial exchange and general rootlessness. In their wake have come several significant studies of this 'New Europe' and its cultural imaginary (e.g. Galt 2006; Király 2015; Mazierska and Rascaroli 2006; Kristensen 2012; Engelen and Heuckelom 2013), though few of these are specifically interested in locating their arguments among discourses on the body.

THE CINEMATIC BODIES OF EASTERN EUROPE AND RUSSIA

One can identify a number of specific scholarly interventions into bodily discourses vis-à-vis Soviet, Russian and Eastern European cinema that have emerged particularly visibly in recent decades, and which have inspired the authors in this volume. Indeed, some topics within this field are more visible than others, and there are certain directors whose work has attracted more widespread attention to the body and corporeal matters, figured in broad terms, than others, such as Sergei Eisenstein, Dušan Makavejev and Jan Švankmajer.[3] There has also been a relatively large amount of work on the Soviet (or Stalinist-era) body in visual culture, both within Soviet Russia (e.g. Attwood 1993; Goscilo 2006a; Kaganovsky 2008; Livers 2004; Haynes 2003) and outside it (e.g. Atanasovski and Petrov 2015; Hanáková 2011; Mroz 2007). Much of this writing explores how the ideal Soviet man and woman were (in theory and representation) moulded through particular bodily practices such as parades, construction activities, Stakhanovite excesses, sporting spectacles, and so on. Given their centrality to concepts of the 'motherland' and the 'fatherland', it is unsurprising that maternal and paternal bodies have also received a fair amount of scholarly attention. In the context of Russian cinema, the body of the father has been identified as an allegorical figure or icon related to the land's paternal rulers, their difficult legacy, and the perceived disintegration of masculine authority in post-communist times (Goscilo and Hashamova 2010: 2–13). In the Polish context, it is the figure of the Polish mother, who is associated with a Romantic, patriotic and martyrological nationalism (Szwajcowska 2006: 15), which stands out as a continual reference point for cinema to deify and deconstruct (see Mazierska and Ostrowska 2006; Ostrowska 1998; see also Daković 1996 on the mother in Yugoslav cinema).

Socio-political and cultural studies conducted on gender in the region are numerous and continue to flourish (see the indispensable bibliography by Livezeanu et al. 2007; also Johnson 2009, Borenstein 2008, Marsh 2013, Thomas 2007), and indeed gender and feminism is a frequent topic of discussion as regards Eastern European and Russian cinema (see e.g. Marciniak 2005; Dánél 2013; Mazierska and Ostrowska 2006; Mazierska 2010b; Portuges 1995; Ostrowska 2005; Ostrowska and Rydzewska 2007; Hanáková 2014; Lim 2001; Jovanović 2015). Research on homosexuality and queer theory in the region is also developing rapidly, with Russia being the most thoroughly studied in this regard (Kulpa and Mizielińska 2011: 2; see e.g. Essig 1999, Štulhofer and Sandfort 2004, Baer 2009). Scholarly analysis that is specifically focused on non-heterosexual cinematic bodies in the region is somewhat sparse, though several authors have begun to 'queer' Eastern European and Russian cinema, finding hidden homosexual undercurrents, as well as to devote attention to more open presentations of homosexuality in film (Griffiths 2008; Jagielski 2013a; Jovanović 2012; Moss 2006). However, many significant studies are available only in the vernacular (for example, Jagielski's 2013b work on homosocial desire in Polish cinema), which has limited their impact outside their native countries.

Recent studies have identified and explored what has been termed a 'meta-genre' of 'corporeal cinema' in Eastern Europe and Russia (Arthur 2006; Imre 2009: 215; Kalmár 2013a and 2013b; Vincze 2016). As Imre has written, such a cinema features a shift from the 'abstraction of language to the expressivity of Bakhtin's "lower bodily stratum"', a transition that emerges particularly during times of crisis (2009: 215). Corporeal cinema, Imre continues, consists of 'grim allegories' that revolve obsessively around the often traumatic historical changes in the region, and include many of the films of Béla Tarr, Alexander Sokurov and Emir Kusturica (Imre 2009: 215). A significant aspect of the studies of such films is their attention to embodied viewing, that is, to the potential bodily impacts of the films on audiences. For example, drawing on his earlier theoretical work, *The Cinematic Body* (1993), Steven Shaviro has explicitly made this connection between 'corporeal' film and the embodied viewer. In an analysis of *Taxidermia*, he points to its 'body-images' as being both allegorical and immediately visceral; the film, he argues, operates by a process of 'affective contagion' which '*forces us to feel*' repulsion, nausea, disgust, and other sensations (Shaviro 2012).

The exploration of 'corporeal cinema' is one significant area, then, where the aforementioned studies of cinematic embodiment are being brought to bear on studies of Eastern European and Russian film. Research on the sensory aspects of cinema has not always been associated with scholarship on this region. Under socialism, censorship tended to be preoccupied with the political implications and literary content of a film, at the expense of its other aspects. Such a focus was echoed in the film criticism of the time and continues to influence much contemporary writing on film in the region, where cinematic works are often judged primarily for their political implications in both press and academia.[4] There are, of course, exceptions to this rule. Particularly of note is the work of Emma Widdis, who, in her writing on pre-World War II Soviet film, explored the ways in which the reconfiguration of the senses through visual culture became 'the ideological foundation of the new [Soviet] order' (2003: 59; see also Widdis 2005, 2012). The films of Andrei Tarkovsky, in their intense focus on the material environment, have also been associated with the haptic and the sensory (Barker 2009; Mroz 2012), while Ágnes Pethő's edited volume *Cinema of Sensations* (2015) includes discussion of Romanian and Hungarian cinema. Various other authors have focused on embodiment and the senses in regional-specific contexts. For example, Elżbieta Ostrowska has explored the textual strategies used in Polish cinema to disembody the female subject and, thus, to relegate it to outside the realm of history, while male bodies, she argues, are represented as sensuous spectacles to serve as a source of spectatorial affect (Ostrowska 2012; see also Mroz 2007; Kalmar 2013a,b; Noheden 2013; Sándor 2014). Research into the senses and embodied viewing in Eastern European and Russian cinema is, however, still relatively slight in volume.

This collection aims to add to this 'body' of research, locating our discussion of the sensory and corporeal within the historical and political. We have aimed to be mindful of Marks's critique of Merleau-Ponty for treating sense experience as 'pre-discursive and, hence, as natural'. Marks argues that 'while much of sensory experience is pre-symbolic, it is still cultivated, that is, learned' (2000: 144–5). The 'order of the sensible', according to Marks, is the 'sum of what is accessible to sense perception at a given historical and cultural moment . . . we can only feel in the ways we have learned it is possible to feel' (2000: 31). This contextualisation of the sensory and of embodiment winds itself throughout the volume. In historical terms, we might also consider that the haptic might be particularly relevant to the region at this point in time, as a strategy to address the gaps in the history of the Soviet Union and Eastern Europe, resulting not only from censorship, but also from a preoccupation with the histories of grand personalities and events rather than private, intimate histories. As Imre has written, drawing on Marks, the films of directors such as Švankmajer and Pálfi exhibit a concern with eliciting repressed memories 'by interrogating the historical layers preserved by objects' and thus confounding 'official history, private recollection, and simple fiction' (2009: 215). In this context a film like *Taxidermia* can be construed as, in part, a work crossing historical epochs whose primary focus is the corporeal adventures of its protagonists. Indeed, the film has become the focus of haptic attention, in the aforementioned work of Shaviro, as well as in texts by Kalmar (2013a) and Strausz (2011), and such a context also informs Małgorzata Bugaj's chapter in this volume.

In taking up the task of intersecting the cinemas of the region with the discourses of the body, the authors in this collection aim to delineate new avenues of research into the cinematic body, while building on the work outlined above. The chapters in this collection have been divided into three sections: 'Wounds and Traumas', 'Transgressions and Pleasures', and 'Carnal Histories', yet it should be noted that the boundaries between these categories are fluid, and many of the chapters touch upon more than one category.

A key factor in post-communist bodily discourse has been the gradual acknowledgement of the bodily traumas of World War II and state socialism, and especially of the Stalinist period. One third of this collection, then, is devoted to exploring wounded and traumatised bodies: bodies suffering from war and work injuries as well as the effects of everyday brutality and alcoholism, the latter seen largely as a means of coming to terms with the deprivations of the state socialist system, but one which also brings traumas of its own. In the first chapter, '"What Does Poland Want from Me?" Male Hysteria in Andrzej Wajda's War Trilogy', Elżbieta Ostrowska examines Andrzej Wajda's early war films: *Pokolenie* (*A Generation*, 1955), *Kanał* (*Kanal*, 1956), and *Popiół i diament* (*Ashes and Diamonds*, 1958). She locates these films within both the vernacular tradition of Romanticism that responds to national trauma, and a broader context of psychoanalysis and the universal traumas of modernity. Using Slavoj Žižek's concept of 'hysterical doubt' and the Polish scholar Michał Paweł Markowski's discussion of melancholia and hysteria, Ostrowska identifies a hysterical subject in Polish Romantic culture and emphasises the uncertainty inscribed within it. She claims that the protagonists of Wajda's War Trilogy are cinematic embodiments of vernacular hysterical male subjects. As hysteria speaks exclusively through the body, the chapter focuses on the haptic potential of the cinematic image as well as specific bodily performances. The excessive bodily spectacles in Wajda's films, which largely fit clinical descriptions of hysterical symptoms, are, the author argues, an attempt to overcome the actual lack of bodily agency and, by extension, male subjectivity. As the chapter explains, owing to various political and cultural circumstances, the Polish masculine subject has constantly been questioned or deprived of its agency. In Wajda's war films male hysteria serves as an embodied metaphor for a politically impotent masculinity as developed within Polish political discourse.

In the second chapter, 'Alcoholism and the Doctor in Béla Tarr's *Sátántangó*', Calum Watt argues that the body ruined by alcohol functions as a synecdoche for the collapse of Hungarian communism, a collapse which is documented through the body in excruciatingly slow and exhaustive detail. The focus of his chapter is on one episode from Tarr's seven-hour-long masterpiece *Sátántangó* (1994), a film about life in a collective farm during the end of communism in Hungary. The episode centres on a reclusive, obese, and severely alcoholic doctor, played by Peter Berling, whose chief pastime is to sit at his desk drinking and recording every aspect of the petty goings-on at the estate in a journal. However, in this episode he finds himself having run out of alcohol and reluctantly resolves that he must leave to get some more. In this hour-long sequence the camera follows the sick man on a veritable odyssey through the rain to the pub where the rest of the peasants are cavorting riotously. As Watt argues, this intimate and yet epic treatment of bodily needs has few equals in cinema. Through a close formal analysis of scenes featuring the doctor, Watt shows that what is often considered the essence of Tarr's style – slowness – is found to have its roots in an attentive depiction of the physical life of the body. In addition, it is typical of Tarr's style to situate the body within a material environment, a theme brought out in *Sátántangó* through vast images of the Great Hungarian Plain, as well as by showing the doctor reading from what seems to be a geological prehistory of Central Europe. Through an engagement with key writers on Tarr (András Bálint Kovács and Jacques Rancière) as well as Gilles Deleuze, the author suggests that there are two temporal modes at work in Tarr's depiction of alcoholism: the heavy present of the body and another time which takes flight from the travails of the body.

Béla Tarr's cinema is also discussed by Hajnal Király in the next chapter, 'Playing Dead: Pictorial Figurations of Melancholia in Contemporary Hungarian Cinema'. She notices that contemporary Hungarian cinema has often been coined as 'dark', depicting an ontological melancholia reflected in what Laura Mulvey termed, after Freud, the 'death drive', that is, the urge of the narration towards a halt (often a melodramatic ending), paired with a preference for a slowness and stillness in the image. But beyond an aesthetics of slow cinema, an aesthetics of the single, painterly image in films seems promising for understanding the specificity of this cinema. Király argues that in films by

Béla Tarr, Kornél Mundruczó, Benedek Fliegauf and Ágnes Kocsis, tableau-like compositions serve as interruptions, revealing the single image as an in-between site where figuration happens. Most of the time, these painterly images relate to the narration metaphorically or allegorically, producing an effect of aesthetic detachment that calls for a pensive spectator and favours the '*lisible*' (readable) over the 'visible'. Király focuses on a corpus of contemporary Hungarian films in which dead or dying bodies are represented in pictorial compositions evoking either Andrea Mantegna's or Hans Holbein's *Dead Christ*, with the aim of identifying 'the figural' conceived as a pure figure that makes sense without a story. She argues that these intermedial images are figurations of melancholia. Relying on Kristeva's controversial gendered interpretation (according to which female artists, unlike men, find it difficult to sublimate melancholia), she explores the dynamics between 'the figurative' and 'the figural' in comparative analyses of films by Hungarian female and male directors. Király concludes by placing the discussion of the figural relevance of paintings in the context of an extended interpretation of anamorphosis, thus proposing a 'phenomenology of the clue' as an approach suitable for defusing the repressed meanings of these films.

Finally, in her chapter 'The Body Breached: Post-Soviet Masculinity on Screen', Helena Goscilo examines male corporeality in post-Soviet cinema. Goscilo argues that, whereas the utopian male body of the Soviet Imaginary hyperbolised and recast in steel or bronze the anatomical ideals of classical antiquity (Mikhail Bakhtin's 'closed body'), post-Soviet cinema typically has featured a male corporeality resembling the open body of apertures and protuberances posited by Bakhtin, but as degraded, marred, and vulnerable rather than celebratory or regenerative. Thus the indomitable heroes of hypertrophied bulk, brawn and beauty in Stalinist films such as Grigorii Aleksandrov's *Circus* (1936), Mikhail Kalatozov's *Valerii Chkalov* (1941) and Mikheil Chiaureli's *Fall of Berlin* (1949) have been superseded by the dramatically violated and traumatised physiques of protagonists in recent films confronting war – Aleksandr Nevzorov's *Purgatory* (1998), Valerii Todorovskii's *My Stepbrother Frankenstein* (2004), Aleksandr Veledinskii's *Alive* (2006) – and those reassessing the Stalinist era: Aleksei German's *Khrustalev, the Car* (1998) and Pavel Livnev's *Hammer and Sickle* (1994). Indeed, the latter explicitly deconstructs the forcible transformation of Soviet citizenry into fantastic icons of Stakhanovite virility and its tragic consequences. Similarly, post-Soviet on-screen crime devastates the male body, and nowhere more vividly than in Filipp Iankovskii's Lermontov-indebted *The Sword Bearer* (2006), which violently imprints all contemporary experience, most of it lethal, on the human form in a world ruled by material values and devoid of communal ideals.

The next section, 'Transgressions and Pleasures', draws together case studies that examine how sexual and 'obscene' corporeality functions vis-à-vis the frame of socialist regulation. In her chapter, 'Borowczyk as Pornographer', Ewa Mazierska discusses the director's representation of sex and the erotic body. It argues that by deciding to be a pornographer (or a creator of erotic art), Borowczyk chose a career path which placed him in conflict with the two dominant ideologies in Poland: Catholicism and state socialism; hence he treated both of them with contempt. That said, there are particular elements of Borowczyk's films that can be seen to thwart the erotic pleasure of his viewers; sexual acts, for example, take place behind curtains or other objects blocking our access to vision, such as pieces of furniture. Such a depiction points to the fact that sexual acts were taboo in the times and places presented by the director, particularly in sites of religious contemplation. Borowczyk breaks this taboo, but only partially, by making his characters engage in sex in churches and convents. Another specific characteristic of his films is their engagement in a discourse about the relationship between body and mind. In Borowczyk's films there is a reversal of sorts between the spiritual and the corporeal – the spirit is thrown from the pedestal, while the body is upgraded. Those who preach about the superiority of mind over body, such as priests and nuns, prove sinful. Those who indulge in corporal pleasures remain innocent. Such innocence is also attributed to animals and humans with bestial tendencies. Ultimately, however, Borowczyk suggests that unity of body and mind cannot be achieved, or that it may only occur when they are on the verge of perishing, in the moment of death. Death in his films is thus presented not as a tragic incident, but as a salvation.

The next chapter, by Nebojša Jovanović, 'Queering Masculinity in Yugoslav Socialist Realist Films', analyses queer male bodies in Yugoslav cinema from the late 1940s to the early 1950s, in order to challenge the assumption that the cinema of that period functioned as a handmaiden of totalitarian ideology. In order to elaborate his point, Jovanović explores the corporeal dimension of queer representations of masculinity in three films from the first decade of Yugoslav cinema. *Život je naš* (*Life is Ours*, Gustav Gavrin, 1948) blurs the boundary between homosexuality and homosociality, *Crveni cvet* (*Red Flower*, Gustav Gavrin, 1953) boasts the very first case of gender cross-dressing in Yugoslav cinema, whereas *Bakonja fra Brne* (*Monk Brne's Pupilii*, Fedor Hanžeković, 1954) features the first protagonist to be unmistakably coded as a homosexual. The queering of these films substantially questions those scholarly narratives that posit that the Yugoslav filmmakers were in cahoots with the socialist ideologues in the joint project of degrading homosexuality as such.

In his chapter 'Geographies of Carnality: Slippery Sexuality in Wiktor Grodecki's Gay Hustler Trilogy', Bruce Williams examines the daring, yet highly contested unmasking of the political and economic realities of the post-communist Czech Republic represented by Grodecki's films *Andělé nejsou andělé* (*Not Angels but Angels*, 1994), *Tělo bez duše* (*Body without Soul*, 1996) and

Mandragora (1997). Williams situates his reading of the films within an examination of the gay sex trade and of Prague as a borderland where the familiar and exotic commingle. Chided by critics as manipulative and even homophobic, Grodecki's films nonetheless, he argues, represent a landmark representation of gay male sexuality in Czech cinema. The chapter examines how the bodies of the young hustlers and porn stars featured in the films are mapped within the shifting turf of a Central Europe in transition. Grodecki's trilogy consists of two documentaries and a dramatised feature, all of which foreground the active complicity of the teenage prostitutes in the dynamics of the sex tourism industry aimed primarily at Western Europeans. Although similar to their clients in their Western appearance, Grodecki's boys offer their customers something exotic that transcends traditional sexual binaries. They are at once consumer goods and proactive marketeers. In a like manner, the three films explore the Czech capital in its fusion of orientalist mystique and Western commercialism. Most importantly, the films are historical documents that uncover the inner workings of the sex market in a time of socioeconomic transformation.

Alexandar Mihailovic similarly focuses on the economies of post-communist (and post-human) queer desire, shifting focus to contemporary Russian cinema, in his chapter 'A Mass Doubling of Heroes: Post-Human Objects of Queer Desire in Vladimir Sorokin and Ilya Khrzhanovsky's *4*'. Mihailovic argues that in their 2004 film *4*, the contemporary Russian novelist and screenwriter Vladimir Sorokin and the filmmaker Ilya Khrzhanovsky create a nightmare fantasy about the intersection of two seemingly unrelated processes of production: in Moscow, a new corrupt industry of processing chemically injected and possibly cloned pig meat and, in the countryside, a community of elderly women who artisanally manufacture a series of eerie life-size dolls out of masticated bread dough. Both processes address anxieties about bodily boundaries being breached or invaded, with the national body becoming tainted or jammed up by what it ingests. Like the pig/human cohabitation and symbiosis that is at the forefront of other scenes in the film, the doll/human cohabitation suggests a moment of cultural anxiety about social reproduction. As Mihailovic claims, the film presents a Russia that is incapable of reproducing itself in ways other than the symbolic and incorporeal; in the film, it is a country that is fertile only in its proliferation of politicised modalities and unsubtle ideological metaphors. In the satirical political critique deployed by Sorokin and Khrzhanovsky, which at first appears to come from a liberal point of view, a homophobic message strong enough to please Russian far-right nationalists is encrypted under layers of anxiety about cloning, a tainted food supply, village poverty, and systemic government corruption. This straight male fear of death through feminisation is projected onto society at large, which is undergoing economic changes in post-capitalism that wreak havoc on individual autonomy.

The chapters in the final section, 'Carnal Histories', conceptualise historical change as a force that acts upon and involves the corporeal and material, reconfiguring perception, bodily experience and bodily imagery, as seen through a cinematic lens. The section opens with David Sorfa's chapter 'The Touch of History: a Phenomenological Approach to 1960s Czech Cinema', which explores the work of two Czechoslovak filmmakers, František Vláčil and Karel Kachyňa. Sorfa outlines how their films employ distinctive formal features, such as shallow focus, action obscured by objects in the foreground and symmetrical image composition, which emphasise the experience of both spectators and characters. The chapter maps this haptic visuality onto the importance of phenomenology as the primary philosophical tendency during this period in Czechoslovakia, and particularly considers Jan Patočka's work on history, freedom and the body. These stylistic tendencies, Sorfa argues, are also a reaction to the dictates of socialist realism. Sorfa's chapter considers three films in detail: Vláčil's *Marketa Lazarová* (1967), often hailed as the most important masterpiece of Czech cinema, and Kachyňa's *Kočar do Vidně* (*Coach to Vienna*, 1966) and *Noc nevěsty* (*Night of the Bride / The Nun's Night*, 1967). While *Marketa Lazarová* is set in the Middle Ages, the action of Kachyňa's films takes place in 1945 and 1958 respectively. All three films are linked by a consideration of Christianity as an institution of political freedom as well as oppression. *Marketa Lazarová* explores the tensions between paganism and formal religion; *Coach to Vienna* presents a dilemma between justified revenge and forgiveness; and *Night of the Bride* explicitly shows religion as an ambiguous counter to communist totalitarianism. In all of these films, the vulnerable human body exists at the intersection of various discourses and displays of power. Sorfa considers these films phenomenologically and argues that their concrete engagement with the experience of the spectator creates a strong connection between the historical and fictional plights of the characters.

Małgorzata Bugaj begins her chapter, 'Corporeal Exploration in Györgi Pálfi's *Taxidermia*', with the observation that in recent decades ample attention within the study of cinema has been paid to the human body, yet few films deal so directly with our physical nature as Hungarian director Pálfi's 2006 film *Taxidermia*. This surreal family saga presents three generations of men obsessed with their corporeal needs. In its reflection on the body, the film juxtaposes the extremes of the human form. On the one hand, it probes the inside and the outside of the body. On the other hand, it investigates Bakhtin's carnivalesque corporealities and considers Baudrillard's notion of the body 'as the finest of the consumer objects'. In contemplating the corporeal exterior, *Taxidermia* celebrates the senses as well as the varied textures and hues of the skin. Revisiting the visceral depths of the body, it imposes its own aesthetics as it exhibits the interior anatomy. Furthermore, while the film begins with grotesque depictions of corporeality and its urges, in its conclusion these are replaced with the image of a modern, constructed physicality whose enslavement to its needs is rebuked. Such a body, emptied of its organic connections and ultimately likened to a taxidermist mount, constitutes a commentary on the contemporary perception of our own physical nature. Tracing *Taxidermia*'s exploration of the human body, Bugaj analyses the film's references to different theories revolving around human corporeality.

In her chapter 'Aerial Bodies in Polish Cinema', Dorota Ostrowska discusses Polish films about aviation made in the period of state socialism: *Sprawa Pilota Maresza* (*The Case of Pilot Maresz*, Leonard Buczkowski, 1956), *Przeciwko Bogom* (*Against Gods*, Hubert Drapella, 1961), *Zniszczyć Pirata* (*To Destroy the Pirate*, Hubert Drapella, 1973), and *Na Niebie i Na Ziemi* (*On the Earth and in the Sky*, Julian Dziedzina, 1974). In tracing how the technology of flying impacts the representation of the body, Ostrowska develops Virilio's notions of the body and technology, which focus on the questions of perception on the one hand and human bonds on the other. The argument is shaped around an element missing in Virilio's discussion of the body–technology dynamic during the Cold War, which is uniquely focused on the Western context and which neglects the particular characteristics of the aerial body under state socialism. The chapter is therefore an attempt to fill in the gap in Virilio's reflection on the body-technology dynamic by discussing the development of a specific representation of the body, referred to here as a 'socialist aerial body', which is impacted not only by the advancements in the technologies of flying, but also by ideological concerns – some of them unique to the socialist context – and by historical shifts under state socialism. What the films discussed here collectively demonstrate is the way in which human bonds, which are a type of affective technology in themselves, and physical disability, affecting the pilot's fields of perception, work as a kind of prosthesis of flying technology in relation to the body. As a result the films show how Virilio's aerial body is reshaped and transformed in the socialist context.

In this volume's final chapter, 'The "Chemistry" of Art(ifice) and Life: Embodied Paintings in East European Cinema', Ágnes Pethő connects the intermedial trope of the *tableau vivant* in recent Eastern European cinema with motifs of historical 'return', variously construed. Focusing on films directed by Pálfi, Mundruczó, Fliegauf, Tarr, and Andrei Zvyagintsev, Pethő traces the ways in which the *tableau vivant* is not conceived primarily as an embodiment of a painting, but rather appears more like the objectification of bodies as images, and something that we can associate with what Mario Perniola considers the 'sex appeal of the inorganic'. Like Király, Pethő draws attention to the 'cadaverous' *tableaux vivants* (among them the recurring cinematic paraphrases of Mantegna's *Dead Christ*), in which a live body is displayed as a corpse, or the other way round – a corpse is presented as an embodied picture, or an object of art made of flesh. Such images enclose almost irreconcilable extremes: from a sensation of corporeality in pictures coming alive as embodied paintings to the distanciating effect generated by conspicuous artificiality and stylisation. In these films the *tableau* becomes a powerful agent in generating metanarratives, offering a comprehensive vision of the world. These references to well-known European paintings, to a universal cultural heritage of 'grand images', can be connected, therefore, to what Lyotard termed the 'figure of return', a movement of '*rétournement*' to a fixed, familiar pattern. By repeatedly showing us bodies dying into art, and ideas reified as images, these films present us with uncanny rituals of 'becoming an image', with a yearning for a reintegration into something universal and lasting, and can be viewed in the context of the reconstructive tendencies of contemporary post-postmodern art.

The image that appears on the cover of this volume, a photograph of a mural entitled 'Love Letter' (2012) in the centre of Łódź, Poland, is evocative of many of the thoughts and affects that are traced throughout the book. The female figure in the mural is at once overtly sexualised and appears as a kind of post-communist Alice in Wonderland – pieces of paper reminiscent of a pack of cards (with an inverted heart symbol) flutter around her. Her body seems to be both emerging from the concrete wall and literally rooted in it, a paradoxical relation that conjures up ideas of the body's embeddedness in, and flights from, its social and spatial contexts. The mural elicits thoughts of the relationships between image, symbol and text. Like many artists and filmmakers, the muralist (known as Aryz) has made the crumbling post-communist architecture his (literal) canvas, and, owing to the *Alice in Wonderland* reference and his own Spanish origin, has drawn attention to the space as a transnational zone of global cultural flows. In what follows, we aim similarly to evoke the complex modes of configuring and rendering the bodies of Eastern European and Russian cinema, in their enchantments and traumas, their pains and pleasures.

NOTES

1. The national origins of Eisenstein and Balázs, who were Russian and Hungarian respectively, suggest an important trajectory of influence that moves from Eastern to Western European theory and practice.
2. This volume does not include chapters on Makavejev, as his representation of the body was recently extensively covered in a special issue of *Studies in Eastern European Cinema* (guest-edited by Greg de Cuir, 2014), of which Ewa Mazierska, Matilda Mroz and Elżbieta Ostrowska are editors.
3. One could argue that these directors are *in general* more discussed outside of their countries of origin than many other Eastern European and Russian directors, who are equally concerned with the body but whose work has simply not garnered equal attention.
4. See, for example, the analysis of the multinational reception of Andrzej Wajda's 2007 film *Katyń*, in Etkind et al. (2012).

WORKS CITED

Arthur, Paul (2006), 'A Meditation on *The Death of Mr Lazarescu* and Corporeal Cinema', *Film Comment*, 42: 3, 44–9.
Atanasovski, Srđan, and Ana Petrov (2015), 'Carnal Encounters and Producing Socialist Yugoslavia: Voluntary Youth Labour Actions on the Newsreel Screen', *Studies in Eastern European Cinema* 6: 1, 21–32.
Attwood, Lynne (ed.) (1993), *Red Women on the Silver Screen: Soviet Women and Cinema From the Beginning to the End of the Communist Era*, London: Pandora Press.
Baer, Brian James (2009), *Other Russias: Homosexuality and the Crisis of Post-Soviet Identity*, Basingstoke: Palgrave Macmillan.
Bakhtin, Mikhail (1965), *Rabelais and His World*, trans. Helene Iswolsky, Cambridge, MA and London: MIT Press.
Barker, Jennifer M. (2009) *The Tactile Eye: Touch and the Cinematic Experience*, Berkeley and Los Angeles: University of California Press.
Baudry, Jean-Louis (1992 [1974]), 'Ideological Effects of the Basic Cinematographic Apparatus', in Gerald Mast, Marshall Cohen and Leo Braudy (eds), *Film Theory and Criticism*, Oxford: Oxford University Press, pp. 302–12.
Berry, Ellen E. (1995), 'Introduction', in Ellen E. Berry (ed.), *Post-Communism and the Body Politic*, New York: New York University Press, pp. 1–11.
Borenstein, Eliot (2008), *Overkill: Sex and Violence in Contemporary Russian Popular Culture*, Ithaca and London: Cornell University Press.
Bourdieu, Pierre (1986 [1983]), 'The Forms of Capital', in John G. Richardson (ed.), *Handbook of Theory and Research for the Sociology of Education*, New York: Greenwood Press, pp. 241–58.
Brzostek, Błażej (2002), *Robotnicy Warszawy: Konflikty codzienne (1950–1954)*, Warsaw: Trio.
Butler, Judith (1990), *Gender Trouble: Feminism and the Subversion of Identity*, New York and London: Routledge.
Courtine, Jean-Jacques (2006), 'The Body', in Lawrence D. Kritzman (ed.), *The Columbia History of Twentieth-Century French Thought*, New York: Columbia University Press, pp. 165–7.
Daković, Nevena (1996), 'Mother, Myth and Cinema: Recent Yugoslav Cinema', *Film Criticism*, 21: 2, 40–9.
Dánél, Mónika (2013), 'Surrogate Nature, Culture, Women: Transylvania/Romania as Inner Colonies in Contemporary Hungarian Films', in Judit Pieldner and Zsuzsanna Ajtony (eds), *The Discourses of Space*, Newcastle upon Tyne: Cambridge Scholars Publishing, pp. 255–83.
De Cuir, Greg, Ewa Mazierska, Elżbieta Ostrowska, and Matilda Mroz (eds) (2014), *Studies in Eastern European Cinema: Special Issue on Dušan Makavejev*, 5: 1.
De Lauretis, Teresa (1984), *Alice Doesn't: Feminism, Semiotics, Cinema*, Bloomington: Indiana University Press.
Doane, Mary Ann (1982), 'Film and the Masquerade: Theorising the Female Spectator', *Screen*, 23: 3/4, 74–87.
Drakulić, Slavenka (1993), *How We Survived Communism and Even Laughed*, New York: Harper Perennial.
Engelen, Leen and Kris Van Heuckelom (eds) (2013) *European Cinema after the Wall: Screening East–West Mobility*, Lanham, MD and Plymouth: Rowman and Littlefield.
Essig, Laurie (1999), *Queer in Russia: A Story of Sex, Self and the Other*, Durham, NC: Duke University Press.

Etkind, Alexander, Rory Finnin, Uilleam Blacker, Julie Fedor, Simon Lewis, Maria Mälksoo, and Matilda Mroz (2012), *Remembering Katyn*, Cambridge: Polity Press.
Foucault, Michel (1979), *Discipline and Punish*, London: Penguin.
Galt, Rosalind (2006), *The New European Cinema: Redrawing the Map*, New York: Columbia University Press.
Goscilo, Helena (2006a), 'Post-ing the Soviet Body as Tabula Phrasa and Spectacle', in Andreas Schönle (ed.), *Lotman and Cultural Studies: Encounters and Extensions*, Madison: University of Wisconsin Press, pp. 248–98.
Goscilo, Helena (2006b), 'Polanski's Existential Body – As Somebody, Nobody and Anybody', in John Orr and Elżbieta Ostrowska (eds), *The Cinema of Roman Polanski: Dark Spaces of the World*, London and New York: Wallflower Press, pp. 22–37.
Goscilo, Helena and Yana Hashamova (2010), 'Cinepaternity: The Psyche and Its Heritage', in Helena Goscilo and Yana Hashamova (eds), *Cinepaternity: Fathers and Sons in Soviet and Post-Soviet Film*, Bloomington: Indiana University Press, 1–25.
Graff, Agnieszka (2007), 'The Land of Real Men and Real Women: Gender and E.U. Accession in Three Polish Weeklies', *The Journal of the International Institute*, 15: 1 <http://quod.lib.umich.edu/j/jii/4750978.0015.107?view=text;rgn=main> (last accessed 21 January 2016).
Greer, Germaine (1993) [1970], *The Female Eunuch*, London: Flamingo.
Griffiths, Robin (2008), 'Bodies without Borders? Queer Cinema and Sexuality after the Fall', in Robin Griffiths (ed.), *Queer Cinema in Europe*, Bristol: Intellect, pp. 129–42.
Grosz, Elizabeth (1999), 'Psychoanalysis and the Body', in Margrit Shildrick and Janet Price (eds), *Feminist Theory and the Body: A Reader*, Edinburgh: Edinburgh University Press, pp. 267–71.
Grosz, Elizabeth (1994), *Volatile Bodies: Towards a Corporeal Feminism*, Bloomington: Indiana University Press.
Hames, Peter (2004), 'Introduction', in Peter Hames (ed.), *The Cinema of Central Europe*, London and New York: Wallflower Press, pp. 1–13.
Hanáková, Petra (2011) 'From Mařka the Bricklayer to Black and White Sylva: Images of Women in Czech Visual Culture and Eastern European Visual Paradox', *Studies in Eastern European Cinema*, 2: 2, 145–60.
Hanáková, Petra (2014) 'The Feminist Style in Czechoslovak Cinema: the feminine imprint in the films of Vera Chytilova and Esther Krumbachova', in Hana Havelková and Libora Oates-Indruchová (eds), *The Politics of Gender Culture Under State Socialism: An Expropriated Voice*, London and New York: Routledge, pp. 211–33.
Haraway, Donna (1991), *Simians, Cyborgs and Women: The Reinvention of Nature*, London: Free Association Books.
Harvey, David (2005), *A Brief History of Neoliberalism*, Oxford: Oxford University Press.
Haynes, John (2003), *New Soviet Man: Gender and Masculinity in Stalinist Soviet Cinema*, Manchester: Manchester University Press.
Ibroscheva, Elza (2013), 'Selling the Post-Communist Female Body', *Feminist Media Studies*, 13: 3, 443–62.
Imre, Anikó (2012), 'Eastern European Cinema from No End to The End (As We Know It)', in Anikó Imre (ed.) *A Companion to Eastern European Cinemas*, Malden, MA and Oxford: Wiley-Blackwell, pp. 1–21.
Imre Anikó (2009), *Identity Games: Globalization and the Transformation of Media Cultures in the New Europe*, Cambridge, MA: MIT Press.
Iordanova, Dina (2003), *Cinema of the Other Europe: The Industry and Artistry of East Central European Film*, London and New York: Wallflower Press.

Jagielski, Sebastian (2013a), '"I Like Taboo": Queering the Cinema of Krzysztof Zanussi', *Studies in Eastern European Cinema* 4: 2, 143–59.
Jagielski, Sebastian (2013b), *Maskarady męskości. Pragnienie homospołeczne w polskim kinie fabularnym/Masquerades of Masculinity. Homosocial Desire in Polish Cinema*, Kraków: Universitas.
Johnson, Janet Elise (2009), *Gender Violence in Russia: The Politics of Feminist Intervention*, Bloomington: Indiana University Press.
Jovanović, Nebojša (2012), 'My Own Private Yugoslavia: Frantisek Cap and the Socialist Celluloid Closet', *Studies in Eastern European Cinema*, 3: 2, 211–29.
Jovanović, Nebojša (2015), 'How the Love Was Tempered: Labour, Romance and Gender Asymmetry in the Classic Yugoslav film', *Studies in Eastern European Cinema*, 6: 1, 33–48.
Kaganovsky, Lilya (2008), *How the Soviet Man was Unmade: Cultural Fantasy and Male Subjectivity Under Stalin*, Pittsburgh: University of Pittsburgh Press.
Kalmár, György (2013a), 'What the Body Remembers. The Memories of Eastern-European Body Cinema: Pálfi György's *Taxidermia*', in Miklós Takács (ed.), *Loci Memoriae Hungaricae: The Theoretical Foundations of Hungarian "lieux de mémoire" Studies*, Debrecen: Debrecen University Press, pp. 196–206.
Kalmár, György (2013b) 'Body Memories, Body Cinema: The Politics of Multi-Sensual Counter-Memory in György Pálfi's *Hukkle*', *Jump Cut*, 55, <http://ejumpcut.org/archive/jc55.2013/kalmarHukkle/index.html> (last accessed 21 January 2016).
Király, Hajnal (2015), 'Leave to Live? Placeless People in Contemporary Hungarian and Romanian Films of Return', *Studies in Eastern European Cinema*, 6: 2, 169–83.
Kristensen, Lars (ed.) (2012), *Postcommunist Film – Russia, Eastern Europe and World Culture: Moving Images of Postcommunism*, London and New York: Routledge.
Kulpa, Robert and Joanna Mizielińska (2011), 'Introduction: Why Study Sexualities in Central and Eastern Europe?', in Robert Kulpa and Joanna Mizielińska (eds), *De-Centring Western Sexualities: Central and Eastern European Perspectives*, Farnham and Burlington, VT: Ashgate, pp. 1–9.
Lim, Bliss Cua (2001), 'Dolls in Fragments: *Daisies* as Feminist Allegory', *Camera Obscura*, 16: 2, 37–77.
Livers, Keith (2004), *Constructing the Stalinist Body: Fictional Representations of Corporeality in the Stalinist 1930s*, Plymouth: Lexington Books.
Livezeanu, Irina, June Pachuta Farris, Mary Zirin, and Christine D. Worobec (eds) (2007), *Women and Gender in Central and Eastern Europe, Russia and Eurasia: A Comprehensive Bibliography*, Volumes I–II, London and New York: Routledge.
Marciniak, Katarzyna (2000), 'Cinematic Exile: Performing the Foreign Body on Screen in Roman Polanski's *The Tenant*', *Camera Obscura: A Journal of Feminism, Culture, and Media Studies*, 43, 1–43.
Marciniak, Katarzyna (2005), 'Second Worldness and Transnational Feminist Practices: Agnieszka Holland's *A Woman Alone*', in Anikó Imre (ed.), *East European Cinemas*, New York: Routledge, pp. 3–20.
Marks, Laura U. (2000), *The Skin of the Film: Intercultural Cinema, Embodiment and the Senses*, Durham, NC and London: Duke University Press.
Marsh, Rosalind (2013), 'The Concepts of Gender, Citizenship, and Empire and Their Reflection in Post-Soviet Culture', *The Russian Review*, 72: 2, 187–211.
Marx, Karl (1977), *Economic and Philosophic Manuscripts of 1844*, Moscow: Progress Publishers.
Marx, Karl and Frederick Engels (1947), *The German Ideology, Parts I and III*, New York: International Publishers.

Mazierska, Ewa (2007), *Roman Polanski: The Cinema of a Cultural Traveller*, London: I. B. Tauris.
Mazierska, Ewa (2010a), 'Eastern European Cinema: Old and New Approaches', *Studies in Eastern European Cinema*, 1, 5–16.
Mazierska, Ewa (2010b) *Masculinities in Polish, Czech and Slovak Cinema: Black Peters and Men of Marble*, Oxford: Berghahn Books.
Mazierska, Ewa and Elżbieta Ostrowska (2006), *Women in Polish Cinema*, Oxford: Berghahn Books.
Mazierska, Ewa and Laura Rascaroli (2006), *Crossing New Europe: Postmodern Travel and the European Road Movie*, London: Wallflower Press.
Mazierska, Ewa and Michael Goddard (2014), 'Introduction: Polish Cinema beyond Polish Borders', in Ewa Mazierska and Michael Goddard (eds), *Polish Cinema in a Transnational Context*, Rochester: University of Rochester Press, pp. 1–20.
Moss, Kevin (2006), 'Queer as Metaphor: Representations of LGBT People in Central and Eastern European Film', in Roman Kuhar and Judit Takásc (eds), *Beyond the Pink Curtain: Everyday Life of LGBT People in Eastern Europe*, Ljubljana: Peace Institute, pp. 249–67.
Mroz, Matilda (2007), 'Fracturing the Marble Façade: Visceral Excavation in Andrezj Wajda's *Man of Marble*', *Senses of Cinema*, 43, <http://sensesofcinema.com/2007/feature-articles/man-marble-wajda/> (last accessed 21 January 2016).
Mroz, Matilda (2012), *Temporality and Film Analysis*, Edinburgh: Edinburgh University Press.
Mulvey, Laura (1989), *Visual and Other Pleasures*, Basingstoke: Macmillan, 1989.
Mulvey, Laura, and Anna Backman Rogers (eds) (2015), *Feminisms: Diversity, Difference and Multiplicity in Contemporary Film Cultures*, Amsterdam: Amsterdam University Press.
Nigianni, Chrysanthi and Merl Storr (2009), 'Introduction', in Chrysanthi Nigianni and Merl Storr (eds), *Deleuze and Queer Theory*, Edinburgh: Edinburgh University Press, pp. 1–10.
Noheden, Kristoffer (2013), 'The Imagination of Touch: Surrealist Tactility in the Films of Jan Švankmajer', *Journal of Aesthetics and Culture*, 5, <http://www.aestheticsandculture.net/index.php/jac/article/view/21111/29896> (last accessed 22 January 2016).
Orbach, Susie (2010), *Bodies*, London: Profile Books.
Ostrowska, Elżbieta (1998), 'Filmic Representations of the "Polish Mother" in Post-Second World War Polish Cinema', *The European Journal of Women's Studies*, 5, 419–35.
Ostrowska, Elżbieta (2005), 'Representations of Female Sexuality in Polish Cinema after 1989: Liberation or Commodification?', *Kinema* 23, 23–32.
Ostrowska, Elżbieta (2012), 'Invisible Deaths: Polish Cinema's Representation of Women in World War II', in Helena Goscilo and Yana Hashamova (eds), *Embracing Arms: Cultural Representation of Slavic and Balkan Women in War*, Budapest and New York: Central University Press, pp. 29–58.
Ostrowska, Elżbieta (2014), 'Agnieszka Holland's Transnational Nomadism', in Ewa Mazierska and Michael Goddard (eds), *Polish Cinema in a Transnational Context*, Rochester: University of Rochester Press.
Ostrowska, Elżbieta and Joanna Rydzewska (2007), 'Gendered Discourses of Nation(hood) and the West in Polish Cinema', *Studies in European Cinema*, 4:3, 187–98.
Parisi, Luciana (2009), 'Adventures of a Sex', in Chrysanthi Nigianni and Merl Storr (eds), *Deleuze and Queer Theory*, Edinburgh: Edinburgh University Press, pp. 72–91.
Pethő, Ágnes (2015), *Cinema of Sensations*, Newcastle upon Tyne: Cambridge Scholars Publishing.
Portuges, Catherine (1995), 'Gendering Cinema in Postcommunist Hungary', in Ellen E. Berry (ed.), *Post-communism and the Body Politic*, New York: New York University Press, pp. 296–314.

Portuges, Catherine and Peter Hames (2013), 'Introduction', in Catherine Portuges and Peter Hames (eds), *Cinemas in Transition in Central and Eastern Europe after 1989*, Philadelphia: Temple University Press, pp. 1–9.
Richardson, Niall (2012), *Transgressive Bodies: Representations in Film and Popular Culture*, Farnham: Ashgate.
Ruffolo, David V. (2012), 'Educating-bodies: Dialogism, Speech Genres and Utterances *As The Body*' in John C. Landreau and Nelson M. Rodriguez (eds), *Queer Masculinities: A Critical Reader in Education*, Heidelberg and London: Springer, pp. 289–305.
Russo, Mary (1994), *The Female Grotesque: Risk, Excess and Modernity*, New York and London: Routledge.
Sakwa, Richard (1999), *Postcommunism*, Buckingham: Open University Press.
Sándor, Katalin (2014), 'Own Deaths' – Figures of the Sensable in Péter Nádas's Book and Péter Forgács's Film', *Acta Universitatis Sapientiae: Film and Media Studies*, 8:1, 21–40.
Shaviro, Steven (1993), *The Cinematic Body*, Minneapolis and London: University of Minnesota Press.
Shaviro, Steven (2012) 'Body Horror and Post-Socialist Cinema: György Pálfi's *Taxidermia*' in Anikó Imre (ed.), *A Companion to Eastern European Cinemas*, Malden, MA and Oxford: Wiley-Blackwell, pp. 25–40.
Shildrick, Margrit, and Janet Price (1999), 'Openings on the Body: A Critical Introduction', in Margrit Shildrick and Janet Price (eds), *Feminist Theory and the Body: A Reader*, Edinburgh: Edinburgh University Press, pp. 1–14.
Shilling, Chris (2005), *The Body in Culture, Technology and Society*, London: Sage.
Sobchack, Vivian (1992), *The Address of the Eye: A Phenomenology of the Film Experience*, Princeton, NJ: Princeton University Press.
Sobchack, Vivian (2004), *Carnal Thoughts: Embodiment and Moving Image Culture*, Berkeley: University of California Press.
Sontag, Susan (1994) [1966], *Against Interpretation*, London: Vintage.
Strausz László (2011), 'Archaeology of Flesh: History and Body-Memory in *Taxidermia*', *Jump Cut*, 53, <http://www.ejumpcut.org/currentissue/strauszTaxidermia/index.html> (last accessed 21 January 2016).
Studlar, Gaylyn (1988), *In the Realm of Pleasure: Von Sternberg, Dietrich and the Masochistic Aesthetic*, New York: Columbia University Press.
Štulhofer, Aleksandar and Theo Sandfort (eds) (2004), *Sexuality and Gender in Post-Communist Europe and Russia*, Binghamton, NY: Haworth Press.
Szwajcowska, Joanna (2006), 'The Myth of the Polish Mother', in Ewa Mazierska and Elżbieta Ostrowska, *Women in Polish Cinema*, New York and Oxford: Berghahn Books, pp. 15–33.
Thomas, Alfred (2007), *The Bohemian Body: Gender and Sexuality in Modern Czech Culture*, Madison: The University of Wisconsin Press.
Turner, Bryan S. (1996), *The Body and Society: Explorations in Social Theory*, 2nd edn, London: Sage.
Turner, William Benjamin (2000), *A Genealogy of Queer Theory*, Philadelphia: Temple University Press.
Vincze, Teréz (2016), 'Remembering Bodies: Picturing the Body in Hungarian Cinema after the Fall of Communism', *Studies in Eastern European Cinema* (in press).
Weiner, Amir (1999) 'Nature, Nurture, and Memory in a Socialist Utopia: Delineating the Soviet Socio-Ethnic Body in the Age of Socialism', *American Historical Review*, 104:4, 1,114–55.
Widdis, Emma (2003), *Visions of a New Land: Soviet Film from the Revolution to the Second World War*, New Haven: Yale University Press.

Widdis, Emma (2005) 'Muratova's Clothes, Muratova's Textures, Muratova's Skin', *Kinokultura* <http://www.kinokultura.com/articles/apr05-widdis.html> (last accessed 21 January 2016).
Widdis, Emma (2012), 'Socialist Senses: Film and the Creation of Soviet Subjectivity', *Slavic Review* 71:3, 590–618.
Williams, Linda (1991), 'Film Bodies: Gender, Genre, and Excess', *Film Quarterly* 44:4, 2–13.

PART I

Wounds and Traumas

CHAPTER I

'What Does Poland Want from Me?' Male Hysteria in Andrzej Wajda's War Trilogy

Elżbieta Ostrowska

In one of his public lectures, Andrzej Wajda complained that Polish literature lacks interesting female characters such as Emma Bovary. According to him, this absence was partly to blame for the historic and endemic parochialism of Polish culture.[1] Regardless of the accuracy of Wajda's critical statement, his choice of Flaubert's heroine as an example of complex femininity is certainly worth consideration. Why does he find her so attractive? Perhaps it is because Emma Bovary is such a departure from the historically dominant Polish model of a femininity that should cherish both national and familial values. Indeed, self-absorbed female hysterics are a rarity in Polish literature. The few who do exist, such as the character of Emilia Korczyńska from the novel *Nad Niemnem* (*On the Banks of Niemen River*, 1888) by Eliza Orzeszkowa, serve as objects of derision.

The relative rarity of female hysteria does not imply that Polish culture is a domain of mental and emotional stability. In fact the very opposite is the case, as it contains an abundance of images of male madness. The figure of the Romantic 'mad patriot', as discussed by Maria Janion in her pioneering study, is the most familiar example (Janion 1989: 10–12). As Janion mentions, Adam Mickiewicz, the most prominent poet of vernacular Romanticism, noted in one of his Parisian lectures that the turbulent history of Poland may have adversely affected the people's mental state. Mickiewicz claimed that when Poland lost its independence in the eighteenth century, the Poles may have consequently lost their senses. Janion discusses numerous examples of both literary and historical figures[2] that settle Mickiewicz's idea on a more empirical base (Janion 1989: 11). In the twentieth century, Polish culture remained within the Romantic paradigm, along with the archetypal figure of the 'mad patriot', which have deeply affected the Polish discourse of masculinity.

The films of Andrzej Wajda are frequently considered to exist within the paradigm of Romanticism (see e.g. Jackiewicz 1961; Lubelski 2000; Lubelski

2009; Nurczyńska-Fidelska 1995; Ozimek 1980; Ursel 1976). Polish critics frequently see the male protagonists of the War Trilogy (*Pokolenie* [*A Generation*, 1955]; *Kanał* [*Kanal*, 1956]; *Popiół i diament* [*Ashes and Diamonds*, 1958]), who are emotional, expressive and often irrational, as Romantic heroes, contemporary incarnations of the archetypal 'mad patriot'.[3] It is not only film critics who approach these films from such a perspective. For example, in his relatively recent study of Romanticism in Polish discourse, the philosopher and historian Marcin Król claims that *Ashes and Diamonds* is in fact a traditional Polish romantic drama owing to the performance of Zbigniew Cybulski, who plays the part of Maciek Chełmicki (1998: 5).[4] In contrast, the review of *Ashes and Diamonds*, written immediately after the film's release by the British critic Peter John Dyer, emphasised Cybulski's generic similarity to both James Dean and Marlon Brando, both icons of troubled Western masculinity. Dyer claims that the Polish actor 'is very much the same, contemporary type – impulsive, sensual, nervous to the point of hysteria and despair, masculine in his awkwardness, almost feminine in his charm' (Dyer 1959: 25).[5] He implies that the protagonist of *Ashes and Diamonds* is a hysterical male, akin to characters played by Dean and Brando, who epitomise a new model of vulnerable masculinity which emerged after the trauma of World War II. Who, then, is Maciek Chełmicki – a Romantic 'mad patriot', or a 'hysterical male'? Are these two critical and, for that matter, cultural claims contradictory? Perhaps one can locate the protagonist of Wajda's film in both paradigms, the vernacular tradition of Romanticism responding to the national trauma along with the cosmopolitan tradition of psychoanalysis and its reaction to the universal traumas of modernity. If this is the case and Maciek Chełmicki is both a Romantic and a hysteric, one may be encouraged to see this symbiosis more generally. Perhaps this interdependence reveals certain features of Polish culture and its gender politics that have remained thus far obfuscated. Perhaps the mask of 'patriotic madness' hides a hysterical component of vernacular masculinity. As hysteria speaks exclusively through the body and always occurs within certain temporalities, cinema is especially capable of representing it.[6] With the affective power of its images, Wajda's War Trilogy has relieved the hysterical impulses that have always been present in Polish culture, albeit in a latent form.

As many critics claim, male characters in the war films of Wajda explore the historical experience of World War II and its aftermath with a particular emphasis upon the emotional, psychological, and existential aspects (see e.g. Coates 2003; Lubelski 2000; Mazierska 2008). However, as Jaimey Fisher notes:

> Experiences of war, in ways hitherto underexplored, do not operate only, or even primarily, on people's minds in ways that they can fashion into material for communication. Rather, wars operate as well, or even predominantly, on the body, on the haptic and affective levels, which

yield a different kind of experience, and representation of it, altogether.[7] (Fisher 2014: 51)

Following Fischer's line of argument, in this chapter I will examine the films of Wajda's War Trilogy and the ways in which they articulate the bodily response to the World War II experience. My focus will be on the ways in which these bodies 'speak' in both the vernacular language of Polish Romanticism and the universal language of psychoanalysis. Moreover, I will look not only at the featured male bodies but also at the cinematic strategies employed in their representation. For Wajda's films do not only present hysterical bodies, but seek also to produce a hysterical effect in the viewer through cinematic form. This effect results from excessive camerawork, ruptures in narrative temporality, and narrative repetitions. In effect, the visual style, like a body in hysteria, creates an alternative language and communicates different meanings from those conveyed by the narrative content.

HYSTERIA, (MALE) TRAUMA AND POLISH ROMANTICISM

In its most familiar use, the concept of hysteria is intrinsically linked with femininity as defined within the patriarchal system.[8] Therefore, its diagnosis has been determined by the gender politics of a given historical moment and cultural milieu. As Julia Mitchell notes, 'in the nineteenth century hysteria and femininity were equated, then male hysteria was "discovered", [and] hysteria "disappeared"' (Mitchell 2000: 246). Mitchell also explains how various aspects of male hysteria are normalised in order to make it either invisible or to identify it as a brief psychotic response to a traumatic experience. In general, patriarchal medical discourse has claimed that women have an internal biological propensity for hysteria, whereas men can only respond hysterically (temporarily) to certain external traumatic factors. Sigmund Freud did not seem to make such a differentiation and he recognised the possibility of both female and male hysteria, a fact which was crucial to the development of psychoanalysis as a universally applicable theory.[9] Moreover, when Freud had his fellowship with Jean-Martin Charcot at the Salpêtrière Clinique in the 1880s, the latter researched male post-traumatic hysteria. In his essay on Charcot, Freud even makes the rather surprising 'discovery' that 'hysteria was far commoner among men than had been suspected' (Freud 1960a: 21; see also Micale 2008: 228–75, Bronfen 1998: 34–40). He also points to a direct link between hysteria and trauma:

> our investigations of . . . hysterical symptoms have revealed causes which must be described as psychic traumas . . . it is possible for one memory

to express its affect by means of bodily phenomena without the other mental processes – the ego – knowing about it or being able to interfere. (1960a: 20)

This strand of studies on hysteria was soon to be abandoned. However, it resurfaced after World War I, when hysteria was identified as a neurosis resulting from shell-shock. This more neutral term, 'neurosis', was invented to keep male hysteria separate from its inferior female counterpart. Despite these linguistic efforts, male hysteria made its bodily emergence and, in consequence, significantly destabilised the normative variants of masculinity. In their study of homosexuality in Polish culture, Paweł Leszkowicz and Tomek Kitliński recognised this effect:

> Hysteria signals the crisis of patriarchal masculinity conceived as a social role and a normative model. The erstwhile dominant and masterful soldier becomes a trembling wreck, whereas the energetic worker sinks into depressive contemplation. An attack of hysteria marks the moment at which the armour (a soldier or worker's uniform) is stripped away to reveal a tragic psychosomatic body trapped by its own disintegration. This body loses the courage and self-control that is demanded from it and slips into a generically female hysteria that also transpires to be a very male condition. With hysteria a new modern psychological model of masculinity emerges that is disintegrated, sensitive, and fragile. (Leszkowicz and Kitliński 2005: 201)

Leszkowicz and Kitliński also comment on the way in which hysteria has functioned in Polish medical discourse before World War II, as exemplified by the *Psychology Textbook* published in Poland in 1939. Although its author, J. Rothfeld-Rostowski, claims that hysteria is determined neither by gender nor by age, he mostly uses examples of male hysteria and links this predominantly with trauma (Leszkowicz and Kitliński 2005: 204). Presenting hysteria in a Polish textbook as a masculine issue may point to a potential conflict with the normative Polish model of masculinity.

In the West, male hysteria is commonly linked with the traumas of modernity. In Poland, the first significant collective trauma was caused by the partitions that took place at the end of the eighteenth century. Vernacular Romanticism, being a response to these events, is therefore often considered to be a post-traumatic cultural formation.[10] These historical circumstances caused a crisis in modern Polish masculinity, yet this has remained either unspoken or hidden behind a smokescreen of 'patriotic madness'.[11] Hysteria is perhaps one of the most significant symptoms of this crisis. While looking at Polish Romanticism from a broader cultural perspective, Leszkowicz and

Kitliński recognise its hysterical component; they see Juliusz Słowacki's poetry as 'entangled in the hysteria of history'[12] (Leszkowicz and Kitliński 2005: 223, 226). By the same token, it can be argued that, in the key scenes of the canonical Polish Romantic plays, the male protagonists' behaviour is reminiscent of hysterical symptoms. For example, at the end of the Great Improvisation scene in Mickiewicz's *Forefathers' Eve*, Konrad, the protagonist, faints and his body seems to undergo an epileptic fit.[13] Likewise, in the key scene of Słowacki's play *Kordian* its eponymous protagonist also faints, which is a symbolic indication of his incapacity to assassinate the Tsar[14] (cf. Chołody 2011: 50, 58). Polish literary critics usually interpret these characters and scenes as a cultural and existential metaphor for the tragic situation of the Polish nation. They approach Polish Romanticism from an aesthetic, historical and philosophical perspective, making the tacit assumption that a psychological approach would be both inappropriate and idle.

Critical resistance, whether conscious or not, to the recognition that certain images from the canonical works of Polish Romanticism embody a hysterical response to historical trauma can itself be a symptomatic gesture. Perhaps it is the absence of psychoanalysis in Polish culture that causes collective 'blindness' to the hysterical component of its Romantic heroes.[15] The literary critic Marek Bieńczyk considers Polish Romanticism to be a formation which prevented psychoanalytical discourse from entering Polish culture[16] (Bieńczyk 1995). As if to overcome this drawback, he employs a psychoanalytical approach in his monograph of the Romantic writer Zygmunt Krasiński. The critic uses the poet's letters written to family, friends and, especially, his lover, Delfina Potocka, to argue that he suffered from Freudian melancholia (Bieńczyk 1990). Michał Paweł Markowski concurs with Bieńczyk's interpretation of Krasiński's writing; however, he argues that it displays not only melancholia but also hysteria.[17] He identifies these two categories as essential features of modernity. While explaining the difference between them, Markowski writes: 'Melancholia calmly brood[s] over lost reality, whereas hysteria does not want to accept it and dramatically fights to link the subject with the reality that does not exist' (Markowski 2009: 61). Unlike the melancholic, the hysteric cannot stop staging the despair that has been caused by his loss. Both melancholia and hysteria, as the Polish critic argues, respond to trauma and in this respect they are analogous rather than oppositional phenomena. Markowski takes this one step further and claims that hysteria can be conceived of as a theatrical staging of melancholia (159). Notwithstanding the problematic nature of the link between hysteria and melancholia, I find Markowski's concept of hysteria effective in approaching the Polish post-traumatic cultural formations initiated by Romanticism in the early nineteenth century, which continued well into the late twentieth century. The Polish Film School, and especially Wajda's War Trilogy, testifies to this continuity. These films responded to the trauma of

World War II yet still remained within the cultural paradigm of Romanticism. The hysterical male bodies featured in Wajda's films forge an important, yet underexplored, link in this chain of tradition.

HYSTERICAL BODIES IN DOUBT

The opening scene of *Ashes and Diamonds*, a flagship of the Polish Film School, takes place in a bucolic rural landscape. Two men lie on the grass; behind them stands a small country chapel. One of them, Maciek (played by Zbigniew Cybulski), is visibly relaxed; his supine body, slightly parted lips and closed eyes make him look peaceful and gentle. His horizontal position contrasts with the verticality of his fellow, Andrzej, who looks nervously about as if anxiously waiting for some eventuality. A little girl approaches from behind and asks Andrzej to open the door of the chapel. The chapel is locked, but he lifts her above his head in order to help her place flowers by the Holy Mother icon above the door. Another man, Drewnowski, gives a loud whistled signal indicating the approach of a military vehicle. Andrzej urgently tells Maciek to stand up. A high-angle camera shot lingers on his body as it stretches horizontally across the frame.[18] He laconically stands, picks up their guns, frantically runs down the hill on which they have been sitting to the nearby road and opens fire on the car. As the open-top vehicle crashes into the hill a passenger is thrown onto the grass. We then see the driver in close-up as the car suffers an explosion and he dies behind the wheel. The other man regains consciousness, picks himself up and runs towards the chapel in order to escape Maciek's fire. Maciek follows him around the chapel and finally shoots him in one of its doorways. The victim bursts into flame as bullets enter his back and he collapses into the chapel. Maciek continues to fire gratuitously at his evidently dead victim; his erect body is tensed and looks as if it is subject to a hysterical fit over which he has no control; a grimace distorts his face and his parted lips reveal clenched teeth.[19] Finally, Andrzej enters the scene and forcibly stops this trance-like act of killing by abruptly lifting Maciek's gun away from the target.

During this brief opening scene the camera shoots Maciek from a multitude of angles and distances; we see him in both close-up and long shots. His constantly moving body seems to be engaged in a perpetual search for its place. Regarding the constant movement of Cybulski's body, Iwona Kurz concludes that 'the protagonist does not feel distress, it is his body that does' (2005: 208). Furthermore, *mise-en-scène* and other cinematic devices structure the opening scene around various oppositions: stillness versus mobility, horizontal composition versus vertical composition, silence versus agitated shouting, and so on. The most conspicuous contrast concerns the representation of the male body.

Figure 1.1 Hysterical act of killing in *Ashes and Diamonds*

Initially, Maciek's body is passive and vulnerable but then it becomes aggressive, predatory and hysterical. Throughout the scene it behaves as if driven by two opposing forces.[20] This bodily expression of conflict is typical of hysteria. In his early reflections on the issue, Freud commented: 'the outbreak of hysteria may almost invariably be traced to a *psychic conflict*, arising through an unbearable idea having called up the *defences* of the ego and demanding repression' (1960c: 206–7). In the opening scene of *Ashes and Diamonds* this internal psychic conflict is projected onto the bodily conflict between the two male characters: Maciek's body resists Andrzej's order. Firstly, he does not stand up quickly enough to undertake the requested action effectively. Secondly, he initially drops a gun while performing a brief and somewhat weird pantomime. Before he explains this to Andrzej with the brief line 'Ants, damn it!', it looks as if the gun is burning his hands, preventing him from touching it. When, finally, he starts shooting, he cannot stop. Andrzej behaves consistently throughout the whole scene; his body easily finds a proper spot for itself within both diegetic and frame space, whereas Maciek frantically traverses these spaces as if unable to settle down in either.[21] When his body stops, it is the result of a spasmodic fit rather than the sign of a completed action. His body not only conveys the internal conflicts of his persona, it experiences conflict autonomously.[22]

Maciek's brief, yet noticeable, delay in undertaking military action can be seen as an initial symptom of hesitancy, and this attains full expression in a number of subsequent scenes in *Ashes and Diamonds*. In one of these, Maciek and Andrzej commemorate their late comrades. They are in a hotel bar listening to a song. At some point Maciek notices glasses filled with spirit on the bar. He sniffs them intently, animalistically, and then he asks his friend whether he remembers 'the spirit at Rudy's place'. When Andrzej initially cannot remember the night, or simply denies it, Maciek curls his body, again like an animal, shouts 'No?', and then ignites the spirit. When describing the scene, Tadeusz Lubelski notes Maciek's hysterical laughter prior to his call upon nostalgia: 'Those were the times, Andrzej! We knew what they wanted from us' (Lubelski 2000: 169). As he says this, he leans back on the bar and stretches out his body in a position of luxuriant peace. His relaxed body physically recalls the war's past when they 'knew what to do', whereas his hysterical laughter signifies his uncertainty about the present and the future.[23]

This *embodied* uncertainty makes a poignant return during the scene in which Maciek and Andrzej converse in the hotel toilet. The former expresses his uncertainty about his patriotic duties in post-war times; specifically, he questions the reason for the planned political assassination. As in the opening scene, the conflict between these two characters is conveyed through both their gestural bodies and their compositional arrangement within the frame. Andrzej's body remains static during most of the conversation as if to mark the stability of his ideological stance. In contrast, Maciek constantly wanders back and forth between the foreground and background, moving respectively closer to or further from his fellow. At one point, he leans his body on the open toilet door and follows its back-and-forth pendulum-like movement from right to left. This excessive movement of Maciek's body occurs in a scene that is otherwise entirely dialogue-driven; thus it is not part of a goal-oriented action, but rather serves to communicate his mental state, specifically his hesitancy about past and future actions.[24] His body compromises his status as an acting subject.

In his reconsideration of subjectivity in the book *The Ticklish Subject* (2000), Slavoj Žižek discusses how it is formed in response to the content of the Unconscious as it is projected onto the figure of the Other. In the course of the discussion, Žižek introduces the notion of 'hysterical doubt'. According to him, the hysterical subject constantly asks the questions 'what am I for the Other? What does the Other want (from me)?' (249). In his essay on melancholia and hysteria in literature, Markowski elaborates on Žižek's discussion, emphasising the uncertainty inscribed in the hysterical subject: 'the hysteric does not know who he is' (2009: 162).[25] As previously mentioned, Markowski identifies the original genesis of the vernacular hysterical subject as an aspect of Romanticism. During the period when the Polish nation-state ceased to exist, the access of the subjective agency of Polish masculinity to the structures of official authority was inevitably compromised. Hence, the Romantic 'hysterical doubt' predominantly concerns aspects of both national and gender identity. In Polish Romantic literature, the male hysterical subject asks not the Žižekian question: 'What does the Other want (from me)?' but rather its vernacular variant: 'What does Poland want from me?'. He tries to find an answer to this question as both a Pole and a man. However, as the protagonists of Słowacki and Mickiewicz's plays show, he can find no answer. His body, which faints or experiences an epileptic fit, communicates not his inability to answer the question, but rather a denial of it.

The hysterical doubt expressed in the question 'What does Poland want from me?' may in fact be more ambiguous than it seems. According to traditional historical accounts, at the end of the eighteenth century Poland lost its independence as a result of the partitions. However, as Jan Sowa argues in his book *Fantomowe ciało króla* (*Phantom Body of the King*), Polish statehood had not actually existed since the end of the sixteenth century. He claims that, with the introduction of an elective monarchy in 1572, the Polish state became a federation of magnate dominions. A centralised monarchical power was replaced with a peculiar form of democracy that privileged each nobleman with the right to elect a king or to veto a bill (2011: 37). Providing a detailed analysis of economic, social, political and cultural factors that affected the Polish state between the sixteenth and nineteenth centuries, Sowa calls the period between 1572 and 1795 the epoch of a 'phantom state'. In this metaphor, he refers to the concept of a phantom limb that is lost yet still exists as a psychic representation. Thus, one can still feel pain originating from a physically non-existent limb. Furthermore, he employs Ernst Kantorowicz's concept of the two bodies of the king, the symbolic and the material, to claim that the Polish-Lithuanian Commonwealth was a *phantom body of the king* – thus, something that has never existed as a Lacanian Real but only as a collective phantasm (Sowa 2011: 38). From this perspective, Polish Romanticism as a post-traumatic cultural formation, becomes a phantasmatic category *per se*. A crucial question concerning Poland's partitions arises: 'What really is the lost object?' The hysterical doubt of the Romantic heroes implicitly conveys uncertainty as to what Polishness is, especially under the conditions of lost statehood.

During the inter-war period (1918–39), when Poland (re)gained its independence, the category of Polishness was again supported by the structures of statehood. However, if one agrees with Sowa's concept of the phantom Polish state in the pre-partitions period, the political attempts to establish the Second Republic as a continuation of the Polish-Lithuanian Commonwealth appears rather debatable. The ambivalence of Polish statehood, and hence national identity as well, continued into the post-World War II period, when 'regaining' independence became even more ambiguous than before, because it also marked the beginning of the Soviet regime. In these circumstances, a hysterical doubt concerning Polish statehood and identity resurfaced. It occurred not immediately after the end of World War II but with a delay typical of traumatic experience. In the second half of the 1950s, when, owing to certain political changes, the textual space of Polish culture opened to more polyphonic meanings and forms, repressed 'hysterical doubts' returned. Wajda's films exemplify this cultural process, and their male protagonists are descendants of the Polish Romantic heroes, not in regard to their devotion to the lost Motherland but rather in terms of their hysterical doubt regarding the identity of Poland and what it 'wants' from them.

(RE)STAGING HYSTERIA

Maciek's frenetic act of killing in the opening scene of *Ashes and Diamonds* is re-enacted in a derisive fashion later in the film. This takes place during a banquet that gathers all the local authorities together in order to celebrate the first day of peace and the beginning of the new communist era. Towards its end, Drewnowski drunkenly re-creates what he witnessed several hours earlier. He steps up onto a long banquet table and runs along it pretending to shoot at the guests with a fire extinguisher (see Hendrykowski 2009: 57). This episode is a grotesquely dramatised reprise of the initial hysterical act of killing. Thus, it foregrounds the performative aspect of the initial event. When, in the first scene, Maciek runs down a hill to the road it looks as if he is entering a stage on which a ritual of killing will take place. In contrast, Drewnowski moves up as he ascends the banquet table and this movement is emphasised by a long low-angle shot. Partly owing to its lack of audibly discernible dialogue, the scene looks akin to a grotesque pantomime.

The theatrical aspect of hysteria has frequently been explored by medical discourse, as exemplified in the famous lectures and demonstrations performed by Charcot in his clinic. Likewise, Freud notes this in his 'General remarks on hysterical attacks' written in 1909, in which he describes hysterical attacks as 'phantasies projected and translated into motor activity and represented in pantomime'[26] (Freud 1960b: 100). In *Ashes and Diamonds*, Drewnowski's drunken pantomime releases the internal shock caused by Maciek's frenetic act of killing, which he witnessed several hours earlier. In a more general sense, the episode, as Didi-Huberman puts it, is '*reinventing the time of the trauma* through an abrupt fiction – of replaying, that is, *restaging* a supposed "first scene"' (2003: 203).

A similar narrative device of performative repetition of an uncontrollable act of shooting occurs in another of Wajda's films, *A Generation*. The character of Jasio Krone, who is initially unwilling to join the resistance movement, finally changes his mind and, in order to prove his commitment, volunteers to execute a German *werkschutz* in a local bar. Like Maciek in *Ashes and Diamonds*, once he starts shooting he appears to be unable to stop. When he eventually succeeds in doing so, he cannot move, as if he is paralysed. After a while, he suddenly bursts out in hysterical laughter. Minutes later, Jasio re-enacts the whole event for his friends. Interestingly, he impersonates all of the characters participating in the earlier scene: the German official, his female companion, and himself while shooting. His friend, Stach, brutally stops this spectacle. However, a few days later, Jasio performs it again. Once more, he imitates the hysterical crying of the woman who witnessed the execution, and then turns away from his friends and starts to sob quietly. There is no liminal point separating the imitated scream of the woman and his sobs. It is as if Jasio has absorbed the trauma that the woman experienced into his own body. He re-enacts the female hysteria to communicate his own terror.

Re-enactment of female hysteria appears to be the only means by which Jasio can express the intense affect of terror. A symbolic transfer between femininity and masculinity occurs here which expresses the hysterical doubt that Jasio experiences about himself as both a gendered man and a Pole. Jasio's initial reluctance to join the underground movement can be seen as a resistance to the normative Polish cultural model of masculine heroism. The film introduces him as living with his senile father, whose only concern is to survive the difficulties of wartime. One evening, Jasio's Jewish friend and erstwhile neighbour, Abram, a refugee from the ghetto, comes to him and asks for help. He says somewhat enigmatically to his Polish friend, 'I've come home, to our home, to you.' What does he mean by 'our home'? Does he simply refer to the apartment building his family used to live in before the war? Or is 'our home' a metaphor for Poland as a space co-inhabited by both Poles and Jews? Finally, what does he mean by: 'I've come . . . to you'? The statement certainly alludes to the friends' former personal relationship, but what kind of relationship was this, one may ask. Does Abram refer to the friendship, or, perhaps, to a mutually recognised but not articulated homoerotic aspect of it? Regardless of the actual meaning of Abram's 'return home', Jasio closes the door on him. Shortly after this encounter, he decides to join the resistance movement and enacts the execution of the German *werkschutz*. Is this to confirm his 'proper' status as a male, as a Pole, or perhaps his Christianity, demanding of him that he love his neighbour? His hysterical behaviour during the execution highlights this confusion. The subsequent re-enactments of the event, in which he repeats the female scream over and over again, reveal his inability to find a stabilised subjective position from which he can speak. He experiences 'hysterical doubt' concerning both the position of Jews in his (Polish) home and his masculinity, which is prone to 'female affects'.

THE HYSTERICAL BODY OF FILMS

A Generation and *Ashes and Diamonds* feature male hysterical bodies that communicate multi-layered trauma. On the one hand, the characters respond to the traumatic events occurring within their fictional realities; on the other, they can be seen to transmit the historical trauma of the Polish male subject. However, it is not only the visual and narrative content of these films that evokes hysterical responses to the traumatic past. The war films of Wajda lend themselves to being interpreted as an embodiment of hysterical response to the past, for not only do they present hysterical characters and behaviour, but their formal structures produce a hysterical effect as well.

In her discussion of the relationship between trauma and hysteria, Mitchell emphasises the importance of memory as it connects these two categories. She argues that both the hysteric and the trauma victim are not only unable to remember things, but also perceive things from the past as if they are still happening; these subjects do not differentiate between perception and memory (Mitchell 2000: 280; see also Coates 2003: 17). Owing to the hysterical effect present in both narrative content and its cinematic rendition, Wajda's war films do not merely work as acts of memory in terms of recollection ('I still remember what happened then'), but rather they re-enact the past as if it still exists in the present ('I see the past events and I still experience them'). The affective excess of the hysterical male bodies marks a nodal point where these various temporalities intertwine, producing a hybrid of the present and the past.

The opening scene of *Ashes and Diamonds*, discussed previously, exemplifies how a cinematic body entangles various temporalities. With a minimal manipulation of the presented action's duration, a momentary effect of arrested narrative development occurs. This happens when Maciek is shooting ecstatically. It lasts too long in a double sense. Firstly, Maciek shoots for longer than is necessary as his victim is already dead, and, secondly, Wajda presents the action for longer than is necessary from the narrative point of view. Despite depicting a frenetic action, the shot becomes a peculiar *tableau vivant* or, as Paul Coates puts it, 'an arrested temporal flow'[27] (2003: 17). The flow of images is 'paralysed' for a brief moment as if halted in a hysterical attack. A similar rupture of standard narrative temporality occurs in *A Generation* during the scene representing Jasio's act of execution. It also lasts 'too long' and the immobilised camera seems unable to move itself, as does he.

Prolonging violent scenes is not rare or exceptional in cinema. Filmmakers often expand the duration of such emotionally and narratively significant moments in order to amplify their impact on the viewer. For this purpose, Eisenstein uses montage, specifically overlapping editing which allows the same event to be shown from various perspectives in order to create an illusion of temporal development where in fact there is none. By contrast, in Wajda's films the slightly prolonged shots 'stop' the narrative for a brief moment and produce a-temporal narrative surplus. Furthermore, when, in both films, these narratively excessive moments of killing are re-enacted, their chronological and linear temporality becomes disrupted. It takes up a circular form that further ambiguates the relationship between the past and the present. In Wajda's films, male bodies in hysterical fits (of killing) induce a temporary change in the mode of narration from that of 'telling' to 'showing'. Hence, the story transforms itself for a brief moment into a spectacle. Respectively, the characters move from the position of narrative agency to the position of an object in a spectacle. 'The spectacle of pain', as Georges Didi-Huberman calls hysteria (2003: 3), is repeatedly performed in all of the War Trilogy films.

TOUCH OF DEATH

In his pioneering study of male subjectivity in Wajda's film, Christopher Caes claims that it is established through the visual spectacle. As he notes, 'the exhibitionist quality of many of the heroes of Wajda's cinema can be linked to the necessity of producing spectacle in order to become a (national) subject' (Caes 2003: 117). He recognises the male body as a pivotal object in these spectacles; however, he links it mainly with a self-narcissistic pleasure operating on both intra- and extratextual levels. Caes argues that the male body in Wajda's films functions as a 'spectacle of the masculine', a 'study of male beauty' but also 'a material sign of the political and sociocultural order that stands behind it' (Caes 2003: 117, 118). Throughout his discussion, he claims that Wajda stages the male body as 'an object to look at'[28] for other characters and the viewer, while not mentioning other possibilities of spectatorial engagement.

As contemporary film theory, or more specifically its strand inspired by phenomenology, claims, cinematic spectatorship does not involve ocular activity only, but engages other senses as well (cf. Marks 2000; Sobchack 2004). That occurs because, as Laura Marks argues, the cinematic image has both optic and haptic qualities that mobilise two different types of perception. As Matilda Mroz explains: 'Optical perception . . . privileges the representational power of the image, allowing the spectator to organise themselves as a masterful subject. Haptic perception, by contrast, privileges material presence in a variety of ways' (2012: 7). In his analysis, Caes focuses exclusively on the optical qualities of the cinematic image to explain the process of male subjectivity formation. However insightful and original this explanation is, it needs to be complemented by an examination of the haptic aspect of the cinematic image to reveal other aspects of vernacular masculinity. Furthermore, such analysis may also help to explain a specific spectatorial engagement pertaining to Wajda's films. Many critics recognise the films' potential intensity; however, most often they see it as originating from purely optical qualities of the image and narrative content, whereas they do not recognise the effect of synaesthesia produced by these films which facilitates embodied spectatorship.

In his war films, Wajda employs various narrative and cinematic devices to produce an effect of embodied spectatorship. First and foremost, all three films of the War Trilogy introduce their characters, whether they are male or female, protagonists or extras, through haptic images of their bodies. In *A Generation*, for example, we see a group of young men who are playing with knives. Each of them takes a knife in his hand and throws it so that it sticks firmly in the ground. Firstly, a sharp metal object fits perfectly with a human hand, and secondly, it can firmly penetrate the solid texture of soil. When Kostek (played by Zbigniew Cybulski), before throwing the knife, touches his forehead with it, it produces a very brief yet intense haptic sensation. When the sharp tip of the knife touches human flesh, it foregrounds its softness and warmth. It makes one feel its corporeal vulnerability.

In the opening scene of *Kanal* there is a brief episode involving a pretty young woman being carried on a stretcher; she is covered with a rather coarse-looking blanket. The image suggests a tactile contrast between a supposedly warm and soft female body and the rough surface of wool. However, when the blanket slips down, it reveals her amputated leg and, in opposition to the previously predicted haptic sensation, the effect of a mutilated body is even stronger. In *Kanal*, the scene of the first encounter between Korab and Daisy, the protagonists also foreground their bodies. First we see the half-naked Korab preparing himself for shaving. He tries the razor on his finger and the sharp blade touches his skin (not as viscerally expressive as the famous analogous image in *Un Chien Andalou*, yet it undoubtedly produces a distinct tactile sensation). As in the opening scene of *A Generation*, this image produces a haptic contrast between human flesh and metal object. When Daisy enters the scene, she tells Korab to stop shaving, whereas he reproaches her for stinking and tells her to wash. Tellingly, the scene introduces the male body as a clean and fragile object, whereas the female body is dirty and needs to be cleansed.

Finally, the opening scene of *Ashes and Diamonds* features a brief ant infestation episode, as Maciek reaches for and prepares the assassins' machine guns. The moment at which he tries to rid himself of the tiny crawling insects from both his hands and his body is likely to induce an instinctive bodily response in many viewers, for it evokes a very common, if not universal, sensory memory. While the episode is certainly of little narrative importance, it delivers exceptional haptic power. The viewer might remain indifferent to the conversation between the characters and, likewise, the setting. The historical distance is also likely to widen the gap between the fictional 'reality' of the film and the contemporary reality of the spectator. However, the introjected sensation of an insect on one's skin lessens the gap between these two in a visceral fashion.

Foregrounding the haptic quality of cinematic images in the openings of Wajda's three war films produces an effect that Julian Hanich calls 'somatic empathy', which he describes as a 'partial parallelism between a character's body and my own body's sensation, affects or motions' (quoted in Fisher 2014: 60). Somatic empathy induces a specific type of identification with characters. It is different from the common affinity and allegiance that are produced by providing the viewer with access to the characters' psychology and emotions. In 'somatic empathy', it is through our body and its sensual and affective memory that we respond and connect to the characters. The opening scenes or episodes of these films include intense 'somatic' stimulants and as such establish a firm ground for spectatorial identification. Thus, the viewer's affective responses to Wajda's characters originate not only from psychological and emotional identification but also from the haptic qualities of the cinematic image.

The most intense moments of somatic empathy in Wajda's films occur in the scenes when the male body, introduced as fragile and vulnerable, is wounded. The moments during which the male body is being penetrated by a bullet are staged in identical fashion in all three films, only the setting being different. In *A Generation*, it occurs on the top of a staircase, in *Kanal* on a crumbled Warsaw street, and in *Ashes and Diamonds* next to a white laundry line.

Despite this different *mise-en-scène*, all the protagonists, Jasio, Korab and Maciek, respond to their wounded bodies in the same way. They look first at the wound, in a state of disbelief that it is *their* body that has been violently

Figure 1.2 Male wounded body in *Ashes and Diamonds*

penetrated. They then touch it as if to get back in contact with their suddenly estranged mortal carcass. Finally, they smell a bloodstain on their hands. A very distinct moment of bodily self-inspection occurs in these scenes. The wound makes them suddenly uncertain of their own body. It is likely that these are moments of a more generally emergent doubt. For as Dennis Slattery notes, 'To be wounded is to be opened to the world; it is to be pushed off the straight, fixed, and predictable path of certainty and thrown into ambiguity' (Slattery 2000: 13). In these brief moments, firstly, a complex process of subjective estrangement of each of the male characters from his body occurs, and then its reintegration into subjectivity takes place. The moment of self-inspection of a wound implicitly points to the twofold sense of the body elaborated in Western philosophical tradition: 'the lived, experienced body (or *Leib* in German), and the body qua physical thing, as it appears when examined like any other extended object (the *Körper*)' (Colombetti 2014: 115). As an object of *embodied* spectatorship, the cinematic wound makes it possible for the viewer not only to perceive the characters but also to experience them in a phenomenological sense. Edith Stein explains this difference: 'my perception of the others as a bearer of experiences is not a judgment (an *Einsicht*, literally a "seeing in") but a feeling (an *Einfühlung*, a "feeling in")' (Colombetti 2014: 173). The haptic quality of the cinematic image in Wajda's war films enables the male protagonist to emerge as a feeling body[29] whose intense presence on the screen ruptures the scopic regime of the visual spectacle.

CONCLUSION

In his war films, Wajda uses the haptic potential of the cinematic image in a range of ways to foreground the bodily presence of the characters. There is a noticeable excess of bodily presence, which is manifested through exaggerated facial gestures and constant body movement. These features are commonly associated with the hysterical body. As Mitchell claims, 'there is no more excessively present body than that of the hysteric (in hysteria the body is always acting and thereby expressing something)' (2000: 221). However, she also notes: 'Excess and absence are once again two sides of the same coin' (Mitchell 2000: 223). The excessive body in hysteria is an attempt to overcome the actual lack of bodily agency and, by extension, one's subjectivity. In some cases it expresses uncertainty concerning subjectivity. Owing to various political and cultural circumstances which have been discussed in the course of the chapter, the Polish masculine subject has constantly been questioned or deprived of its agency. Vernacular masculinity responded to the ambiguities and uncertainties regarding itself with its hysterical body, which emerged during the period of Romanticism and continued throughout the twentieth century.[30] Wajda's protagonists communicate these twists and doubts concerning their masculinity with their hysterical bodies. For them, as for their Romantic ancestors, 'Hysteria's moment is the moment when the displaced ego reasserts itself as a subject, fragile but too insistent' (Mitchell 2000: 343). The hysterical body represents the only possible way of exercising subjectivity, for the narrative agency of Wajda's protagonists is either significantly weakened or absent from the outset. Through the effect of somatic empathy, male hysteria serves as an embodied 'communicable metaphor' (Micale 1995: 194) for a politically impotent masculinity as developed within Polish political discourse.

NOTES

1. 'The protagonist of Polish literature tends to be a young boy, between 18 and 20, sometimes 22, a cadet or an officer, fighting for Poland. Can such a hero be interesting? Hardly. On the other hand, just look – Emma Bovary, all these women in Dostoyevsky – how beautiful it all is, how profound. These women teach me more about the world than men do' (Wajda 2000: 276–7).
2. Tadeusz Rejtan, an envoy to the Polish Sejm, is perhaps the best-known example of 'patriotic madness'. His madness and suicidal death are commonly interpreted as a response to the Third Partition of Poland. As Janion reconstructs his legend, he initiates what she calls 'a syndrome of Polish madness' (Janion 1989: 18–19; see also Mazierska 2008: 38).
3. In her book *Masculinities in Polish, Czech and Slovak Cinema*, Ewa Mazierska considers the Romantic figure of the 'mad patriot' as crucial for establishing a certain model of Polish masculinity that is also represented in the films of the Polish Film School. However, she discusses this 'madness' only within the familiar context of Polish Romanticism as producing a certain model of heroism (Mazierska 2008: 38–40, 45–53).
4. Maria Janion discusses Wajda's affinity with Romanticism in several essays (1980, 1991). Foreign critics also recognise it (see, for example, Coates 2003: 29–30). Michael Goddard presents an inspiring perspective on the issue in his essay 'Wajda, Grotowski and Mickiewicz: The Dialectic of Apotheosis and Derision' (2003: 132–45).
5. Polish critics also frequently compared Cybulski to James Dean (see Toeplitz 1962; Afanasjew 2008; Lubelski 2009). Likewise, they occasionally describe Maciek's body as hysterical, without, however, binding it to psychoanalytical discourse (see, for example, Kurz 2005: 208).
6. As Jaimey Fisher usefully notes: 'Cinema serves well in tracing such elusive textual effects on the body, affect, and perception: it offers both deliberately structured narratives and collectively staged events that help clarify the mechanisms of pre- or protocognitive affect, experience, and the body' (Fisher 2014: 51).
7. Bodily expression of war trauma is characteristic of the paintings by Wajda's favourite Polish post-war artist, Andrzej Wróblewski, especially his cycle of *Executions*. They often depict disfigured, dismembered and contorted male bodies in a brief moment of death. Interestingly, these dying bodies often look as if they are experiencing an epileptic or hysterical fit. The bodily disfigurement can recall paintings by Francis Bacon, who used the nineteenth-century photographs of hysterical men taken at the Salpêtrière Clinique

for his work. Unlike the photographs of female hysterics, these have never been publicised (see Micale 2008: 216–27).

8. It needs to be emphasised that there is nothing like a commonly accepted and precise definition of hysteria. Elisabeth Bronfen explains: 'The persistent inability of medical professionals to find a universal, systematic definition for hysteria ultimately illustrates that hysteria can have no autonomous and original identity outside its discursive formations' (1998: 102).

9. In his essay on trauma in Wajda's films, Paul Coates makes references to the Freudian double concept of trauma (2003: 16).

10. In her essay, Ewa Graczyk defines Polish national culture as centred around the century-long lack of independence and Polish Romanticism as its hegemonic cultural paradigm that survived until the end of the twentieth century (Graczyk 1995: 35). Likewise, in her essay on Mickiewicz, Maria Żmigrodzka identifies Polish Romantic cultural heritage as a collective 'source of suffering' (Żmigrodzka 1995: 190).

11. Traditional critical reception of Polish Romanticism recognises the importance of the motif of madness (see Kowalczykowa 1977; Chołody 2011), whereas the authors undertaking revisionist analysis of the cultural formation argue for its secondary importance. Agata Bielik-Robson identifies the categories of 'holy madness' and 'romantic fever' as 'romantic epiphenomena', not crucial components of Romanticism as a philosophical and cultural system (Bielik-Robson 2008: 79).

12. Interestingly, in their analysis of Polish Romanticism, Leszkowicz and Kitliński identify the popular Romantic digressive poems as a hysterical genre *per se* (2005: 234). They also reveal the hysterical aspect of Słowacki's poetry and relate it to the problem of sexuality and, specifically, bisexuality (226).

13. In his essay Goddard argues that many of Wajda's characters are analogous to Konrad from *Forefathers's Eve*, in that they embody the idea of 'the transcendent or monumental subject' (2003: 138). While I agree with this interpretation, I would also argue that it significantly overlooks the fact that Konrad, as well as many other Romantic heroes, is an embodied subject.

14. In his letters to family and friends, Zygmunt Krasiński often mentions his epileptic fits. In his monograph of the poet, Marek Bieńczyk argues that these epileptic symptoms signify a psycho-emotional discord caused by the historical circumstances. He writes: 'Horror of History directly touches Krasiński, it haunts him and brings about the destructive fever. In its sickness, Body imitates History . . . However, this relationship occurs also in its reversed form. History affects body, causes its different reactions, yet it does not work as its passive recipient of the impulses sent by History. Body talks about History not only by means of its own movements but also by means of images imposed on it' (Bieńczyk 1990: 96, quoted in Chołody 2011: 69).

15. This is not to claim that psychoanalysis has been entirely absent in Polish culture and critical discourse. In her book on Romantic philosophy, Agata Bielik-Robson emphasises the importance of Stanisław Brzozowski's criticism of Polish Romanticism. She writes: 'Brzozowski demonstrated willingness to look at the romantic formation from the new perspective of then emerging discourses of Nietzscheanism, Marxism, and psychoanalysis' (Bielik-Robson 2008: 76).

16. Bieńczyk characterises Polish Romanticism as a cultural formation based on a Manichean conflict between Good and Evil, and that belief, one may add here, survived into the post-World War II era. According to Bieńczyk, the anti-utopian nature of Freudian psychoanalysis did not respond to the needs of an oppressed society and, hence, it expressed a refusal to accept it on both a clinical and critical level (Bieńczyk 1995: 28).

However, he also points to some traces of psychoanalytical structures implicitly present in Polish Romanticism that critical reception has marginalised or erased. He concludes that Polish Romanticism discovered the realm of the Unconscious, yet instantly sealed it up (Bieńczyk 1995: 34).

17. In his letters, as Markowski argues, Krasiński describes his bodily torments, such as vomiting, migraine, convulsions, visions, acoustic hallucinations, which medical and literary discourse commonly identifies as hysterical symptoms (Markowski 2009: 145).

18. Although the horizontal composition in this shot is not as spectacular as in the opening shot of *Rebel Without a Cause*, because the former was filmed in academic ratio whereas the latter was filmed in Cinemascope, in both cases frame composition is used to foreground the male body as passive and vulnerable.

19. While describing the opening scene in his monograph on *Ashes and Diamonds*, Marek Hendrykowski identifies Maciek's behaviour as a 'murderous passion' (Hendrykowski 2009: 99). In a similar vein, Stanisław Ozimek emphasises the affective excess of the scene. While describing Maciek's behaviour in the scene, he writes about his 'wild eyes, open lips revealing clenched teeth' his 'frantic madness' and 'almost erotic abandon' (Ozimek 1980: 47, 57). In his compiled biography of Zbigniew Cybulski, Jerzy Afanasjew calls his acting very expressionistic and rough: 'He is not afraid of screaming. He is not afraid of howling and crying' (Afanasjew 2008: 179). In general, critical reception of Cybulski's rendition of the character of Maciek emphasises the affective excess of his acting style.

20. Paul Coates also emphasises various oppositions in the opening scene, and also discusses Maciek as a contradictory figure (Coates 2005: 30).

21. His restlessness and constant movement can be seen as a bodily expression of Caes's remark about a Polish national subject that is 'enjoined to occupy an impossible position' (Caes 2003: 130).

22. In this interpretation I draw on the general idea of embodiment that, as Giovanna Colombetti explains, is based on the premise that 'the mind is not an immaterial Cartesian substance, a thinking thing, but neither (and more controversially) is the brain its minimally sufficient physical basis. Rather the mind is enacted or brought forth by the living organism in virtue of its specific organization and its interaction with the world' (Colombetti 2014: xiv). Similarly, Richard Shusterman, in his theory of somaesthetic, writes about a somatic style in which a split between body and mind ceases to exist: 'Somatic style . . . is not simply an external image of character but an integral expression or aspect of it, because character is not merely a secret inner essence but rather something intrinsically expressed or constituted through somatic behaviour, demeanour, and attitude' (Shusterman 2012: 319).

23. In her monograph on Andrzej Wajda, Janina Falkowska sees Maciek as 'uncertain as to which political orientation would prevail, many Polish citizens were virtually forced to co-operate with the winning party against their inner wishes' (2007: 57). Likewise, Tadeusz Lubelski notes the political doubt that Maciek experiences (2000: 171).

24. The scene was shot as a first one, and it was Cybulski's hesitant movement that Wajda was delighted with. He saw it as a key clue to the character of Maciek Chełmicki (Afanasjew 2008: 160).

25. In a similar vein, Juliet Mitchell links hysteria with destabilised identity: 'the serious hysteria sufferer shifts the register from a position of place in any world order into a crisis of identity. The "Where am I?" becomes the "Who am I?"' (Mitchell 2000: 342).

26. Although in this specific essay Freud refers to hysteria caused by sexual repression, it could also be applied to hysteria caused by a traumatic event.

27. In his study of hysteria, Didi-Huberman emphasises that its discourse frequently utilises the form of *tableau* (2003: 203–10).
28. Mazierska also notes Maciek's 'to-be-lookedness', yet she does not link it with a specific model of national subjectivity as Caes does, but rather interprets it as an object of 'visual pleasure' (Mazierska 2008: 50; see also Warkocki 2013).
29. In her discussion of hysteria, Mitchell employs the concept of the 'feeling body'. According to her, hysteria erases the traditional division in Western thought between mind and body. It is feeling that plays a crucial role in that process: 'Both the mind and the body feel. Or perhaps one should say that feelings such as joy or pain, guilt or jealousy do not distinguish between mind and body' (Mitchell 2000: 205, 207). Therefore, the hysterical body is an affective body that does not express emotions but constitutes the very origin of these. If body and mind are both experiencing the same emotion at the same time it removes the possibility of one controlling the other.
30. Paul Lerner makes a similar claim in relation to German masculinity and hysteria: 'In peacetime and war, male hysteria bespoke the economic and military failings of German masculinity' (2003: 2).

WORKS CITED

Afanasjew, Jerzy (2008), *Okno Zbyszka Cybulskiego. Brulion z życia aktora filmowego połowy XX w.*, Warszawa: Prószyński i S-ka.

Bielik-Robson, Agata (2008), *Romantyzm, niedokończony projekt. Eseje*, Kraków: Universitas.

Bieńczyk, Marek (1990), *Czarny człowiek. Krasiński wobec śmierci*, Warszawa: Instytut Badań Literackich PAN.

Bieńczyk, Marek (1995), 'Czy romantyzm jest odpowiedzialny za brak psychoanalizy w kulturze polskiej?', in Dorota Siwicka and Marek Bieńczyk (eds), *Nasze pojedynki o romantyzm*, Warszawa: Instytut Badań Literackich PAN, pp. 27–34.

Bronfen, Elisabeth (1998), *The Knotted Subject. Hysteria and Its Discontent*, Princeton, NJ: Princeton University Press.

Caes, Christopher (2003), 'Catastrophic Spectacles: Historical Trauma and the Masculine Subject in *Lotna*', in John Orr and Elzbieta Ostrowska (eds), *The Cinema of Andrzej Wajda: The Art of Irony and Defiance*, London: Wallflower Press, pp. 116–31.

Chołody, Mariusz (2011), *Ciało-dusza-duch. Dyskurs cielesny w romantyzmie polskim (fragmenty)*, Poznań: Wydawnictwo Poznańskie.

Coates, Paul (2003), 'Wajda's Imagination of Disaster: War Trauma, Surrealism and Kitsch', in John Orr and Elzbieta Ostrowska (eds), *The Cinema of Andrzej Wajda: The Art of Irony and Defiance*, London: Wallflower Press, pp. 15–29.

Coates, Paul (2005), *The Red and the White: The Cinema of People's Poland*, London and New York: Wallflower Press.

Colombetti, Giovanna (2014), *The Feeling Body: Affective Science Meets the Enactive Mind*, Cambridge, MA and London: MIT Press.

Didi-Huberman, Georges (2003), *Invention of Hysteria: Charcot and the Photographic Iconography of the Salpêtrière*, trans. Alisa Hartz, Cambridge, MA and London: MIT Press.

Dyer, Peter John (1959), 'Ashes and Diamonds', *Films and Filming*, 5:11, 24–5.

Falkowska, Janina (2007), *Andrzej Wajda. History, Politics, and Nostalgia in Polish Cinema*, New York and Oxford: Berghahn Books.

Fisher, Jaimey (2014), 'The Haptic Horrors of War: Towards a Phenomenology of Affect and Emotion in the War Genre in Germany, 1910s to 1950s', *Seminar: A Journal of Germanic Studies*, 50: 1, 51–68.
Freud, Sigmund (1960a), 'Charcot', in *Collected Papers*, vol. 1, authorised translation under the supervision of Joan Riviere, New York: Basic Books, pp. 9–23.
Freud, Sigmund (1960b), 'General Remarks on Hysterical Attacks', in *Collected Papers*, vol. 2, authorised translation under the supervision of Joan Riviere, New York: Basic Books, pp. 100–4.
Freud, Sigmund (1960c), 'The Etiology of Hysteria', in *Collected Papers*, vol. 1, authorised translation under the supervision of Joan Riviere, New York: Basic Books, pp. 183–219.
Goddard, Michael (2003), 'Wajda, Grotowski and Mickiewicz: The Dialectic of Apotheosis and Derision', in John Orr and Elzbieta Ostrowska (eds), *The Cinema of Andrzej Wajda. The Art of Irony and Defiance*, London: Wallflower Press, pp. 132–45.
Graczyk, Ewa (1995), 'Przeżyć dzień, napisać księgę?', in Dorota Siwicka and Marek Bieńczyk (eds), *Nasze pojedynki o romantyzm*, Warszawa: Instytut Badań Literackich PAN, pp. 35–43.
Hendrykowski, Marek (2009), *Wajda's Ashes and Diamonds*, transl. Peter Langer, Poznań: Wydawnictwo Naukowe UAM.
Jackiewicz, Aleksander (1961), 'Powrót Kordiana', *Kwartalnik Filmowy*, 4, 23–37.
Janion, Maria (1980), 'Wajda i wartości', in Maria Janion, *Odnawianie znaczeń*, Kraków: Wydawnictwo Literackie, pp. 112–19.
Janion, Maria (1989), *Wobec zła*, Chotomów: Verba.
Janion, Maria (1991), 'Egzystencja ludzi i duchów. Rodowód filmowej wyobraźni Andrzeja Wajdy' in Maria Janion, *Projekt krytyki fantazmatycznej: szkice o egzystencji ludzi i duchów*, Warszawa: Wydawnictwo PAN, pp. 110–19.
Kowalczykowa, Alina (1977), *Romantyczni szaleńcy*, Warszawa: Państwowe Wydawnictwo Naukowe.
Król, Marcin (1998), *Romantyzm. Piekło i niebo Polaków*, Warszawa: Res Publica.
Kurz, Iwona (2005), *Twarze w tłumie. Wizerunki bohaterów wyobraźni zbiorowej w kulturze polskiej lat 1955–1969*, Warszawa: Świat Literacki.
Lerner, Paul (2003), *Hysterical Men: War, Psychiatry, and the Politics of Trauma in Germany, 1890–1930*, Ithaca and London: Cornell University Press.
Leszkowicz, Paweł and Tomek Kitliński (2005), *Miłość i demokracja. Rozważania o kwestii homoseksualnej w Polsce*, Kraków: Aureus.
Lubelski, Tadeusz (2000), *Strategie autorskie w polskim filmie fabularnym lat 1945–1961*, 2nd edn, Kraków: Rabid.
Lubelski, Tadeusz (2009), *Historia kina polskiego. Twórcy, filmy, konteksty*, Katowice: Videograf II.
Markowski, Michał Paweł (2009), *Życie na miarę literatury. Eseje*, Kraków: Wydawnictwo Homini.
Marks, Laura U. (2000), *The Skin of the Film*, Durham, NC: Duke University Press.
Mazierska, Ewa (2008), *Masculinities in Polish, Czech and Slovak Cinema: Black Peters and Men of Marble*, Oxford: Berghahn Books.
Micale, Mark S. (1995), *Approaching Hysteria: Disease and Its Interpretations*, Princeton, NJ: Princeton University Press.
Micale, Mark S. (2008), *Hysterical Men. The Hidden History of Male Nervous Illness*, Cambridge, MA and London: Harvard University Press.
Mitchell, Juliet (2000), *Mad Men and Medusas: Reclaiming Hysteria*, New York: Basic Books.
Mroz, Matilda (2012), *Temporality and Film Analysis*, Edinburgh: Edinburgh University Press.

Nurczyńska-Fidelska, Ewelina (1995), 'Romanticism and History. A Sketch of the Creative Output of Andrzej Wajda', in Ewelina Nurczyńska-Fidelska and Zbigniew Batko (eds), *Polish Cinema in Ten Takes*, Łódź: Łódzkie Towarzystwo Naukowe, pp. 7–19.

Ozimek, Stanisław (1980), 'Konfrontacje z Wielką Wojną', in Jerzy Toeplitz (ed.), *Historia filmu polskiego 1957–1961*, vol. 4, Warszawa: Wydawnictwa Artystyczne i Filmowe, pp. 11–128.

Shusterman, Richard (2012), *Thinking through the Body: Essays in Somaesthetic*, New York: Cambridge University Press.

Slattery, Dennis Patrick (2000), *The Wounded Body: Remembering the Markings of Flesh*, Albany: SUNY Press.

Sobchack, Vivian (2004), *Carnal Thoughts: Embodiment and Moving Image Culture*, Berkeley: University of California Press.

Sowa, Jan (2011), *Fantomowe ciało króla. Peryferyjne zmagania z nowoczesną formą*, Kraków: Universitas.

Toeplitz, Krzysztof Teodor (1962), 'Zbyszek – polski James Dean', *Polska* 20.

Ursel, Marian (1976), 'Legenda romantyczna w polskiej szkole filmowej', in Jan Trzynadlowski (ed.), *Polska Szkoła Filmowa. Poetyka i tradycja*, Wrocław: Zakład Narodowy Ossolińskich, pp. 65–90.

Wajda, Andrzej (2000), *O sobie. O sztuce. O polityce*, Maria Malatyńska (ed.), Warszawa: Pruszyński i S-ka.

Warkocki, Błażej (2013), 'Nie na sprzedaż', in Zespół K. P. (ed.), *Wajda. Przewodnik Krytyki Politycznej*, Warszawa: Wydawnictwo Krytyki Politycznej, pp. 147–60.

Žižek, Slavoj (2000), *The Ticklish Subject: The Absent Centre of Political Ontology*, London and New York: Verso.

Żmigrodzka, Maria (1995), 'Czy Mickiewicz zamordował Kochanowskiego? Interpretacje romantycznej interpretacji', in Dorota Siwicka and Marek Bieńczyk (eds), *Nasze pojedynki o romantyzm*, Warszawa: Instytut Badań Literackich PAN, pp. 189–203.

CHAPTER 2

Alcoholism and the Doctor in Béla Tarr's *Sátántangó*

Calum Watt

INTRODUCTION: ALCOHOL IN THE FILMS OF BÉLA TARR

Alcohol is a constant presence in the films of Béla Tarr. Tarr gives special significance to heavy drinkers and their bodies, which are frequently figured as hunched or ruined. This is a theme that persists throughout Tarr's career, from his first films to his averred final work, *A torinói ló* (*The Turin Horse*, 2011). An early short film, *Hotel Magnezit* (1978), shows an old man being kicked out of a hostel, partly because of his drunkenness. The main character of Tarr's second film, *Szabadgyalog* (*The Outsider*, 1980), loses his job as a nurse in a mental hospital also on account of his drinking. In *Macbeth* (1982), Tarr's television adaptation of Shakespeare's play, Tarr retains – where many productions drop – what is arguably the most famous drunkard speech in English literature, that of the Porter who imagines he is a gatekeeper of Hell (played by Ferenc Bencze, perhaps alluding to his role as the barman in Zoltan Fabri's *Az ötödik pecsét* [*The Fifth Seal*, 1976]). In *Kárhozat* (*Damnation*, 1988), the anomic protagonist Karrer (Miklós Székely B.) is a nomad who sits around in bars giving nihilistic monologues. In a notable moment from Tarr's last film, *The Turin Horse*, a drunkard (Mihály Kormos) appears at the remote house of the main characters to ask for pálinka – a Hungarian fruit brandy, and the most frequent drink of choice in Tarr's films – before giving a long speech prophesying apocalypse.

The key focus of this chapter, however, will be on one extended episode from Tarr's seven-hour-long magnum opus, *Sátántangó* (*Satantango*, 1994), namely the third of the film's twelve sections, which occurs a little over an hour into the film and is centred around a reclusive, obese and severely alcoholic doctor. The film as a whole, set in the closing days of the Hungarian communist era, tells the story of a crumbling farm collective and the return of one of their number, Irimiás (Mihály Vig), long thought dead, who deceptively promises a better future in a new collective. The film primarily follows the fortunes of its protagonists as they variously drink and dance together and scheme against each other, but also follows a young girl in the run-up to her suicide and the activities of the false messiah who cons the group out of their savings. The doctor's chief pastime is to sit at his desk drinking and obsessively, voyeuristically looking out of his mould-encrusted windows and recording every aspect of the petty goings-on at the estate in a journal. In the episode under discussion in this chapter, entitled 'To Know Something', he carries out his daily business, has a minor fall in his home, and, having run out of pálinka, reluctantly resolves that he must leave home to get some more. The doctor's journey leads him through the estate in the rain to the pub where the rest of the peasants are cavorting riotously. This hour-long episode is notable for following this sick man almost in real time, literally step by step and drink for drink, making it an intimate and yet epic treatment of bodily needs and a veritable odyssey. Never before has the physical effort involved in the life of an alcoholic body been so exhaustively documented. As this chapter progresses I will pursue this idea of an 'alcoholic body' in relation to two theoretical notions: firstly, how the body is situated within the film's world and how that world can be said to 'weigh down' on the body; and secondly, how alcoholism can be seen as a reaction to this world, one which creates subjective temporal distortions. These ideas are informed respectively by the work of the French philosophers Jacques Rancière and Gilles Deleuze.

Sátántangó's doctor is played by Peter Berling, a German actor, writer and producer, perhaps best known for starring in some of Werner Herzog's films with Klaus Kinski – *Aguirre, der Zorn Gottes* (*Aguirre, the Wrath of God*, 1972), *Fitzcarraldo* (1982) and *Cobra Verde* (1987) – and for being involved in the productions of early films by Rainer Werner Fassbinder. More recently, Berling has also become known as a writer of historical novels set in the Middle Ages. The choice of Berling is unusual in the context of Tarr's films in that Tarr does not normally cast professional actors for key roles, preferring amateurs. This is because, as András Bálint Kovács observes in the first monograph in English on Tarr, Tarr prizes the expressive physical characteristics of his actors, especially their faces, rather than any psychologically realistic acting (Kovács 2013: 15). In practice what this means is that a great deal of time in Tarr's films is given over to simply observing the physical bodies of the characters. Acting as such takes a secondary role in the doctor's episode as the shots focus on the very being or presence of Berling. Berling is an actor who has always been known for his large frame, and it can be said that in Tarr's films the characters are closely identified with their bodies: in the first place they are physical beings caught on camera rather than the social role or persona they are playing. Post-synchronised sound is used in *Sátántangó* and the dubbing into

Hungarian is not particularly tight, which means that although we see Berling it is not him that we hear. Before moving on to the theoretical considerations mentioned above, this chapter will focus firstly on a formal analysis of how the doctor's character is created through a combination of Berling's pro-filmic body and the film's sound design.

PHYSICAL BODIES, MATERIAL WORLDS

The episode in question begins with a shot showing a view seen through binoculars. Through the binoculars the doctor's neighbour Futaki (Miklós Székely B.) can be seen looking out of his window from his house across the yard, while the sound of bells tolling can be heard. In the context of the film, which has a non-linear temporal structure, this is understood as a reprise of the opening episode and thus locates the time as early in the morning. The significance of the apparently phantom bells only becomes clear later in the film. The sight seen through the binoculars moves to a dribbling tap in the middle of the yard. As the camera continues to move around the yard, hens can be seen pecking amid the dirt and general flotsam littering the place. The camera stops at the corner of a rooftop for a moment, before coming down the side of the building to the dirt in front of it where a shaggy dog eating scraps fills the frame. The camera rests in front of the dripping tap. It is at this point that we have the first cut and are presented with a close-up of the doctor's profile, his head filling the right-hand side of the frame while the binoculars he is looking through, and his large, spade-like hands holding them, fill the left-hand side. The sound of the bells fades away and the doctor puts the binoculars away with the heavy scratching sound of an old desk drawer being opened and closed. He leans forward and we hear the sound of the friction and rubbing of his clothes. The camera dollies backwards and reframes the doctor so that we can see the far corner of the desk he is sitting at, on which there are set a small wooden board, three small glasses of different sizes, a shallow, overflowing tin ashtray and a tall, broad bottle filled with a clear liquid. He then reaches for the bottle and pulls the top from it with a brief anticipatory exhalation. He pours a drink into the middle-sized glass, stops to look at it, then tops it up a little. He then takes the smallest, shot-sized glass and, producing a small glass jug full of another clear liquid, fills it to the brim. The tinkling, needling sound of liquid being measured is here met by the increasing sound of harsh and congested breathing. The contents of both of these glasses are then poured into the larger glass, which is brought to the doctor's lips. It later becomes evident that the large bottle contains pálinka and the small jug contains water. The doctor takes two sips, pursing his lips, and replaces the glass, keeping one eye on the window. He draws from the ashtray a nearly spent cigarette and takes a light drag before setting it back and exhaling again; the respiration involved in smoking that can be heard here seems to introduce a regularity to the pattern of breathing we have been hearing until now. The camera reframes again as the doctor opens the main drawer of the desk and takes out a number of small exercise books. He takes the board from the desk and balances it against the open drawer as he sorts through the exercise books, choosing one and replacing the others. The board, it becomes clear now, is a rest for writing on. Producing a pen, the doctor opens the book, looks at his watch and begins to write. As he does so, the camera slowly reframes again to give a close-up side-view of the doctor's face, similar to the framing at the beginning of the shot. The doctor speaks as he writes, slowly and gutturally, dictating to himself, with a pause for breath and a clearing of the throat between every couple of words. Here, as elsewhere, it is as if the recorded sound of his voice comes not from in front of his mouth but from under his throat. He is detailing exactly what has just been seen, that his neighbour Futaki was startled early in the morning and was looking out the window, and the doctor adds his own interpretation: Futaki is 'afraid of death'. He then looks up, allowing us the clearest view so far of his face: he has a short, greyed beard, suggestive more of neglect than design, and heavy bags under his eyes. We do not see his whole head, for the frame cuts off above the forehead. In these close-ups, the doctor is often framed in such a way that the line of his brow to his chin fills the entire central vertical axis of the frame, with his nose to the back of his neck occupying the entirety of the right-hand side of the frame. His girth is such that his chest extends the whole breadth of the frame. He looks out of the window. His lip curls as he exclaims

Figure 2.1 The doctor looks out of the window (*Sátántangó*)

words to the effect of 'Don't worry Futaki, you and the others will all be dead soon'. His lip uncurls and he continues to stare out of the window, the camera remaining fixed on his expression for almost half a minute before the next cut.

Together, these two shots introducing the doctor take up almost eight minutes. I relate the sequence in such detail because much of the film consists precisely in these apparently insignificant actions and everyday, banal minutiae studied over the course of slow camera movements and long sequence-shots. The actions add up to more than the sum of their parts and the scenes resist a cursory synopsis. Though the slow pace is the most frequent observation made about Tarr's films, Kovács is correct to identify what it is that this pace consists of, and that is not merely duration as such, nor the suggestion of 'nothing happening', but the scrupulous attention to the details of the characters' everyday actions and processes: in other words, a form of *'radical continuity'* in which apparently trivial details are not passed over (Kovács 2013: 114). The episode with the doctor is one of the most outstanding examples of this. The essence of viewing Tarr's film consists in close observation; significantly, this is also what the doctor's activity consists of. As Erika Balsom writes, '[t]hrough the extension of time and the deployment of cinematic scale, Tarr engages in a sort of magnification of the world, rendering the miniature gigantic' (Balsom 2007: 28). Although Balsom is referring primarily to visual elements, this observation can be made about the auditory elements as well. The voice is almost constantly present on the post-synchronised soundtrack, but nearly all of it is non-verbal: it is thick with breaths, grunts, sniffs, groans, purrs and wordless murmurs. It is not merely non-verbal; much of it is what would normally be considered involuntary – coughs, splutters, sudden gasps. Even more intimate than the sound of breathing is the sound of the moisture in the mouth and inside the cheeks: sounds that ordinarily seem to exist only between one's own ears. Even the doctor's grimaces when drinking the pálinka or smoking are audible as the briefest intakes of breath. In this way, by magnifying the sounds of the doctor's mouth and throat, the film accords with the analyses of Davina Quinlivan, for whom breathing, as an aspect of film form and diegesis, can inter-subjectively make the viewer aware of their own breathing and engender a degree of insight into a character's interiority (Quinlivan 2012: 131–41). As I argue below, in the case of *Sátántangó* this interiority is to be understood in a physical rather than an emotional sense.

The doctor's speech during these sequences is a low rumble, like a tractor's wheel through dirt; the pitch is hoarse and deep, coming from a cavernous chest, while the timbre records the harsh friction in the throat of the ill man. It is in this way that *Sátántangó* is marked by what Michel Chion calls 'materializing sound indices': 'the qualities of a sound that direct our attention to the physical nature of its source, to whatever it is that is blowing, scraping, rubbing – the indices of resistance of the real, reminding us that a voice does not issue from the pure throat of an angel but from a body' (Chion 2009: 244). The use of sound in Tarr's film has a Bressonian materiality, but with none of the lightness or sense of metaphysical import associated with Bresson. It registers the weight of the world that the body is made to suffer. The proximity with the doctor into which the sounds project us is matched by the movement of the dolly shots, weaving closely around his body and often coming to settle around or behind his heavy-set shoulders. Emphasis is also given to sounds such as the dragging of boots on the floor and the rustling of paper, sounds which suggest not only the gross materiality of the world that is the doctor's study, but also his heavy presence embedded within that world. When the doctor sits in his chair, prominence is given to the pained sounds of the joints of the chair and the creaking of the wood. Later in the episode we hear him urinating, which from the sound of the sparse tinkling and the pained breaths seems forced or difficult – or perhaps he is just extremely dehydrated. Likewise when the doctor draws in the third shot, following the two discussed, we hear the scraping of the cheap pencil on the paper, as if to testify to inscription less as a means of intellectual signification or creation than as a mode of physical labour or exertion. When he writes and the action of the hand is mirrored in the speech of dictation, the slowness of this writing seems to be a measure of effort or determination rather than care. From the sounds, we are given to hear something of how he feels, how it feels to be him in his world – and this feeling is essentially corporeal. What he thinks or feels psychologically is only given in what he actually verbalises, either to himself or as he writes in his journal. What he does say – as with the remark that Futaki and the inhabitants of the farm will all die – is often somewhat cryptic. While emphasis is given to the characteristics of the pro-filmic bodies of Tarr's characters, they are at the same time approached through a process of somatic empathy rather than intellectual or psychological understanding. Characters are in the first instance bodies, not thoughts or feelings.

It is clear that some time has passed between the third and fourth shots of the sequence. This is evident from the depleted volume of pálinka in the bottle and confirmed by the reframing of the camera, which tracks towards the doctor's left side, from the antechamber of the doorway into his study, where previously the camera had orbited around his right shoulder and his view of the window. As the camera tracks in, he reads from what seems to be a geological prehistory of Central Europe. The text describes how in the prehistoric past the lowland sea – where today the Hungarian Great Plain is located – had subsided, leaving a lake the size of Hungary's famous Balaton. There is a moment of bathos as, exhausted even by reading two lines of academic prose, he then falls asleep. The camera continues to track in to rest on an extreme close-up of his slumped head, snoring. This is the only direct reference in the film to where it is supposed to be set (besides the fact of the characters speaking Hungarian). It is a relatively obscure reference, especially for the non-Hungarian viewer, but is clearer in the source novel by László Krasznahorkai. In the chapter in the novel to which this episode corresponds, there are three such quotations from a geological history, and the first of these quotations opens the chapter. The doctor is reading a text by the noted Hungarian geologist László Bendefy (1904–77), identified in the text as 'Dr Benda' (Krasznahorkai 2012: 58).[1] In the novel these geological motifs are related to the characterisation of the personality of the doctor by obsessiveness and anxiety; his is a 'probably pathological love of order' (Krasznahorkai 2012: 52). He has arranged his living space in such a way that all his needs can be met from the chair at his desk and he is strongly averse to leaving his 'observation post' to go to his front door, much less leave the house. Though in the film he is irascible, his determination to document everything he sees and his concern to conserve it in his memory as a stay against chaos is more strongly emphasised in the book. Drinking, watching and keeping order are his means of exercising control in a world of ineluctable deterioration. Chaos and changes in the world's natural landscape are hypostasised in the novel as a generalised 'wrecking process' and a 'sinister, underhanded process of decay' (Krasznahorkai 2012: 54). The geological references appear to testify to this chaos. This is partly allied to the closing of the estate, conceived of as just another moment in a natural history, but it is also seen in an even broader context as a cosmic phenomenon (there is one shot in which a poster of the solar system can be observed on the wall next to the desk). While in the film the doctor falls asleep after reading the text, in the novel he ponders 'whether he was reading a work of prophecy regarding the earth's condition after the demise of humanity or a proper work of geological history based on the planet on which he actually lived' (Krasznahorkai 2012: 58). In this respect, the doctor's rituals bear out the anthropologist Mary Douglas's remark that drinks do not just organise social gatherings, but also construct an 'ideal world'; they 'make an intelligible, bearable world which is much more how an ideal world should be than the painful chaos threatening all the time' (Douglas 1987: 11). In this respect, the doctor of the novel bears comparison with the visitor from *The Turin Horse*, for whom 'everything's in ruins. Everything's been degraded . . . they've acquired everything in a sneaky, underhand fight' (the question of who 'they' are in the monologue takes on metaphysical associations). Despite the apparent Nietzschean overtones of godlessness and eternal return in this speech from *The Turin Horse*, in more than one interview Tarr has dismissed this speech as nothing beyond the vision of an alcoholic awaiting his next drink:

> This is someone's monologue who just needs some spirit, he's just coming and waiting for his bottle and during all this time he is talking talking talking talking, like someone in the next bar, you know, and that's

simple; nothing more, and of course the people are in the bar, and the alcoholic people they are talking always about serious things. (Sbrizzi 2011)

When the doctor does leave the house, he wears a fur-lined coat that resembles that of the visitor in *The Turin Horse*. Both coats have a large collar that can be turned up, such that when followed by the camera from behind the wearer resembles a large, dark, headless mass.

The relation between the landscape and the body is one that Jacques Rancière has investigated in his book on Tarr's films. Characterising Tarr's style, Rancière writes:

> Through the pane of a window, in a small town in Normandy or on the Hungarian plain, the world slowly comes to be fixed in a gaze, to be etched on a face, to weigh down upon a body's posture, to fashion its gestures, and to produce that part of the body called soul: an intimate divergence between two expectations: the expectation of the same, habituation to repetition, and the expectation of the unknown, of the way that leads toward another life. (Rancière 2013: 64)

Rancière here usefully indicates how in Tarr's films the body and the world are closely interconnected. The 'world' here must be understood not merely as in the metaphysical determination that Rancière sometimes gives it, but also in the sense of the specificity of the physical Hungarian landscape I have evoked above. The world 'weighs' on the body through the sense of life's onerousness, but also in the way that chaos and decay, the material change of the world, encompass bodily ageing and deterioration at the same time as tectonic movements and rock formations. As well as making a conceptual argument, Rancière is evidently thinking of a formal construction that can be repeatedly observed in Tarr's films – a perfect example is the opening shot of *Damnation* – in which a shot can ostensibly show the outside world, before the sequence-shot tracks back to reveal it as the view through a window and even after that, tracking back to behind a shoulder, to be the view of a character. By starting the doctor's episode with the view through binoculars, Tarr situates him within the physical world, the world that is 'fixed in a gaze'.

WITHDRAWAL

After a brief visit from Mrs Kráner (Irén Szajki), the local woman who brings him his necessaries so that he does not need to leave the house, the doctor gets up from his chair and turns about. He tries to reach around the wall for a light

ALCOHOLISM IN BÉLA TARR'S *SÁTÁNTANGÓ* 61

switch above a bookcase. He misses it and loses his balance, bringing down the bookcase with him as he falls to the floor, unconscious. This action is shot in a single take, and after he has fallen the camera lingers in a close-up, slowly tracking over his enormous frame from his head to his foot. An undefined period of time passes in the interval before the next shot, which shows him crawling to his bed in the corner of the room. Sitting on his bed, he murmurs to himself: 'It seems I got pretty drunk.' He appears to be in a state of incipient alcohol withdrawal; the beads of sweat that can be seen on his face show that his skin is clammy. He also seems to be in pain as he pulls himself upright to open a drawer, grimacing as he sets himself back down on the bed. He prepares a syringe from the drawer and undoes his trousers to expose a buttock. The needle is a fiddly object in his enormous hands and he flicks it unceremoniously before giving himself a shot (of what is unclear). With a harried expression, still breathing deeply, he sits, dishevelled and with his belly hanging out from his trousers, clearly very unwell after suffering a minor fall in his own home. (Though he does not take a shot in the novel, it is more explicit there that he is suffering from a tightness in his chest.)

In the next shot, the doctor is framed from the doorway to his left in a relatively long shot, as he had been in a previous frame discussed above. At this point, as he attempts to fix himself another drink, it becomes clear that he has run out of pálinka. This is a fact that he then records in his journal: 'Today I ran out of the last drop of fruit brandy. It looks like I need to leave the house.' The distant framing, following the more involving, moving close-ups of earlier, coupled with the simplicity of this statement, slowly enunciated

Figure 2.2 Out of drink (*Sátántangó*)

at the same time as its inscription in the journal, creates a moment of deadpan humour (a not inconsiderable effect in this film). The humour lies partly in the rendering of an apparently innocuous task – leaving the house – into a Herculean physical ordeal, something meriting noting in a logbook (as if he might not come back), and partly in the ostensible absurdity of the doctor's resolve to continue drinking even after this episode of falling over and his acknowledgement of drunkenness. Alcohol as a motivation or pathology is a matter of both bathos and pathos – after the potential seriousness of the fall it is both absurd and pathetic (in the etymological sense) to continue drinking. Indeed, it is in this latter sense that the doctor's condition is considered by other characters in the story. When on the way to refill his bottle shortly after this, as he takes refuge from the rain in a large barn he meets two prostitutes – to whom he is more civil than to Mrs Kráner – and neither appears remotely shocked or surprised by his condition. They talk about the doctor matter-of-factly as being not far from death. 'He hasn't got a lot of time left', says one, as he leaves. 'You'd hardly recognise him', the other replies.

It turns dark. The doctor approaches the tavern, from which accordion music is playing and where the young girl of the collective, Estike (Erika Bók), is looking through the window. (One might note in passing the perhaps-implied comparison between the raucous drinking of the peasants in the bar and, closely followed in the timeline, the method by which Estike commits suicide, believing she is ascending into heaven: by consuming poison.) In the circular narrative of *Sátántangó* this is a moment that is seen more than once in the course of the film; at this stage we are seeing it from the perspective of the doctor. The other characters in *Sátántangó* are heavy drinkers also. Sitting in the bar earlier in the timeline, the schoolteacher Halics (Alfréd Járai) complains of 'this demand from the liver' in a speech nominally about drying off from the rain. The cart driver Kelemen (Barna Mihók) rambles interminably in that same scene and becomes abusive when drunk. After the characters all leave the estate later in the film and settle down for their first night away, even the religious fanatic Halics's wife (Erzsébet Gaál) is seen during the night sneaking a drink from their bottle of spirit. According to Tarr, the whole cast were drunk during the shooting of the dance sequence in the tavern (Romney 2001). The dance, when viewed on its own and especially with its hypnotic accordion music, suggests an alternative, redemptive aspect to drinking distinct from the rituals of the doctor. This is similar to the extraordinary opening shot of *Werckmeister harmóniák* (*Werckmeister Harmonies*, 2001), in which the staggering bar-room drunkards are choreographed by the main character Valuska (Lars Rudolph) to mimic the movements of the planets and thus to evoke cosmic harmony. This again suggests Douglas's remark that drinks construct an ideal world – here less a private sanctuary, as with the doctor, but a situation where everything is in its ordained place.

Estike goes to the doctor as he approaches the tavern and grabs onto his arm. When she lets go, the doctor slips in the mud and collapses again. He gets up and shouts to the girl, whom he has frightened, not to run away. He follows her into the woods. There is a cut, no more music can be heard, and the doctor is dragging his feet much more slowly among the trees; he is clearly lost. On the horizon can be seen three figures walking on the road. The doctor calls out very weakly to them before collapsing next to a tree. The image fades out and then in, bringing us to the following morning. The doctor is found lying among the leaves by the cart driver, Keleman. The doctor is disoriented and unable to stand. In another take remarkable for its uninterrupted length, Keleman brings him to his old wooden cart and steadies him against the side. Keleman takes out a box from the back and sets it on the dirt as a step. He guides the doctor to the step and helps him up to the cart. The doctor is unsteady and grips his bottle. Keleman has to push his bottom and lift his leg to physically get him into the cart, then push his feet in off the edge, as if he were a heavy lifeless load. He lifts the back flap of the cart up and tosses the step in as well, hitting the comically non-responsive doctor. Keleman gets into the saddle and the camera cranes up as the cart drives off. The camera then stops and remains fixed, and the take continues until the cart has almost disappeared over the horizon and is completely out of shot. A voice-over – not the voice of the doctor – speaks:

> My heart – he thought again and again. He longed to lie in a warm room, and be taken care of by sweet little nurses, sipping hot soup, then turn towards the wall. He felt light and easy and the conductor's scolding echoed long in his ears: You shouldn't have done it, doctor. You shouldn't have done it . . .

The episode thus ends with the doctor fading into the distant landscape. At the same time the voice-over raises him into the discursive narration. The 'lightness' he feels and the reversion to a fantasy of convalescence suggest the evanescence of his bodily form.

Although this might give us to think the doctor has died, the final episode of the film returns to him, almost five hours later in the film's running time than we had seen him last. The shot is a familiar composition, framing the doctor from the doorway on his left and shows him returning to his home, which is untouched since he went away. He has his bottle, clearly having filled it up on the way home, and before turning on the light or even taking off his coat and hat he pours himself a drink, uncut with water. He sits down, burping. The camera slowly tracks towards him as he fills up the bottle on his desk from his larger bottle with the aid of a funnel. Still wearing the same clothes as before, he sits back in his chair, staring out of the window. We can hear the sound of his deep breathing and the trickling of the rain outside; things are apparently much as they were before. He has, however, clearly recovered some of his health. There is a cut to the doctor's window, steamed-up on the inside and with water running down the outside. We then hear him writing in his journal, confirming that this is not some kind of flashback:

> During the thirteen days I spent in hospital Mrs Kráner didn't turn up again. Everything is like I'd left it. Neither of them dares to leave the house. They must be lying on their beds, snoring or staring at the ceiling. They haven't a clue that it is this dull inertia that leaves them at the mercy [of] what they most fear.

The camera reframes from the window, slowly panning left and dollying round to frame the doctor's head from his right. Again his bitterness is in evidence, as in his rhetorical address to Futaki, in imagining an existential indolence on the part of his neighbours. The irony is that they have in fact departed from the estate at this point and left him behind. At this point the phantom bells that recur throughout the film can be heard, and the doctor decides to investigate. He is in better physical shape now and makes his way out to the chapel, a short distance from the estate over the Plain. It turns out that a madman is clanging the damaged bell in the ruined chapel. The doctor returns home and says 'I must be crazy! I've mistaken the bells of the sky for the sound of the knell.' This is a moment of demystification, an anti-climactic pay-off at the end of a seven-hour film – evidence, as Kovács puts it, of 'the superior world as the great con' (Kovács 2004: 241). That is to say, all that there is in the Tarr universe is the material world, with no apocalypse to come from an external or transcendental sphere.

CONCLUSION: THE TWO MOMENTS OF ALCOHOLISM

In the final shot of the film we see the doctor back in his house, first collecting the objects on his desk into a small box and then proceeding to board up the window through which he normally conducts his observations. With each plank of wood he nails to the wall the shot becomes progressively darker up to the point of a complete blackout. At this point the final speech of the film is heard, spoken by the doctor in the same tone and pace as when he dictates and writes, observed earlier in the film:

> One morning at the end of October not long before the first drops of the insufferably long autumn rains fell on the parched sodic ground on the western side of the yard for the stinking bog to make the tracks until

the first frosts impassable and the town cut off, Futaki was woken by the sound of bells. Closest eight kilometres to the south-west on the old Hochmeiss field was a solitary chapel but not only [was] no bell there, even its tower collapsed during the war . . .

On one level this is an ingenious conceit – the opening voice-over of the film uses the same words, suggesting that the whole film is circular, written by the doctor – to structure the story, but it also shows the distance with which the doctor holds events. Speaking these two sentences takes the doctor two and a half minutes of the film's runtime, during which time there is only darkness on-screen, giving the words an unusual heaviness. There is no transcendent world – the bells are the evidence of this – but as the doctor responds to this revelation by immediately going home to write, what is shown is that there is instead a world of memory and of story which can take flight from the material world. In this sense, we can add to Rancière's remarks about the relation between the body and the world those of Gilles Deleuze, who in *The Logic of Sense* (1969) gives a subtle account of the temporal distortions specific to alcoholism:

> Alcoholism does not seem to be a search for pleasure, but a search for an effect which consists mainly in an extraordinary hardening of the present. One lives in two times, at two moments at once . . . The other moment may refer to projects as much as to memories of sober life; it nevertheless exists in an entirely different and profoundly modified way, held fast inside the hardened present which surrounds it like a tender pimple surrounded by indurate flesh. In this soft center of the other moment, the alcoholic may identify himself with the objects of his love, or the objects of his 'horror and compassion', whereas the lived and willed hardness of the present moment permits him to hold reality at a distance. (Deleuze 2004: 179–80)

The alcoholic self is divided in these two times tensely balanced through this corporeal image of the pimple. Deleuze is thinking of Malcolm Lowry's modernist, stream-of-consciousness novel *Under the Volcano* (1947), a novel about the final day in the life of an alcoholic, the temporal structure of which, set over the course of a single day, bears comparison with that of Krasznahorkai's novel. While for Rancière the body is weighed down and conditioned by the world in which it lives, Deleuze is describing a particular response to the world in which one tries to hold reality and the time of the world at a remove – a response which, as achieved through drinking, can be tragic, lonely and self-destructive. I want to suggest, in conclusion, that the extreme long takes of Tarr's film evince these two 'times': those slow takes, meticulously rendered through framing and sound, of the doctor's profane, solitary, everyday labours – of drinking, urinating, sitting in a chair – relate to the hardened present, while other points at which the camera lingers patiently and the doctor looks on are those of his 'horror and compassion' – such as this moment of writerly composition in the darkness, the fascination of geological timescales, the imagined activities of others and the cart ride into the distance. This, I think, goes some way towards suggesting why *Sátántangó* returns to the doctor at its close, and how the portrait of the doctor achieves its haunting effect.

NOTE

1. I am grateful to Anna Batori for this suggestion. In turn, this reference calls to mind Hungary's national poet, Sándor Petőfi, who is known for his relation to the Great Plain and to whose poetry Tarr paid tribute in his less well-known short film *Utazás az Alföldön* (*Journey on the Plain*, 1995), shot soon after *Sátántangó*. Another of the key themes of Petőfi's verse, it will be noted, is alcohol and its pleasures. The film is Tarr's most overt treatment of the Plain.

WORKS CITED

Balsom, Erika (2007), 'Saving the Image: Scale and Duration in Contemporary Art Cinema', *CineAction*, 72, 23–31.
Chion, Michel (2009 [2003]), *Film, A Sound Art*, trans. Claudia Gorbman, New York: Columbia University Press.
Deleuze, Gilles (2004 [1969]), *The Logic of Sense*, trans. Mark Lester with Charles Stivale, ed. Constantin V. Boundas, London: Continuum.
Douglas, Mary (1987), 'A Distinctive Anthropological Perspective', in Mary Douglas (ed.), *Constructive Drinking: Perspectives on Drink from Anthropology*, Cambridge: Cambridge University Press, pp. 3–15.
Kovács, András Bálint (2004), '*Sátántangó*', in Peter Hames (ed.) *The Cinema of Central Europe*, London: Wallflower Press, pp. 237–43.
Kovács, András Bálint (2013), *The Cinema of Béla Tarr: The Circle Closes*, New York: Wallflower Press.
Krasznahorkai, László (2012 [1985]), *Satantango*, trans. Georges Szirtes, London: Tuskar Rock Press.
Quinlivan, Davina (2012), *The Place of Breath in Cinema*, Edinburgh: Edinburgh University Press.
Rancière, Jacques (2013 [2011]), *Béla Tarr: The Time After*, trans. Erik Beranek, Minneapolis: Univocal Publishing.
Romney, Jonathan (2001), 'Out of the Shadows', *The Guardian*, 24 March, <http://www.theguardian.com/film/2001/mar/24/books.guardianreview> (last accessed 11 January 2015).
Sbrizzi, Paul (2011), 'A Conversation with Béla Tarr (*The Turin Horse*)', <http://www.hammertonail.com/interviews/a-conversation-with-bela-tarr-the-turin-horse/> (last accessed 11 January 2015).

CHAPTER 3

Playing Dead: Pictorial Figurations of Melancholia in Contemporary Hungarian Cinema

Hajnal Király

AN 'AESTHETICS OF SLOW' – AND BEYOND

Contemporary Hungarian cinema has often been conceived by its Western critics as being 'dark', 'extremely slow' and minimalistic, emanating a melancholia that reaches an ontological and even cosmic dimension in Béla Tarr's films, especially in *A torinói ló* (*The Turin Horse*, 2012).[1] Intriguingly, Tarr's films following the fall of the Iron Curtain, as well as those of a younger generation of filmmakers from the last decade, do not usually deal with the immediate external – historical, political or social – causes of this melancholia. The films of Kornél Mundruczó, Benedek Fliegauf, Szabolcs Hajdu and Ágnes Kocsis, to mention just a few directors following Tarr in terms of slowness and minimalism, are characterised by a lack of direct reference to a specific event, place and time. Their stories could happen anywhere and anytime, which brings these films in line with a trend in European and international arthouse cinema, called 'slow' or 'contemplative' by critics. Tarr's films in particular are often cited as examples of films that foreground duration, 'a cinema of walking' or minimalism, along with works of Kiarostami, Angelopoulos, Tsai Ming-liang, Gus Van Sant, Hou Hsiao-hsien, Kim-ki Duk, and Pedro Costa, to name a few directors from around the world (Flanagan 2008). The discourse around the aesthetics of slow cinema (mostly taking the form of blogging, discussions around films and articles related to the topic[2]) helps to isolate certain stylistic and narratological traits that unify films and directors from different countries, such as a slow pace, a preference for duration, the long-take instead of continuity editing, non-events or ritualistic repetition over action, minimalism of style and acting, and so on. These discussions also create a rather strong camp of sceptics claiming that the term 'slow' is relative, that it does not necessarily exclude event, and that the phenomenon has always existed in cinema, and culminated in modernism, with the films of Bresson and Antonioni (Bíró 2006; Flanagan

2008; Shaviro 2010). From this point of view, the discourse of slow cinema is just a 'recycling' of already existing theoretical stands on neorealism and modernism that obfuscates interpretation and creates confusion (as in the case of Angelopoulos, whose films are often characterised as 'contemplative cinema' and who is also frequently seen as a late modernist).[3] According to Steven Shaviro (2010), 'contemplative cinema' can easily become a cliché, based on a routinised style. Shaviro accuses contemplative cinema of being 'nostalgic and regressive', stating that only a few filmmakers can transcend this with 'a hunger for all dimensions of life', as in the case of a few Korean directors, for example (Shaviro 2010).[4] When writing about 'the fullness of minimalism', Yvette Bíró also points out the trap that narrative minimalism hides:

> The fullness of guarded storytelling is a rare gift, but it offers deep sensation only in a particular case if it is able to intimate that the visible foreground does comprise more than the obvious, and beyond the incidental events a more substantial experience exists. (2006)

I argue that the discourse of slow cinema, although emphasising the priority of the image over narration, does not sufficiently cover the variety and degree of visual mannerisms, framing practices and intermedial references, nor the figurative potential of the image in disclosing its cultural and psychological content. Expanding more on this aspect of many slow films may help us to find the individual, cultural specificities inside a global trend and deal with the differences even within the oeuvre of the same director.[5] While accepting certain traits of 'slow cinema' as characteristic of contemporary Hungarian cinema in general (slow pace, minimalism of dialogues and acting, and a preference for silence, for non-actors and, in the case of Tarr and Fliegauf, for a 'cinema of walking'), I also contend that the 'non-event' does not fully apply to these films, not even to all the work of Béla Tarr. In the films of Kornél Mundruczó, Benedek Fliegauf and Ágnes Kocsis that I chose for analysis, there is always a story; things happen, even though at a slower pace. And more than that: there is a lot happening *in* the frame and *with* the image. Matthew Flanagan lists this tendency for rigorous framing among the characteristics of 'slow cinema', recalling the Bazinian distinction between the image that reveals reality and the image that adds to reality (2008). The latter, paired with the deliberate retreat from representing actual events, is responsible for the mannerist formalism of these Hungarian directors that is greatly detectable in the composition, lighting and figurative content of the frame. Thus, beyond the still open discourse of 'slow cinema', this aestheticising tendency has its place in a wider context of an ongoing debate over the 'aesthetic' in the arts, which urges us to re-establish the distance between reality and artistic representation. According to Lyotard, art must 'renounce its claims to representation and seek out new ways of revealing that every representation is condemned to a forgetting – the presence of the Other, the trauma of an event – that is constitutive of thought, and only able to be remembered as forgotten' (Lyotard 1990: 18). In a similar vein, Giorgio Agamben argues that aesthetics is 'the very destiny of art in the era in which, with tradition now severed, man is no longer able to find, between past and future, the space of the present, and gets lost in the linear time of history' (Agamben 1999: 69). Jacques Rancière's concept of the régime or politics of the aesthetic, which he refers to in his analyses of contemporary art, also emphasises the importance of the difference between meaning (sens) and what offers itself to our senses. As he points out, in the aesthetic régime of art – which is not a chronological account of art – the artwork

> is not an appearance drawn from a reality that would serve as its model . . . It is given in a specific experience, which suspends the ordinary connections not only between appearance and reality, but also between form and matter, activity and passivity, understanding and sensibility. (Rancière 2009: 30; see also Tanke 2011: 73)

In line with this philosophical background, starting in the 1980s a number of critical works in film and media studies proposed a new approach to aestheticism by claiming the necessity of examining the figurative potential of films and the realignment of film studies with cultural studies (see for example, Straw 1981, and Kuntzel 1978, 1980). The Hungarian-born theorist Yvette Bíró also argued that film creates a 'profane mythology', a metaphoric, metonymic and symbolic 'writing' that anticipates a 'visual thinking' on the part of the spectator, who will be then able to 'read' the film (1982: 42). This line of thought culminated in David N. Rodowick's *Reading the Figural, or, Philosophy after the New Media* (2001), which conceives the figural as a meta-theoretical discourse of media, detectable in intermedial exchange. Rodowick also links his preoccupation with the figural to 'the last stage of the era of the aesthetic', characterised by 'the unconscious fear that Art may never have existed – and will never be able to exist in the economic age that desires it as a supplement to alienation and lack of freedom' and 'the split in consciousness that attempts to repress the economic and the political in the aesthetic' (2001: 138).

Rodowick uses examples from Western art, but the tendency towards aestheticisation, intense figural and/or figurative representation that effaces issues of social actuality, is also valid for the contemporary Hungarian films under analysis. They show an increased preference for mythical, biblical and allegorical allusions (see Tarr's *The Turin Horse* and Mundruczó's films *Johanna*, 2005, *Delta*, 2010 and *Fehér isten* [*White God*], 2014), utopian stories (Fliegauf's *Womb*, 2010), rigorous framing and stylised camera movement (Fliegauf's *Dealer*, 2004 and *Csak a szél* [*Just the Wind*], 2012), or figuration (use of metaphors and symbolism) through the colour palette and diegetic music (Kocsis's *Friss levegő* [*Fresh Air*], 2006 and *Pál Adrienn* [*Adrienn Pál*], 2011). The observation of the critic Gábor Gelencsér that the winners of the 2006 Hungarian Film Week reveal a preoccupation with the 'images of the body' (Gelencsér 2006) is true for most Hungarian films of the last decade. In these the 'empty', 'absent' body – which, according to Drew Leder, means not a void but 'being-away', a being that is away from itself (Marks 2000: 132) – becomes a mere surface on which the figurative meaning inherent to the story can be projected. The visually 'alienated' body, devoid of bodily functions and emotions, has been commonly interpreted by critics as a figuration of the loss and deception that characterises the post-communist era (Strausz 2011), but is also symptomatic of an artistic attitude that chooses the 'aesthetic' over the social or political. This tendency towards aestheticisation finds its most eloquent expression in a preference for isolated images that, owing to their composition, colouring, tone and mood, become close or strikingly identical references to Andrea Mantegna's *Lamentation over the Dead Christ* (*c*.1480) and Hans Holbein the Younger's *The Body of Dead Christ in the Tomb* (1520–2).

In order to discover the meanings repressed in this aesthetic gesture, in the following analyses of contemporary Hungarian films I propose – in addition to the theoretical background of visual figuration – a cultural and psychoanalytical approach to the artistic sublimation of crisis through beauty, as discussed by Julia Kristeva in *Black Sun: Depression and Melancholia* (1989). After an in-depth analysis of Béla Tarr's *The Turin Horse*, an ultimate example of the last stage of slow cinema, where the moving image 'regresses' into the earlier state of the still image and the painterly composition, I will proceed with the interpretation of similar painterly references and the figurative role of framing in other contemporary Hungarian films. I will argue that the recurrent depiction of dead or ailing bodies evoking either Andrea Mantegna's or Hans Holbein's paintings is a figuration both of loss in the post-communist era and of artistic melancholia. This will inevitably lead to a comparison of the representation of melancholia by the male directors and the female director under analysis, departing from Kristeva's implied 'gendered melancholia' and its interference with artistic sublimation (1989: 69–86). I will conclude with the contextualisation of these painterly references within the wider phenomenon of clue-images, rebuses and diagrams in the visual arts, as well as in the discourse on 'the figural' provided by Lyotard (2011), Deleuze (2004) and Rodowick (2001).

TRAPPED BY THE LONG TAKE: *THE TURIN HORSE*

The work of Béla Tarr is paradigmatic of the repression of the political in the aesthetic: as András Bálint Kovács, his monographer, points out, he is a radical aesthetic filmmaker rather than a political activist. Kovács also convincingly argues that Tarr gave up filmmaking after having practically exhausted the aesthetic possibilities of the long take and, at the same time, having managed to separate definitively the aesthetic from the political. Through the in-depth analyses of Tarr's work in his book *The Circle Closes* (2013), Kovács demonstrates how the growing length of the shot in Tarr's films systematically not only isolated the characters of his films from the actual story and the historico-political narrative, but also liberated the filmmaker from the urge to document real events and to adhere to the mainstream trends of filmmaking. Thus the very long shot became a figure of entrapment: that of the character, going around in circles and ending up in the same or worse situation than she/he was; that of the body of the spectator, tied to his chair for up to seven hours, almost under hypnosis; and finally that of the filmmaker who has reached the apotheosis of this form of expression. As Kovács points out, narrative circularity is another figure of entrapment in Tarr's films:

> The expression of this human situation represented as a trap from which there is no escape is the focus of Tarr's films, and circular narrative structure and extreme narrative slowness are the most conspicuous stylistic tools Tarr uses in service of this expression. Circularity expresses the trap situation, slowness gives birth to something I would call *the time of hope*, hope that after all there is a way out of the circle when there is not. (Kovács 2012: 5)

This narrative slowness and circularity can be interpreted as a figure of entrapment depicting the post-communist situation. The hope of a new start outlines new goals that mobilise people, but in the process the lack of means or lack of access to the new economic infrastructure, or old anxieties, make them divert from the road and end up in the same place or worse. However, such a situation is not exclusively applicable to Eastern Europe or Hungary. It applies as well to the actual worldwide economic crisis or, more generally, to the general condition of a 'humiliated and insulted' humanity, always the focus of Tarr's artistic preoccupations, as formulated in an interview on *The Turin Horse*:

> Yes, somehow this is an anti-Creation story. Somehow it's attempting to show a very simple – 'okay, we are doing our daily life'. The same routine, but every day is different, and every day just becomes bleaker, bleaker, and by the end is just suffocating. That's all – in a very quiet and very silent way. No apocalypse . . . Nothing. Just the simple pain of living. (Levine and Meckler 2012)

In *The Turin Horse*, the entrapment appears as final: the characters cannot leave the house, because of severe weather conditions, and their life is reduced

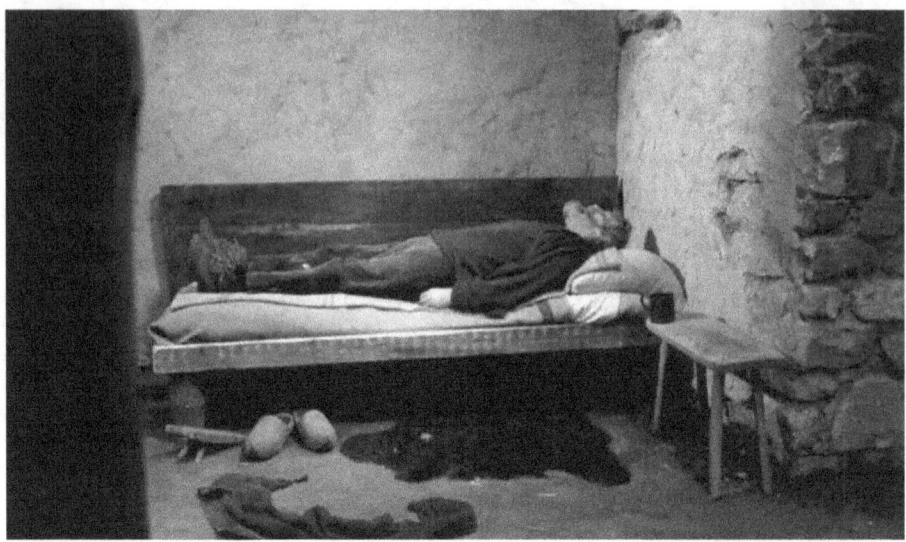

Figure 3.1 The father lying on the bed in a pose evoking Hans Holbein's *Dead Christ* (*The Turin Horse*)

to one daily meal or sitting and lying on the bed. The film shows the father's body posed as a figure in Holbein's painting *The Body of Dead Christ in the Tomb* or Mantegna's *Lamentation over the Dead Christ*, both intermedial references that isolate the still image from the narrative background to transform it into a concentration of repressed, unspeakable meanings.

As Thierry Kuntzel (1978, 1980), Angela Dalle Vacche (1996), Raymond Bellour (2002), Susan Felleman (2006) and, recently, Belén Vidal (2012), among others, have argued, traditionally the function of painterly compositions or references in cinema has been to render visible what is hidden in the story: that which cannot be said, only shown. Visibility here does not mean only 'available for the sight', but rather, as Rodowick formulates, 'it refers to what can be rendered as intelligible and therefore knowable in a society' (2001: 53).

In the case of Béla Tarr and the Hungarian directors following in his footsteps in terms of minimalism and preference for the long take, the film–painting intermedial shift can be interpreted as the emergence of the figural, also called by Lyotard 'the other of signification' (Lyotard 2011: 13). In Rodowick's approach the figural can be detected in the shifts between media: 'Wherever physical distribution is replaced by electronic storage, retrieval, and retransmission, there one will find the figural' (Rodowick 2001: 49). I argue that, besides condensing hidden narrative meanings, the figural emerging as a painterly reference disrupting narration in these films is meant to render visible death and the death drive, as unspeakable contents inherent in melancholia, also called asymbolia or the impossibility of signification and figuration. As Julia Kristeva puts it: 'If I am no longer capable of translating or metaphorizing, I become silent and I die' (1989: 42). Thus the figural becomes the figure of the non-figurable, of the immaterial and, ultimately, death. Or, as Olivier Schefer playfully formulated in his essay seeking a definition of the figural: the figure of the non-figurable is a dis-figuring figure, dis-figured, engaging in a logic of 'dissembling resemblances' (1999: 920).

In her analysis of the works of the melancholic artist Marguerite Duras (together with Holbein, Dostoyevsky and Nerval), Kristeva points out that the crisis of thought, speech and representation that characterises melancholia is closely related to political, economic and legal collapse (Kristeva 1989: 218). *The Turin Horse* appears as the ultimate representation of this connection: Béla Tarr isolates the single image in painterly compositions, reminding us of Holbein's in its minimalism and in the solitude of the figure, reaching, as Kristeva puts it, the extinction of all artificiality right inside the same, thoroughly mannered artificiality (1989: 125). What Kristeva calls the competition between the form and death in Holbein's painting, film in general, and Tarr's work, *The Turin Horse* in particular, translates as the death drive, or the tendency of the narrative and moving image to freeze, and of time to become space, as described by Laura Mulvey (Mulvey 2006: 70). The role of the still or stilled image in a film, a photograph or a painting, assumes Raymond Bellour, is to show the invisible and unspeakable by breaking visual fascination, 'stopping its movement, decomposing and transposing it into writing' (Bellour 1975: 25). These still moments, comparable to the 'pregnant moment' of the painting or the photographic 'punctum' of Barthes, are always related, according to Bellour, to exceptional events, such as birth and death (Bellour 2002: 129). The death drive, the 'principle of the figural' according to Rodowick, links 'dreamwork' with 'filmwork', revealing desire as a constitutive factor of film genres and styles.

Rodowick identifies in the Deleuzian taxonomy of images a distribution between two concepts of history: that of Hegel, based on causality, continuity and orderly unfolding, and that of Nietzsche, denying the importance of the origin and succession of actions, believing instead in time and event and conceiving the subject as a complex site crossed by discursive, libidinal and social forces that both constrain and enable the possibilities of agency (Rodowick 2001: 190–2). This duality is a possible clue to Tarr's allusion to Nietzsche in the prologue of *The Turin Horse*. In this film, an extreme version of his previous works, action and real acting are replaced by long close-ups of the characters' faces that seem to condense their whole history: their helplessness and silent resignation to change their situation of entrapment in a house surrounded by hostile natural forces. As Kovács points out, extending movement into duration and 'providing the sensation of being inside and outside at the same time' is 'one of the specificities of Tarr's long takes' (2012: 50), an aesthetic attitude embodied in the face of the old man with one eye closed and the other open (as if looking outwards and inwards at the same time).

In the prologue of the film, a seemingly minor incident with the Turin horse from the period of mental decay of Nietzsche's life, a scene charged with grief, is recalled, which may also be seen as a coded call to discover the detail, the small visual incidents, absences and excesses that make us read these images as texts. The figural effaces narrative, emerging, as always in Tarr's films, on the almost undetectable verge between the movement and time images. The systematic isolation of the character from all narrative – private or historical – becomes complete in this last film: the circle closes. The character *as* figure is re-framed *as* painting, an ultimate form of aesthetic entrapment and isolation. The reference, Holbein's painting, is all about this: in it Christ's body is strangely alone, extracted from all historical and biblical narrative. As Kristeva notes, it is more this isolation, a compositional factor, than the colouring and lighting that is responsible for the melancholic charge of this painting. In Tarr's film, just as in Holbein's painting, beauty, 'the admirable face of loss' (Kristeva 1989: 100), becomes a solution that sublimates the (personal, social, political) crisis.

SUBLIMATION OF CRISIS THROUGH BEAUTY

In Béla Tarr's last film the long take is used to the extreme of its artistic possibilities. The extraction of the single image (evoking Holbein's and/or Mantegna's painting) from narrative could be interpreted as an act of mourning both over a suffering humanity and over the end of the 'era of the aesthetic', an exhaustion of the means of representation. A similar tendency, to sublimate melancholy through beauty, that is, a reference to these two prominent paintings of Western visual culture, representing the last scene of Christ's Passion, or other painterly stylisation (composition, lights, colours), can be also identified in the films of Kornél Mundruczó, Benedek Fliegauf and Ágnes Kocsis.

This is not an exclusively Hungarian phenomenon. As Ágnes Pethő points out, the references to paintings about the dead Christ can also be encountered in arthouse films from other post-communist countries (Pethő 2014: 57). Moreover, Mantegna's painting is often referred to in contemporary Russian films, for example in Zvyagintsev's *Vozvrashcheniye* (*The Return*, 2003) and *Izgnanie* (*The Banishment*, 2007). According to Pethő, these 'cadaveric' *tableaux vivants* are paradoxical figurations of death, which can be interpreted both as an allegory of the 'lost father', bearing political undertones in the context of contemporary Russian history, and as a 'figure of return' to mythical narratives, thematising the relationship between 'image' and 'medium' (2014: 60). Hence we may question the preference for these two paintings

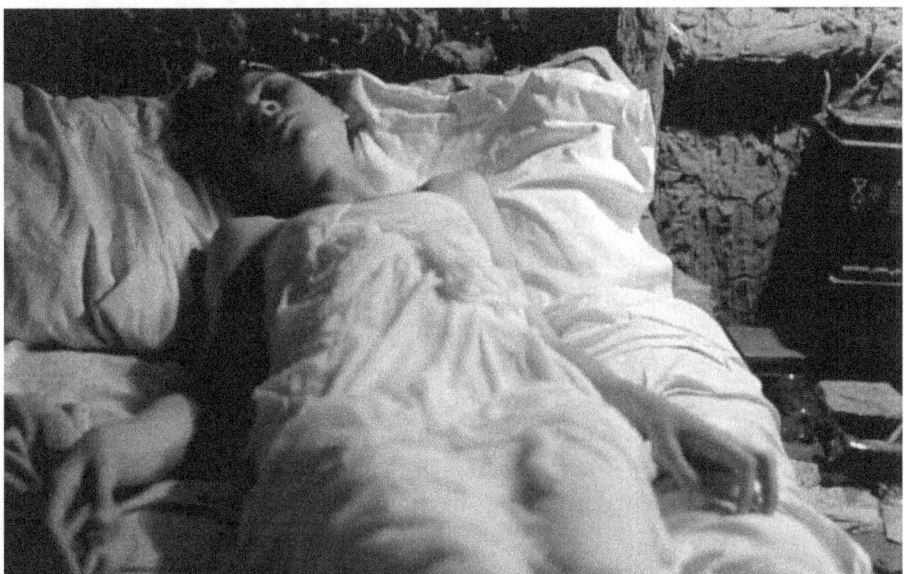

Figure 3.2 Reference to Mantegna's painting in Fliegauf's *Delta*

over other representations of the dead Christ. What is the connection between these two paintings, produced forty years apart, in two different countries, Italy and Germany? To whom are these references addressed? As has often been pointed out by art historians and summarised by Kristeva in her aforementioned essay on Holbein (1989: 105–38), both paintings are famous for providing an unconventional representation of the dead Christ. They emphasise the finitude of the physical body of the Son of God either by distortion (in the case of Mantegna's painting) or by a colouring that makes the body look cadaverous, as in Holbein's piece. In addition, the presence of mourners in the composition of Mantegna's painting and the claustrophobic tomb in that of Holbein shows death as irreversible, emanating a deep grief over loss, a melancholia even for those who are not familiar with the painters' work. In the context of the fast spreading of Reformation and Renaissance humanism (affecting both Germany and Italy, then powerful centres of Catholicism) that shook the world order, the 'irregularities' of these two paintings, signalling a paradigmatic change in the representation of Christ's body, also translate as a loss of faith in the Resurrection. Moreover, as Kristeva also implies, in the case of Holbein the painting also sublimates the personal and artistic crisis of the artist's life divided between his home, a protestant Germany, and the court of the Catholic Henry VIII. Accordingly, for those who happen to know the two paintings, their repetition in these films may be more than a figuration of a loss of faith in a better future in a post-communist context; it can be also seen as a visual code meant to raise issues of representation, reveal the cinematic dispositif through intermedial exchange, address spectatorship and cultural references, and consequently facilitate the emergence of the figural.

The concept of the image that adds to reality (a figurative or figural meaning) rather than showing it also appears in Fliegauf's *Just the Wind* (2012), inspired by racist atrocities against Romas that occurred in Hungary in 2007 and 2008. As the director himself has emphasised in an interview (Fliegauf 2012a), he was more preoccupied with the representation of the status of the 'victim' and of the sense of fear than with the reconstruction of the actual events. While combining the very long shot with a camera angle that follows the characters closely, in the style of Gus van Sant or of the 'cinema of walking',[6] the film displays an aesthetically distant imagery that does not give much space to moral judgement or empathy. The characters are constantly on the move; only the last scene showing their dead bodies in the morgue betrays a certain amount of tenderness through the camera that witnesses closely their being carefully cleaned and dressed. Fliegauf was criticised for trying to avoid generalisations of racism by using stereotypes of the 'good' member of the majority population (the boss of the Roma mother, Rigó, gives her a pack of clothes and kisses her) and the 'bad', aggressive members of the Roma community. However, Fliegauf is breaking a basic stereotype: instead of showing Romas as a noisy, menacing group, he is isolating the characters from each other in order to reveal the alienated individual, left alone with their anxiety (Fliegauf 2012b). In this way he manages to be 'political' without actually making a political statement, in accordance with the 'politics of the sensible' described by Rancière as a reconfiguration of appearances, a reframing of problems and a redefinition of what can be seen and said (Rancière 2009: 25).

A slowing down of the action and movement in the films of these directors also corresponds to what psychoanalysis calls 'the learned helplessness of the melancholic', who, instead of fighting back or escaping, chooses to withdraw and 'play dead' (Seligman 1975: 26 and Kristeva 1989: 36). Slowness is always paired with minimalistic, and disturbingly clumsy, dialogue, in striking contrast with the neat, carefully planned images and mannered camera movements. Often the words do not fit the situation and the lines of dialogue simply do not match, which again corresponds to the description of melancholia by Kristeva as something which it is impossible to symbolise verbally:

> Faced with the impossibility of concatenating, they [the melancholics] utter sentences that are interrupted, exhausted, come to a standstill. Even phrases they cannot formulate. A repetitive rhythm, a monotonous melody emerge and dominate the broken logical sequences, changing them into recurring, obsessive litanies. (1989: 33)

The impossibility of the characters symbolising and expressing themselves verbally is reflected by the last words of the dealer in the homonymous film by Fliegauf (2004): 'I have no ideas anymore.' This statement can also be read as depicting a mannerist contemporary Hungarian cinema that has exhausted its expressive means. Fliegauf himself indirectly reflects on this in an interview when he argues that, after the desperate darkness of *Dealer*, films like *Just the Wind*, inspired by real events, could represent a 'new way' for Hungarian cinema (Fliegauf 2012a). But he could not fully avoid a certain mannerism and stereotypical attitude that many contemporary Hungarian films are accused of by Hungarian critics. Miklós Sághy, for example, argues that these films export 'images of poverty' to the West (Sághy 2013), while Mónika Dánél criticises, from a postcolonial theoretical point of view, the stereotypical representation of women, either destroyed by a patriarchal order or acting as a dark force seeking revenge (Dánél 2013). Moreover, Ágnes Pethő sees the references to Western paintings as an effort of Hungarian cinema to (re)connect with European art (Pethő 2015). As Giorgio Agamben points out, this mannerism, achieved by an imitation of styles and direct references, reveals art as a 'phantasmatic operation', closely related to the melancholia of the artists:

> Painters become melancholics because, wishing to imitate, they must retain the phantasms fixed in the intellect, so that afterward they can express them in the way they first saw them when present; and, being their work, this occurs not only once, but continually. They keep their minds so much abstracted and separated from nature that consequently melancholy derives from it. (Agamben 1993: 25)

Thus an ingenious use of frames – in *Dealer* (2004), for example, the protagonist is often 'pushed' to the edge of the frame – may be seen as figuring the liminality of both the melancholic's existence and an artistic position. In *Johanna* (2005), directed by Mundruczó, the body of the nurse who heals terminally ill patients with sex is systematically isolated from other bodies and all worldly signification, and even framed as a Catholic saint (an allusion to the legend of Saint Joan). Undeniably under the influence of films by Lars von Trier such as *Breaking the Waves* (1996), *Dancer in the Dark* (2000) and *Dogville* (2003) – von Trier has also been lately preoccupied with the representation of melancholia (in *Melancholia*, 2011) – *Johanna* also uses the alienating effect of the musical genre: the characters express themselves in long opera recitatives. Atonality, lacking the harmonies of classical music and adapting to the rhythm of speech, emphasises the monotony of the verbal interactions, and adds to the melancholic effect provided by the lighting and colour palette of the images.

While both *Dealer* and *Johanna* separate melancholic bodies through framing, in *Adrienn Pál* (2010) by Ágnes Kocsis, which concerns a nurse working in the intensive care unit of a clinic, the eating disorder of the character appears, on the contrary, as a desperate attempt by the body *to fill the frame*: always located in the centre, the body appears as if growing towards the edges, sometimes even overflowing beyond them. This figuration of the desire to fill an inner void is paired with a narrative conceivable as self-therapy, a quest for the 'real self'.

Kocsis in *Adrienn Pál* and Mundruczó in *Johanna* are relying visually on what Rodowick calls, after Foucault, the 'spectacular' organisation of the clinic (2001: 55). However, the representation of terminally ill and dead bodies in the two films differs in terms of the spectacle offered to the eye, which raises the issue of a 'gendered (representation of) melancholia', also discussed by Kristeva in her book.

A GENDERED FIGURATION OF MELANCHOLIA?

In *Adrienn Pál* the still bodies of patients appear mostly in the same frame as the nurse (sometimes as extensions of her body), as figuration of her melancholia, and as metaphors for her immobility, feeling of emptiness and 'learned helplessness'. The monitors that she watches all day long, which register the extremely low vital functions of patients in intensive care, have, like her eating disorder and oversized body, a similar symptomatic and metaphoric function. The wall of monitors, a version of Foucault's Panopticon, which became a major figure of our contemporary culture of supervision, here appears as another figure revealing the psychological profile of the nurse: a person who cares for too many others to the detriment of herself, and who ends up feeling extremely lonely and becomes susceptible to melancholia. In fact, it is her care for the other – a friend from childhood – which encourages her to set off to discover her own past and ultimately find her true self.

In *Adrienn Pál* figuration is subordinated to narration and serves to symbolise underlying psychological processes. The quest for the (feminine) self, which makes these films a logical continuation of a 'feminine' cinematic tradition initiated in Hungary by Márta Mészáros, is deeply marked by a tone of self-confession and a preference for the 'journal' form (*Napló gyermekeimnek* [*Journal to my Children*], 1984, *Napló szerelmeimnek* [*Journal to my Lovers*], 1987, *Napló anyámnak és apámnak* [*Journal to my Mother and Father*], 1990). Just as in the films of Mészáros, the reframing of other media in the film of Kocsis – the news, the electrocardiographic data screens, the radio in *Adrienn Pál* – both mirror and serve psychological processes (either as means of self-understanding and thus self-therapy, or as compensation). But while in Márta Mészáros's films the achievement of (feminine) self-consciousness is only conceivable in a political and historical context, the communist and post-communist condition becoming obsessively re-presented and reframed through inserts of documentary footage, in the films of Kocsis no such reference is made. In *Adrienn Pál* narration is symptomatic in terms of revealing the alienation (from the Mother, i.e. the archaic object of loss, from her own self) of the female melancholic, only to take her back, at the end of a circular journey, to the mother and her true self. Alienation is conveyed through a lack of colour (the white robe of nurse Piroska makes her body 'dissolve' into the white background of the hospital), the eating disorder and the oversized body, and the lack of communication. In *Adrienn Pál*, the name of an old female patient stirs up childhood memories in the expressionless nurse. These memories about a friend, Adrienn Pál, shake her up from lethargy and urge her, as if by magic, to find her. During her quest she meets other schoolmates who, interestingly enough, happen to remember her better than Adrienn Pál, who thus turns out to be a sort of 'alter ego' of the protagonist. The circular journey leads her finally to an old patient, the mother of a man who also used to know the girl Adrienn Pál. The return to the mother figure coincides with a higher level of self-understanding and appears as a rather optimistic outcome. The appearance of a mother figure also coincides with a new start and the promise of a romantic relationship.

In Kornél Mundruczó's *Johanna* the representation of melancholic bodies does not meet such an impulse of narrativisation, but rather offers a pure visual spectacle enhanced with sombre, highly stylised colours alternating with bright lights and X-ray images, as well as compositions reminiscent of Mantegna's *Lamentation Over the Dead Christ*. This latter painting gives, according to Kristeva, a rather anatomic vision of the body of the dead Christ: with the soles of the feet turned towards the spectators, in a shortened perspective, 'the body appears here with a brutality approaching the obscene' (1989: 117). Deleuze's views on Bacon's representations of Christ also seem valid for a cinematic representation of pale bodies that look cadaverous in greenish lights: 'Christ's body is fashioned by a truly diabolical inspiration that makes it pass through all the "areas of sensation", through all the "levels of different feelings"' (Deleuze 2004: 10). As in Bacon's paintings, it is not the invention of new forms that is important here, but, as Deleuze argues, the capturing of forces: 'Invisible forces of isolation, dissipation and deformation' (2004: 69). Something that already belongs to the domain of 'the figural'.

For Kristeva, melancholia itself is a 'secret force', even 'a form of modern sacredness', a source of artistic creativity. As one of her interpreters, Tsu-Chung Su, argues, it is also

> a gendered dialectic in the sense that melancholia as feminised asymbolia or loss of words and meanings, and melancholy writing as the recovery of words and meanings and of the ability of signification are two dynamic, dialectical events that occur under melancholia. (2005: 175)

The difference between figuration-narrativisation in the film of Ágnes Kocsis and the emergence of the figural as pure visual sensation and a discourse on visual technologies as means of empowerment over the (female) body in that of Mundruczó is similar to the difference implied by Kristeva's interpretation of works by male and female melancholic artists. Kristeva shows how melancholic male artists (Nerval, Dostoyevsky and Holbein) *distanciate* themselves from the Mother-Thing (the unspeakable, archaic object of loss, the initial loss in the process of individuation, giving consistency in the imaginary to the secret and untouchable horizon of our loves and desires) (Kristeva 1989: 27, 141). While male artists can isolate this loss as a single image and ultimately sublimate it, the only female artist discussed, Marguerite Duras, *interiorises* this object and is not capable of distanciation. As feminist critics and Su have also pointed out, Kristeva in her book posits the cultural empowerment of the male artist through language, in contrast to an incomplete signification (a 'strange artifice') that she identifies in Duras's work, both literary and cinematic (see Doane and Hodges 1992: 75; Su 2005: 185).

Engaging further in the discussion of the cultural implications of Kristeva's analysis would lead too far, not to mention the risk of falling into the error of generalisation based only on a couple of Hungarian films or an essentialist approach restating the male artist's ability to signify and the female artist's inability to express melancholia through signification. Instead, to avoid qualifying distanciation through language as a 'better way' of sublimation than interiorisation (as implied by Kristeva), I argue that the different representations of melancholia in Kocsis's *Adrienn Pál* and Mundruczó's *Johanna* in fact correspond to two different 'languages of mood' (Kristeva's term 1989: 21). Besides colours and symptomatic body-images there is another language, which E. Ann Kaplan in her analysis of the film *Nathalie Granger* (1972) by Marguerite Duras calls 'the politics of silence' as 'a female strategy to counter the destructive male urge to articulate, analyze, dissect' (1983: 95). In contrast to Kristeva's already-mentioned remarks, Kaplan emphasises Duras's ability to show 'in a powerful way how a crisis can be worked through without words which, given phallocentric culture, would permit only certain, male-style actions and understandings' (Kaplan 1983: 95). In Kocsis's film female silence figures like a language of resistance instead of a sign of obedience or powerlessness, as propagated by a patriarchal culture. It becomes a force of resistance against patriarchal discourse present in the phone calls of the husband and his memorable phone message announcing the break-up, all meant to control Piroska and blame her for an unhappy marriage. But male authority, conveyed by a distant voice reaching her through a technological device, crashes against the indifferent silence of Piroska, who does not always follow orders. The silent determination of the female melancholic thus appears as a driving force that in both films helps the female protagonists to deal with crisis.

In Mundruczó's *Johanna* the silent actions of the nurse to heal patients with touch are opposed to the (male) doctors' distanciating medical gaze paired with authoritarian verbalisation, a disruption that leads to the elimination of the nurse under the accusation of subversion and witchcraft. Both male and female melancholia — the doctor's fetishistic approach to Johanna and Johanna's own helplessness — are embedded in a meta-narrative discourse on the cinematic dispositif that, according to Gwendolyn Foster, shares with medical technology the same preoccupation to 'capture the body' (1999: 11). *Johanna* is a palimpsest of discourses on cinematic entertainment/spectatorship, a scientific/ cinematic inquiry into the body and into Foucauldian concepts of regulation and control. Accordingly, the representation of melancholic, dying/ailing bodies either as X-ray images or recalling the composition of Mantegna's painting or the colouring of Holbein's piece already belongs to the domain of the figural, which emerges in these intermedial shifts between media and technologies.

As we have seen, while the film of Kocsis narrativises and figures female melancholia as the impossibility of separating from the Mother-Thing, in the case of Mundruczó the narrative only serves as a background for figuration, or for the emergence of the figural. In both *Adrienn Pál* and *Johanna* the titles are names of women that figure as 'lost objects' in the narrative. But while in the former film this object is recovered in the end as the protagonist's old/true self, in the latter, although it seems recovered, it is lost again and this loss can be only compensated through sublimation, a re-mediation into a fetishistic, technological or painterly image.

In Mundruczó's films and Tarr's *The Turin Horse*, the stories tend to be archetypal, with mythical undertones, as if these directors were trying to find a narrative for their 'ready-made' images and stylistic effects and not the other way around, to enhance narrative complexity with an original figuration. We can consider in this light Mundruczó's *Delta* (2010), about a young man who returns home from abroad to the region of the Delta of the Danube in Romania and ends up killed by the villagers after trying to settle down outside the village with his sister. The film contains carefully planned images, significations and effects, a mixture of mythical and Biblical references such as the prodigal son, the miraculous catch of fish, the feeding of a crowd with five loaves of bread and two fish, the last supper, and ritual settling and killing: in sum, a profane Messianic story. Interestingly enough, the script is signed by Yvette Bíró herself, which makes this film a kind of 'exercise' or application of her theoretical ideas about 'visual thinking' from *Profane Mythology*. The single, still, carefully framed image of melancholic characters is one of the main components of this artificiality, enhanced with lighting effects and evoking, for example, Vermeer's style, turning the female body into a silent painting. As we have seen, extracted from narrative, these images can emerge with the force of the figural and thus sublimate grief and death. As Kristeva argues:

> Sublimation alone withstands death. The beautiful object that can bewitch us into its world seems to us more worthy of adoption than any loved or hated cause for wound or sorrow. Depression recognizes this and agrees to live within and for that object, but such adoption of the sublime is no longer libidinal. It is already detached, dissociated, it has already integrated the traces of death, which is signified as lack of concern, absentmindedness, carelessness. Beauty is an artifice; it is imaginary. (1989: 99–100)

Having in mind the cultural implications of a gender-specific representation of loss, I argued above that despite the apparent similarities in artistic representation — such as minimalism, use of long shots, and unidentifiable space–time coordinates — the film of Ágnes Kocsis is different from those of the male artists as regards the degree of aesthetic mannerism. Kocsis's story of a female melancholic represents a process of self-understanding and thus the possibility of a new start, even though it is culturally conditioned by the interiorisation of the Mother-Thing. By contrast, in most films of Tarr, Mundruczó and Fliegauf, there is no possibility of narrative liberation through action or revelatory encounters: the loss appears definitive, without the possibility of redemption. The characters are the 'living dead' and most of them are dead by the end of the films, which makes the recurrent image of still or dead bodies a major artistic tool of the sublimation of melancholy through beauty, that is, painterly compositions.

This preference for still images isolating the body as the body of Christ is, however, completely independent from all religious possibilities of figuration. It rather belongs to what Deleuze calls in his analysis of Francis Bacon's work 'the atheistic game' of painting (2004: 8). Most importantly, the figure isolated in a painting or *as* a painting becomes an icon, an image. To all these films, of both male and female directors, one can apply what Belén Vidal has pointed out concerning 'the shifting spaces of the figure: from presence to absence; from body to ghost; from actuality to desire; but also from past (history) to present (consciousness)' (2012: 44).

THE IMAGE AS CLUE

Before concluding, I would like to reiterate the main questions raised by the unmistakable preference of contemporary Hungarian filmmakers for representing dead or ailing bodies, often in painterly compositions. I argued that the 'aesthetics of slow cinema', a phrase which is still being developed, is not yet nuanced enough to cover the variety of films that use long shots and emphasise duration and the figurative role of the single image instead of Hollywood-style continuity editing. These films demonstrate big differences in terms of degree of mannerism and its power to reveal cultural, political or philosophical meanings. Hence, I have opted for already existing aesthetic approaches to the role of still(ed), photographic or painterly images in cinema, interpreted as revelatory in showing unspeakable content, such as death or religious concepts, which makes the phenomenon comparable to the 'pregnant moment' of paintings. Julia Kristeva's analysis of the paintings by Holbein and Mantegna as examples of a sublimation of melancholia – the unspeakable sense of loss – has here provided the psychoanalytical background for the interpretation of the numerous references to these particular paintings in contemporary Hungarian cinema, drawing attention, at the same time, to the role of figuration (colours, composition) and the figural. While figuration makes sense alongside the story, the figural is a 'force' that works without the story; it makes visible what cannot be said, the immaterial: as such, the figural emphasises the act of looking. It makes us see differently, by changing angles, visibility, colours, shapes and/or the frame. As such, it corresponds to the extended concept of anamorphosis, originally an optical device used in painting and meant to re-form by de- and recontextualisation. As the 'other of signification', it traditionally had the role of revealing the unspeakable and concentrating the meaning of the story depicted in the painting. Just like one of its types, the mirror anamorphosis, in which a distorted drawing or painting can be seen un-deformed in a mirror placed on it, anamorphosis in film can function as a mirror in which truth or meaning, hidden or distorted in narration, becomes exposed to contemplation. As Daniel Collins points out,

> to observe anamorphic images, one must be an 'eccentric observer', that is, an observer who is not only a bit 'eccentric' in the usual sense of the term (i.e. strange), but an observer who is willing to sacrifice a centric vantage point for the possibility of catching a glimpse of the uncanny from a position off-axis. (1992: 73)

Recalling Lacan's expression 'trap for the eye' and Barthes' 'gap in the garment' to describe anamorphosis, Collins sees its importance 'not as an alternative to the way we experience artworks ... but as a metaphor for accepting information from unfamiliar places and unexpected sources' (1992: 186). This is perfectly in line with Donald Kunze's approach to anamorphosis 'as a general principle': as Kunze points out, it 'is the idea that multiple meanings can be materially and mutually supported within the same material circumstances. Such conditions are so pervasive that anamorphosis is almost inseparable from the phenomenology of the clue' (2012). I argue that a phenomenological approach to puzzling, intermedial images seen as clues to the film as a whole can be a productive way of revealing the social and psychological content behind the calculated mannerism of contemporary Hungarian cinema.

In many contemporary Hungarian films the *mise en abyme* created through the reframing of other media (painting, photograph, video, television) functions as a mirror anamorphosis, revealing, condensing and interpreting hidden psychological processes. As Kristeva points out, if you cannot see the death in Holbein's painting – because it cannot be represented – you can find it in the shape of the line and the composition, metamorphosed in the volume of objects and bodies, as in the case of the anamorphosis of the skull in Holbein's *The Ambassadors* (1533) (1989: 127). According to Lyotard, the change in our way of looking at this painting (the lateral gaze) 'inverts the relation between visible and invisible, signifier and represented scene', giving us 'the signification unseen for direct vision'. His conclusion, that 'the anamorphosis instructs us that reading requires that one die to representation, to the phantasy of presence' (2011: 378), is just the extended version of his definition of the figural as 'the Other of signification'.

As discussed above, the distorted, seemingly shorter, dead or sick bodies appear in some Hungarian films as intermedial individual references to Mantegna's painting, rendering visible death in all its nakedness and obscenity. Belén Vidal coins tableau-like compositions as 'the irruption of painterly textures' in the film:

> By tableau I refer to the various effects provoked by the irruption of painterly textures and still moments in the temporal system of the film shot, as indexes of self-reflexivity in the visual text. The emphasis on framing as artifice is often achieved through double-framing devices that introduce an immobile frame within the mobile (film) frame, usually with the inclusion of paintings or photographs in the mise-en-scène. However, instances of temporal and spatial manipulation of the shot should also be considered: fixed framings, long takes, slow motion, zooms or superimpositions strain the narrative as a whole, drawing our attention to the visual textures of the film. This 'overwriting' of the shot throws into relief tensions between discursive and figural dimensions of film. (2012: 111)

An elaborate use of anamorphosis as the figural *par excellence* can be encountered in Benedek Fliegauf's *Dealer*. Right at the beginning, in the menu of the DVD, the puzzling image of an unidentifiable object visually evoking the sci-fi genre makes us believe that by pushing the play button we are entering an enigma, a riddle. As such, this image possesses all the qualities of a diagram, a rebus or a hieroglyph, considered the model of figural activity by both Deleuze (2004: 102) and Ropars (as discussed by Rodowick 2001: 89) and defined by

Lyotard as a 'space of transformation triggered by desire' (see Vidal 2012: 41). The enigmatic image will be deciphered only in the very last scene of the film, only after we are taken through a journey on one day of the young drug-dealing protagonist's life. His stops are marked by melancholic bodies, drug addicts, and his severely depressed widowed father. We find out that his mother died in an accident when he was a child − she fell out of the window − and in a highly dramatic scene of unspeakable loss we see father and son contemplating the hollow where the body of the mother hit the ground. Thus the last scene of the suicide of the dealer can be interpreted as a figuration of the desire of the melancholic to reunite with the lost object, the Mother-Thing, to fill the empty hollow of the womb of the mother. After taking an overdose, the dealer lies down in a tanning bed, also called a 'sun bed', a version of the 'black sun' (a metaphor used by Nerval for melancholia and chosen by Kristeva as the title of her book). This bed also recalls the tomb in Holbein's painting, a narrow space enclosing the body without any hope of resurrection: death is represented as irrevocable and a final solution for the melancholic. Only when the image becomes still and, in a suggestive representation of the aesthetic moment, is distanciated and thus extracted from narrative do we recognise the opening hieroglyph. The work of condensation established by the figurability of the tanning bed enclosing the body might be understood, in Rodowick's words, 'as forging a correspondence between three discursive registers − that of narrativity, of figural representation, and of the enunciation of fantasy − whose boundaries are mobile, permutable, and by no means distinct' (2001: 88). In this distorted image, in the figural reconciling the claustrophobic composition of Holbein's *Dead Christ* and the optical bravura of *The Ambassadors* we can recognise not only the dead body, but death itself, its unspeakable solitude and melancholia.

To summarise, Hungarian filmmakers representing the generation that grew up after the change of regime, in their effort to figurate and sublimate the sense of loss and the death drive, to bridge the gap between the unconscious and aesthetic representation, inside and outside, often use intermedial references to Holbein's and Mantegna's paintings. These are not simple clichés, compositions that are always already on the canvas or the screen, as Deleuze puts it in his book on Francis Bacon (2004: 87). As I argued above, they have the status of the figural, owing to the disruption they cause in the narrative flow, their work of condensation and displacement and their force to render visible 'what is unavailable to conscious consideration save in the form of secondary revision' (Rodowick 2001: 80). Like true mannerists, these filmmakers are not inventors of forms: they anamorphosise already existing forms by excess, re- and de-contextualisation or distortion. Instead of depicting actual political or social events, they transform the single image itself into *an aesthetic event*.

This work was supported by a grant from the Romanian Ministry of National Education, CNCS − UEFISCDI, project number PN-II-ID-PCE-2012-4-0573.

NOTES

1. For example, Peter Hames mentions 'miserabilism' and discusses the 'inherent melancholy of the long take' in his overview of Tarr's films (2001), Rose McLaren writes about a 'dry, dark type of comedy' (2012), while Ira Jaffe, in her book on slow cinema (2014: 124), in the chapter dedicated to Tarr uses expressions like 'death-haunted', 'the unbearable heaviness of life' and 'nothingness' to illustrate the peculiar atmosphere of Tarr's films.
2. Many of these discussions are hosted on the blog *Unspoken Cinema: Contemporary Contemplative Cinema*. Among the representative contributors to the discourse are Jonathan Romney (2000), Yvette Bíró (2006), Harry Tuttle (2007), Matthew Flanagan (2008), Steven Shaviro (2010), and Antony Fiant (2014). The many points of view are gathered in a recent collection edited by Tiago de Luca and Nuno Barradas Jorge, entitled *Slow Cinema* (2015).
3. In this respect, see Lydia Papadimitriou's review of Andrew Horton's *The Films of Theo Angelopoulos: A Cinema of Contemplation* and of *The Last Modernist: The Films of Theo Angelopoulos*, ed. Andrew Horton. The latter collection contains essays by Bordwell and Jameson, among others, representing a different approach from Angelopoulos's: while Bordwell emphasises his modernism, Jameson praises his originality in representing the unrepresentable of the collective (Papadimitriou 1999).
4. Shaviro mentions the names of the Korean directors Bong Joon-ho, Park Chan-Wook and Kim Ki-Duk. In his conclusion, he considers slow cinema as a 'way of simulating older cinematic styles', of 'flattering classicist cinephiles and of simply ignoring everything that has happened, socially, politically, in the last 30 years' (Shaviro, 2010).
5. As in the case of Béla Tarr, whose work shows an increasing preoccupation with the frame and composition, or Abbas Kiarostami's films ranging from references to Persian miniatures, through art-theoretical considerations of visual representation to an exploration of issues of spectatorship.
6. The American director also considers himself a disciple of Tarr. See, for example, his essay written for the MoMA Béla Tarr Retrospective Catalogue (2001).

WORKS CITED

Agamben, Giorgio (1993), *Stanzas: Word and Phantasm in Western Culture*, Minneapolis: University of Minnesota Press.
Agamben, Giorgio (1999), *The Man without Content*, Stanford: Stanford University Press.
Bellour, Raymond (1975), 'The Unattainable Text', *Screen*, 16:3, 19–28.
Bellour, Raymond (2002), 'L'Interruption, l'instant', in Raymond Bellour, *L'Entre-Images. Photo, Cinéma, Vidéo. Les essais*, Paris: Éditions de la différence, pp. 109–34.
Bíró, Yvette (1982), *Profane Mythology: The Savage Mind of Cinema*, Bloomington: Indiana University Press.
Bíró, Yvette (2006), 'The Fullness of Minimalism', *Rouge*, 9, <http://www.rouge.com.au/9/minimalism.html> (last accessed 28 August 2014).
Collins, Daniel L. (1992), 'Anamorphosis and the Eccentric Observer: inverted perspective and the construction of the Gaze', *Leonardo*, 25: 1, 72–82.
Dalle Vacche, Angela (1996), *Cinema and Painting: How Art Is Used in Film*, Austin: University of Texas Press.
Dánél, Mónika (2013), 'Surrogate Nature, Culture, Women: Transylvania/Romania as Inner Colonies in Contemporary Hungarian Films' in Judit Pieldner and Zsuzsanna Ajtony

(eds), *The Discourses of Space*, Newcastle upon Tyne: Cambridge Scholars Publishing, pp. 255–83.
Deleuze, Gilles (2004), *Francis Bacon: The Logic of Sensation*, London and New York: Continuum.
De Luca, Tiago and Nuno Barradas, Jorge (2015), *Slow Cinema*, Edinburgh: Edinburgh University Press.
Doane, Janice and Devon Hodges (1992), *From Klein to Kristeva: Psychoanalytic Feminism and the Search for the 'Good Enough' Mother*, Ann Arbor: University of Michigan Press.
Felleman, Susan (2006), *Art in the Cinematic Imagination*, Austin: University of Texas Press.
Fiant, Antony (2014), *Pour un cinéma contemporain soustractif*, Vincennes: Presses Universitaires de Vincennes.
Flanagan, Matthew (2008), 'Towards an aesthetics of slow in contemporary cinema', *16:9*, 6: 29, <http://www.16-9.dk/2008-11/side11_inenglish.htm> (last accessed 28 September 2014).
Fliegauf, Benedek (2012a), 'An interview with András Vágvölgyi and Zsuzsa Debre about *Just the Wind*', <http://www.civiljutub.hu/play.php?vid=9518#.VB8osfmSxFs> (last accessed 21 September 2014)
Fliegauf, Benedek (2012b), 'Director's comments on *Just the Wind*'. <http://www.filmpressplus.com/wpcontent/uploads/dl_docs/JustTheWind-Notes.pdf> (last accessed 22 January 2015)
Foster, Gwendolyn Audrey (1999), *Captive Bodies: Postcolonial Subjectivity in Cinema*, Albany: SUNY Press.
Gelencsér, Gábor (2006), 'Testi Mesék' [Bodily Tales], *Beszélő*, 11:3, <http://beszelo.c3.hu/cikkek/testi-mesek> (last accessed 21 September 2014).
Hames, Peter (2001), 'The melancholy of resistance: the films of Béla Tarr', *Kinoeye* 1:1, <http://www.kinoeye.org/01/01/hames01.php> (last accessed 21 January 2016).
Jaffe, Ira (2014), *Slow Movies: Countering the Cinema of Action*, London and New York: Wallflower Press.
Kaplan, E. Ann (1983), *Women and Film: Both Sides of the Camera*, London and New York: Routledge.
Kovács, András Bálint (2013), *The Cinema of Béla Tarr: The Circle Closes*, London and New York: Wallflower Press.
Kristeva, Julia (1989), *Black Sun: Depression and Melancholia*, New York: Columbia University Press.
Kuntzel, Thierry (1978), 'The Film Work', *Enclitic*, 2:1, pp. 38–61.
Kuntzel, Thierry (1980), 'The Film Work 2', *Camera Obscura*, vol. 5, pp. 7–68.
Kunze, Donald (2012), 'Anamorphosis', <http://art3idea.psu.edu/boundaries/documents/anamorphosis.html> (last accessed 30 September 2014).
Levine, Matt and Jeremy Meckler (2012), 'Listening to the World: A Conversation with Béla Tarr', *Walker Magazine*, <http://www.walkerart.org/magazine/2012/bela-tarr-turin-horse> (last accessed 10 March 2014).
Lyotard, Jean-François (1990), *Heidegger and 'The Jews'*, Minneapolis: University of Minnesota Press.
Lyotard, Jean-François (2011), *Discourse, Figure*, Minneapolis and London: University of Minnesota Press.
McLaren, Rose (2012), 'The Prosaic Sublime of Béla Tarr', *The White Review*, 6 December, <http://www.thewhitereview.org/features/the-prosaic-sublime-of-bela-tarr/> (last accessed 21 January 2016).
Marks, Laura U (2000), *The Skin of the Film: Intercultural Cinema, Embodiment, and the Senses*, Durham, NC and London: Duke University Press.

Mulvey, Laura (2006), *Death 24x a Second. Stillness and the Moving Image*, London: Reaktion Books.
Papadimitriou, Lydia (1999), 'Review about Andrew Horton's *The Films of Theo Angelopoulos: a Cinema of Contemplation* (Princeton, NJ: Princeton University Press, 1997, 227 pp.) and about Andrew Horton (ed.): *The Last Modernist: the Films of Theo Angelopoulos* (Trowbridge: Flicks Books, 1997, 138pp.)', *Screen*, 39: 2, 210–18.
Pethő, Agnes (2014), 'The *Tableau Vivant* as a "Figure of Return" in Contemporary East European Cinema', *Acta Universitatis Transylvaniae, Film and Media Studies*, 9, 51–76.
Rancière, Jacques (2009), *Aesthetics and its Discontents*, Cambridge: Polity Press.
Rodowick, D. N. (2001), *Reading the Figural, or, Philosophy after the New Media*, Durham, NC and London: Duke University Press.
Romney, Jonathan (2000), 'Are you sitting comfortably?' *The Guardian*, 7 October. <http://www.theguardian.com/film/2000/oct/07/books.guardianreview> (last accessed 29 September 2014).
Sághy, Miklós (2013), 'Szegénységfilmek mint kulturális exportcikkek' [Poverty-Films as Cultural Export Products], *Élet és irodalom*, 57:38, <http://www.es.hu/saghy_miklos;szegenysegfilmek_mint_kulturalis_exportcikkek;2013-09-19.html> (last accessed 21 September 2014).
Schefer, Olivier (1999), 'Qu'est-ce que le figural?', *Critique*, 630, 912–25.
Seligman, Martin E. P. (1975), *Helplessness: On Depression, Development, and Death*, San Francisco: W. H. Freeman.
Shaviro, Steven (2010), 'Slow cinema vs. Fast Films', <http://www.shaviro.com/Blog/?p=891> (last accessed 29 September 2014).
Strausz, László (2011), 'Archeology of Flesh. History and Body-Memory in *Taxidermia*', *Jump Cut* 53 (Summer). *http://www.ejumpcut.org/archive/jc53.2011/strauszTaxidermia/3.html* (last accessed 22 January 2016).
Straw, Will (1987), 'The Discipline of Forms: Mannerism in Recent Cinema', *Cultural Studies*, 1 (October), 361–76.
Su, Tsu-Chung (2005), 'Writing the Melancholic: The Dynamics of Melancholia in Julia Kristeva's Black Sun', *Concentric: Literary and Cultural Studies*, 3:1, 163–91.
Tanke, Joseph J. (2011), 'What is the Aesthetic Regime?', *Parrhesia*, 12, 71–81.
Tuttle, Harry (2007), '(Technical) minimum profile: unspoken cinema', <http://unspokencinema.blogspot.hu/2007/01/minimum-profile.html> (last accessed 29 September 2014).
Van Sant, Gus (2001), 'The Camera is a Machine', in *Bela Tarr Retrospective Catalogue*, New York: MoMa.
Vidal, Belén (2012), *Figuring the Past: Period Films and the Mannerist Aesthetic*, Amsterdam: Amsterdam University Press.

CHAPTER 4

The Body Breached: Post-Soviet Masculinity on Screen

Helena Goscilo

> The masculine body seeks to be Rambo, not Rimbaud.
> Antony Easthope, *What a Man's Gotta Do*

MODES OF THE SIGNIFYING BODY

In his renowned study *Rabelais and His World* (1984), Mikhail Bakhtin posits two contrasting bodily paradigms. The more familiar is the classical version, exalted in Western culture – 'a strictly completed, finished product', 'isolated, alone, fenced off from all other bodies', pruned of 'protuberances and offshoots . . . its apertures closed' (Bakhtin 1984: 29). Indebted to Greek aesthetics and revived during the Renaissance, this canonical form, popularised through the nude in art, showcases the ideals of beauty and proportion mirroring divine sublimity, argues Kenneth Clark. It is a body that 'furnished the mind of Western man with a pattern of perfection from the Renaissance until the present [that is, twentieth] century' (Clark 1957: 14). What Bakhtin finds incomparably more productive is its slighted, frequently censored counterpart: the body of carnival and grotesque realism. Celebrated most memorably by Rabelais and explored by Boccaccio, Cervantes, Hieronymus Bosch, Breughel the Elder, Lucian Freud, Egon Schiele, Oleg Kulik, Vladimir Sorokin,[1] Italian film directors Federico Fellini and Lina Wertmüller, as well as gay camp, this is 'the unfinished and open body . . . blended with the world, with animals, with objects' (Bakhtin 1984: 26–7). This uncanonical form comprises the 'lower bodily stratum', excess, 'apertures and convexities . . . the open mouth, the genital organs, the breasts, phallus, the potbelly, the nose' (Bakhtin 1984: 26).[2] Unlike Bakhtin, who privileges the carnivalesque body as life-affirming and regenerative, Clark largely perceives it as degraded and shame-driven during the Gothic and later periods. Tellingly, his selection of representative images tends to spotlight diminished and broken forms rather than aggressively robust, radically exuberant physicality.[3] In contemporary Russian culture, the body of grotesque realism has little to do with celebration; lacking vitality and joy, it resembles the marred and disabled body lamented by Clark, sooner aligned with the Gothic than with the utopian musculature of Soviet classicism.[4]

The status of the nude in Russian culture plays a decisive role here. During the nineteenth century, Russian art – significantly, bypassed by the Renaissance, with enormous consequences – favoured portraiture and landscape over the nude, which Russian literature, apart from Nikolai Gogol's Bosch-like phantasmagoria, likewise circumspectly euphemised or sidestepped, its references to bodily activities confined largely to the intake of food and drink.[5] Subsequently the prudishness of official Soviet ideology mandated that cultural production favour the harmonious, often abstracted, classical body, which, regardless of gender, rarely shed clothes and symbolised power, strength, and endurance – features that Soviet propaganda programmatically emphasised as the defining qualities of the state, the nation, and the New Man. Sartorial preferences, no less than bodily shapes and movements, conveyed ideological probity or deviance. While film equated negative female characters, such as foreigners, domestic traitors, and women of 'loose morals', with scant or 'decadent' clothing, heavy make-up, and coquettish mannerisms,[6] suspect males hid behind sunglasses and an unSoviet ('unmanly') preoccupation with their looks. Their antipodes, the New Soviet Men, wore uniforms or simple, unobtrusive clothing. Physical appearance, including fashion, was coded unambiguously and audiences could easily decipher its moral valences.[7] Naked flesh, however, was nowhere in sight, and even partially clothed bodies rarely appeared on-screen. In viewers contemplating it, the male body may have elicited admiration but not desire, for, unlike its American counterpart (for instance, Marlon Brando as Stanley Kowalski stripped down to his 'wife beater' in *A Streetcar Named Desire* [1951] or Paul Newman as the bare-chested rebel in *Cool Hand Luke* [1967]), the Soviet body could hardly have been more desexualised.[8]

If the post-revolutionary body of the avant-garde and the 1920s strived for gender neutrality (one need only recall Varvara Stepanova's unisex clothes designs), starting in the 1930s gender differentiation reflected the militarism of Stalin's policies for men and his retrograde endorsement of maternal and domestic duties for women. This disparity in functions notwithstanding, bodies of both genders – solid, relentlessly energetic, and able to withstand all trials – were idealised as part of the New Order that would lead to the future utopia. Political and sports parades offered opportunities for the display of streamlined young physiques whose smoothly orchestrated movements resembled the co-ordinated operation of animated machines.[9] This practice corroborated Antony

Easthope's notion that '[t]he most important meanings that can attach to the idea of the masculine body are unity and permanence. [A masculine image] clear in outline and firm in definition' shores up identity (Easthope 1992: 53). This classical body, like the Soviet body politic, would be 'opened up' and dismantled only after the implosion of the Soviet Union – a process dramatically visible in film, where the orderly strength and propriety of the Soviet male body was displaced by violent, vulnerable, exposed post-Soviet bodies of apertures and excrescences – anatomies under siege reflecting the chaotic, volatile, beleaguered Russia humiliated by its loss of empire and intent on both rejecting and nostalgically recuperating its rapidly receding past.

CANONICAL BODIES ON SCREEN UNDER STALIN AND KHRUSHCHEV

Not the female, but the male body incarnated Soviet values, as attested by sculptures of hypertrophied musculature, paintings of Herculean Stakhanovites, and films featuring everyday life and popular culture under Stalin. As Rigmaila Salys's excellent study of Grigorii Aleksandrov's musical comedies notes, one of the iconic and most celebrated Soviet films of the 1930s, Aleksandrov's *Tsirk* (*Circus*, 1936), epitomised the decade's revival of the Greek ideal of beauty outlined by J. J. Winckelmann (Salys 2009: 177). Tellingly, a chief attraction of the circus life depicted on-screen showcases the impressively proportioned physique of Ivan Martynov (Sergei Stoliarov) as he 'flies' through the air – admittedly, fully clothed, but the contours of his body visible under his Flash Gordon outfit.[10] That strapping body as spectacle and symbol was an object of veneration for both circus spectators within the diegesis and Stalin-era movie audiences. And Freud's notion of flying as symbolising male erection certainly buttresses the image of machismo projected by Stoliarov's risk-defying flight.[11] Little wonder that the actor subsequently would make a career of embodying the epically-proportioned 'bogatyr' adept at miraculously heroic feats in stirring film adaptations of fairy tales and epic tales, such as Aleksandr Rou's *Vasilisa prekrasnaia* (*Vasilisa the Beautiful*, 1939) and *Kashchei bessmertnyi* (*Kashchei the Deathless*, 1944), and Aleksandr Ptushko's *Sadko* (1952) and *Il'ia Muromets* (1956). Clearly, fantasy and power attached to Stoliarov's physical endowments, for during the Thaw he was cast in leading roles in sci-fi movies, such as *Taina dvukh okeanov* (*The Mystery of Two Oceans*, 1955) and *Tumannost' Andromedy* (*The Andromeda Nebula*, 1967).[12]

Martynov's circus flight was essentially a metaphor literalised in *Valerii Chkalov* (1941) – Mikhail Kalatozov's idealising film about the unruly, record-setting ace pilot under Stalin's tutelage, who likewise possesses a quintessentially Soviet male body, robust and powerful, usually encased in a black leather jacket and reflecting a 'broad Russian spirit' capable of heroic exploits and colossal stoicism. With only slight variation, the same masculine paradigm obtains in Aleksei, the stalwart Stakhanovite of Mikheil Chiaureli's *Padenie Berlina* (*Fall of Berlin*, 1949), who overcomes what initially seems a serious head injury and psychological castration vis-à-vis Stalin's supreme machismo, to triumph over the Nazis and his own heavy-handed bashfulness before Natasha, his Stalin-deifying beloved, whom he effortlessly lifts and carries as though she were the proverbial light feather. Such physical monuments of macho splendour could grapple with all challenges, as if already prepared to be cast in bronze or stone as models for the adulation of future generations.

Chkalov's conquest of air space is grounded in history, as is the case of Aleksei Mares'ev/Meres'ev (1916–2001), a fighter pilot during World War II who, despite being an amputee, returned to World War II aerial combat, earning more than a dozen decorations. In her Lacan-indebted monograph, *How the Soviet Man Was Unmade* (2008), Lilya Kaganovsky argues that both Boris Polevoi's *Povest' o nastoiashchem cheloveke* (*Story about a Real Man*, 1946/7) and Aleksandr Stolper's screen adaptation (1949), which hagiographed Mares'ev's achievements, depict a vulnerable Soviet body, incapacitated and hospitalised. Indisputably, Meres'ev's body in both texts undergoes suffering, but it manifestly does so only to underscore how the Soviet spirit overcomes any physical hardship through patriotism and superhuman will. Indeed, whereas the real-life Mares'ev spent more than a year recovering and learning to use his prosthetic legs, editing in the film reduces that process to a matter of minutes.[13] In fact, the film surpasses the novel in driving home the invisibility of Meres'ev's prostheses, which enable him to dance, recapture his reputation as a daredevil pilot, and enjoy a traditional, loving family life. Like many other Soviet films, Stolper's resembled contemporary posters, inasmuch as both genres shrank from depicting the male body not only as naked, but also as penetrable, defenceless, and incapable of miraculous restoration.[14] That body's integrity derived from and symbolised the claimed integrity of the Soviet Union and the integration of all within it.

POST-SOVIET BODIES

> The human body is essentially something other than an animal organism.
> Martin Heidegger

Unsurprisingly, the protracted enervation and subsequent dissolution of the Soviet Union inflicted upon the male body a plethora of carnivalesque indignities and invasions, regardless of the eras portrayed on-screen. All too quickly, the notorious *chernukha* of perestroika and the 1990s – the naturalistic preoccupation with the seamier, physiological aspects of life, marked by violence, drunkenness, casual sex, squalid settings, sordid behaviour, and the perception of life as a dead end – rapidly overturned decades of Soviet decorum and celluloid puritanism.[15] The male body that during the Soviet era had symbolised state aspirations now dramatised their debacle within an analogous semiotic system. Hence the 'marks of the Tsar' popularly believed to legitimate claims to the throne, imprinted on Pugachev's exposed body in Aleksandr Proshkin's *Russkii bunt* (*Russian Revolt*, 2000), prove false, merely externalising his lust for power, which ultimately leads to his horrendous decapitation.[16] Similarly, in Pavel Chukhrai's *Vor* (*The Thief*, 1997), the tattoo on Tolian's back, which to the savvy audience betrays the owner's stint in prison, inscribes his self-serving amoralism, which eventually results in his violent death at the hand of his surrogate son.[17] More circumspect films, such as these and Sergei Bodrov's *Kavkazskii plennik* (*Prisoner of the Mountains*, 1997), contain sequences in which men briefly appear on-screen fully or partially naked – itself a departure from Soviet practice. In all three cases and others, however, the directors ensured that specific circumstances rationalise the nakedness: a visit to the *bania* (sauna) in the first two and an army physical examination in the third instance. Even so, the boy Sania's anxiety about the size of his penis in *The Thief* and his surrogate father's reassurance touch on a topic of physiology that even in scenes at the *bania* was tabooed under the Soviet regime. In sum, these films left no doubts that the post-Soviet exposure of the male body, most often in a non-heroic, far-from-classical form, was part of the new Russian cinema's unglamorous explorations of the recent and distant past.

A more disturbing instance, not of the male body's nudity, but of its penetrable apertures, occurs in Aleksei German's unflinching, phantasmagoric *Khrustalev, mashinu!* (*Khrustalev, the Car!*, 1998), where the military brain surgeon General Iurii Glinskii is 'brutally raped and sodomized by a gang of criminal thugs in the back of a closed truck en route to the gulag' (Hoberman 1999). In a country where even today the incomparably more common violation of women remains largely unacknowledged, that sequence carries extraordinary shock value. The reticence in Soviet cinema – as well as other cultural genres – about forcible physical violation may be inferred from Mikhail Kalatozov's *Letiat zhuravli* (*The Cranes Are Flying*, 1957): the protagonist Veronica's rape is shot in such stylised fashion that viewers unused to radical mediation by the camera in the interests of visual euphemism have difficulty understanding that a rape actually occurs. By contrast, German, without explicitly dwelling on Glinskii's anal penetration, does not rely on the camera to soften the impact of Glinskii's grisly fate, which cannot be misinterpreted.

Putrefaction of the male body during late-Soviet dreary desolation and corruption, as well as the state's callous approach to soldiers' deaths in the Afghan war, received comparably horrifying treatment in Aleksei Balabanov's *Gruz 200* (*Cargo 200*, 2007), focused on the Orwellian year of 1984. In addition to dramatising a psychopathic policeman (Aleksei Poluian)'s rape with a bottle of a young woman, Angelika (Agniia Kuznetsova), after which he chains her to a bed in the squalid apartment he shares with his demented, alcoholic mother (Valentina Andriukova), the film wallows in rotting and rutting bodies: the corpse of Angelica's fiancé, transported as cargo from Afghanistan back to the USSR,[18] decays beside the hysterical young woman, along with the bodies of those men whom the voyeuristic, impotent policeman forces to have sexual intercourse with her. Reduced to meat, male flesh here is nothing more than fodder for military purposes or for sexual manipulation terminating in arbitrary extinction. Determined to arraign late-Soviet society, Balabanov in his sweeping, hyperbolic satire of negative 'types' projects all manner of ills onto the body, and, despite Tony Anemone's earnest plea for the film's quality, *Cargo 200* rarely moves beyond the shock tactics of *chernukha*.[19]

THE BODY IN WAR

> Combat exercises a profound attraction to the masculine imagination, whether in fictional or documentary form.
>
> Antony Easthope, *What a Man's Gotta Do*

If such revelations of Stalinist-era and late-Soviet excesses finally introduced manifestly traumatised bodies to Russian audiences,[20] on-screen war and its aftermath likewise jettisoned Soviet triumphalism to expose the incalculable physiological and psychological price of armed conflict. Whereas, under Putin, World War II has remained sacrosanct on the post-Soviet screen, the wars in Afghanistan and Chechnya have sooner inspired scenarios parading not glorious victory, but the incalculable cost in human life and humaneness.[21] That cost is painfully imaged in numerous films, such as Valerii Todorovskii's signally titled, award-winning *Moi svodnyi brat Frankenshtein* (*My Stepbrother Frankenstein*, 2004), where Pavlik, the (eloquently) illegitimate, traumatised son of an established Moscow physicist, appears on his father's doorstep, physically and emotionally scarred, a patch over one no-longer-existent eye. A maimed veteran of the Chechen war, Pavlik incarnates paranoia, fantastic delusions, and instant readiness to eliminate all enemies, however putative.[22] Todorovskii materialises his mutilated psyche in his body, particularly his one eye, which symbolically distorts and circumscribes his vision of the world, in which everyone outside the family constitutes a potential foe to be eradicated. Here, too, as in *The Thief*, father and son visit the *bania*, allowing for shots of their and other men's bare bodies, as well as demonstrating a disquieting example of Pavlik's 'monstrousness' when he reacts with uncontrollable violence to a man who has merely appropriated their *venik* – an officially trained kneejerk response for which his father carries but disavows responsibility.[23]

Predictably, the Chechen war yielded many films lamenting its destruction of young men's lives and limbs. Aleksandr Veledinskii's *Zhivoi* (*Alive*, 2006)[24] dramatises the inability of the amputee Kir (Andrei Chadov), who survives the war physically, to adjust psychologically to his family, his former girlfriend, so-called 'normal life', and a blighted, materialistic society, to which he returns after the grim travails of combat. Unlike Stolper, Veledinskii does not hesitate to show the young man's difficulty with his prosthetic leg or the damage to his psyche, which prompts violent reactions of the sort that become automatic in enlisted men trained to kill. Like Pavlik's eye-patch in *My Stepbrother Frankenstein*, Kir's prosthesis, which at times he cannot adequately manipulate, externalises his psychological instability, imprinting it on his body, which from the outset is slated for the death that he eventually meets, joining the two comrades whose ghosts accompany him throughout much of the film.[25] Like Fedor Bondarchuk's bombastic, award-winning *9-aia rota* (*9th Company*, 2005), *Alive* highlights military male bonding, for the genre permits men

> to behave towards each other in ways that would not be allowed elsewhere, caressing and holding each other, comforting and weeping together, admitting their love . . . War's suffering is a kind of punishment for the release of homosexual desire and male femininity . . . [which] only war allows. (Easthope 1992: 66)

Such a genre-based suspension of traditional macho constraints, coupled with Soviet privileging of militarism, accounts for the popularity of war films in a culture notorious for its misogynistic homosocialism.

War as a weapon guaranteed to wreck men's physical (as well as moral and mental) health and wholeness receives its most extreme articulation in *Chistilishche* (*Purgatory*, 1998), a savage television movie about the Chechen war or, more precisely, the calamitous assault on Grozny in 1994–5.[26] Scripted and directed by the ultranationalist former Duma deputy Aleksandr Nevzorov, the film, which focuses on the day of 4 January 1995, operates by propaganda – rank prejudice against Chechens, women and black people – and the sensationalism of shoreless gore. Bodies in the film exist exclusively to burst into flames, undergo amputation, crumple under tanks, and erupt in fountains and pools of blood when shot by any and all weapons in their vicinity. It is as though Nevzorov decided to overturn all Soviet prohibitions against physical display, and to showcase, unremittingly and usually in close-up, every conceivable bodily devastation visited upon combatants. A Russian general's eyeball falls out and, after merely shoving it back into his eye-socket, in the spirit of 'a man's gotta do what he's gotta do', he returns to the more immediate task of slaughtering the enemy; Baltic female snipers on the Chechens' side laugh as they aim their weapons at male genitalia and, in what the director presumably conceives as 'justice', perish in the same mode, shot in the crotch; a Russian soldier is crucified, and the camera returns obsessively to the pinkish-red fluid unconvincingly passed off as blood pouring out of his open mouth. Such scenes, like the mangled bodies they feature, pile up non-stop, with virtually nothing occupying the screen apart from the bloody destruction of human flesh, which appears as dismembered stumps resembling chunks of meat.

Virtually no male body in the film survives intact, and almost all movement involves something fatal entering and exiting the human form, ripping it apart. As Easthope trenchantly observes, Joseph Conrad's 'the horror, the horror' is partly 'an image of the body in pieces, literally "blown away"' (Easthope 1992: 64). Not celebratory carnival, but dark doom defines this trajectory. In light of the epigraph from the 136th Psalm superimposed on-screen before the film actually begins – with heavy irony, offering thanks to God for his mercy, which 'endureth forever' – one may be tempted to interpret *Purgatory* as a pacifist statement. Anyone so credulous, however, would have difficulty explaining the overkill: other than brief instances of the Russians' failure to make radio contact, the film comprises nothing but vicious annihilation, encouraging the conclusion that Nevzorov simply enjoys contemplating the ghastly spectacle he produces, which lacks a narrative, consisting, as it does, of a senseless gallery of scenes comprising carnage and mayhem. Though on first glance the story 'Smert' Dolgushova' ('Dolgushov's Death') in Isaak Babel's *Konarmiia* (*Red Cavalry*, 1925) might seem a literary precedent for this depiction of bloody slaughter – the narrator, Liutov, confronts the soldier Dolgushov holding his bloody intestines in his hands as he begs to be shot – Babel's sophisticated treatment of aesthetics, spirituality, and military violence during the Civil War and his confinement of the plot to a single, though gruesome, incident, could hardly be more remote from Nevzorov's exclusive emphasis on the transformation of bodies into bleeding pulp during armed conflict.

While the one-dimensionality and opaqueness of Nevzorov's *Purgatory* resists analysis on anything other than psychiatric grounds, two films of dissimilar quality, divided by a decade, urge sustained attention because of their complex notion of the male body and its (in)capacities: Sergei Livnev's startling *Serp i molot* (*Hammer and Sickle*, 1994), which during the first post-Soviet decade not only engaged the Frankenstein scenario, but also marked a watershed in celluloid representation of the male body;[27] and Filipp Iankovskii's *Mechenosets* (*Sword Bearer*, 2006), pitched at a different, younger audience, yet in some ways novel and far-reaching in its symbolic implications. Both films have recourse to fantasy, which tropes their central concerns.

MASCULINITY CONSTRUCTED, DECONSTRUCTED AND MONUMENTALISED IN *HAMMER AND SICKLE*

> Divided into knowable parts the body can be reassembled
> as though it were a rational order . . . or a machine.
>
> Antony Easthope, *What a Man's Gotta Do*

Livnev's bold *Hammer and Sickle* literalises the Stalinist-era metaphor of creating the New Man by dramatising a clandestine operation that trans-sexualises the female worker Evdoiia (Dusia) Kuznetsova into the manufactured male ideal, Evdokim Kuznetsov (Aleksei Serebriakov), whose subsequent life unfolds as a series of image-consolidating Soviet pseudo-achievements.

The first half-hour of the film, which focuses on the metamorphosis, spotlights the power of the penis as potential phallus, devoting an entire frame to the upright member at the Frankensteinian venue in which the operation

Figure 4.1 DVD cover of *Hammer and Sickle*, the newly-minted Evdokim

transpires. Given the building's former identity as a monastery, the procedure suggests the usurpation of divine creation by the omnipotent secular lord – Stalin (Vladimir Steklov) – whose experiment at sociopolitical engineering fails, leaving most participants in the project dead.[28] Once the body and penis become united, Evdokim must learn the basics of both biological difference (standing when urinating; penetrating the nurse Vera Raevskaia [Evdokiia Germanova] in his first bout of sexual intercourse as a male) and behaviour appropriate to Stalinist masculinity: Stakhanovite labour on the metro, participation in political committees, marriage to a fellow Stakhanovite from the countryside, adoption of a girl orphaned by the Spanish Civil War (1936), and so forth. These experiences incrementally invest the penis with phallus-power.

Yet the repeated performance of socially approved rituals of gendered behaviour as a mode of acquiring conventional gender identity, as proposed by Judith Butler (1990), fails to take hold in Evdokim's case,[29] for painful discrepancies ravage his post-operative self. These include the possession of physical male attributes that disturbingly collide with his memories of experiences as a woman – memories revived during intercourse with Vera and during a chance encounter with his former male lover at a restaurant bar; and his unfulfilling state-arranged marriage to Elizaveta (Alla Kliuka), which lacks the love he nurtures for Vera, the woman who shares the secret of his 'male birth' and who initiated him into sex as a man. In other words, through the battlefield that is Evdokim Kuznetsov, the film dramatises what seems to be the disabling distance between sex and gender while also distinguishing between theory and praxis as regards notions of identity, love, and social advancement.

Those conflicting categories are played out on the site of Evdokim's body – a body, as he eventually learns, that belongs to him only nominally, for the state that reconstructed it also claims it to further its own political aims. That body, in fact, serves the state's interests by building the Moscow metro, appearing at countless official functions, becoming the model for the male figure in the iconic sculpture by Vera Mukhina (Larisa Uromova) of *Rabochii i kolkhoznitsa* (*The Male Worker and the Female Kolkhoz Laborer*, 1937) – subsequently adopted as Mosfilm's instantly recognisable logo – and, finally, by lying as a silent, inert figure in the museum bearing Evdokim's name. *In his name that museum generates a large-scale mythology showcasing him as a heroic New Soviet Man, paralysed when shot saving Stalin's life, though in reality he was shot trying to kill Stalin as the architect of his personal tragedy. Evdokim's helpless body *qua* museum exhibit, as Alexander Prokhorov's outstanding article argues, is the apotheosis of the Stalinist enterprise, whereby, hovering between life and death, the living body becomes a static imitation (Prokhorov 2000: 30).[30] That imitation facilitates an endless proliferation of

Soviet myths elaborated by officialdom and the museum's keeper, in this case Elizaveta Kuznetsova, who uses Evdokim's body for sexual pleasure and for her own aggrandisement in the spurious name of love. For Aleksei (Avangard Leont'ev), Stalin's aide and his chief representative throughout the film, Evdokim's helpless body permits the accumulation of whatever tales Aleksei cares to circulate about the glory of Soviet heroes exemplified by Evdokim. And for visitors to the museum, that body is 'living proof' of Soviet men's courage, devotion to the nation, and readiness to sacrifice their lives for their glorious leader.

Evdokim's insistence on personal subjectivity and therefore agency as he attempts to strangle Stalin – 'I'm going to live as I want' (*Ia budu zhit' kak ia khochu*) – betrays his failure to understand the meaning of his transformation from Dusia to a Soviet masculine icon. The external attributes of his success, such as his car, his spacious residence, and the positions he holds, like the penis surgically sutured to his body, constitute the state's investment in malleable matter that must be shaped in accordance with official ideology and decrees. Dispelling Evdokim's delusions, Stalin points out that he (and the system instituted by him) 'created' Evdokim from a 'hysterical broad' (*istericheskaia babenka*), and this creation has no life independent of the creator's will. Evdokim's sole means of escape, whereby he can reclaim his subjectivity and his body, is to leave life permanently; hence his smile of happiness when his adopted daughter, Dolores, shoots him dead with his own gun. Ultimately, then, Evdokim's acquired penis never attains the status of a phallus, which in *Hammer and Sickle* and in Stalin-era films such as *The Fall of Berlin* belongs exclusively to Stalin.

In a sense, Mukhina's sculpture, which depicts the male wielding the urban hammer while the female holds the sickle – identified with the retrograde countryside – incarnates in steel Evdokim's personal dilemma: the inability to reconcile his new Stakhanovite masculinity with his origins as a rural woman. His inability, in turn, metonymises the unsuccessful national policy of *smychka* introduced during the 1920s: the need to bring together the countryside and the city, to unite the agricultural sphere with urban industry, a feat yet to be achieved in Russia.

What is particularly striking about Stalinism as conceived in Livnev's poorly distributed film is the primacy of visibility, of physicality. That trait likewise marks other post-Soviet films reassessing the Stalin era,[31] such as Ivan Dykhovichnyi's *Prorva* (*Moscow Parade*, 1992), which highlights dazzling official displays within the urban landscape as a contrastive background for humans who lose lives, parts of their bodies, and illusions under the Soviet system's pitiless indifference to its citizens' desires and ultimate fates. As in *Hammer and Sickle*, the state inscribes its values and imperatives on the individual and collective body. Whereas Stalinist cinema registered the male body's wounding and pain as essentially a stage to be vanquished with maximum speed by the iron will of the New Soviet hero, post-Soviet revisitations of Stalinism such as Livnev's *Hammer and Sickle* dwell on that body's humiliation, torments, disintegration, and seemingly inevitable death.[32]

MY WEAPON, MYSELF IN *THE SWORD BEARER*

> I did not come to bring peace, but a sword.
>
> Matthew 10: 34

Superficially, the death-strewn plot of Filipp Iankovskii's *Sword Bearer* (based on an identically-titled novel by Evgenii Danilenko) has the semblance of yet another crowd-pleaser for young Russian audiences addicted to both violence and fantasy.[33] Sasha Strel'tsov (Artem Tkachenko),[34] a brooding young man with longstanding family problems, returns to his 'roots', only to be attacked viciously by his resentful former classmates. He responds by maiming the group's jealous leader, reducing him to a hospitalised vegetable. Bella (Tat'iana Liutaeva), the aggressive mother of the luckless youth, persuades her criminal lover, Klim (Aleksei Gorbunov), to wreak revenge, but Sasha manages to dispatch him in hideous fashion – only one in a sequence of men he kills, including his biological father. Hunted by the police, Sasha pretends to kidnap the daughter of the police detective on his trail (Leonid Gromov) to gain entry into the psychiatric ward where Katia (Chulpan Khamatova), his newly acquired love interest, has been confined as an unforeseen consequence of Sasha's fatal activities. When the couple escape from the mental institution on a motorcycle, the police pursue them by car, helicopter, and on foot. Along the highway Katia is shot by a policeman and expires in Sasha's arms by a remote, isolated seashore, where the detective, Roshchin, finds him, wracked by grief.

While the plot differs little from that of numerous forgettable Russian B-films, it conveys neither the film's philosophical-literary aspirations nor the camerawork that abets them. Granted, *The Sword Bearer* contains a glut of violent, gut-wrenching scenes focused on the body, notably the sequence in which Sasha's erstwhile classmates attack him, prompting his blood-curdling, savage response, and above all the sight of Klim's bloody upper torso slowly crawling across the floor of a café after Sasha has sliced him in half. But far from being an action/criminal movie intended to entertain the bloodthirsty, *The Sword Bearer* attempts to translate into the modern visual idiom one of Russian literature's most revered canonical works: Mikhail Lermontov's *Demon*, which he began in 1829 and continued revising until his death in 1841.

The *dominanta* throughout Lermontov's creative career, cast in various recognisable guises, the Byron-inspired Demon is an existential figure, shuttling between heaven and hell (i.e. on earth), exiled from the former yet yearning to be redeemed through love. His passion for the earthly Tamara, however, induces him to kill her beloved and, inadvertently, to cause her death, leaving him a tragic exile from heaven and happiness. Obviously, Sasha's sense of inalienable loss, his rootlessness, lack of 'home', estrangement from those around him, murder of Katia's lover, and responsibility for her death all Demonise him. Moreover, his oblique confession to a sympathetic priest (Nikolai Shatokhin) is a clever equivalent for the confessional nature of the Demon's anaphoric avowals to Tamara ('I swear by the first day of creation,/I swear by its last day,/I swear by the ignominy of a crime . . .').[35] But what is original, if not necessarily successful in the film, is Iankovskii's exteriorisation of the tragic Demon's dire ability to exterminate others: the prosthetic sword that extrudes from Sasha's right hand whenever he feels threatened or enraged.

Internalised in Lermontov as the Demon's fatal will, in the film the sword becomes part of Sasha's body – a fitting parallel for the post-millennial transposition of the Soviet Union's ever-abstract discourse into traumatised physicality. That weapon, with which he presumably was born and over which he seems to possess little control, cripples his former classmate and demolishes not only Klim, but also several other males, including – as revealed in a flashback to Sasha's childhood – his adoptive father. Whereas, in the religious mythology of Romanticism espoused by Lermontov, father was God, in *The Sword Bearer* the paternal figures on whom he wreaks vengeance are two flawed, earthly fathers: his biological sire, who abandoned the family, and the abusive second husband of Sasha's mother (Nadezhda Markina). Paternity here, as in countless post-Soviet films, is either inadequate or absent.[36]

Investigating Sasha's murder of his father, the perceptive detective Roshchin guides viewers' thoughts by wondering aloud why Sasha leaves women unharmed. Indeed, homicide in *The Sword Bearer* is gender-specific, and though Bella insists on revenge for her son's incapacitation, it is men who bear weapons, enact violence, and are beaten or slaughtered. Their bodies constitute the stage for melodrama, as was indeed the case during Russia's lawless 1990s. Most of the men whom Sasha exterminates in the film appear in a negative light: a vagrant intending to rape a little girl; Sasha's father (who abandoned the family and would not pay alimony) and fist-wielding stepfather; a shifty character who attempts to sell Sasha a knife that proves a MacGuffin;[37] Katia's foul-mouthed lover and his henchman; and the quartet of criminals who on Klim's orders unwisely try to best Sasha in their cell. Since only the priest and Roshchin, whom Sasha never harms, emerge as moral beings, one might think that Sasha functions as the agent of legitimate justice in the film. Such a notion, however, is dispelled when he slaughters all the police personnel transporting him to jail in a closed truck; though Iankovskii in this instance refrains from exhibiting their corpses, the stream of blood pouring out of the truck as Sasha escapes leaves no doubts as to what remains of the men within it. Not only Sasha, but most males in the film express themselves primarily through violence: male rage leads to a series of bleeding, mangled or dismembered bodies – precisely the spectacle that Soviet cinema eschewed, harnessing male violence to honourable defence of the nation.

Sasha's responsibility for multiple men's deaths extends to Katia's, however indirectly, and Iankovskii conveys as much through bodily movement. Throughout, the body is the couple's chief means of communication, and words seem so irrelevant to their relationship that they exchange (first) names only after they elude the police and relax in the car of the priest who aids their efforts at flight. Editing ensures that their first sexual intercourse, with Sasha's body near-naked, takes place immediately after they meet and in silence.

Their subsequent lovemaking in the apartment is orchestrated as a wordless dance: as both turn gracefully in a circular motion, Katia's head limply falls back while his hands caress her face. Iankovskii reprises that choreography for Katia's death: on the motorcycle, her head drops back at the same angle after she is shot, and as she dies, he strokes her face with identical gestures. Repetition here is predicative: his love, like the Demon's, is lethal, inevitably condemning her to death – a fact he acknowledges to himself and the priest when he tells

Figure 4.2 Sasha and Katia in bodily communication (*The Sword Bearer*)

the latter, 'She shouldn't be with me'.[38] This awareness, as well as his parting remark to the priest that it is too late for him to turn to God, confirms Sasha's sacrifice of Katia to his own desires – precisely Lermontov's scenario.

What is the significance of a sword that, under specific circumstances, becomes a death-dealing part of one's body and is perpetually a potential extension of it? However one interprets the prosthesis, it clearly has a symbolic function. In the film's contemporary social context, early established as that of crime-riddled Russia, the sword may be viewed literally as a means of self-protection. Given the film's recuperation of Lermontov's narrative poem and its symbolism, however, the retractable weapon surely represents a metaphysical/psychological response to the injustice of God's world. As a 'tool' of rebellion, it evokes the Romantic era, when poets such as Shelley and Byron, following Milton, placed God on trial for an arbitrary, dehumanising world and championed Satan as his principled insurgent antagonist. That Sasha's situation symbolises man's place in the universe may be deduced from his a priori, unwilled possession of the sword; after all, in a flashback Iankovskii shows him as a child unexpectedly discovering it and, significantly, attempting to amputate his hand to rid himself of the 'fatal gift' – an attempt he repeats as an adult in a fit of despair. The automatic extrusion of the sword parallels the inborn ability of Lermontov's hero to annihilate at will his rival for Tamara. The capacity to destroy, in other words, is a given, independent of the individual's volition, and the bandage that Sasha winds around his right hand signals his status as a vulnerable victim of his unwanted power. If the sword symbolises man's revolt against the fundamental inequity of God's world, Iankovskii's script ultimately cannot sustain the symbolism of this grand conception, for Sasha is not only a victim, but also a violent killer. Like Lermontov's Demon, he perpetually moves between good and evil, capable of both.

Visually, Iankovskii leaves no doubts about the metaphysical nature of Sasha's dilemma: the film consistently and fruitfully exploits associations of water with religious elements, and movement along the vertical axis.[39] In narratively mysterious yet symbolically pregnant mode, Sasha is first seen crossing water in a ship, the camera lingering for a considerable time on the turbid depths, into which a large object has been tossed;[40] at virtually all turning points or moments of intensity, rain pours down on him: when he attempts to sever his sword-extending arm, twice as he stands on the ship's deck, when he kills his biological father, when he and Katia escape from her apartment by car, when he reclines atop a roof, and so forth. The film's conclusion likewise locates Sasha beside water. Traditionally a trope for spiritual cleansing and simultaneously chaos, water in the film has the same ambivalence as Sasha's very being.

Furthermore, though the film's setting shifts from a provincial town to an urban environment, and then to the forested far north, Iankovskii names no specific location, implying that the human condition is eternal, unchanging, and universal. And the camera emphasises the metaphysical nature of Sasha's dilemma, inasmuch as high and low angle shots throughout the film draw attention to the vertical of heaven/hell. Isolated and aloof, Sasha, like Lermontov's Demon, contemplates life around him from an elevated perspective: on the roof of a rotunda, from which, with a white pigeon (dove of peace?) beside him, he surveys the cityscape below. Shortly afterwards, he encounters his potential salvation, incarnated in Katia, on the second-floor landing of a staircase he has ascended. Finally, at the seashore, he raises his sword-arm heavenward, to cut through and bring down the helicopter and Roshchin into the water. And, as he agonises over Katia's dead body, cradled in his arms, the camera zooms upward in an aerial shot that shows Sasha utterly alone, a speck in the wild, depopulated landscape – a highly effective image of existential solitude. As if these analogies with Lermontov's protagonist were insufficient, the film's debt to Mikhail Vrubel's paintings of *The Demon*, convincingly argued by Vlad Strukov (2010: 180–2), consolidates *The Sword Bearer's* fundamental inseparability from the Romantic narrative poem. Similarly, Artem Tkachenko's tall, narrow body, whether clothed or exposed, is frequently shot in such a way as to evoke the elongated forms of El Greco's religious paintings. It is no exaggeration to say that Iankovskii conceives of the body – suffering, bloodied, mutilated and segmented – as emblematic of the human condition. Not coincidentally, Katia's two dreams of Sasha, who may seem merely a killer, envision him as a victim, his face streaked with blood.

Iankovskii's film is uncommonly laconic because its protagonist expresses himself predominantly through the body: taciturn and unforgiving, as an adult he never speaks to his mother or the father he kills, exchanges no words with those he stabs or slices to death, and never declares his love for Katia. His laconism is a polar contrast to the Demon's verbal seduction of Tamara and the logorrhea favoured by Soviet cinema, which infused the male body with ideology, yet found it necessary to drive its points home through lengthy speeches instead of assigning that function to editing and camerawork.[41] To understand all that may be understood about Sasha, the viewer merely needs to watch his eloquent body at rest and above all in action, which cinematographer Marat Adel'shin tracks from a variety of angles. As a major innovative aspect of the male body in contemporary Russian film, the sword that he cannot jettison suggests, on the one hand, humans' timeless instinct for self-protection, and, on the other, the inborn violence of masculinity.

Like *Hammer and Sickle*, though in an appreciably different mode, *The Sword Bearer* draws a definitive distinction between genders, literalised and narratively elaborated in Livnev's film and troped in Iankovskii's. Whereas Livnev restricts his purview to the Stalinist phase of the Soviet era, Iankovskii's perspective is broader and philosophical, notwithstanding the film's installation of post-Soviet realia. Both works are part of the larger cinematic trend starting in Russia's 1990s of communicating experience through male bodies that, given the country's parlous state, inevitably showcase the non-canonical body, rejecting the closed, idealised body of the Soviet period. One need only compare the prosthetic feet of Aleksei Meres'ev in Aleksandr Stolper's adaptation of Boris Polevoi's socialist realist novel, *Story of a Real Man*, to Sasha Strel'tsov's somatic prosthesis to appreciate how the iterated, unsettling emphasis on the latter contrasts with the downplaying of the former, in the insistence that the Soviet male body could triumph over any 'alien' element, even absorbing it into its reassuringly heroic, resilient form. In current Russian cinema such a scenario could only elicit ironic scepticism from audiences by now habituated to a steady parade of celluloid male bodies materialising the violence and profound uncertainty characterising post-Soviet Russia. Yet neither period has shared the West's discovery of the cinematic male body as an object of desire, voyeurism and sensual pleasure. Such a body has been displayed off-screen, however, by the country's current president, the sexualisation of whose physique he himself has promoted while narcissistically parading its vigour. As under Stalin, so during Putin's reign, the leader's body is supreme and must be impervious to the slings and arrows from which the average man suffers, for in addition to its individual status, it is a symbolic 'kremlin' – the royal body described by Ernst Kantorowicz, inseparable from the body politic. In post-Soviet Russia that mythologised body, impregnable and spectacular but absent from the screen, can belong only to Vladimir Putin.[42]

NOTES

1. See especially the photograph album *V glub' Rossii* (1994), on which Kulik and Sorokin collaborated and which shows animals and humans in varying degrees of bodily intimacy.
2. As Antony Easthope notes, ideally in the male body 'what holes remain must be firmly shut' (Easthope 1992: 52).
3. A quintessential degradation and diminishing of the male body is represented by the Austrian Expressionist Egon Schiele's often-autobiographical portraits, such as *Standing Nude* (1910).
4. For an examination of the body within Soviet and post-Soviet culture in general, see Helena Goscilo (2006), 'Post-ing the Soviet Body as Tabula Phrasa and Spectacle', in Andreas Schönle (ed.), *Lotman and Cultural Studies: Encounters and Extensions*, Madison: Wisconsin University Press, pp. 248–96.
5. See Ronald LeBlanc, *Slavic Sins of the Flesh: Food, Sex, and Carnal Appetite in Nineteenth-Century Russian Fiction*, Lebanon, NH: University of New Hampshire Press/ University Press of New England, 2009. See also Otto Boele's investigation of sexuality in *The Kreutzer Sonata* and his study of Mikhail Artsybashev's *Sanin: Erotic Nihilism in Late Imperial Russia* (Madison: University of Wisconsin Press, 2009).

6. For an original examination of this predicative image, see Alexander Prokhorov, 'She Defends His Motherland: The Myth of Mother Russia in Soviet Maternal Melodrama of the 1940s', in *Embracing Arms: Cultural Representation of Slavic and Balkan Women in War*, ed. Helena Goscilo and Yana Hashamova, Budapest and New York: Central European University Press, 2012, pp. 59–80, esp. p. 66.
7. The definitive Anglophone monograph on Socialist fashion and its ideological associations is Djurdja Bartlett, *FashionEAST: The Spectre that Haunted Socialism*, Cambridge, MA: MIT Press, 2010; on pre-Soviet Russian fashion, Christine Ruane, *The Emperor's New Clothes: A History of the Russian Fashion Industry 1700–1917*, New Haven CT: Yale University Press, 2009. Articles on more circumscribed topics within the semiotics of Russian and Soviet fashion include John Bowlt, 'Constructivism and Early Soviet Fashion Design', in *Bolshevik Culture*, ed. A. Gleason, P. Penez and R. Stites, Bloomington, IN: Indiana University Press, 1985, pp. 203–19; Helena Goscilo, 'Keeping A-Breast of the Waist-land: Women's Fashion in Early-Nineteenth-Century Russia', and Ol'ga Vainstein, 'Female Fashion, Soviet Style: Bodies of Ideology', both in *Russia*Women* Culture*, ed. Helena Goscilo and Beth Holmgren, Bloomington: Indiana University Press, 1996, pp. 31–63 and pp. 64–93; Emma Widdis, 'Sew Yourself Soviet: The Pleasures of Texture in the Machine Age', in *Petrified Utopia*, ed. Evgenii Dobrenko and Marina Balina, London and New York: Anthem Press, 2009, and 'Dressing the Part: Clothing Otherness in Soviet Cinema before 1953', in *Insiders and Outsiders in Russian Cinema*, ed. Stephen M. Norris and Zara M. Torlone, Bloomington: Indiana University Press, 2008, pp. 48–67.
8. Even today, a study of male bodies in Russian film, such as Peter Lehman's monograph two decades ago on the Hollywood male body on-screen, is inconceivable. See Peter Lehman, *Running Scared: Masculinity and the Representation of the Male Body*, Philadelphia: Temple University Press, 1993.
9. Indeed, during the 1920s literary works such as Iurii Olesha's *Zavist'* (Envy, 1927) and posters by Iurii Pimenov and a host of other graphic artists illustrated the utopian yearning to transform bodies into machines. The imperative of strengthening and honing the body accounted for the official promulgation of *fizkul'tura* (disciplining and training the body) and sport. On this phenomenon see David L. Hoffmann, 'Bodies of Knowledge: Physical Culture and the New Soviet Man', in *Language and Revolution: Making Modern Political Identities*, ed. Igal Halfin, London and Portland, OR: Frank Cass, 2002, pp. 269–86; Mike O'Mahony, *Sport in the USSR: Physical Culture – Visual Culture*, London: Reaktion Books, 2006; *Euphoria and Exhaustion: Modern Sport in Soviet Culture and Society*, ed. Nikolaus Katzer, Sandra Budy, Alexandra Köhring and Manfred Zeller, Frankfurt and New York: Campus Verlag, 2010; and James Riordan, *Sport in Soviet Society*, Cambridge: Cambridge University Press, 1977 and several other volumes and articles authored by him.
10. George Mosse ascribes the lack of exposed Soviet male bodies to 'conformity with Lenin's and Stalin's devotion to respectability' (Mosse 1996: 130).
11. See Sigmund Freud, *The Interpretation of Dreams*, trans. James Strachey, New York: Avon Books, 1965, Chapter 6E, pp. 385–439.
12. I am indebted to Alexander Prokhorov for this information and for his generous response to an earlier draft of this chapter.
13. While I applaud the originality of Kaganovsky's thesis, I find it lopsided, inasmuch as it ignores the larger picture, whereby the maimed, mutilated and suffering bodies that she emphasises exist chiefly in order to focus on their triumphant recovery and superiority to mundane, unwounded bodies. In short, not maiming but the lack of it signalled a failure,

for the devastated body that tested the moral fibre of the New Soviet Man inevitably recovered, so as to bring glory to the state, and therefore represented a stage, and not an identity, as implied in Kaganovsky's argument. After all, how many devastated Soviet male bodies in socialist realist works never conquered their infirmities?

14. For a comparison of Stolper's film with Louis Gilbert's *Reach for the Sky* (1956), a biopic of Douglas Bader, likewise an amputee-ace but in the British air force, see Helena Goscilo, 'Slotting War Narratives into Culture's Ready-Made', in *Fighting Words and Images: Representing War across the Disciplines*, ed. Elena V. Baraban, Stephan Jaeger and Adam Muller, Toronto: University of Toronto Press, 2012, pp. 132–60, especially pp. 147–50.
15. For a list of perestroika films deemed part of the *chernukha* mania, see Graham (2000) pp. 10–11. The article discusses celluloid *chernukha* during the period from the late 1980s to the early 1990s.
16. The film is an adaptation of Aleksandr Pushkin's *Kapitanskaia dochka* (*The Captain's Daughter*, 1836).
17. On tattoos in Soviet culture, see Helena Goscilo, 'Texting the Body: Soviet Criminal Tattoos', in *Cultural Cabaret: Russian and American Essays in Memory of Richard Stites*, ed. David Goldfrank and Pavel Lyssakov, Washington, DC: New Academia Publishing, 2012, pp. 203–30.
18. The official code word for such transportation was gruz 200, which gave the movie its title, but such a degrading depersonalisation operates for all bodies in the film.
19. For a sympathetic review that struggles to rescue the film from the category of *chernukha*, see Tony Anemone, 'Aleksei Balabanov: *Cargo 200* (*Gruz 200*, 2007)', *KinoKultura*, No. 18 (October 2007), <http://www.kinokultura.com/2007/18r-gruz.shtml> (last accessed 4 April 2016).
20. A cinematic return to Stalinism entailed manifold physical, formerly interdicted displays on-screen, as illustrated by such films as *Serp i molot*, *Khrustalev, mashinu!*, *Prorva*, *Ancor, eshche ancor*, and many others. On this tendency, see Larsen (2000).
21. Therefore, it is worth comparing these films with Fedor Bondarchuk's neo-Soviet *Stalingrad* (2013), which records the decisive, mortality-heavy battle that turned the tide in World War II, portrayed by Bondarchuk as a love story(!) against the background of supreme Soviet heroism. Similarly, Bondarchuk's *The 9th Company* (2005), while detailing Russia's losses in the Afghan War, underlined male bonding and machismo under fire, earning Vladimir Putin's absurd statement that the film rendered him optimistic about the future of Russian cinema. So much for Andrei Zvyagintsev, Kira Muratova, Aleksandr Sokurov, Valerii Todorovskii, and a host of talented younger directors, who precisely avoid the nationalistic, militaristic flag-waving that Bondarchuk espouses.
22. For an incisive, wide-ranging analysis of the film, see Mark Lipovetsky, 'War as the Family Value: Failing Fathers and Monstrous Sons in *My Stepbrother Frankenstein*', in *Cinepaternity: Fathers and Sons in Soviet and Post-Soviet Film*, ed. Helena Goscilo and Yana Hashamova, Bloomington: Indiana University Press, 2010, pp. 114–37.
23. The *venik* is an object resembling a shortened broom made of twigs or branches, used in the *bania* to stimulate blood circulation by hitting the body.
24. Symptomatically, the film won several Russian awards but would hardly attract a wide audience abroad.
25. For a sympathetic review of the film, see Elena Monastireva-Ansdell, 'Staying Alive in the Age of Blockbusters: War, Youth, Popular Culture, and Moral Survival in Alive', *KinoKultura*, No. 17 (July 2007), <http://www.kinokultura.com/2007/15r-alive.shtm> (last accessed 5 January 2008).

26. The supervising producer was the 'oligarch' Boris Berezovsky (1946–2013), an implacable opponent of Putin and his policies after Putin virtually drove him out of the country.
27. For earlier commentaries on the film, see Larsen (2000) pp. 107–15 and Prokhorov (2000); also Kaganovsky (2008).
28. The death toll speaks eloquently of the enterprise as an abortive effort on the part of the Soviet state and its overseer: those who do not survive the film include the doctor, Mariia (Marina Kaidalova), who performs the operation; her husband, Amvrosii Bakradze (Nodar Mgaloblishvili), helpless to prevent her extermination by Stalin's order; the nurse, Vera, killed by the NKVD; and the 'created man', Evdokim, shot by his adoptive daughter in what can only be called inadvertent euthanasia.
29. The operation, however, idiosyncratically illustrates Butler's notion of sex as also constructed.
30. That imitation parallels the numerous monuments dotted around the Soviet landscape. In a sense, during Stalinism all males were but pale imitations of The Leader.
31. On films intent on revisiting Stalinism, see the excellent article by Larsen (2000).
32. For a survey of the kindred phenomenon in Soviet and Russian films about World War II, see Tatiana Smorodinskaya, 'The Fathers' Ear through the Sons' Lens', in *Cinepaternity*, pp. 89–113.
33. In fact, the Russian MTV movie awards nominated the film for Best Villain, Best Action Sequence, and Best Kiss (!). The very nominations indicate a young audience.
34. The choice of surname is both heavy-handed and misleading, for it conjures up the verb 'streliat', which means 'to shoot'.
35. *Klianus' ia pervym dnem tvoren'ia / Klianus'ego poslednim dnem, / Klianus' pozorom prestupleniia* . . .
36. For the insoluble dilemmas of post-Soviet Russian paternity, see Goscilo and Hashamova, *Cinepaternity* and the items cited in its bibliography.
37. Sasha commits his murders with his hand-sword and actually has no need of a knife unless that blade operates independently of his will. So the acquisition of a knife, which could lead the police astray, in fact informs the viewer that Sasha cannot fully (or even partially?) control the sword that, despite repeated efforts, he is unable to extricate from his hand.
38. *Ona verit mne . . . so mnoi [ei] nel'zia.*
39. Bakhtin identifies that axis with the timelessness of religious works, such as Dante's *Divina Commedia* (*Divine Comedy*, early fourteenth century), and the chronotope of spirituality.
40. The enigmatic image may be a subjective recollection of the dead body of Sasha's stepfather, which, in one of the film's several flashbacks, his mother and Sasha as an adolescent toss into the water.
41. In that sense, once the experimental 1920s ended, Soviet cinema became uncinematic and radically logocentric, as registered in M. Iampol'skii, 'Kino bez kino', *Iskusstvo kino* 6 (1988): pp. 88–94.
42. Post-Soviet 'spectacular bodies' include those in Aleksei Uchitel's *Vos'merka* (*Break Loose*, 2013), based on Zakhar Prilepin's novel *Vosm'erka* about four OMON members, and Gleb Orlov's *Poddubnyi* (2014), a biopic about the remarkable wrestling champion Ivan Poddubnyi. In both cases, there is little aesthetic or erotic pleasure in contemplating the bared male bodies that either engage in mindless, brutal violence or trounce professional wrestling opponents. Those symbolic attributes of the American cinematic 'hard bodies' investigated so insightfully by Yvonne Tasker (1993/1995) and, especially, Susan Jeffords (1993) are irrelevant to these films.

WORKS CITED

Bakhtin, Mikhail (1984), *Rabelais and His World*, trans. Hélène Iswolsky, Bloomington: Indiana University Press.
Butler, Judith (1990), *Gender Trouble: Feminism and the Subversion of Identity*, New York: Routledge.
Clark, Kenneth (1957), *The Nude: A Study in Ideal Form*, New York: Pantheon Books.
Easthope, Antony (1992), *What a Man's Gotta Do: The Masculine Myth in Popular Culture*, London: Routledge.
Goscilo, Helena (2006), 'Post-ing the Soviet Body as Tabula Phrasa and Spectacle', in Andreas Schönle (ed.), *Lotman and Cultural Studies: Encounters and Extensions*, Madison: Wisconsin University Press, pp. 248–96.
Goscilo, Helena and Yana Hashamova (eds) (2010), *Cinepaternity: Fathers and Sons in Soviet and Post-Soviet Film*, Bloomington: Indiana University Press.
Graham, Seth (2000), '*Chernukha* and Russian Film', *Studies in Slavic Cultures*, I, Pittsburgh: University of Pittsburgh: 9–27.
Hoberman, J. (1999), 'Exorcism: Aleksei German Among the Long Shadows', *Film Comment*, <http://www.filmcomment.com/article/exorcism-aleksei-german-among-the-long-shadows> (last accessed 26 January 2016).
Hoffmann, David L. (2002), 'Bodies of Knowledge: Physical Culture and the New Soviet Man', in *Language and Revolution: Making Modern Political Identities*, London and Portland, OR: Frank Cass, pp. 269–86.
Jeffords, Susan (1993), *Hard Bodies: Hollywood Masculinity in the Reagan Era*, New Brunswick, NJ: Rutgers University Press.
Kaganovsky, Lilya (2008), *How the Soviet Man Was Unmade: Cultural Fantasy and Male Subjectivity under Stalin*, Pittsburgh: University of Pittsburgh Press.
Larsen, Susan (2000), 'Melodramatic Masculinity, National Identity, and the Stalinist Past in Postsoviet Cinema', *Studies in 20th Century Literature*, 24:1, 85–120.
Mosse, George L. (1996), *The Image of Man: The Creation of Modern Masculinity*, New York and Oxford: Oxford University Press.
Prokhorov, Alexander (2000), 'I Need Some Life-Assertive Character or How to Die in the Most Inspiring Pose: Bodies in the Stalinist Museum of Hammer and Sickle', *Studies in Slavic Cultures* I, Pittsburgh: University of Pittsburgh: 28–46.
Salys, Rimgaila (2009), *The Musical Comedies of Grigorii Aleksandrov: Laughing Matters*, Bristol: Intellect.
Strukov, Vlad (2010), '"For All Who Draw The Sword Will Die by the Sword": The Symbolism of Filipp Iankovskii's *Mechenosets*', *Studies in Russian and Soviet Cinema*, 4:2, 171–85.
Tasker, Yvonne (1993/1995), *Spectacular Bodes: Gender, genre and the action cinema*, London and New York: Routledge.

PART II

Transgressions and Pleasures

CHAPTER 5

Borowczyk as Pornographer

Ewa Mazierska

He's without doubt one of the most interesting and unusual directors of all time, and his movies will make you question your preconceived ideas of what a movie can/should be. Cynical smut peddler or misunderstood maker of art movies? You decide. I'm still thinking about it!

From a review published on IMDb

BOROWCZYK IN THE EYES OF HIS CRITICS AND HIS OWN

Most authors writing about the cinema of Walerian Borowczyk follow a simple narrative. It goes like this: until a certain moment in his career, either finishing with his emigration from Poland to the West, or up to his making of *Blanche* in 1971, he was an avant-garde artist. In the West he became a pornographer and the longer he lived there, the more his films adhered to the overall low standards of this genre. For example, Michael Richardson, who devoted one chapter to Borowczyk in his book *Surrealism and Cinema*, writes about *La Marge* (*The Margin* or *Streetwalker*, 1976) and *Interno di un convento* (*Behind the Convent Walls*, 1978) as follows: 'These two films seem to have sealed his fate by giving critics the ammunition they needed to dismiss Borowczyk as a simple purveyor of pornography, and it is certainly difficult to understand how he could have made two such ordinary, even vulgar, films from such promising material' (Richardson 2006: 117). Borowczyk's story is thus one of a steady decline, even if punctuated by some attempts to reverse this downward trajectory, such as making his only full-length fiction film, *Dzieje grzechu* (*The Story of Sin*, 1975), in Poland. His nadir was directing *Emmanuelle 5* (1987), the fifth instalment of a history of one of the sexiest women in the world. This film through its very title betrays its belonging to the category of pornography (as opposed to erotic art) and to commodities produced in a serial way, by directors whose names viewers are not meant to remember. Borowczyk's trajectory appears to be even sadder owing to its colonial inflection; he can be seen as a male version of an Eastern woman who goes to the West in the hope of finding there a home and true love, only to be put in a brothel and exploited by her hosts. The only difference is that in his case he was exploited by the Western producers of porn, and this exploitation afforded him a comfortable life, complete with a *château* in France.[1]

I do not intend to undermine the factual side of this narrative. Indeed, the early Borowczyk made films classified as avant-garde and the late Borowczyk specialised in genres marked by excess, such as pornography (even if only of the softcore variety) and horror, and by the same token until recently valorised negatively. Troubled productions of Borowczyk's later films, his battles with their sponsors and censors, and the existence of these works in many butchered versions, often underlined by their appearing under several titles, for example *Dr Jekyll and his Wives*, *The Strange Case of Dr. Jekyll and Miss Osbourne* and *Borowczyk's Dr Jekyll* (Barefoot 2009: 242) in the case of his adaptation of Robert Louis Stevenson's novella, point to his existence not as an auteur, realising his unique artistic vision, but as a 'rent boy', working hard to please his clients and distract his detractors. However, I argue that the two stages of Borowczyk's career have much in common, as they reveal the sensibility of a graphic artist, interested in the materiality and 'touchability' of objects, more than that of a storyteller (Wiącek 2009: 248), and more of the approach of a rag-picker, collecting antiquities and curiosities, as described by Walter Benjamin (Eiland and McLaughlin 1999: ix–x), than that of a historian interested in a grand history. These features, however – namely shunning grand, or indeed any, narrative, and breaking down barriers between high and low art – render Borowczyk a postmodern figure, indeed a postmodern artist before the term was introduced to film studies: a postmodern avant-gardist.[2]

Off-screen, Borowczyk, sincerely or not, presented himself as a kind of Reichian figure, who believed that by acting on our sexual impulses we achieve freedom, harmony with people and inner peace. In a much-quoted interview with Andrzej Markowski, published in 1975, he said: 'Eroticism is one of the most moral parts of life. Eroticism does not kill, exterminate, encourage evil or lead to crime. On the contrary, it makes people gentler, brings joy, affords fulfilment and leads to a selfless pleasure' (Markowski 1975: 17). Wilhelm Reich believed that free love would ultimately lead to socialism understood as a system of total emancipation, unlike fascism, against which he created his theory (Reich 1972).

In his edification of the sexual and bodily aspects of human life, Borowczyk can be compared to another trans-national filmmaker from Eastern Europe,

Dušan Makavejev. However, there are important differences between their works and reputations. Makavejev was a self-declared communist, willing to criticise the mistakes of the communist parties, in Yugoslavia and elsewhere, but never questioning the principles of Marxism, especially the very idea of egalitarianism. Moreover, Makavejev was rarely accused of being a pornographer, because sex in his films appears never to be merely for sex's sake, but is linked to politics, especially the specific economies of socialism and capitalism. Borowczyk never went as far into the politics of eroticism or indeed any other politics as his Yugoslav counterpart. Throughout his life he remained contemptuous about politics, regarding it as a sphere of human activity demanding compromises, prone to corruption and, unlike art, addressing groups of people rather than individuals, hence not worthy of the attention of an artist. I will categorise his attitude to specific political systems as that of a 'radical refusenik', a type common in Eastern Europe, and in Poland especially. 'Radical refuseniks' were hostile towards state socialism, and unwilling to differentiate between the practices of state socialism and the Marxist ideal of communism. They also lacked enthusiasm for Western capitalism, regarding it as philistine and by the same token 'softly' totalitarian. Ultimately they were apolitical; this was also their survival strategy while living in their own country. Instructive from this perspective is an interview given by Borowczyk's collaborator, Jan Lenica, in 1991, in which he admits that the charm of animated film in communist Poland was that it was more or less free from political interference. The same was largely true about animated film for adults in Western Europe, which was less dependent on commercial pressures than mainstream film; hence both systems allowed the filmmaker to act as an *auteur* and remain faithful to their own interests (Benedyktowicz 1992: 253–5).

Borowczyk's own writings, collected in two books published in Poland, are full of rants against people, usually some minor Polish film journalists (as the major ones tended to ignore his art), and the star of his only Polish film, Grażyna Długołęcka (Borowczyk 2001, 2008), and ideas and institutions, such as the Catholic Church in Poland, but ultimately he does not refute his adversaries with rational arguments but chastises them simply for daring to say bad things about him. Against those who accuse him of pornography Borowczyk uses two contradictory arguments. On the one hand, he attempts to elevate the 'erotic' to the position of the most important aspect of human life and subject for art, as in the quoted interview. On the other hand, he insists that he was always much more than a pornographer, namely a great artist, and the proof of that is his making films which are not primarily concerned with the pleasures of the body, such as *Goto, l'île d'amour* (*Goto, Island of Love*, 1969) and *Blanche*. With this goes a playing down of the erotic dimension of some of his films, such as *La bête* (*The Beast*, 1975), which he describes as 'not so much an erotic film as a film about the mechanism of a dream' (Borowczyk 2010: 88) or a disavowal of those of his films which represent sex at its most explicit, most importantly *Emmanuelle 5* (1987), which he presents as a film which he signed without really directing it, except for two short episodes (Borowczyk 2008: 97).

In my opinion, such an inconsistent approach to one's work reflects not only Borowczyk's difficulty in coming to terms with his difficult position after he had left Poland, but also the various discourses on sexuality which the director encountered in his professional life and which he had to negotiate to maintain (at least in his own eyes) the status of an artist. Let me thus present these discourses, before identifying the salient features of Borowczyk's take on sexuality and the body.

NO COUNTRY FOR A PORNOGRAPHER, OR BOROWCZYK'S EROTIC INTERESTS IN NATIONAL CONTEXTS

Borowczyk began his career in Poland as an avant-garde artist and filmmaker in the mid-1950s, and gained recognition as a creator of animated film, largely working with Jan Lenica, a filmmaker who had a similar background in graphic arts. Borowczyk left Poland in 1958 (Borowczyk 2008: 28). His main period of artistic activity in Poland thus largely coincides with Władysław Gomułka's 'thaw', which started in 1956 and finished around the end of the 1950s. Hence, his trajectory might be seen as typical for an Eastern European dissident artist who enjoyed working in his own country during a period of liberalisation and left when censorship tightened. Borowczyk, however, claims that it was not censorship that was the reason why he decided to leave Poland, but an opportunity to work in France.

I take this confession at face value, but suggest that, although direct censorship was not the cause of his emigration, a more subtle censorship was, namely the general cultural climate which was not conducive to making films of the type he made later in his life, namely films about love, sex and the pleasures of the body, as testified by the fact that up until the 1970s Polish cinema lacked filmmakers seriously interested in sexual relations, except, of course, Borowczyk. The chief Polish jester, and Borowczyk's favourite critic, Zygmunt Kałużyński (Borowczyk 2008: 35), once said jokingly that when a Polish man in a film undoes his fly, bullets from a rifle fall to the ground. When Polish filmmakers do overcome their fear of eroticism and show naked bodies and sexual intercourse, in Kałużyński's opinion 'they are so sad, so simply without heart that they fail to arouse the viewer' (Kałużyński 1976: 184). He summarises his argument by saying that there is 'no erotic climate in Polish films' (Kałużyński 1976: 184; on the attitude of Polish culture to love see also Mazierska 2008: 131–76).

The negative attitude towards, or the lack of interest in, sex in Polish cinema can be explained by the influence on filmmakers of three ideologies and three centres of power in the 1950s: the communist state, the Catholic Church, and the political opposition. The state regarded sex not as an aim in itself, but as a means of populating the country with people willing to work for socialism. Sex for its own sake was regarded as a frivolous subject for art, especially at a time when Poland economically lagged behind the West and the socialist bloc was surrounded by enemies, whose decadence was in part reflected in their laissez-faire attitude to sex. It is worth mentioning that Gomułka himself was a prudish man, outraged by any bodily excess, such as in the performances of the Polish actress who has often been compared to Brigitte Bardot, Kalina Jędrusik (Kurz 2005: 164). Socialist realist films, following the Party line, tend to connect desire for erotic fulfilment with excessive consumption and the shunning of work. An example is the depiction in *Baza ludzi umarłych* (*Damned Roads*, 1959), by Czesław Petelski, of Wanda, the only woman among a group of men heroically working in the God-forsaken mountain region of Poland, who is promiscuous and has an extravagant dream about new stockings and moving to the city, where houses are furnished with bathrooms, rather than contenting herself with washing her body in a basin and purchasing what is available in the village shop, namely alcohol, which satisfies the men.

Paradoxically, the attitude of the Polish state in the matter of sex was similar to that of the Catholic Church. For the Church, sex was a means of reproduction. Moreover, the Church regarded bodily transgressions, especially those committed by women, as the gravest sins. Catholic girls were (and still are) taught to remain 'pure', which meant avoiding sexual relationships before marriage. Even the fact that Catholic priests, the mediators between God and the ordinary folk, are required to be celibate points to the superiority of a sex-free, spiritual existence over life driven by the needs of the body.

Finally, the political opposition to state socialism might not have been hostile to sex, but regarded it as of secondary importance. During Borowczyk's creative years in Poland, rehabilitating Home Army fighters or exposing the sins of Stalinism was more important for 'progressive' Polish filmmakers, such as Andrzej Wajda and Andrzej Munk, than showing Poles finding the meaning of life by experiencing orgasm, as poignantly demonstrated by Kałużyński's anecdote. Although, as Iwona Kurz argues, the 'thaw' addressed not only political liberalisation but also in some measure personal liberation, as reflected by the fact that literature and cinema started to be produced in the name of 'I' rather than 'us' (Kurz 2010: 221), sexual liberation played in it a marginal role at best.

Not surprisingly, throughout the remaining part of his career, on- and off-screen, Borowczyk shows aversion to the oppressive, totalitarian state, most importantly in *Goto*, and to the Catholic Church, in films such as *The Beast*, *Les héroïnes du mal* (*Immoral Women*, 1979) and *Behind the Convent Wall*.

On some occasions, his aversions to the Church and to the communist state are conflated, as in this passage from his book: 'The monopolised communist press, looking for an alliance with the Catholic press, to flatter the religious bigots and attract voters, found a scapegoat in Borowczyk-the pornographer' (Borowczyk 2008: 34). The least obvious aversion is Borowczyk's antipathy towards the Polish political opposition, but this can be deduced from his sour remarks about Andrzej Wajda and Krzysztof Zanussi, symbols of the resistance of Polish cinema to the state within the prescribed parameters of the state-funded art. He writes, for example, that Zanussi is the least talented and the grimmest representative of the Polish variation of 'l'art pompier' (ibid.: 50). Of all these three centres of moral authority, the Church is treated by Borowczyk with the greatest hostility. This is not surprising, given that of the three it was the most critical of the pleasures of the body. The favourite target of Borowczyk's satire are priests, to whom the director attributes all the cardinal sins. His criticism is not particularly original or courageous; however, in the Polish context it was, until recently, unacceptable.

The France of the 1960s, where Borowczyk started his international career, came across as a more conducive environment for developing 'erotic investigation'. France is traditionally regarded as a 'country of love', not least because many of its best writers are renowned for a sophisticated treatment of the subject. Sexual liberation was also an important motif in the French and Western liberation movements of the 1960s, which culminated in May '68 (Badiou 2010: 49–50). Sex and love was also an important subject in the works of French New Wave directors such as Jean-Luc Godard, Eric Rohmer, Jacques Rivette, Claude Chabrol and Roger Vadim, whose *Et Dieu . . . créa la femme* (*And Woman . . . Was Created*, 1956) prefigured the French New Wave. Borowczyk could thus have felt more at home in the New Wave circle in France than among the directors belonging to the Polish School. This is proved by the fact that he was friendly with filmmakers belonging to the so-called Left Bank Group, a 'subset' of the *Nouvelle Vague*, particularly with Chris Marker. As Jonathan Owen observes, Chris Marker loaned both his name and his pet owl Anabase to Walerian Borowczyk's short animation *The Astronauts* (*Les Astronautes*, 1959), the Polish director's first film after his emigration to France, and a few years later, Borowczyk's wife Ligia Branice appeared briefly in Marker's celebrated 'stills movie' *The Pier* (*La jetée*, 1962) (Owen 2014: 215–16). Moreover, Borowczyk's films share similarities with the products of such artistic and literary movements originating in France as the post-Surrealist literary group OuLiPo (ibid.: 224). Furthermore, he adapted the works of an author close to the Surrealists, André Pieyre de Mandiargues, including, in 1976, *La Marge* (1967).

However, Borowczyk was on the fringe of the French New Wave, and with the passage of time his links with this movement faded away and he pursued his own career path. This, in my opinion, resulted from the fact that he came from Eastern Europe and had a different approach to sexuality from that pertaining to the New Wave directors. For Eric Rohmer, sex is to be approached by the intellect, and it is always one element in a larger scheme of things. His narratives are populated by characters who deliberate regarding whether to give in to their passions or not and are usually able to control their desire. Moreover, sex follows intellectual interest or even a decision to get married, rather than other way round. Godard, like Borowczyk, has a special affinity with the figure of the prostitute. Godard uses it in, among other films, *Vivre sa vie* (1962) and *Deux ou trois choses que je sais d'elle* (*Two or Three Things I Know about Her*, 1966); Borowczyk in *Goto, The Story of Sin* and *Cérémonie d'amour* (*Love Rites*, 1987) and *Immoral Women*. However, for these two filmmakers this figure has different connotations. For Godard, prostitution represents the fate of a woman conditioned by the harsh reality of capitalism and a metaphor for capitalist labour and the circulation of commodities. Accordingly, his prostitutes tend to be sad, alienated workers. It is unlikely that films such as *Vivre sa vie* and *Two or Three Things* make their viewers masturbate. For Borowczyk, by contrast, prostitution yields pleasure to a woman, her partner and the film's audience and often is a means to empower women by giving them control over the bodies and minds of their lovers and over their own, as well as monetary gain. These positive associations of (any) sex are confirmed off-screen by Borowczyk, who on various occasions claimed that sex is always a good thing, as previously mentioned. Godard, I believe, would not say such a thing under any circumstances; for him there is no 'naked' sex, as there is no 'naked' image – they always exist in a specific economic and cultural context. Borowczyk also seems to have much in common with Jacques Rivette. Some of their films are close to surrealism. They present events which belong to a dream and characters who yearn to enter a different reality, as in Rivette's *Céline et Julie vont en bateau* (*Celine and Juliet Go Boating*, 1974) and Borowczyk's *Jekyll et les femmes* (*The Strange Case of Dr. Jekyll and Miss Osbourne*, 1981). The mundane, which usually means bourgeois reality, bores them; they want to move beyond it. By the same token, the films of both directors are populated by artists and perverts, and frequently these categories are conflated. Painters try to capture the beauty of a naked female body, in the case of Rivette most importantly in *La belle noiseuse* (1991). However, Borowczyk and Rivette's takes on eroticism are different. Rivette's gaze is less erotic, and erotic relations in his films tend to represent something else; in his films there is never eroticism for eroticism's sake.

I believe that, even if Borowczyk was ripe for producing pornographic works upon his arrival in France, this shift was facilitated by the changes that occurred in French cinema at the end of the 1960s, which included the political radicalisation of the filmmakers who appeared closest to him, such as

Chris Marker and Jean-Luc Godard. Borowczyk, who, as already mentioned, identified socialism, Marxism and any form of leftism with the system ruling in Eastern Europe and was distrustful of any politics, was not prepared to embrace their political programme or even engage with it critically. Moreover, never having the right temperament to produce narrative-driven films (which is the case with many avant-garde filmmakers and those making animation for adults), he had little option other than to move to pornography, not least since this genre, by his own account, proved very profitable. His turn to pornography might have been facilitated by the inclusion of sexually explicit material in the 1970s work of such important filmmakers as Nagisa Oshima, Pier Paolo Pasolini and Miklós Jancsó. Borowczyk returned to Poland in the mid-1970s to make *The Story of Sin*, based on the novel by Stefan Żeromski of the same title. This return might seem like a strange break in his by this time well-established international career, but I see it as a logical decision, owing to the fact that the Poland of the 1970s was more accommodating towards his interests and tastes than in the 1950s and 1960s. The 1970s was a period when the pragmatic authorities practically stopped proselytising about the principles of Marxism-Leninism and tried to maintain good relations with the West (hence inviting back the émigré artist was good propaganda for this policy). Moreover, during this period there was greater pressure than before to produce profitable films. Turning to the classics of Polish literature and putting naked flesh on-screen could be seen as a perfect way to achieve this objective, as well as – as the cynics might say – a means of deflecting the attention of the population from the subject which really mattered, namely 'hard' politics. Borowczyk's adapting of Stefan Żeromski's bestseller was like hitting two birds with one stone. It is also worth mentioning that by this point Polish cinema had produced some work which, from the perspective of representing sexuality, was no less daring than what Borowczyk produced in the West, such as *Trzecia część nocy* (*The Third Part of the Night*, 1971) by Andrzej Żuławski, an artist of a similar sensibility to Borowczyk. However, Borowczyk did not stay in Poland for long, which might be explained by the worsening economic situation in the country in the second half of the 1970s and the domination of the Cinema of Moral Concern during this period, which again (not unlike during the triumphs of the Polish School in the second half of the 1950s) rendered Borowczyk a 'foreign body' on Polish soil. After this episode the artist seemed to have little choice but to return to his usual fare, namely 'low' genres. It is also worth mentioning that in the 1970s and 1980s many of his films were French–Italian co-productions. In the 1970s Italy became the capital of (s)exploitation, hence a natural place for the pornographer to go, providing confirmation also that Borowczyk had crossed a symbolic Rubicon dividing pornography from art. My next question is, what is this director's specialism as a pornographer? In order to answer this question, I shall begin with a definition of this concept.

PORNOGRAPHY SWANN'S WAY

Definitions of pornography are contested, but they contain a common core. Firstly, as Susan Sontag notes, pornography occurs when we deal with the explicit portrayal of sexual subject matter, as opposed to veiled and detached descriptions and depictions, which are the prerogative of art (Sontag 2009: 39). This explicitness is meant to lead to sexual arousal. For this reason Linda Williams lists pornography with melodrama and horror, as they are all low, 'jerking' genres, forcing the viewer to react bodily: weep, be frightened, or, as is the case with pornography, masturbate (Williams 2000: 209–11). Secondly, pornography is a strictly commercial activity; it is produced to sell quickly. For this reason, it is regarded as exploitative, most importantly of actresses, whose bodies are displayed or even engaged in actual sex (in hard core pornography) for the delectation of a male audience, on whose 'low instincts' the pornographers play. No wonder that pornography attracted much criticism from feminists such as Andrea Dworkin (known for her radicalism), who wrote:

> The word *pornography*, derived from the ancient Greek *pornē* and *graphos*, means 'writing about whores'. *Pornē* means 'whore', specifically and exclusively the lowest class of whore, which in ancient Greece was the brothel slut available to all male citizens. The *pornē* was the cheapest (in the literal sense), least regarded, least protected of all women, including slaves. She was, simply and clearly and absolutely, a sexual slave. *Graphos* means 'writing, etching, or drawing'.
>
> The word *pornography* does not mean 'writing about sex' or 'depictions of the erotic' or 'depiction of sexual acts' or 'depictions of nude bodies' or 'sexual representations' or any other such euphemism. It means the graphic depiction of women as vile whores. In ancient Greece, not all prostitutes were considered vile: only the *porneia*.
>
> Contemporary pornography strictly and literally conforms to the word's root meaning: the graphic depictions of vile whores, or, in our language, sluts, cows (as: sexual cattle, sexual chattel), cunts. The word has not changed its meaning and the genre is not misnamed. The only change in the meaning of the word is with respect to its second part, *graphos*: now there are cameras – there is still photography, film, video. (Dworkin 1981: 199–200)

These descriptions point to the difference between pornography and erotic art, but also to the difficulty of marking a boundary between the two. Some descriptions or depictions of sex are explicit, yet are regarded as non-pornographic, as exemplified by the works of Henry Miller, such as *Tropic of Cancer* (1961). Some (high) artists attempted to elicit immediate bodily reactions from their audience; this was the case with Viennese Actionism. Thirdly, profit is often seen as the main motive of producing some high art and, in any case, it is difficult to establish, especially in contemporary times, which art is produced for money and fame and which for more sublime reasons. Finally, while there is no doubt that certain forms of pornography result from the exploitation of women, as when the actresses are the object of violence or when they are coerced to play in films or pose for photographs, in other types of pornography the issue of exploitation is problematic because some women choose pornography as their career and claim to enjoy revealing their bodies or even having sex in front of the camera. Borowczyk himself wrote that 'pornography' belongs to the discourse of police or law, rather than art; it is a means to shame and intimidate (Borowczyk 2008: 55). This opinion he shares with Susan Sontag, who observes that pornography is typically seen through the lens of morality (Sontag 2009: 36–8). Moreover, he pointed to the fact that the criteria for pornography are historically and culturally specific: what is classified as pornography for one generation might not be seen this way by another (Borowczyk 2008: 55). The work of Henry Miller and, in the Polish context, Żeromski proves this point.

Similarly, it is not easy to classify Borowczyk according to the above criteria: artistic versus pornographic, exploitative versus liberating, commercial versus arthouse.[3] In some ways, he is a plain pornographer, because many of his films are centred on corporeal pleasures and their plots are simple. This is the case with *Contes immoraux* (*Immoral Tales*, 1974), *Immoral Women*, *Lulu* (1980) and *Emmanuelle 5*. Several of his full-length films, such as *Immoral Tales* and *Immoral Women*, are made up of shorter films, as if he lacked material to fill a full-length feature film, which is also a criticism directed at pornography, seen as narratively 'thin'. Furthermore, Borowczyk's films tend to have fragmented, episodic structures and the transitions between parts of his films are rough. *Emmanuelle 5* represents the extreme case from this perspective, but this observation also pertains to *The Beast*. Their organising structure is repetition, not progression. However, this is also a typical feature of the avant-garde. Borowczyk's own proper avant-garde films are from this perspective similar to his pornographic films. Their organisation is spatial rather than temporal; they move from one item in the collection to the next, rather than from what was before to what will be next. Borowczyk is preoccupied with worlds frozen in time, and by the same token decadent works, be it 'Goto, island of love', the château where the action of *Blanche* is set, or the aristocratic residence in *The Beast*, where nothing of importance has changed for centuries. His characters repeat what their ancestors did, which can be explained either by the power of tradition or by human instinct, most importantly sexual instinct. Borowczyk's fascination with the Catholic Church might have something to do with its durability and the way Borowczyk sees it as following elaborate rituals, established centuries ago, yet governed by the immense sexual energy of its servants.

At the same time, something blocks the erotic pleasure of viewers of Borowczyk's films, or at least the target audience for pornography, namely men who want to see 'everything'. To use the title of his film as a metaphor, we can say that he shows us sex 'behind the convent walls'. The sexual acts take place behind curtains or other objects blocking our access to vision, such as pieces of furniture. Sex is represented in this way in *Behind the Convent Walls* and *Love Rites*. Furthermore, sexual acts are often performed in darkness, in a church or a convent, or in dimly lit boudoirs, as in the two films previously mentioned, as well as in *The Story of Sin* and Borowczyk's adaptation of Robert Louis Stevenson's novella, *Docteur Jekyll et les femmes* (*The Strange Case of Dr. Jekyll and Miss Osbourne*, 1981). Such a depiction points to the fact that sexual acts constitute a taboo in the times and places presented by the director, and, most importantly, they are forbidden in the sites of religious contemplation. Borowczyk breaks this taboo, but only partially, by making his characters engage in sex in churches and convents, but in a coy way.

I also argue that Borowczyk's films belong not so much to pornography as to meta-pornography, because what interests him is not really the naked female body, but its pictorial representation. In this respect he reminds me of Swann from Proust's *Remembrance of Things Past*, who used to look at real people as incarnations of characters from art or mythology, for example naming one of the servants working in the household of Marcel's parents 'Giotto's Caritas'. Borowczyk shares with Swann such a fascination with what endures and returns. His focus on the representation of nudity is conveyed by frequent images of people painting, photographing or filming bodies, as in *The Beast*, *Lulu*, *Emmanuelle 5* or *Margherita*, constituting the first episode of *Immoral Women*. Borowczyk's films are also populated by voyeurs, often using complex devices, such as specially devised holes in the wall or optical instruments to peep at female bodies, as in *Blanche*, *Immoral Women* and *The Strange Case of Dr. Jekyll and Miss Osbourne*. To counteract this pleasure, there are also devices to block access to these bodies, as in *Margherita*, in which Raphael Sanzio, commissioned to paint frescoes in a church, designs a complex system of scaffolding, including traps, to prevent people from peering at his work. These devices point to the contradictory way cinema works, as discussed by, among others, Christian Metz: it both allows us to see things and, equally, obstructs our access to full vision by such devices as framing or lighting (Metz 1985). One also gets an impression that Borowczyk's men do not love and desire real women, but their images. This is excellently conveyed in *Margherita*, when Raphael, after making a portrait of the beautiful baker, caresses the canvas with her painted breast, as if it were real flesh. Such a confusion between the animate and inanimate pertains also to surrealism and Romanticism, two movements with which Borowczyk as an avant-garde artist is connected. His male characters often want women to conform to specific images. In *The Story of Sin* Niepołomski shows Ewa images of love-making from the Kamasutra, as if he wanted to transform this 'girl from a Polish gentry mansion' into a hot, oriental woman. Miss Osbourne receives as a gift from her fiancé Dr Jekyll a painting by Vermeer, 'Woman in Blue Reading a Letter'. This painting, which in the narrative is described as an image of a pregnant woman, can be seen as an allusion to Jekyll's expectation that his future wife will be a traditional woman, reconciled to her role as a mother and a woman waiting for her husband, while he, in the disguise of Mr Hyde, commits the most hideous sexual crimes. In *The Beast* we see images of women who used to live in the mansion and of the beast these women encountered, as if somebody wanted history to repeat itself so that the women behave in the same way as their female ancestors. Even the king, when meeting Blanche in the film of the same title, tells her that she reminds him of a woman whom he encountered during the crusades. This requirement for women to conform to a specific image might be seen as a metaphor for the patriarchal demand that women adjust to men's ideals, rather than creating their own identities and histories. By the same token, this requirement sentences women to eternal imperfection, because reality cannot match the ideal, especially when the ideal is lost or buried deep in male memory.

However, Borowczyk's women do not easily acquiesce to men's demands to fit a specific image, but fight over the matter. In this respect the stories of Margherita and Miss Osbourne are the most poignant. At first, when inspecting the paintings by Raphael, Margherita questions the truthfulness of her body ('Is my mouth like that?'), as if accepting the primacy of an image over her (material) existence. Later, however, she challenges the painter, claiming that 'my body is not like that, I have dark hair' and demanding that he corrects his painting to account for her true appearance. He refuses, saying that 'one has to lie to say the truth', which can be understood, metaphorically, as a need to ignore real women in art, to convey some eternal truth about them,[4] but Margherita does not accept such rhetoric. Her eventual murder of Raphael can be seen as her taking revenge on the painter for not being faithful to her real self. Miss Osbourne, against Dr Jekyll's will, refuses the image of a domesticated woman, which her fiancé imposes on her, by taking a bath in the same substance as changes Dr Jekyll into the wild, murderous and über-sexual Mr Hyde. Consequently, she also becomes a vampire-like and sex-hungry figure. Finally, the prostitute Myriam in *Cérémonie d'amour* (*Love Rites*, 1987), the last film directed by Borowczyk, not only resists the man's pressure to adhere to his ideal image of a woman, to play according to his rules, but establishes her own rules, her own 'love rites', and requires the man to play according to them, to be an actor in a theatre of which she is the director.

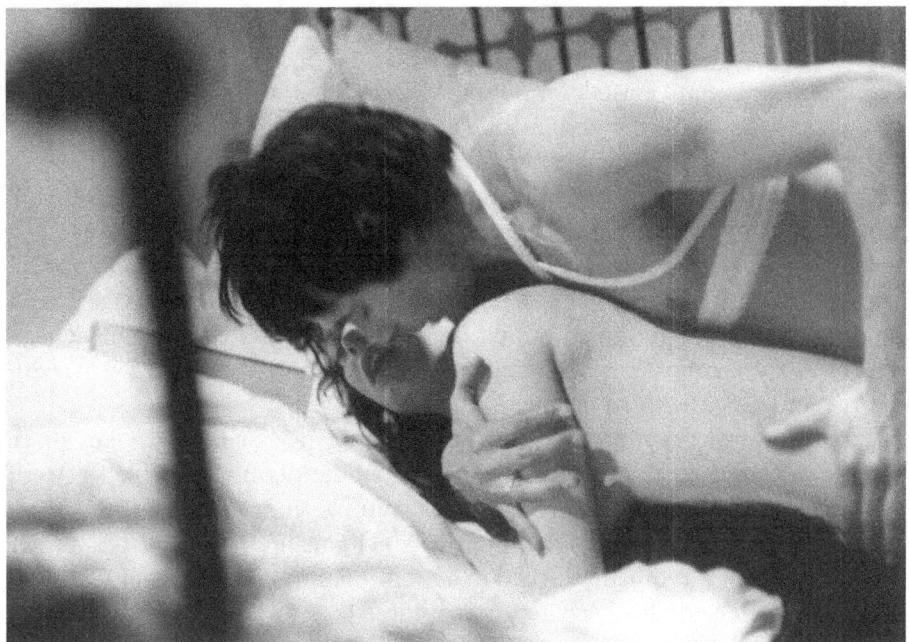

Figure 5.1 Łukasz and Ewa in *The Story of Sin*

It is worth mentioning that there is a specific trajectory in the way Borowczyk represents women. First, he focused on women as the victims of patriarchy; such women were played by his wife, Ligia Branice. In his later films, which feature Marina Pierro, women overpower men, either by forcing them to comply to their sexual requirements or by killing them. From this perspective, Ewa Pobratyńska, in his Polish film *The Story of Sin*, is a transitional figure, or perhaps she merges these two types of women. She begins her life as a typical girl from a good, though impoverished, house of the Polish gentry: virginal, modest and unaware of the power of her body. However, after meeting a man who would become her first lover, Łukasz Niepołomski, she shows an immense appetite for sex and is later able to destroy men with her sexuality.

However, she operates within the confines of patriarchy, as she is subjugated and controlled by men, that is, her pimps, and even Niepołomski, who makes her love him yet ultimately betrays her. Hence, we can see Ewa in two ways: as a victim of men who take advantage of her innocence, or as proof that even within the confines of the patriarchal order some women are able to achieve sexual satisfaction. Borowczyk's women also frequently strive for sexual satisfaction without male assistance. An example is the master's daughter in *The Beast*, whose sex with the servant is constantly interrupted by the master asking the servant to do something for him. When this occurs, however, the young woman does not stop enjoying herself, but continues, using the edge of the bed as a sex toy. The nuns in *Behind the Convent Wall* constantly frolic and masturbate. One of them even uses a wooden stick with an image of Christ as a surrogate penis. Marceline, the heroine of the second episode in *Immoral Women*, uses a white rabbit for sexual stimulation and Lucy, the heroine of *The Beast*, who is the last in a long line of women living in the mansion of the l'Esperances, has sex with the beast.

Even when Borowczyk's women have 'ordinary' sex with men, Borowczyk films it in a way that gives the impression that their sex is propped up by a certain object, such as a helmet touched by the feet of Margherita and Raphael during their intercourse, and later with money, with which Margherita caresses herself and her lover. Solipsistic sex or sex mediated by an object can be seen as a metaphor for pornography, which is a kind of *ménage à trois*, with the voyeur being the third partner.

Finally, Borowczyk often shows that an exchange of money takes place when women engage in sex, but this fact does not undermine their self-esteem or reduce their sexual pleasure. On the contrary, money gives the women extra pleasure and empowers them in their relationship with men. It is rather the lack of money and being locked in a monogamous relation, as in *Goto* and *Blanche*, which cause his heroines unhappiness.

Borowczyk is also a Swann-style pornographer because he chooses for his films women of great beauty and perfect bodies, which seem to be untouched by the physical and moral decay that surrounds them. The only, even if partial, exception to this rule is *The Story of Sin*, where Ewa's body reflects her history: the discomfort of pregnancy, the pain of childbearing and simply hard work, be it in an office, a factory or a brothel. One wonders what made Borowczyk represent the 'Polish body' differently from the 'foreign bodies'. One possible answer is that he simply knew Poland better, and we tend to idealise what we do not know well. The realistic representation of the body in distress might also reflect his dislike of the actress playing Ewa. Finally, such an approach might testify to his awareness that in Poland he catered for a different type of audience: not the purveyors of (cinematic) sex but more likely an arthouse audience, who do not need to be wooed by the images of perfect bodies.

On account of his extensive quotation from Western art, his tableau-like shots and his emphasis on pictorial effects, Borowczyk can be considered under the rubric of 'intermediality'. Elsewhere in this collection Ágnes Pethő maintains that this phenomenon in Eastern European cinema might suggest a desire on the part of Eastern European directors to reconnect their cinema with Western high art and dissolve the boundary between cinema and pictorial art. However, she also argues that each form of intermediality is different and reveals local references. Pethő's argument certainly holds true with reference to Borowczyk. His affinity with intermediality can be regarded as his way of defending himself against the accusation of being a pornographer by pointing to his proficiency in the history of art. However, it can be also regarded as a way of criticising high art as a patriarchal tool, a means of immobilising the female body and subjugating it to male desires.

BODY AND MIND

Borowczyk's films can also be regarded as meta-pornographic because, instead of simply showing us the joys of the flesh, they also engage in a discourse about the relationship between body and mind. In his writings Borowczyk presented his views on this subject, mainly apropos *The Beast*, when he said: 'An animal is in a sense the closest and dearest creature to people, although how different from him! It is half way between a man and God. In the relationship (or intercourse) with a woman, an animal is the addressee of Love' (Borowczyk 2009: 89). These words (like the entirety of Borowczyk's philosophy) are not clear, but what one can get from them is an edification of the unconscious and corporeal side of life. Borowczyk also mentions that animals and animality function in culture as 'scapegoats'; we displace onto animals and our animal instincts what we do not approve in ourselves as humans (Borowczyk 2009: 89). His views on corporeality and animality have, again, something in common with those of Wilhelm Reich, who claimed that human beings are different from animals not because humans are less sexual than animals but because they are more so: 'Man is distinguished from the animal not by a lesser sexuality but by a more intensive one (readiness for sexual activity at all times)' (Reich 1972: 130–1). Hence, if sexuality is what differentiates people from God, animals indeed stand in the middle between (asexual) God and humans; they are not below but above humans. For Reich, this also means that restricting the human need for sex, forcing people to 'sublimate', that is, project their desires into a different sphere of life, is immoral.

The issue of mind versus body/nature is also a topic discussed by the characters in Borowczyk's films. On one side of this discussion are religious people, most importantly Catholic priests and nuns. According to the rule, presented by Georges Bataille, that in a theistic philosophy there is God on the one hand and nature on the other (Bataille 1997: 268), they argue that human nature is sinful. People can only reach God by renouncing or at best controlling their nature, which means their sexual urge. However, this is, as Borowczyk suggests, unnecessary, cruel and barely possible. Hence, the worlds that Borowczyk constructs on-screen bear resemblance to a concentrationary universe, in which people are imprisoned to prevent them from committing crimes of the flesh. Such a function is fulfilled by a convent in *Behind the Convent Walls*, the castle in *Blanche* and the Goto island. Against them are pitted those who either reject the body–mind dualism, typically associated with Cartesianism, or accept it, but valorise the body differently, not as inferior but as superior to the soul. Here we can list Łukasz Niepołomski in *The Story of Sin*, who places above the Catholic faith Oriental religions, which reject the body–mind dualism, regarding them as different forms of the same substance.

Borowczyk, of course, aligns himself with those who worship the body. In his films we observe a reversal of sorts between the spiritual and the corporeal – the spirit is thrown from the pedestal, the body is upgraded. This is achieved by showing numerous 'crimes of the mind', committed by those who preach the superiority of mind over body, such as priests and high-ranking nuns. These church functionaries advocate in public the need to remain chaste and ascetic, but in private indulge in sins such as greed, gluttony and alcoholism, as well as paedophilia and voyeurism, and are cruel towards those placed in their care. Jakub Majmurek observes that in Borowczyk's films 'the institution of the Church is hiding the excesses of desire, which hidden "behind convent walls", only externally repressed, are bursting with perverse energy' (Majmurek 2015: 160). This makes the priests and nuns doubly sinful: they are super-lecherous and hypocritical.

By contrast, those who indulge in corporeal pleasures, such as Ewa Pobratyńska in *The Story of Sin* or the young nuns in *Behind the Convent Walls*, remain innocent. Such innocence is also attributed to animals and humans with bestial tendencies, such as the half-wit heir to the aristocratic property in *The Beast* and Marceline in *Immoral Women*. The former, who spends most of his life breeding horses, and eventually changes into a beast, comes across as innocuous, unlike his plotting relatives. Similarly, Marceline, frolicking with her white rabbit on the grass of the country house owned by her parents, comes across as pure and good, unlike her parents, who maliciously kill her rabbit in order to force her to conform to their lifestyle. Importantly, the attempts to 'rescue' zoophiles and human beasts from their bestial tendencies not only fail, but bring the opposite result from the one intended, namely mayhem and murder. The contrast between the animals and zoophiles and 'healthy' society is underscored by the motif of meat. Borowczyk often shows images of killing animals or meat being displayed in such a way that one is aware that the corpses were once alive. There is thus a poignant contrast between those who love animals and are loved by them in return and those who kill animals to stuff their bodies. Again, Borowczyk shows in this way the crude materialism, barbarity and hypocrisy of those who preach the superiority of the human mind over the body, and the purity of those who supposedly gravitate towards the 'body pole'.

Ultimately, however, Borowczyk suggests that unity of body and mind cannot be achieved or that it only happens when they are on the verge of perishing, at the moment of death. Death in his films is presented not as a tragic incident, but as a salvation. We feel relieved seeing the death of Ewa in *The Story of Sin*, of the nuns in *Behind the Convent Wall*, of the vampire-like

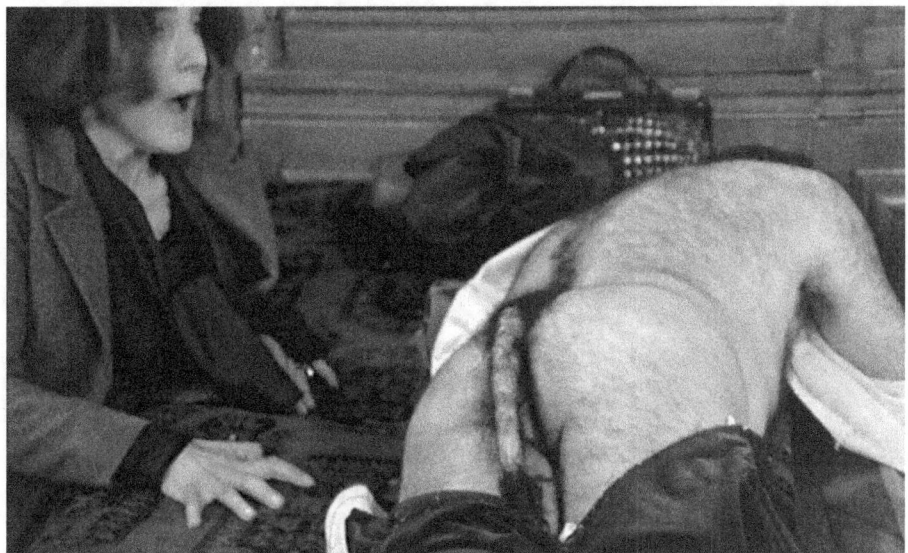

Figure 5.2 Humanity and bestiality in *The Beast*

characters in *Dr. Jekyll and Miss Osbourne*, and even of Hugo Arnold in *Love Rites*. Such an apotheosis of Thanatos can be linked to the movements with which Borowczyk was connected, most importantly Romanticism and surrealism. Equally, it can be seen as a reflection of his Polishness. It is worth quoting here Andrzej Banach, the author of the book *Erotyzm po polsku* (*Eroticism Polish Style*), who draws attention to the death-like images of love and lovers in the work of Polish painters such as Wojtkiewicz, Malczewski, Beksiński and Starowieyski, concluding: 'Polish Romanticism invented Polish death, a patron of lovers' (Banach 1974: 46).

However, even if Borowczyk borrows from the existing traditions of representing love and sex, he gives this topic his own twist and places it in the context of low, namely 'jerking' genres. He is thus a postmodern director, since he broaches serious subjects in popular work, yet without undermining their seriousness.

CONCLUSIONS

In one of the films by Jean-Luc Godard and Anne-Marie Miéville, *Numéro deux* (1975), the voice-over belonging to Miéville asks whether the film can be both political and pornographic; a question echoed by Borowczyk's troubled fan whose words I chose as a motto for my chapter. For the authors of *Numéro deux* it is a rhetorical question; for them it can be both. By the same token, pornographic work can also be a work of art. I agree, and in this chapter have tried to demonstrate that Borowczyk's films are at the same time pornographic, political and philosophical. The director not only shows the pleasures of the flesh, but creates a specific discourse about them. I believe that this discourse will resist the passage of time, while the strictly pornographic side of his work, the way he presents human flesh, for the audience who developed their taste on the new forms of pornography, most importantly that offered by the internet, might appear dated.

NOTES

1. Borowczyk's fate is not untypical. Other Eastern European directors who emigrated to the West during the Cold War were also offered work in pornography, especially at the beginning of their careers. For example, Aleksandar Petrović, upon leaving Yugoslavia, was asked to write a script for *Emmanuelle 2* (1975). The leading Yugoslav auteur agreed to do it, but his contract included a clause stating that his name would not appear in the credits (Sudar 2013: 252). This is a reverse situation to that of Borowczyk, who signed *Emmanuelle 5* without allegedly directing it. Moreover, although Roman Polanski never made porn, his first contract in the West was with a company specialising in 'soft porn'. One also notices that the films of Eastern European directors, once they are in the West, significantly gain in nudity.
2. In her seminal essay on pornography Susan Sontag quotes Adorno, who argues that works of pornography lack the beginning-middle-and-end form characteristic of literature (Sontag 2009: 39). However, the same can be said about many works classified as experimental or avant-garde. The difference is that in the case of pornography such a structure is attributed to the ineptness of its author, while in the case of the avant-garde it is attributed to his/her intention of breaking with the constraints of narrative, mainstream art.
3. This might be why his work is omitted from Linda Williams' *Screening Sex* (2008).
4. Ironically, such a position was also taken up by the ideologues of socialist realism, who advised the artists to sacrifice ordinary realism to capture a deeper truth of history.

WORKS CITED

Badiou, Alain (2010) [2008], *The Communist Hypothesis*, trans. David Macey and Steve Corcoran, London: Verso.
Banach, Andrzej (1974), *Erotyzm po polsku*, Warszawa: Wydawnictwa Artystyczne i Filmowe.
Barefoot, Guy (2009), 'Lost and Found in Translation and Adaptation: Walerian Borowczyk and *Docteur Jekyll et les Femmes* (1981)', in Richard Ambrosini and Richard Dury (eds), *European Stevenson*, Newcastle upon Tyne: Cambridge Scholars Publishing, pp. 241–52.
Bataille, Georges (1997), 'The Object of Desire and the Totality of the Real', in Fred Botting and Scott Wilson (eds), *The Bataille Reader*, Oxford: Blackwell, pp. 264–70.
Benedyktowicz, Zbigniew (1992), 'Rozmowa z Janem Lenicą (6 września 1991)', in Marta Fik (ed.), *Między Polską a światem: Kultura emigracyjna po 1939 roku*, Warszawa: Krąg, pp. 253–8.

Borowczyk, Walerian (2001), *Moje polskie lata: Dzieje grzechu 2000*, trans. Lidia Brokowska, Warszawa: Hypnos Media.
Borowczyk, Walerian (2008), *Co myślę patrząc na rozebraną Polkę*, Warszawa: Rytm.
Dworkin, Andrea (1981), *Pornography: Men Possessing Women*, London: The Women's Press.
Eiland, Howard and Kevin McLaughlin (1999), 'Translators' Foreword' to Walter Benjamin, *The Arcades Project*, Cambridge, MA: Harvard University Press, pp. ix–xiv.
Kałużyński, Zygmunt (1976), *Wenus automobilowa: Obyczaje współczesne na ekranie*, Warszawa: Państwowy Instytut Wydawniczy.
Kurz, Iwona (2005), *Twarze w tłumie*, Izabelin: Świat Literacki.
Kurz, Iwona (2010), 'Dziwki, anioły i rycerze a „moment nowoczesny" w polskim kinie po 1956 roku', in Mariusz Zawodniak and Piotr Zwierzchowski (eds), *Październik 1956 w literaturze i filmie*, Bydgoszcz: Wydawnictwo Uniwersytetu Kazimierza Wielkiego, pp. 220–32.
Majmurek, Jakub (2015), 'Sex and the Sacred: The Obstacles to Desire Becoming its Objects', in Kamila Kuc, Kuba Mikurda and Michał Oleszczyk (eds), *Boro, L'Île d'Amour: The Films of Walerian Borowczyk*, Oxford: Berghahn Books, pp. 159–65.
Markowski, Andrzej (1975), 'Erotyka łagodzi obyczaje', *Kino*, 4, 16–18.
Mazierska, Ewa (2008), *Masculinities in Polish, Czech and Slovak Cinema*, Oxford: Berghahn Books.
Metz, Christian (1985), 'Story/Discourse: Notes on two kinds of voyeurism', in Bill Nichols (ed.), *Movies and Methods*, vol. II, Berkeley: University of California Press, pp. 543–8.
Owen, Jonathan (2014), 'An Island Near the Left Bank: Walerian Borowczyk as a French Left Bank Filmmaker', in Ewa Mazierska and Michael Goddard (eds), *Polish Cinema in a Transnational Context*, Rochester, NY: University of Rochester Press, pp. 215–35.
Reich, Wilhelm (1972) [1951], *The Sexual Revolution: Toward a Self-Governing Character Structure*, Plymouth: Vision.
Richardson, Michael (2006), *Surrealism and Cinema*, Oxford: Berg.
Sontag, Susan (2009) [1967], 'The Pornographic Imagination', in her *Styles of Radical Will*, London: Penguin, pp. 35–73.
Sudar, Vlastimir (2013), *A Portrait of the Artist as a Political Dissident: The Life and Work of Aleksandar Petrović*, Bristol: Intellect.
Wiącek, Elżbieta (2009), 'Niemoralny moralista w młodopolskiej masce: Wokół *Dziejów grzechu*', in Sebastian Jagielski and Agnieszka Morstin-Popławska (eds), *Ciało i seksualność w polskim kinie*, Kraków: Wydawnictwo Uniwersytetu Jagiellońskiego, pp. 239–60.
Williams, Linda (2000), 'Film Bodies: Gender, Genre, and Excess', in Robert Stam and Toby Miller (eds), *Film and Theory: An Anthology*, Oxford: Blackwell, pp. 207–21.
Williams, Linda (2008), *Screening Sex*, Durham, NC and London: Duke University Press.

CHAPTER 6

Queering Masculinity in Yugoslav Socialist Realist Films

Nebojša Jovanović

INTRODUCTION

This chapter takes a closer look at Yugoslav socialist realist films of the late 1940s and early 1950s, tackling their overt queer motifs and characters, as well as apparently non-queer motifs that were recognised as queer by some viewers.[1] Admittedly, the combination of 'queer' and 'socialist realism' might seem rather improbable to some film critics and scholars of Yugoslav cinema – and, by extension, of Eastern European cinema. That should not be surprising given the persistence of the totalitarian-model view of the socialist past, which sees arts and culture through the unsound polarities of 'artist versus regime', 'art versus propaganda' and 'dissent versus dogma'. Whereas the modernist *novi film* of the 1960s is venerated as the anti-dogmatic summit of filmmaking under Yugoslav socialism, the chronically under-researched classic films of the socialist realist ilk are usually deemed its dogmatic antipode, nothing but the misuse of cinema for spreading the Party's noxious ideas and invectives.[2] How, then, is one to connect the notion of queer – 'by definition *whatever* is at odds with the normal, the legitimate, the dominant' (Halperin 1995: 62) – with the propaganda that advanced communist rule as the only acceptable one? Apparently, the relation between them must have involved the vanquishing of anything queer.

Let me illustrate that vantage with a few examples. In his variant of the anti-socialist backlash, the Serbian film critic Zoran Janković maintains that Yugoslav cinema was but a reliable handmaid of ideology: 'Here and there a hint at those who are sexually different would appear [on film], and yet, following the pressure of the strong paw of the state under which they created, the film directors persistently refused to make sexual minorities visible' (2008: 188). Even worse, he argues, the filmmakers demonised queers through negative stereotypes. Or, consider how the well-known Croatian film critic

Nenad Polimac (2010) labels Czech émigré director František Čap as 'the first maltreated gay filmmaker in Yugoslavia', while neither offering a shred of evidence about the abuse nor mentioning other filmmakers who allegedly suffered the same fate. There is only insinuation that the Yugoslav socialist regime naturally persecuted gay filmmakers, Čap being the first.

I beg to differ. To begin with, instead of deeming it a totalitarian dungeon, I see socialist Yugoslavia as a complex socio-political, economic and cultural project suffused with a number of contradictions and paradoxes that cannot be adequately grasped if one reduces them to the crass narratives of 'binary socialism' (Yurchak 2006), which offer variations on the 'good dissidence versus evil tyranny' theme. I propose that we turn to other concepts and methodologies in order to challenge the totalitarian-model platitudes. One of the most salient is Foucault's concept of apparatus (*dispositive*), which posits that socio-historical complexities must not be reduced to the mechanisms of top–bottom control and repression; instead one should explore them in terms of 'a thoroughly heterogeneous ensemble consisting of discourses, institutions, architectural forms, regulatory decisions, laws, administrative measures, scientific statements, philosophical, moral and philanthropic propositions – in short, the said as much as the unsaid' (1980: 194). In the context of Yugoslav socialism, the concept of apparatus challenges the thesis that the Yugoslav regime had been imposing homophobia by means of its 'strong paw'. Instead of figuring as the targets of ideological disparagement, homosexuality and other 'sexual deviances' – to use the vocabulary of the era – were actually being constantly redefined, discussed and valued at different social sites and by many social agents in early Yugoslav socialism.

Indicative of the complex dynamics of the gender/sex apparatus is Yugoslav jurisprudence. In the early years of the socialist state (1945–51), the Yugoslav courts still prosecuted male-to-male 'unnatural acts' by applying the penal code of the Kingdom of Yugoslavia, which punished homosexual acts with up to five years' imprisonment. The new criminal code of 1951 brought the first legal principle that treated same-sex acts in socialist Yugoslavia: according to Paragraph 186, any man who engaged in 'unnatural acts' would be sentenced to up to two years in prison. Whereas for authors like Janković the very existence of this act can be seen as unambiguous proof of the inherent homophobia of the Yugoslav totalitarian regime, those who do not accept the totalitarian model will notice that Paragraph 186, first, did not criminalise female homosexuality, and, second, was the first step towards the gradual loosening of the legal status of male homosexuality, which would culminate in the 1970s in homosexuality being decriminalised in half of the country (the republics of Slovenia, Croatia, Montenegro, and the autonomous province Vojvodina). The fact that the decriminalisation encompassed some federal units and not others testifies to the fact that Yugoslav socialism was not as monolithic and uniform in terms of the law as the totalitarian model presumes.

The logic of apparatus and its complexities enables us to recast Yugoslav cinema in at least two ways. Instead of being relegated to the propagandist conceit and the arena of top–bottom repression, as in the totalitarian-cinema model, cinema turns into a dynamic constellation of ever-changing and sometimes conflicting discourses, practices and agents. Accordingly, the films – including the socialist realist films – should be analysed as works that might have many ideologies, including mutually contradictory ones (Klinger 1997).[3]

Second, we should finally acknowledge that cinema was integral to the gender/sex apparatus of Yugoslav socialism. Far from merely reflecting the gender order of the socialist country, Yugoslav films imbued the public imaginary with a relentless streak of celluloid femininities and masculinities of different class backgrounds, locations, ages and ethnicities; of romances that led to happily-ever-after unions or to fatal dead-ends; of narratives of marriage, family and kinship as historically shifting yet ever-fundamental social tenets; and so on. In both propelling and questioning manifold ideas, fantasies, values, and norms about gender and sexuality, cinema figures as one of the royal roads to Yugoslav socialist modernity and its gender order.

The three films discussed below represent major cinematic contributions to the queer-related aspects of the apparatus of sexuality in Yugoslav socialism. Specifically, the representation of male bodies in these films testifies tellingly to the ways in which Yugoslav cinema designated early on the queer characters and motifs that defy the totalitarian-model assumptions.

UNBRIDLED HOMOSOCIALITY

The fourth Yugoslav feature film, and the very first to be set in the post-war socialist present, *Život je naš – Ljudi s pruge* (*Life is Ours – The People from the Railway*, Gustav Gavrin, 1948), follows one of the many 'youth labour brigades' that contributed crucially to the reconstruction of the war-ravaged country. I have already pointed out that the film introduced male privilege in the on-screen designation of labour in Yugoslav cinema: despite the officially proclaimed politics of gender equality, *Life Is Ours* was the first of the films that rendered men as natural born workers, defined primarily by their professional skills, achievements and work ethics, while relegating women to beings of romance, who do not relate to work directly, but through their male partners (Jovanović 2015).

Throwing some light on the film's queer underside will further that account. Let me approach the issue via the diary of Vladimir Pogačić, Gustav Gavrin's fellow director. According to the entry of 11 March 1948, the cinematographer of *Life Is Ours*, Mile Marković, had a quarrel with Gavrin and his first assistant Sava Popović after the film's premiere: 'He told them that the boys in the film behave and look "like faggots'" (Pogačić 1994: 68). Since Pogačić says nothing else about the incident, how are we to account for Marković's dismissive remark?

In my view, the cinematographer reacted to the fact that the bonding between the male brigadiers had gained an upper hand over the heterosexual romances. The film has two heterosexual love stories, but, being underdeveloped in terms of narration, they pale in comparison with the flamboyantly enthusiastic brotherhood and camaraderie of the young boys, who make up the vast majority of the characters and occupy most of the screen time. One is tempted to say that desire, being repressed in the heterosexual domain, erupts in the homosocial one and connotes the homosexual – a slippage well elaborated in queer scholarship ever since Eve Kosofsky Sedgwick proposed a continuum between the homosocial and the homosexual in her seminal study *Between Men* (1985).

At its most elemental, *Life is Ours* entails homosocial privilege by screening male and female bodies – and the respective types of youthful masculinity and femininity – in significantly different ways. First, the brigade girls are marginalised through their overall thin screen presence and exclusion from the labour activity that makes for the principal spectacle of the film. But even when the girls are on-screen, their corporeality is additionally contained in several ways, primarily by means of framing. The camera prefers to show them in long shots and medium long shots, as if trying to keep a distance between the girls and the viewers. For example, it is not until 53 minutes have elapsed that we can see the face, in a medium close-up, of the main female character as she eyes her sweetheart. In addition to this striking lack of close ups of female faces, the film apparently tries to prevent even erotic titillation by generally fully dressing up the girls, either in traditional peasant tunic-style dresses or in work clothes. Although this systematic de-eroticisation can be seen to be in line with the imperative of the 'revolutionary asceticism' that allegedly dominated early Yugoslav cinema (Ranković 1982), it has to be said that *Life Is Ours* was unprecedented in that regard. Simply, no other film of the period tried so hard to contain female corporeality.

The extent to which *Life Is Ours* restricted its representations of femininity becomes fully evident only if the film's images of female bodies are compared to its images of male bodies. The boys do not only dominate the film in terms of screen time and action; the camera also grants them more detailed and spectacular displays of their faces and physiques. The film zeroes in on the young men's facial expressions in order to convey a wide range of their emotions and thoughts. For example, the inner transformation of a selfish coward into a selfless comrade is conveyed with a long-held close-up of his face. However, the same does not apply to, say, a Muslim girl, who undergoes an even more radical change: she decides to unveil her face, quit the pre-modern patriarchal tradition and join the brigade. One of the effects of such different screenings of masculinity and femininity is that the boys appear to have a richer emotional life. Consequently, this adds to the impression of the intense emotional exchange that makes the stuff of the homosocial bond between the young brigadiers. Untainted by the more pronounced heterosexual motifs and representations of femininity, these intense all-male emotional rapports eventually trigger the homosexual connotations and impressions that Marković referred to.

Those undertones are additionally supported by the immediacy of the bodily contact between the boys, in a series of scenes that celebrate the closeness and tenderness that they enact when they are together, often in couples. Given that the only touch between a girl and a boy happens near the end of the film, when she timidly rubs off some dirt from his sleeve, why the man-to-man contacts steal the show is understandable: not being recognised as properly erotic, homosocial contact is utterly uninhibited, unlike heterosexual contact. Of course, one can assume that the filmmakers saw the carefree relation to the body as immanent in the camaraderie characteristic of young male peers, additionally amplified by their joint participation in a revolutionary project. And yet, the final effect of those comradely attachments boasts a certain excess that challenges an innocent reading. Consider the scene of a boy saying to his buddy: 'Once we depart [after the work is done], you will forget about me . . .' Again, such a charged exchange is precisely what is foreclosed from the film's (heterosexual) love stories: as if the most romantic lines in the film, after being denied to the heterosexual couples, surface in the homosocial layer of the film and irrevocably taint it with a queer nuance.

Whereas in action and buddy films it is the spectacle of violence that provides male characters with the opportunity to get as close as possible, both physically and emotionally (Wyatt 2001), in *Life Is Ours* it is the spectacle of physical work with its underlying macho ethic of camaraderie. The privileged space of homosocial bonding lies at the very centre of the construction site: the tunnel that the brigade has to dig through a Bosnian mountain. In the penultimate scene of the film, the camera zeroes in on the two very young boys who dig the tunnel using newly-arrived modern equipment. As they drill the rock, naked to the waist, they exchange ecstatic looks as if enchanted with their own strength and bond. It is a veritable triumph of budding virility and togetherness. In the climax of the scene the boys drill through the underground torrent, which spurts all over them. The spectacle of labour and camaraderie instantly bursts into a spectacle of pure masculinity: the jets of water splash onto the boys' faces and over their naked torsos in a way that would give a Pet Shop Boys video a run for its money. Ever the symbol of nature at its most untameable, the water invites the most obvious and obscene reading: the unstoppable torrent gives body to the boys' impulses that they themselves could not keep in check. Carried away by the illusion of their own power, they do not realise that their budding virility and male bonding are also a liability, an accident waiting to happen.

Of all early Yugoslav films, *Life Is Ours* is arguably the ultimate example of what Vicko Raspor, the most renowned film critic of the era, decried as 'cinematic primitivism' (1988: 34). For all its imperfections, however, the film remains noteworthy as the first Yugoslav feature that rendered visible the interstice between the homosocial and the homosexual.[4] It is exemplary of the films that fall 'supposedly within the domain of "straight male" friendship, yet which cannot adequately contain the threat of homosocial bonding' (Wyatt 2001: 55), that is, the threat that homosocial bonding will ultimately be recognised as homosexual bonding. While these films do not designate overt homosexual rapport, they nevertheless 'suggest that homosociality unconstrained by social conventions can foster a homosexual relationship' (Wyatt 2001: 55). The socially approved institutional framework – the dominantly male working brigade – neuters the sliding along the homosocial/homosexual continuum, but only to an extent. The spectacle of unbridled male bonding in the film eventually proves to be too overwhelming to completely defuse the homosexual colouring with a mere reference to the imperative of the construction of the bright socialist future. Hence, although we can assume that many filmgoers deemed *Life Is Ours* an ode to camaraderie and the socialist cause, Marković's reaction indicates that some audiences might have interpreted it in terms of homosexual innuendo.

We can only guess what in the film shocked its own cinematographer, but whatever the case, it certainly did not picture homosexuality in a pejorative way. Marković's derision expresses his own prejudice and probably the shame that his creations would be recognised as 'faggots' by the wider audience. As the previous analysis makes clear, nothing in the film itself pertains to a homophobic attitude in general, let alone to some particular totalitarian homophobia.

REVOLUTIONARY DRAG

Gavrin's sophomore film *Crveni cvet* (*The Red Flower*, 1950) tells the story of the soldiers of the Yugoslav royalist army captured in April 1941 and interned in a POW camp in Germany. The film's principal protagonists are the members of a communist cell; they are pitted not only against their Nazi captors, but also against the anti-communist expatriates, the officers and soldiers still loyal to the Yugoslav prince and government in exile. Although the film is thus also set in an exemplary homosocial setting, I will not tackle the general representations of homosociality in the film, but a single, more obvious queer motif: gender cross-dressing.

In the second part of the film the communist prisoners launch a musical revue that is supposed to bring some joy to their fellow inmates, but is also an act of resistance. The entire show is a distraction: while the Nazi officers are attending it, a communist inmate plans to sneak into the administration offices and destroy an incriminating document. The leader of the communist cell explicitly stresses that the most important act of the revue will happen 'behind the scenes'.

The musical number that interests us here opens with a stereotypical *mise-en-scène*: a bar; the bartender polishes the glass; a gentleman in a white suit sits on a bar stool and nonchalantly enjoys a glass of brandy and a cigar. After a musical cue, a female voice starts singing off-screen (and off-stage), catching the man's attention and attracting his gaze, and a lanky feminine silhouette enters the frame and approaches him. We first see the black contour of her body from the back, and when she turns away from the man in white towards the camera/audience, we realise that she is a man with a wig, in make-up and a dress. Seductively gazing at the audience and singing a sorrowful tune about desire and loss, 'she' strikes a full-blown diva pose. The act seems to be as good as it gets in the improvised theatre of the POW camp. The audience is flabbergasted and even the Nazi officers appear to be impressed by the spectacle.

This scene inscribes *The Red Flower* among the World War II films that employ drag, the most popular of which was *This Is the Army* (Michael Curtiz, 1943) (Bérubé 1990; Eberwine 2007). One should also notice that the use of drag as a strategic ruse in Gavrin's film anticipates the famous *The Bridge on the River Kwai* (David Lean, 1957), where the English POWs perform a drag routine in order to divert the Japanese guards from the captives who plant the explosive under the newly-finished bridge. However, I argue that in comparison with the drag scene in Lean's film, cross-dressing in *The Red Flower* is more complex. Although originally concocted as a superficial conceit, the revue and its drag acts eventually outgrow their original function, unlike in Lean's film; starting as a means to an end, they evolve into an end in itself.

The rest of the revue adds to this interpretation. What follows the bar lady act is an equally unabashed number that plays with another type of identification. An ensemble of inmates in blackface sing the song 'The Black Jim' (*Crnac Džim*), impersonating the slaves in the antebellum South who decry their exploitation by their white masters and announce their eventual rise to freedom. In his analysis of *The Jazz Singer*, Michael Rogin reminds us that blackface minstrelsy is also a type of cross-dressing: 'blackface is racial cross-dressing. Just as the white man in classic American literature uses Indians to establish an American identity against the old world, so the jazz singer uses blacks' (1992: 441). The tradition of blackface is nothing if not controversial, for in the conflict of interpretation that surrounds it one can deem it as promulgating or subverting racism, depending on the context and reception. In the context of the anti-fascist resistance in *The Red Flower*, blackface unambiguously signifies interracial political identification *par excellence*: it both delivers an all-too-obvious slap to the racist politics of Nazism and is a moment in the communists' reappropriation of the anti-slavery movement as an important precursor of their own anti-fascist struggle.

The gender and racial cross-dressing are short-circuited in the rest of the revue. In the act that follows 'The Black Jim', the inmates dressed as majorette girls share the stage with the performers who represent different nations and ethnic groups worldwide, conveniently reduced to iconic stereotypes: an Uncle Sam, a Chinese man, an Arab. In the final act they are joined by the performers from the previous numbers, joyfully singing about international solidarity and a better world. When the 'bar lady' stands next to the 'Chinese man', with whom she exchanges cheerful, triumphant glances, an annoyed German officer insists that 'the Chinese coolie should be removed away from the white woman'; the director of the show sarcastically apologises: 'Would you prefer a Japanese?'

The Red Flower thus aptly illustrates Richard Dyer's argument that we should not deem stereotypes to be necessarily abusive or pejorative (1993: 11–18). The Nazi officer knows very well that before him is just a jumble of the most blatant caricatures crammed into a cardboard utopia, and yet he gets provoked, perfectly aware that even such a shabby spectacle still channels meanings and values that confront his ideology. Complexities like these elevate the revue from only a charade into a genuine act of political struggle, in which the queer cross-dressing aligns with pejorative stereotyping into a universal politics of internationalism and equality. We can thus turn the relationship between the sabotage and the revue upside down: the former is little more than a MacGuffin serving as a pretext for having the spectacular show suffused with revolutionary cross-dressings.

The queer performance in *The Red Flower* is notable for one more reason: the 'bar lady' does not deliver merely a glamorous performance, but a performance of glamour. The importance of this cannot be overstated in the context of the early Yugoslav cinema, when glitz and glamour were still associated with pre-war bourgeois femininity and, worse, with collaboration. Already the first Yugoslav feature, *Slavica* (Vjekoslav Afrić, 1947), is illustrative in this regard. Contrasting working-class poverty with bourgeois excess, the film fuses erotic unrestraint with the luxury and leisure characteristic of the latter. The party of the rich – a wild mix of music, dance and alcohol – unravels literally under the sign of the naked enraptured female body. Along the same lines, the first two films directed by Pogačić – *Priča o fabrici* (*Story of a Factory*, 1949) and *Poslednji dan* (*The Last Day*, 1951) – also feature the glamorous *femme fatale*-style antagonists who plot against socialist rule and side with the remnants of the pre-war bourgeoisie and fascist forces.

And yet, there were films that vindicated glamour, or, rather, a specific femininity associated with it. The representation of the nightlife in Belgrade during wartime in *Besmrtna mladost* (*Immortal Youth*, Radoš Novaković, 1948) culminates in the spectacle of a tap dancer, who works in a night club in which the local girls mingle with and date Nazi soldiers. Although the tap-dance routine can be deemed an outright collaborationist activity, the film does not invest it with ideological resentment but designates it as a veritable bodily spectacle that channels nothing but the dancer's own enjoyment in dancing as such. The very same Afrić who vilified the rich women who drink, dance and flirt with the occupiers in *Slavica*, in his second film, *Barba Žvane* (*Uncle Žvane*, 1949), created Nineta, a glamorous diva who sings for the occupying forces and even falls in love with a Nazi soldier, yet nevertheless functions as a positive character who even manages to save the life of the titular protagonist. Even more pronouncedly than the tap-dancer in *Immortal Youth*, Nineta connotes a certain type of virtue, which not only utterly vindicates her collaboration, but elevates her love affair with the Nazi soldier into pure bliss, as rendered by one of the most romantic scenes of lovemaking in early Yugoslav cinema.

The Red Flower also approvingly designates glamour as the performance of a spectacular femininity that, although a product of the bourgeois world, cannot be reduced to it, and lends itself to a revolutionary appropriation. By deploying a cross-gender act, the film actually goes much further than *Immortal Youth* and *Uncle Žvane* in revealing the performative nature of glamour: the flamboyant femininity, which conveys it, is a far cry from any presupposed feminine essence, be it mystical, spiritual or natural. Although *The Red Flower* was hardly a critical success, two of its formal details appear as strokes of genius with regard to queer performance. First, the 'bar lady' does not exist outside the revue segment in some authentic male identity. The actor Kiro Vinokić does not play a Petar or a Marko who happens to wear the wig at one point and drops it afterwards – the end credits list him as the 'bar lady' only. This is not to suggest that a designation of cross-dressing as an identity-shifting process would be wrong or less emancipating. It is just that the film's specific strategy accentuates the performative quality of (glamorous) femininity more than it posits gender cross-dressing as a transitory mimicking in the life of a man. Secondly, instead of being sung by Vinokić or some other man, in falsetto or imitating a female voice, the 'bar lady' act is performed by an actual female singer; the film, however, does not suggest that the Vinokić character lip-syncs to a recorded track, but treats the female voice as his own. The significance of the voice is punctuated by the fact that we hear the bar lady even before we recognise her as a cross-dressed man. Attaching an authentic female voice to a male body, the film makes the 'bar lady' an even more volatile performance, literally an effect of montage of seemingly incongruent gender elements. In this way, the queerness of the film's drag act reaches the point of paroxysm.

QUEER VIRTUE

A year after the cross-dressing in *The Red Flower*, Yugoslav cinema gave birth to its first homosexual character, or, rather, the first character who was unambiguously coded as homosexual although not explicitly labelled that way. It was Tetka (played by Milivoj Presečki), one of the more prominent supporting characters in *Bakonja fra Brne* (*Monk Brne's Pupil*, Fedor Hanžeković, 1951), an adaptation of the eponymous novel by the realist author Simo Matavulj (1892). Set in Dalmatia in the 1870s, the film details the growing pains of the peasant boy Ivo who leaves his poor, craggy village for a cloister in order to become a monk, only to be slowly yet irreversibly corrupted by his mentor Brne and the rest of the sinful clergy.[5] Some of the monks are nicknamed in a *nomen est omen* fashion: whereas Žvalonja – Big-mouth – points to the monk's insatiable gluttony, Tetka's nickname pins down sexuality as his defining trait, as it literally means 'aunt', jargon for a feminised homosexual (similar to 'queen').

Over the course of the film Tetka undergoes a veritable transformation, punctuated by three scenes. The first is set shortly after Ivo's arrival. 'Who is that new boy?', asks Tetka, checking out the newcomer with a piercing gaze. The scene decidedly obscures the line between the homosexual and the paedophilic: the shot straightforwardly frames the monk as a predator who feasts his eyes on the kid. In his late fifties or early sixties, clothed in a dark robe, his big nose protruding from a skinny, unattractive face, Tetka would perfectly embody a child-molesting priest at its most caricaturised even today.

However, the film soon significantly recasts the monk. In the next appearance, another monk slaps Ivo for no real reason, in an act of sheer caprice. Seeing the incident, Tetka swiftly approaches the boy and, waving a flower in his hand, tells him in a mild voice 'I am the one you should not be afraid of . . .', and playfully waves the flower in front of him. Any notion that Tetka might be a predator is gone. Everything about his demeanour – his body movements, mannerisms, the melody of his voice – couples his homosexuality with a feminised posture that effectively undoes any real paedophilic threat, and the generally comical air of the scene dissolves the last fears about him as a potential menace. When the monk proceeds down the corridor, the camera shoots him from the back, capturing his joyful flower-waving and hip-swinging; his protégé, Ivo's peer, mockingly imitates the monk's *tante* step, while walking behind him. In sum, the film seems to suggest that no man so vehemently feminised and ridiculed by a kid could ever hurt a child.

Figure 6.1 *Monk Brne's Pupil* (1951): Monk Tetka at his most feminine

And yet, the flaming jester is not Tetka's final persona. As Ivo secretively returns to his room late at night after drinking with his peers, he spots the monk in front of the statue of the patron saint in the hallway. Hidden in the shadows, the boy observes how Tetka dusts the statue off and decorates it with flowers. Despite its institutional frame, the ritual appears surprisingly intimate. However, once Tetka leaves, another monk, who appears to be enviously spying on his nocturnal actions, quickly shows up and puts out the candle that was lit before the statue. After the other monk is gone, Ivo brings the burning candle from his own room, lights the candle again and piously looks at the figure of the saint.

The scene thus establishes Tetka as a genuinely devout believer who literally keeps the flame of faith alive, surrounded and despised by the other priests who are blasphemy incarnate. In the eyes of the boy, who is still a believer himself, the monk offers an authentic role model of piety. In this way, the film soothes the mockery of the previous scene, suggesting that one should respond to the monk with a benevolent and empathic laugh, instead of ridiculing him with a contemptuous sneer. Tetka is finally transformed into a quixotic guardian of the genuine faith that is misused and betrayed by the hypocritical religious institution.

This positive status of queerness is complemented by the film's criticism of the heterosexual erotic life of the monks. Although they officially live in celibacy, the monks indulge in clandestine affairs with the local women. The film posits that such a heterosexual affair is actually the worst thing that can happen to Ivo: his romance with a tavern girl can persist only as an illicit relationship that would eventually poison their love. In the light of this moral, the case of Tetka becomes more complex. Whereas the straight desire of the monks results in the secret affairs that corrupt their lives and those of their lovers, Tetka's implied same-sex desire is ultimately rendered as benign. By the end of the film Ivo adopts virtually all the bad habits of the monks, remaining untainted only by Tetka's queer desire. Hence, one could interpret the monk's queerness as something which, *stricto sensu*, is not a sin: it neither affects others negatively, that is, entails devastating social consequences, nor stands in the way of sublime feelings, such as true faith. If anything, Tetka's example testifies that queerness perfectly aligns with what is most virtuous, true and noble in us.

CONCLUSION

A chapter of this length and with this particular focus cannot do justice to the historical shifts in different discourses on homosexuality and queerness in Yugoslav socialism. However, the analysis of the socialist realist cinema of early Yugoslav socialism firmly refutes the totalitarian-model preconceptions.

In the latest assessment of the debate on socialist realism in Yugoslav cinema, Miranda Jakiša criticises scholars who use socialist realism as 'a term of vituperation' (2015: 20). Siding with those who do not overestimate its role in Yugoslav cinema, she asserts that, since we can endlessly debate how much of it there was in early Yugoslav cinema, it is more important to establish that, first, the socialist realist aesthetic as such is more complex than its detractors would like to admit; and thus, second, that the presence of socialist realist conventions and traits does not necessarily mean that the early Yugoslav films are aesthetically poor and politically conservative. It is for the same reasons that I have not chosen to attempt to establish the level of socialist realism in the films I have analysed here. Instead of isolating specific socialist realist features and conventions, I strategically take these films as socialist realist, since they were produced when socialist realism, as Raymond Williams would argue (1977: 121–7), was the dominant aesthetic in Yugoslav cinema, before becoming residual from 1952 onwards.

The analysis of *Life Is Ours*, *The Red Flower* and *Monk Brne's Pupil* unambiguously evinces how misguided is the presumption that the early Yugoslav films – indisputably affected by close political control of cinema – were locked in an orbit of conservative, dogmatic meanings and values when it comes to queer motifs.[6] Not only did socialist realist Yugoslav cinema offer a complex and non-derogatory screening of queerness, but it did not challenge this screening by derogatory counter-images. To the best of my knowledge, not a single film made during this period reviles homosexuality or other queer experiences by blatantly attaching them to a villain in the well-known Hollywood style. Hence, if the queer motifs in allegedly monolithic and insipid socialist realist cinema were anything but simple and unambiguous, one should do better than approaching these – and many other – films with totalitarian-model presumptions. Only thus will one be able to grasp the vicissitudes of queer sexuality in socialist Yugoslavia in all their unpredictability and complexity.

NOTES

1. This chapter furthers the theses previously presented in my essays in Bosnian/Croatian/Serbian, both published in 2014: 'Seksologija, muška homoseksualnost i film u socijalističkoj Jugoslaviji', in L. Duraković and A. Matošević (eds), *Socijalizam na klupi: Jugoslavensko društvo očima nove postjugoslavenske humanistike*, Pula, Zagreb: Srednja Europa, CKPIS, Sveučilište Jurja Dobrile u Puli, Sa(n)jam knjige u Istri, pp. 125–52; and 'Kvir paralaksa i jugoslovenski film', in J. Blagojević and O. Dimitrijević (eds), *Medju nama: Neispričane priče gej i lezbejskih zivota*, Belgrade: Heartefact, pp. 310–23. I am deeply indebted to Franko Dota for sharing his groundbreaking, still unpublished research on legislation concerning homosexuality in socialist Yugoslavia.
2. See, for example, the work of Greg DeCuir, Jr (2011), and Senadin Musabegović (2008).
3. In this regard, I draw on the work of scholars who see socialist realism as non-monolithic and irreducible to the 'regime versus art' dichotomy (Clark 2000; Kaganovsky 2008; Lahusen and Dobrenko 1997).
4. One could also argue that the homosocial/homosexual slippage was caused precisely *by* the film's flaws, such as the bad performances of the young, untrained actors, and some technical mistakes; for example, the unrefined editing of a simple exchange between the two boys might easily entice an impression that they stare at each other intensely and thus lustfully. That being said, the technical primitivism can only partially account for the 'faggot' effect, as there is much more to the overall queer dimension of the film (different regimes of representation as regards female and male corporeality, and so on).
5. Daniel J. Goulding curiously sets the film in the Renaissance, and also asserts that Ivo 'learns to combine spiritual progress with a discerning and lusty appreciation for worldly pleasures' (2002: 44) – a misguided remark as the film insists that the clergy's 'lusty appreciations for worldly pleasures' is a hypocrisy that denies any true spirituality.
6. Given Polimac's totalitarian-model vantage, one should not be surprised that he excludes even such a remarkable, positively-valued queer as Tetka from his account of the 'gay moments in YU cinema' (2007).

WORKS CITED

Bérubé, Allan (1990), *Coming Out Under Fire: The History of Gay Men and Women in World War II*, Chapel Hill: University of North Carolina Press.
Clark, Katerina (2000), *Soviet Novel: History as Ritual*, Bloomington and Indianapolis: Indiana University Press.
DeCuir Jr, Greg (2011), *Yugoslav Black Wave: Polemical Cinema from 1963–72 in the Socialist Federal Republic of Yugoslavia*, Belgrade: Film Centre Serbia.
Dyer, Richard (1993), *The Matter of Images: Essays on Representation*, London and New York: Routledge.
Eberwine, Robert (2007), *Armed Forces: Masculinity and Sexuality in the American War Film*, New Brunswick, NJ and London: Rutgers University Press.
Foucault, Michel (1980), *Power/Knowledge: Selected Interviews and Other Writings, 1972–1977*, New York: Pantheon Books.
Goulding, Daniel J. (2002), *Liberated Cinema: The Yugoslav Experience, 1945–2001*, Bloomington: Indiana University Press.

Halperin, David M. (1995), *Saint Foucault: Towards a Gay Hagiography*, Oxford and New York: Oxford University Press.
Jakiša, Miranda (2015), 'On Partisans and Partisanship in Yugoslavia's Arts', in Miranda Jakiša and Nikica Gilić (eds), *Partisans in Yugoslavia: Literature, Film and Visual Culture*, Bielefeld: Verlag, pp. 9–28.
Janković, Zoran (2008), 'Nikad pokoran: *Marble Ass* Želimira Žilnika', in Dejan Ognjanović and Ivan Velisavljević (eds), *Novi kadrovi: Skrajnute vrednosti srpskog filma*, Belgrade: Clio, pp. 185–234.
Jovanović, Nebojša (2015), 'How the Love Was Tempered: Labor, Romance and Gender Asymmetry in the Classical Yugoslav Film', *Studies in Eastern European Cinema*, 2, 33–48.
Kaganovsky, Lilya (2008), *How the Soviet Man Was Unmade: Cultural Fantasy and Male Subjectivity under Stalin*, Pittsburgh: University of Pittsburgh Press.
Klinger, Barbara (1997), 'Film History Terminable and Interminable: Recovering the Past in Reception Studies', *Screen*, 2, 107–28.
Kosofsky Sedgwick, Eve (1985), *Between Men: English Literature and Male Homosocial Desire*, New York: Columbia University Press.
Lahusen, Thomas, Dobrenko, Evegny (eds) (1997), *Socialist Realism Without Shores*, Durham, NC and London: Duke University Press.
Matavulj, Simo (1892), *Bakonja fra Brne: Njegovo djakovanje i postrig*, Belgrade: Srpska književna zadruga.
Musabegović, Senadin (2008), *Rat: Konstitucija totalitarnog tijela*, Sarajevo: Svjetlost.
Pogačić, Vladimir (1994), *Imaginarni zapisi 1*, Novi Sad and Belgrade: Prometej, Prosveta, YU film danas.
Polimac, Nenad (2007), 'Gay momenti u YU kinematografiji', *Jutarnji list*, 12 May, <http://www.jutarnji.hr/gay-momenti-u-yu-kinematografiji/173995/> (last accessed 21 June 2015).
Polimac, Nenad (2010), 'Povratak Františeka Čapa, prvog gay šikaniranog filmaša u Jugoslaviji', *Jutarnji list*, 5 June, <http://www.jutarnji.hr/povratak-frantiseka-capa/817039/> (last accessed 21 June 2015).
Ranković, Milan (1982), *Seksualnost na filmu i pornografija*, Belgrade: Prosveta, Institut za film.
Raspor, Vicko (1988), *Riječ o filmu*, Belgrade: Institut za film.
Rogin, Michael (1992), 'Blackface, White Noise: The Jewish Jazz Singer Finds His Voice', *Critical Inquiry*, 3, pp. 417–53.
Williams, Raymond (1977), *Marxism and Literature*, Oxford and New York: Oxford University Press.
Wyatt, Justin (2001), 'Identity, Queerness, and Homosocial Bonding: The Case of *Swingers*', in Peter Lehman (ed.), *Masculinity: Bodies, Movies, Culture*, New York and London: Routledge, pp. 51–66.
Yurchak, Alexei (2006), *Everything Was Forever, Until It Was No More: The Last Soviet Generation*, Princeton, NJ and Oxford: Princeton University Press.

CHAPTER 7

Geographies of Carnality: Slippery Sexuality in Wiktor Grodecki's Gay Hustler Trilogy

Bruce Williams

The title of this chapter suggests 'space' in several senses of the word. First, on a cartographic level, it speaks to the liminal position between East and West of Central Europe – and specifically the Czech Republic and its capital, Prague – and to the socio-cultural ambiguities such a setting implies. On a more metaphorical level, it references the corporeal dynamics of the teenage gay hustler trilogy of Wiktor Grodecki and the shifting turf of sexuality and sexual practice that define the films. The two spaces are closely merged in Grodecki's films, inasmuch as the economic and political realities of the Czech Republic led, in the years following the fall of communism and the Velvet Divorce, to the reconfiguration of Prague as Europe's sex tourism mecca. It is in yet another liminal space that the critical reception of Grodecki's trilogy is housed. All the while lauded in festivals in both Europe and North America by predominantly heterosexual audiences, the films have met with acerbic critique in both academic studies and popular-press reviews for reason of their heterosexist perspective and implicit adulation of traditional family values (Horton 1999; Moss 2006a; de Villiers 2007). The trilogy is comprised of two documentaries and one feature film, the latter purportedly based on real-life situations and co-authored with a hustler. All three were released within the four-year period immediately following the split between the Czech Republic and Slovakia. The first film, *Andělé nejsou andělé* (*Not Angels but Angels*, 1994) presents interviews, mostly utilising talking-heads, with 19 young men between the ages of 14 and 19, who work as male prostitutes in Prague. Its successor, *Tělo bez duše* (*Body without Soul*, 1996) follows suit structurally and stylistically, but shifts its attention to teenaged boys working in Prague's gay porn industry. Finally, *Mandragora* (1997) is a feature film, combining the above themes of gay prostitution and pornography, which focuses on the pathos of a small-town runaway to Prague and the hardships and tragedies that befall him. To a large extent, Grodecki's own biography mirrors the East/West dynamics present in the trilogy. Born in Warsaw in 1960, Grodecki studied at the Polish National Film School in Łodz. Following a period of residence in the USA, he returned to post-communist Eastern Europe in 1992, and it was at this juncture that he became interested in what was transpiring in Poland's neighbour to the south. Indeed, Grodecki's career did not blossom as far east as Poland. Rather, he became best-known for the Czech-language hustler films made in Prague.

My intention in this chapter is neither to add to the extensive allegations of Grodecki's manipulation and heavy-handedness that to date have characterised critical discourse on the trilogy, nor to redeem the films from such reproach. Rather, I seek to map, even if provisionally, the bodies of the young males within the shifting confines of the political and economic transformations that define their workspace. I will argue that the vacillation of these bodies between ambiguous and contradictory positions, a process which mirrors the cultural dynamics of Prague itself, serves to debunk prevailing mythologies of the Czech Republic's post-communist context.

PRAGUE, THE WESTERNMOST EAST

As Kevin Moss (2006a) has argued, the Czech capital lies to the west of Vienna, yet has always held 'a special place in the Orientalist construct of Eastern Europe' (n.p.). Indeed, the 'heart of Europe' is associated more with the East than with the West.[1] To elucidate such an assertion, I will draw upon both linguistic and cultural processes at play in the relationship between the historical Czech lands and their neighbours. Moss reminds us of Larry Wolff's study of the western 'invention' of Eastern Europe during the Enlightenment, and references specifically an anecdote involving Mozart's arrival in Prague. Wolff's study foregrounds the composer's bafflement at the Bohemian language, and stresses that Mozart, who had a strong knowledge of a number of Western European tongues, mockingly treated his entourage to nonsense utterances and silly nicknames in compensation for the language's difficulty as the group travelled west to Prague (Wolff 1994: 106–15). Language is but one of the spheres in which the Czech world is most distanced from mainstream Western Europe, but it serves as a gateway to more extended dynamics. One can argue that the history of the Czech language has been a peek-a-boo process. J. F. N. Bradley explains that, following the 1620 Battle on the White Mountain, the Czech language became the vehicle of communication of the lowest of classes. Songs, poems and proverbs appeared in Czech, while more highbrow works were written in Latin or German (Bradley 1971: 97). Ewa Mazierska has further explained that the 'Czech revival' of the eighteenth century, which 'led to the spread of literacy and the creation of the new Czech elite of teachers, engineers and scientists . . . was carried through largely by rediscovering, codifying and researching the Czech language' (Mazierska 2010: 9).

Nonetheless, the study of Czech was only rarely taken on by non-natives. Some 230 years after Mozart's arrival in Prague, the language of the Czech Republic still remains less studied in the West than those of its neighbours. During the Cold War, it was much easier in the Anglo-Saxon world to find materials for learning Polish or Hungarian than for learning Czech. Granted, this may have been because there are considerably fewer speakers of Czech than of other Slavic or Eastern European languages. Today, while Polish boasts some 40 million speakers, there are roughly only 10 million speakers of Czech. Moreover, from 1918 to 1992, unlike Poland or Hungary, Czechoslovakia was divided between speakers of two main languages, and hence neither language gained the prestige of other Eastern European languages.[2]

I must stress, moreover, that the Iron Curtain contributed greatly to the 'near' and 'far' dynamics of Czechoslovakia. Tourism from the West was not terribly difficult, yet visa regimes remained in place. In fact, in the early 1950s, Czechoslovakia was designated as off-limits to American citizens by the US State Department.[3]

Czech(oslovak) culture, as well, has evoked a combined proximity to and detachment from the West. 'Prague', a popular 1966 French song released by Israeli-born Rika Zaraï, presented the Czechoslovak capital as a virtual double for Paris. It was easy for French listeners to relate to the cityscape defined in the romantic love song and to conjure up its imagery. Nonetheless, something was slightly amuck. By virtue of the singer's birthplace and Hebrew accent in French, the song aroused associations with the Middle East, or at least of something lying well to the east of France. Prague became at once familiar and exotic. In a similar manner, Alain Robbe-Grillet's film *L'Eden et après* (*Eden and after*, 1970) and its companion-piece *N. a pris les dés* (*N. Rolled the Dice*, 1971) were filmed in part in nearby Bratislava. Discussing the earlier film at a March 1977 screening at the Annenberg Center of the University of Pennsylvania in Philadelphia, Robbe-Grillet argued that he chose the Czechoslovak location to suggest something which conveyed Paris, but was not quite recognisable. The film, which depicts the activities of bored university students who meet at the Mondrianesque Café Eden to indulge in drugs and ritual games of chance and torture, combines the familiar with the exotic. The students view a documentary on Tunisia, and set off from Bratislava (or Paris!) to the island of Djerba, where they attempt to solve a mystery related to an abstract painting. They thus depart from something similar to Paris, but oddly different, to a far more exotic world. Like Zaraï's song, Robbe-Grillet's film treads a tightrope between East and West, between Czechoslovakia (as a proxy for France) and the Middle East.

The attitudes of westerners to sexual practices in this ambivalent part of Central Europe reflect the geographical, linguistic and cultural energy suggested above. Citing Edward Said's description of the Arabic world as a place promising 'sexual experience[s] unobtainable in Europe' (Said 1978: 190), Moss (2006a) argues: 'The Slavs' sexuality, like their language [has been] inscrutable and therefore open to Western projection' (np). Moss further references Matti Bunzl's study of Prague as a haven for sex tourism. Bunzl argues that Austrian men felt that Czechs had a different sort of sexuality from the homo/hetero binary of Austrian society. They were 'available', 'passionate', and 'pan-sexual'. The Czech Republic's lower age of consent, moreover, combined with economic disparity, led younger boys to be more available in Prague than in Vienna (Bunzl 2000: 83).

THE TOURIST GAZE AND SEX TOURISM

The post-colonial dynamic suggested by Moss and Bunzl, particularly in the light of gay male sexuality and the fascination with the youthful body that characterise Prague's sex trade, implies a reworking of Annette Kolodny's notion of 'the lay of the land'. Kolodny likens the westward expansion of the USA to the violated female body, and her descriptions of the processes of 'eroticism, penetration, raping, embrace, [and] enclosure' (Kolodny 1975: 150) can be reconceived to encompass the geographical space of Prague and the corporal condition of the city's tender-aged male prostitutes. A land that is 'eastern' all the while lying slightly to the West is indeed being laid. These processes recall the notion of the 'tourist gaze', a concept discussed at length by John Urry and Jonas Larsen. Positing the tourist gaze as a global phenomenon, Urry and Larsen explore how tourist patterns in a particular society cannot be explained without examining what is happening in other places. The result of such interconnectedness is that 'different countries, or different places within a country, come to specialise in particular kinds of objects to be gazed upon' (55). One can thus understand how the combination of the growth of post-Fordist consumerism in Western Europe and the Americas, coupled with the economic transformations in the post-communist Czech Republic, has played a role in the development of Prague as object of an (eroticised) tourist gaze.

The visual dynamics of the tourist gaze are underscored by the fact that the concept had its origins in ethnographic photography (Clifford 1988; Volkman 1990). The tourist gaze describes the ideological framework through which both the cultural ethnographer and the recreational tourist are manipulated in their confrontation with the cultural Other. Volkman posits the tourist gaze as a symptom of the West's 'relentless desire to collect the world' (91).

She extends the definition of 'collection' far beyond the realm of souvenirs and photographs to the objectification of culture itself. Volkman argues: 'The objectifiers are not merely international capitalists who control the great tourist industry (the largest in the world). They are also the indigenous people caught up in complex relations with that industry and the appetites it stimulates' (91). Although Volkman's research focuses on the Toraja culture of southern Sulawesi in Indonesia, the tourist gaze and its co-dependent dynamics can circulate in cross-cultural contacts that are considerably less different one from the other than those which Volkman describes. For instance, in my earlier discussion of the film *Miss Mary* (1987) by the Argentine director María Luisa Bemberg, I have examined the tourist gaze with reference to British/Argentine cultural interactions and to issues of social class (Argentine upper-crust, British nannies) (Williams 2003). In this case, the tourist gaze functions in a context in which it is hard to know just who the natives are, a situation the film's protagonist, a British governess in Argentina, herself decries at the opening of the film. Grodecki's films also examine a case of cultural colonialism among those who are 'not-so different'.

Closely related to the tourist gaze is the phenomenon of sex tourism. Martin Oppermann (1998) opens his extended discussion of the interface between sex tourism and prostitution with a generalisation that can well be extended to the Czech context and to Grodecki's films. He asserts:

> The term sex tourism invariably evokes the image of (white) men, usually older and in less than perfect shape, traveling to developing countries, may they be in Asia, Africa, Latin America, or the Caribbean, for sexual pleasures generally not available, at least not for the same price, in their home country. Commonly, it is considered to be an economic (return) flow from the economic prosperous to the less well-off nations. (Oppermann 1998: 1)

The studies that appear in Oppermann's edited collection focus primarily on Indonesia, Sri Lanka, Thailand and Vietnam. The work includes references to homosexual prostitution, most notably the phenomenon of 'beach boys' in Sri Lanka. Yet these references are stereotypically couched in the book's index under such categories as 'anal sex', rather than categorised as homosexual per se.

In what is, for the purpose of my analysis, a study more appropriately grounded in cultural and economic theory, Chris Ryan and Michael Hall explore the liminality implied by both ends of the sex tourism dyad. They argue that 'both tourist and prostitute are symbols of, and actors seeking, needs generated by a wider social context formed by the modern era ushered in by the Industrial Revolution' (Ryan and Hall, 2001: 1). For

Ryan and Hall, both tourist and prostitute occupy two distinct liminal zones. They stress:

> The one, the tourist, is enacting a socially sanctioned and economically empowered marginality, while the second, the prostitute, is stigmatised as a whore, a woman of the night, as the scarlet woman. Yet, as will be described, such stigmatization is now being challenged, made ambiguous and respectability being sought by emphasizing the role of female labour within the terminology of being a sex worker. (2001: 1)

From the above introductory remarks, the heterosexual bias of Ryan and Hall's research is evidenced. Nevertheless, they do devote a chapter to gay and lesbian tourism, which focuses on such venues as Goa, Sri Lanka, the British Virgin Islands, Australia, and New Zealand.

In sum, despite book-length examinations of sex tourism, the above-referenced study by Bunzl is one of the few to explore the phenomenon with regard to homosexual sex and the Czech Republic. Like the tourist gaze of Bemberg's *Miss Mary*, the gay sex trade in Prague is defined by far fewer physical differences than those, let us say, between a German and a Vietnamese. What is at play is a certain level of subtlety and the debunking of the notion of Slavic homophobia in favour of a more fluid and destabilised sexuality. In the context of Grodecki's films, the heteroflexibility of a number of the young hustlers imbues Prague with the dual positioning of near and far, similar and different, European, yet 'orientally' exotic.

CRITICAL DISCOURSE ON GRODECKI

The three most extensive critical examinations of Grodecki's films all appeared between nine and eleven years following the production of the final part of the trilogy, and all were written from a queer studies perspective. Kevin Moss (2006a), Nicholas de Villiers (2007) and Robin Griffiths (2008) shed divergent light on the works, yet overlap in a good number of their central assertions. Their discussions have devoted considerably more attention to the documentaries *Not Angels but Angels* and *Body without Soul* than to the feature film *Mandragora*. While Griffiths focuses most of his attention on the earlier (and visually less disturbing documentary), Moss splits his analysis almost equally between the two non-fiction works. De Villiers, for his part, focuses his arguments more heavily on *Body without Soul*.

Moss's argument brings to the forefront similar problematical points regarding Grodecki's films, yet he is somewhat more redemptive in his critique. For Moss, *Not Angels but Angels* is 'heavily-handed and manipulative'.

Citing a blurb on a video box for the film, which foregrounds that the young hustlers' 'frankness and need to talk become the engine that drives the film', Moss argues that 'Grodecki's films are both highly manipulated and highly manipulative in ways that serve to enforce "normal" sexuality while demonstrating "abnormal" sexual practices' (Moss 2006a, np). This negative stance notwithstanding, Moss, in a discussion of the attitudes towards sex of *Mandragora*'s protagonist, stresses that, even though the young man appears to assume a passive role, 'the power dynamic may not be as straightforward (pun intended) as Grodecki would like us to think'. Moss concludes that 'It's these queer moments that slip past Grodecki's controlling heterosexist gaze that make the film worth watching' (Moss 2006a, np).

Similar ambiguity is expressed in Robin Griffiths' analysis of the three films. Griffiths, in a manner similar to that of Moss, stresses that Grodecki's masquerade of objectivity and frankness, particularly in what concerns investigations into the 'heart of darkness' of the gay sex trade in Prague, is offset by the director's presentation of a triptych that is 'ideologically slippery, exploitative and yet, undoubtedly queer' (Griffiths 2008: 130). Despite the manipulative nature of Grodecki's films, Griffiths deems the trilogy as

> an important means for both mapping and interrogating the unknown territories of the [gay] margins, thereby documenting narratives of self-discovery, emergence and a necessary sense of identity and solidarity – in all its 'problematic' manifestations – at a time of quite sweeping moral, economic and socio-cultural transformation . . . Grodecki's trilogy combined narrative, testimony and cinematography to produce texts that lent themselves quite readily to multiple readings both locally and globally . . . his work indelibly marked a timely, first step in the emergence of a post-communist 'queer' cinema that by resisting the oppressive regimes of the 'normal', had begun to articulate the synonymously painful yet productive pleasures of a region that was struggling to find its way in a new world order. (Griffiths 2008: 139–40)

Griffiths' observations on the two documentaries recall, but do not specifically reference, Clifford and Volkman's notion of the tourist gaze. He emphasises the fact that

> the true exploiters presented here are not the supposedly malevolent western sex tourists that have flocked to the region, but those home grown pimps and pornographers (all apparently 'straight' family men) who have come to realize the very lucrative potential that this new pink economy holds. (Griffiths 2008: 137)

Nicholas de Villiers' exploration of Grodecki's documentaries draws a connection between these films and Pasolini's *Love Meetings*, particularly in what concerns prostitution, the corruption of young men, and individual responses to homosexuality. Arguing that Grodecki views the issue more in terms of affect than economics, de Villiers foregrounds the director's exploration of 'spiritual and emotional degradation' and his creation of a 'confessional atmosphere' (de Villiers 2007: 347). De Villiers has, as his stated goal in writing about Grodecki, Larry Clark, Andy Warhol and others, '[not to] choose who is "correct" in their cinematic technique (since each has remarkable similarities), but to make their enterprise seem more strange, more open to critique, and not to imagine that every instance of talking about sex, or making sex talk, constitutes a liberation from control or surveillance' (359). In this respect, de Villiers draws our attention to the complexity and ambiguity of Grodecki's enterprise.

ANGELS OF THE NEW WORLD ORDER

De Villiers explores how the two films, especially *Not Angels but Angels*, deals with the sociopolitical and economic realities of post-communist Prague. He notes that the description on the DVD cover of the Water Bearer Films release of *Not Angels but Angels* is considerably more political than that of its successor, and stresses the impact of the western consumerism to which the young men have fallen prey in the wake of the socio-political transformations in the Czech capital. The chapter titles of the DVD reflect this dynamic. Among them are 'On the Job', 'International Trade' and 'Economics'.

De Villiers stresses that *Not Angeles but Angels* is considerably less claustrophobic than the latter film inasmuch as it reveals Prague's Central Station more prominently as the epicentre of solicitation, and also interviews the young subjects in several nightclubs, thereby opening up to social places as opposed to simply the bedroom (de Villiers 2007: 352). The film, moreover, includes interviews with a pimp, mostly occurring in a park near Central Station, in which the man, who appears to be in his thirties, describes the techniques he uses to introduce the young men to their tricks. Although we are only on occasion privy to the actual questions posed by the interviewer, the interviewees' responses appear, for the most part, as monologues spoken in Czech. The prostitutes who know English, however, speak this language, although they are sometimes difficult to understand. In all cases, the interviews are subtitled in either Czech or English, as appropriate. De Villiers, moreover, has pointed out that the hustlers of *Not Angels but Angels* spend more time discussing what they like and dislike about their job than their companions in *Body without Soul*.

Moss (2006a) includes in his analysis of *Not Angels but Angels* a discussion of why the English title of Grodecki's film is far more evocative than the original Czech. *Anděle nejsou anděle* rather prosaically translates as 'Angels are not angels'. In contrast, the English version evokes an episode in Bede's *Ecclesiastical History of the English People* that tells of a pope who catches sight of two English slave boys in a Roman market and is told that they are Angles. He replies that they are not Angles, but rather angels; their beautiful faces suggest that they should be the co-heirs of the angels in heaven (Bede 1969: 540–604). In this respect, it is the English title of the documentary that implies more the corporeal dynamics that will be the focus of my discussion here.

Arguing that Grodecki needs 'only to highlight the sexual activities of the boys in order to evoke the disapproval of the audience', Moss draws upon Gayle S. Rubin's 'hierarchies of sexual value' (Rubin 1993), and includes in his discussion her graph of how society has separated sexual activities into a 'charmed [inner] circle' and 'the outer limits'. Such notions as heterosexual, vanilla, procreative, 'at home', etc. lie safely within the inner circle, while homosexual, S&M, 'in the park' are relegated to the outer limits. We note immediately that the sex acts discussed by the interviewees in *Not Angels but Angels* belong, by and large, to the latter category. The only exception is that more emphasis is devoted to sex with a partner than to sex by oneself or in a group.

Both Moss and de Villiers have noted the use of classical liturgical music in *Not Angels but Angels*, specifically Bach's *Saint Matthew Passion* and Mozart's *Requiem*. For Moss, such a device provides a shocking contrast to the young men's narrations about their work and sexual practices. De Villiers, on the other hand, views the musical choices as evidence of the film's inherent homophobia given that the music, and specifically the *Requiem*, tends to drown out the boys' comments. He stresses that the distributor, Water Bearer Films, specialises in foreign, arthouse and gay films; hence, a connection is made between *Not Angels but Angels* and the 'artsy' or highbrow. Moss and de Villiers fail to mention yet another piece of classical music used extensively throughout the film, the 'Aria' from Heitor Villa-Lobos' *Bachiana brasileira No. 5*, performed by the soprano Barbara Hendricks.[4] This work, a song with minimal lyrics and extended bars sung by the soloist while articulating only vowels, lacks the ecclesiastical underpinnings of the Bach and Mozart works. It is significant to note that the *Bachiana brasileira No. 5* was one of nine works by the Brazilian composer that were intended to emulate the style of Bach, hence the work's title. Although it is arguably one of the *Bachianas* that most heavily draws upon Brazilian folklore, these references are subtle indeed. To many listeners, the work appears very European.[5] The choice of the *Bachiana brasileira No. 5* is significant for another reason. The non-liturgical nature of Villa-Lobos's composition may, to older gay men, recall the use of classical music in gay porno films of the 1970s, which perhaps was due to lower royalty rates for needle drops for works in the public domain performed by lesser-known orchestras than would have been the case with songs by well-recognised contemporaneous pop singers.

Moss and de Villiers further mention the images of massive statues of angels that are interspersed with images of the young hustlers. When one considers the English title of the film and its references, such a device becomes especially evocative. Indeed, the statues, shot from low angles, constitute a more harmonious fit with the liturgical music than do the bodies and talking heads of the young prostitutes. They evoke the majesty of a Central European capital, and, like the classical music, contribute a sense of elegance and dignity that contrasts sharply with the boys' narrative. High art is revered and exalted by the educated; hustlers are deprecated by the masses. The angels are fully adults, and their corporeal perfection contrasts with a certain level of imperfection of the adolescent bodies of the young men being interviewed. Some of the boys are chubby, still sporting baby fat, while others are lanky. In both cases, they provide counterpoint to the adult voluptuousness of the semi-nude female statues. One of the hustlers, moreover, has a very spotty face, which could be due either to a bad case of teenage acne or to the early stages of AIDS. Of equal importance are relatively few shots in which the boys are shown as full bodies; most often taken in or near Central Station, these shots depict the hustlers as unwashed and grungy, anything but angels.

The works of classical music and sculpture decidedly contribute a sense of elegance and dignity that contrasts sharply with the boys' bodies and narratives. Their deployment in Grodecki's film may well align gay viewers with the highbrow culture in which they purportedly circulate. To an extent, the use of the statues and music places Grodecki's film safely in the realm of the arthouse. Yet the contrast between high art and the young hustlers' bodies holds even more disturbing implications. A work of art has meaning and dignity of its own, and can be deemed timeless. The hustlers' work, on the other hand, is often portrayed as transitory. An English-speaking hustler who grew up in New York City views prostitution as a temporary means of employment that will lead him to an eventual career as a gangster. Other youths suggest that they will sell their bodies only as long as their desirability lasts. For some, the ultimate end of their work as prostitutes may well be death, given their fear of AIDS.

The corporal dynamic of the young hustlers recalls, to a certain extent, the linguistic concept of the subject of a reflexive verb. Under the most promising of circumstances and when free from the control of a pimp, they are at once subject (the sellers) and object (the sold). Even more propitious is that they retain the goods once sold; hence, the oldest profession can be very lucrative. Nevertheless, Grodecki's film caustically foregrounds the ambivalent economic situation of the boys. To this effect, another linguistic analogy is appropriate, that of the middle voice, in which it is unclear whether the subject of the verb is an agent or a recipient. The middle voice is at once more economical and more ambivalent than a reflexive verb. In a sentence such as 'The glass shattered', it is difficult to clearly define the role of the 'glass'. Does it act? Is it acted upon? Such a metaphor allows us to question to what extent the teenaged prostitutes are agents or victims, or a fusion of both.[6]

The young men appear very aware of their bodies as commodity, and Grodecki's camera is complicit in this dynamic. Its zooms into the faces of the talking heads appear subtly copulative, and suggest a blow job, one of the stocks-in-trade of the boy subjects. The young men discuss with candour what they are willing or not willing to do, or which acts they perceive as 'normal' or 'not normal'. Several concur that they will charge the least for simply giving a trick a hand job; giving a blow job will be expensive. At times, there is an additional charge for performing a sex act without a condom. As one young man tells his tricks, 'If you are going to mess up my body, it will cost you'. Most consider masturbation or oral sex within the realm of 'normality'. One hustler even goes so far as to say that he enjoyed defecating and urinating into the mouth of a trick! What remains more problematical is the concept of anal sex. This seems especially threatening to those hustlers who identify themselves as straight. In any case, getting fucked is the act that the young men, by and large, least want to perform, and for which they charge the most. The interviews with the young hustlers are, particularly towards the end part of the film, intercut with the faces of older men contemplating the boys in a club. The men do not speak, yet their intent is clear from the lustful gazes. A close-up of a postcard which a hustler has received from a trick who has offered to take him to California underscores the importance of the anus in the trade. Depicted on the card is a group of people who have dropped their drawers and are mooning the camera. A caption reads, 'Guess which one is me!' Such a device suggests that the relationship between hustler and trick included active anal sex on the part of the youth.

A seemingly unrelated sequence also involves an older man. In a long-shot, we see a very thin, middle-aged man jumping around naked in what appears to be a workplace. Although his penis is never exposed, the camera reveals much more of his body than it does of those of the young hustlers. His persona may well anticipate the middle-aged pornographer featured in *Body without Soul*. Nonetheless, visual depictions of the young bodies are not entirely absent. Digitally distorted images of the youths engaged in sex acts, inserted throughout the latter part of the film, show the hustlers with each other rather than with their tricks. Despite the distortion, both the nature of the acts and the relative ages of the participants are clear. The penis and the anus are frequently featured in these images. The fact that the boys appear with each other rather than with a trick provides a seamless transition between *Not Angels but Angels* and *Body without Soul* inasmuch as the images suggest the porno films in which teenage boys are featured that become the primary subject of the latter film.

CUTTING AND PENETRATING: *BODY WITHOUT SOUL* AND *BOY PORN*

De Villiers describes the broad framework of *Body without Soul* as one of 'revulsion for homosexual sex and "dirty old men"', and stresses that such a stance appears 'through tone, the type of questions asked, music, images inserted for "punctuation" and framing' (348). The film is far more disturbing and complex than its predecessor, particularly in its portrayal of a pornographer whose day job entails performing autopsies. Over the course of the final third of the film, the interviews with the young porn stars and sequences of porn shoots are intercut with details of an autopsy. By virtue of the coroner's work, the intersection between teen prostitution and death is rendered considerably more prominent. Once again, Prague as a site for the exploitation of young men is rendered clear; the film's title is superimposed over a cityscape of the Czech capital. Another title highlights the economic dynamics at play and indicates the exchange rate between the Czech crown and the US dollar.

The early interviews in the film continue along the lines of *Not Angels but Angels*. The young men describe their first encounters, the prices they charge for specific acts, and the different sexual acts preferred by distinct nationalities. While Germans mainly opt to perform oral sex on the boys, Czech johns want everything. One youth explains how he evokes the fear of AIDS in order to charge a higher price for sex without a condom. In what might be deemed a contradiction of Ryan and Hall's ascription of economic privilege to the sex tourist, another rent boy stresses that his German, Austrian and Swiss clients pretend to be rich, but cannot afford to buy him a good dinner. A discussion of human trafficking is included, and a hustler describes how boys are often transported across the border under car seats or in the trunk. Grodecki also presents a sequence simulating the filming of the story about a runaway youth who walks around Prague and ends up as a porn star. Such a story provides a bridge to the trilogy's third film, *Mandragora*. The discussions, moreover, are characterised by a good deal of homophobia. One participant claims that homosexuality is inhuman, and traces the topic back to Adam and Eve and their children. The unseen interviewer dumbfounds him by asking, 'What if Adam and Eve's children were gay?' Unlike *Not Angels but Angels*, we hear more of the questions asked by the interviewer. The comments made by the youths thus appear to be more of a dialogue.

The interviews soon move from discussions of prostitution to discussion of the youth's participation in porno films. They discuss how the youngest boy usually gets the main part, and how participants are expected to perform everything. Often, the pornographer demands oral or anal sex between tricks. One youth articulates that he likes to fuck because it reminds him of sex with a woman, and that he is especially fond of sex with pre-pubescent boys.

In tandem with the autopsy scenes, a boy stresses, 'I sell all the parts, the complete body.' The boys appear to discuss what the body consists of – 90 per cent water combined with meat and bones. Combining the notion of soul and body that defines the film's title both in Czech and English, one affirms, 'The soul wants the money, the body sells itself.' Another muses, 'My body I sell, but my soul is for someone else.' One points out a poignant irony, that hustlers care for their souls and forget their bodies; when they realise this, it is too late. Such a position recalls a discussion in Godard's *Vivre sa vie*, in which it is argued that an act of prostitution does not imply the selling of the soul.

The film introduces a middle-aged pornographer, who explains how, by virtue of his work as a photographer, he was introduced to a pornographer in the Netherlands. He stresses the economic challenges of the job and that, with all costs considered, he only makes approximately sixty dollars per film. International clients may refuse to pay for the films if they do not like the backdrop or if the stars do not ejaculate for a full nine seconds. The latter claim recalls Linda Williams' discussions of the pivotal role of the 'money shot' in pornography (Williams 1989: 8). Over the course of his years in the business, he has used some 150 boys in thirty films. The filmmaker clarifies

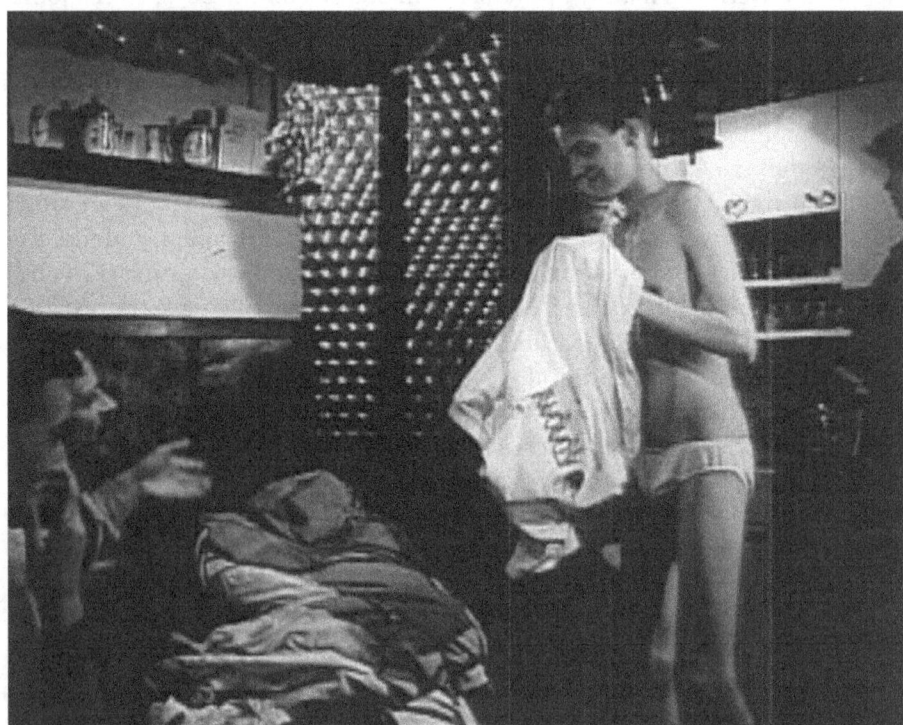

Figure 7.1 A new young porno star in Wiktor Grodecki's *Body without Soul*

that the young men who star in his films tend to be either low-lives, who have run away from their village and have ended up as fourteen-year-old criminals, or exhibitionists who do not care about who will see them or how much they will get. The pornographer is seen briefing his stars on the need to produce an erection without delay; they must not masturbate before the shoot. Moreover, the boys must be flexible and open. 'If you go to a porno shoot not expecting to get fucked', he explains, 'you are like a gravedigger who goes to a cemetery without a shovel and a coffin.' Such a comment accentuates the film's linkage between sex and death, particularly in what concerns the risk of AIDS the hustlers and porn stars confront on a daily basis.

The pornographer segues from a discussion of the rectum and the buttocks to recollections of his eight years as a pathologist. He initially took a job in a surgical ward because he wanted to see what the body looked like from the inside. He then became a police coroner. Drawing a connection between autopsies and gay sex, the pornographer compares the opening up of the body to the opening up of the anus. A parallel is drawn between two tools, a knife and a dildo. And, by extension, a sharp knife is like a hard penis. The man brags that he can completely dissect a body in five minutes, a remark that recalls the time constraints he imposes on his young stars' orgasms. The pornographer's comments are juxtaposed with images of the young men showering together prior to a shoot. Penises are shown in chiaroscuro. Grodecki cuts between the shower sequence and the preparation for the autopsy in such a way that the boys appear to watch the pornographer as he changes from his Bestman Video Team jacket to his protective coat and cap. The pornographer stresses that he never protects himself completely, a choice that mirrors that of having unprotected sex. As the protagonist cuts open a body, he discusses the perfection of porno films and his control of the actors. As is the case with his autopsies, he is detailed in his work. He asserts that the morgue has thus influenced his style of directing.

The theme of death is underscored by a young man who speaks while in a partially-reclined position, surrounded by fake candles. Of the interviewees, his remarks appear among the most genuine. And these are also intercut with the autopsy. The pornographer begins by removing the tongue and throat, and proceeds to the lungs and inner organs. It is implied, but not stated, that the rectum is the ultimate destination of the process. Like balls on a Christmas tree, the testicles frivolously provide a coda to the event.

The foreign market for which the films are designated is made clear by a close-up of a video box touting the title *Sommerträume* (Summer Dreams), as well as by an interview with a young man in front of a wall-sized image of the New York City skyline, which appears in an undisclosed location. (The image will figure more prominently in *Mandragora*.) The same actor, moreover, is shown featured in an advertisement for AIDS prevention. The presence of this youth and the setting in which he speaks illustrate a number of contradictions – lip service towards safe sex coupled with dangerous behaviour, Prague as both consumer of the West and (eastern) haven for sex tourism.

CHRONICLE OF A DOWNFALL FORETOLD: *MANDRAGORA*

Andrew J. Horton refers to *Mandragora* as 'highly middle-class' and 'middle-of-the-road'. Asserting that if it were not for 'the explicit nudity and conversation about sex, [it would be] the sort of film that every parent would want to show their teenage children' inasmuch as it reinforces traditional family values, Horton reminds us that five of the prizes that the film initially won were awarded in Geneva, which he describes as 'one of the most smugly middle-class cities in Europe' (Horton 1999, n.p.).

As Moss (2006a) points out, the mandragora, or mandrake, is a plant which, according to East Indian folklore, 'grows under the gallows from the sperm of hanged men' (np). He adds that the life that grows out of this death is 'already condemned, infected, illusory' (n.p.). It is essential to note that the folklore surrounding the mandrake is widespread throughout Europe, the Middle East, and South Asia. D. C. Allen has viewed the plant in terms of biblical references to it, and observes that in Genesis 30: 14–17, Leah bore Jacob a son with the help of fecundating mandrakes. He stresses that the mandrake is related to both lust and fecundity in the Bible (Allen 1959: 396). In a 1905 paper presented at the American Academy of Arts and Sciences, Charles Brewster Randolph foregrounded the traditional belief that the mandrake grew in a form that resembled the human body (494). He explores folkloric accounts that the plant grows from the urine voided at death by men unjustly hanged, and that it visually resembles the entire human body, including the genitals (Randolph 1905: 495). In literature, from the poetry of John Donne to the *Harry Potter* series, the mandrake has been celebrated. The destructive behaviour attributed to the plant is evidenced in 'El talismán', a 1909 short story by Spanish writer Emilia Pardo Bazán. The story tells of the death of a baron in a train wreck after his prized mandrake, to which he has attributed his wealth, is stolen and thrown into a sewer. For our purposes here, we note that the baron has a Hungarian name, which by extension associates the mystique of the mandrake with Central Europe. Almost a hundred years later, in Guillermo del Toro's *El laberinto del fauno* (*Pan's Labyrinth*, 2006), a film set during the Spanish Civil War, a faun gives a young girl a mandrake to cure her sick mother. The plant's healing properties are successful, but the mother dies after the plant is thrown into a fire. The film textualises the mandrake's

GEOGRAPHIES OF CARNALITY   161

human characteristics as it writhes and cries while perishing. The above examples reveal the close relationship in folklore, literature and art between the mandrake, sexuality and death.

Mandragora can well be described as an anti-*Bildungsroman*. It opens in the Moravian town of Prerov as the protagonist, Marek, breaks the window of a store selling Western merchandise, from which he steals a jacket. At the back of the window display, one sees an image of the Manhattan skyline, which reappears on the wall of the fashionable Hotel Praha, where Marek and his friend David later turn tricks. Yet in Prague, it is the young men's bodies that become the commodities for sale, not the foreign goods proffered in the little shop in Prerov. This juxtaposition is far more complex than it originally appears, inasmuch as it plays upon the geographical ambiguity of the Czech capital, and especially, the city's East/West dynamic. As a backdrop for Marek's theft of the jacket, the presence of the Manhattan skyline juxtaposes the western source of the goods the young man from the 'East' could not possibly afford. In the hotel, the cityscape alludes to the western market into which the young men have become integrated. Nonetheless, such integration is illusory, for when David is sodomised by a billiard cue in the hotel in front of the Manhattan backdrop, one senses a strong dichotomy between the perpetrator and the young victim, for whom western capitalism has proven at once exploitative and violent.

Moss has devoted special attention to a sequence in which a British trick asks Marek to stand nude on a rotating pedestal, holding a sword and

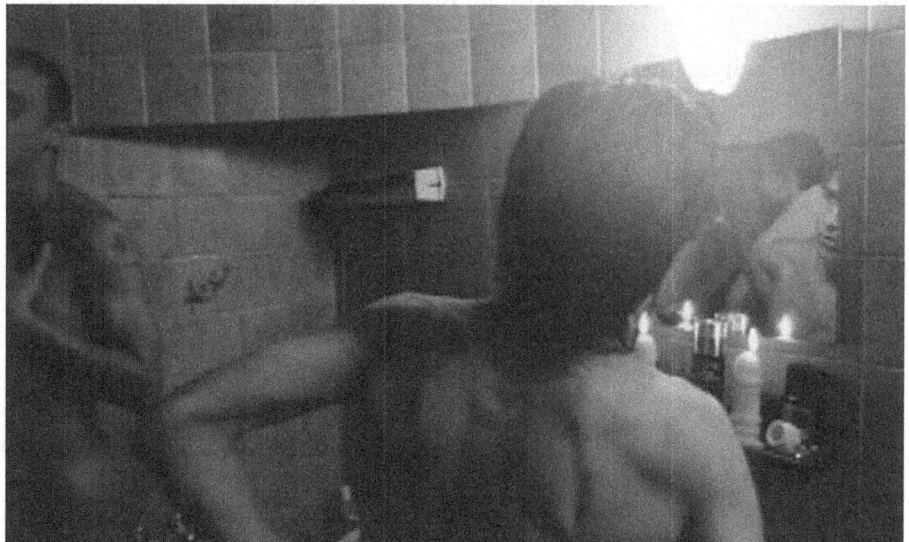

Figure 7.2 Young hustlers in Wiktor Grodecki's *Mandragora*

imitating the pose of Donatello's David. Focusing on the scene's dialogue, Moss argues:

> The dialogue perfectly captures the process of objectification, in which the object is there purely for the enjoyment of the owner/viewer, who in this case apparently reaches orgasm through verbalizing the aesthetic experience. But it points to the problem of colonization, since the viewer's knowledge is expressed in complex English Marek can't understand. Marek is reduced to being an object, an immobile statue for the viewer's pleasure, but which viewer – the Englishman or the film audience? (Moss 2006a, n.p.)

Moss's observations regarding the interplay of voyeurism and language in this sequence are most insightful, especially inasmuch as he points out that, although Germans are described as the primary customers for both the young male prostitutes and the porno films in which they are featured, the language of hegemony is English. Nevertheless, the sequence needs to be examined in its entirety. One notes that as the English voyeur expounds how the youthful body has been an object of contemplation in high art, Marek, in spite of his complete lack of understanding, appears somewhat complicit in the process. Nevertheless, there is a considerable divide implied between the artistic ideal and Marek's own body. The statue of David implies the aesthetically perfect. Despite the beauty of Marek's form, we have come to know the youth as rather base and often dirty, given the conditions under which he is forced to live. As the trick's monologue continues and the pedestal rotates, Marek's penis becomes slightly erect. The dynamics recalls the above-mentioned notion of the 'tourist gaze', particularly in light of the youth's participation in the fantasies of the coloniser. Grodecki, however, concludes the sequence with an abrupt and disturbing change, one that recalls the notion of planned obsolescence. The Englishman goes from worshipping Marek's physical perfection to noting that his testicles are too big for a great work of art. Declaring that he will rectify the situation, the trick manipulates the young man's testicles, inducing considerable pain. Marek as consumer good is proven defective, and it is implied that the older man will find a replacement for his sadistic game of adulation/debasement.

THE CITY AND BODY AMBIVALENT

The young rent boys in Grodecki's films are undeniably complicit in the tourist gaze that characterises both gay sex tourism and gay pornography destined for western markets. They are at once objects for consumption and clever marketeers; they are European in appearance, yet exotic to clients used to sexual binaries. Specifically, they promise sexual treats that can only be bought at a higher price in Germany, Austria, or the USA. In a like manner, Prague as a city plays upon its dual position as orientalist outpost and western shopping mall. It is so close to escape to, yet so very different. Considered together, these two dynamics attest to the liminality of both the geographical location of the Czech Republic and the economics of the trick/hustler dyad. Moss (2006b) has underscored a process at play in this context that, all the while addressing the circulation of western images of LGBT people in Eastern Europe, can by extension be applied to such sex tourism. He asserts, 'Nationalist and homophobic discourse in Central and Eastern Europe has consistently claimed that homosexuality is not a native phenomenon, but instead something learned from the West' (265). Ewa Mazierska has further linked Grodecki's homosexuality/West association with the gayness/AIDS connection he posits. Nonetheless, she argues for the film's importance given that it is the 'best-known film about homosexuals in the country'. Whether or not Grodecki was cognisant of the complexities of the social and cultural discourses that converge in his films is of little consequence. They constitute valid and disturbing documents of a specific time and space. They invite us to uncover the dynamics of one (hopefully small!) aspect of homosexuality in the early years of the post-communist Czech Republic.

NOTES

1. The expression 'the heart of Europe', which has defined Prague in popular culture, and has also been used in reference to Poland, may well be misleading. If one considers Europe as the space stretching from Finisterre to the Ural mountains and from the northernmost point of Norway to the southern Greek Islands, the 'heart of Europe' can more accurately be applied to Vilnius. In either case, Europe's centre lies, in Cold War terms, well behind the Iron Curtain.
2. The difficulty of obtaining materials for learning the Czech language continued well into the 1990s, when one could purchase Czech-language courses with accompanying audio materials exclusively at the most basic level. It is only in the last few years that the Czech Republic's membership of the EU and the development of the Common European Framework of Reference for Languages have led to the ready availability of language learning materials oriented towards the advanced and superior levels. Today, the availability of teaching and learning materials at the advanced/superior C1 and C2 levels of the European Framework is on a par with that of materials for Hungarian, which had traditionally been more prevalent, despite the purported difficulty of the language for westerners.
3. As Genovese and Spitzer explain, the US State Department began, in July 1951, to stamp passports 'not valid for travel to Czechoslovakia'. The following year, it made the same annotation for Albania, Bulgaria, Communist China, Hungary, Poland, Romania and the Soviet Union. In 1955, Czechoslovakia, Hungary, Poland, Romania and the Soviet Union were removed from the list.

4. The most famous recording of the 'Aria' from *Bachiana brasileira No. 5* was made in 1958 with the composer himself, Heitor Villa-Lobos, conducting the Catalán soprano Victoria de los Angeles. Given the singer's acclaim as an interpreter of the works of Rossini, Bizet, Puccini and many others, once again, the Brazilian piece is imbued with considerable Europeanness.
5. Given that one of the most famous recordings of the 'Aria' was made by the Russian soprano Galina Vishnevskaya, and a heavy Russian accent can be heard in her rendering of the lyrics and the vowels, the work may well be associated with Russia. In any case, the Brazilian rhythms and other musical nuances are lost upon most lovers of classical music not specialised in Brazilian composers. The *Bachianas brasileiras* can indeed transport the listener to Eastern or Central Europe. An interesting linguistics phenomenon comes into play here. Due largely to the similarities between the /l/ sound and certain vowels in Russian and Brazilian Portuguese, the two accents can be confused in English. Hence, the choice of the *Bachiana brasileira No. 5* to be played alongside the music of Bach and Mozart is not purely coincidental, and may well evoke for educated listeners an Eastern European context.
6. The English language has yet another phenomenon that mirrors, to an extent, the middle voice. The expressions 'She was attacked by a bear' and 'She got attacked by a bear' are not a hundred per cent synonymous. The use of the verb 'got' implies a certain level of agency on the part of the subject. Maybe she was approaching the bear too closely or antagonising it. In any case, she was not entirely an innocent victim. In the case of Grodecki's film, the young prostitutes are never completely guiltless with regard to the misadventures they sometimes endure.

WORKS CITED

Allen, D. C. (1959), 'Donne on the Mandrake', *Modern Language Notes*, 74:5, 393–7.
Bede (1969), *Bede's Ecclesiastical History of the English People*, Oxford: Clarendon.
Bradley, J. F. N. (1971), *Czechoslovakia: A Short History*, Edinburgh: Edinburgh University Press.
Bunzl, Matti (2000), 'The Prague Experience: Gay Male Sex Tourism and the Neo-colonial Invention of an Embodied Border', in Daphne Berdahl, Matti Bunzl and Martha Lampland (eds), *Altering States: Ethnographies of Transition in Eastern Europe and the Former Soviet Union*, Ann Arbor: University of Michigan Press, pp. 70–95.
Clifford, James (1988), *The Predicament of Culture: Twentieth-Century Ethnography, Literature, and Art*, Cambridge, MA: Harvard University Press.
De Villiers, Nicholas (2007), 'How Much Does It Cost for Cinema to Tell the Truth of Sex? Cinéma Vérité and Sexography', *Sexualities*, 10:3, 341–61.
Genovese, Michael and Robert J. Spitzer (2005), *The Presidency and the Constitution: Cases and Controversies*, New York: Palgrave Macmillan.
Griffiths, Robin (2008), 'Bodies without Borders? Queer Cinema and Sexuality after the Fall', in Robin Griffiths (ed.), *Queer Cinema in Europe*, Bristol: Intellect, pp. 129–42.
Horton, Andrew J. (1999), 'Going Down and Out in Prague and Prerov: Wiktor Grodecki's Mandragora', *Central Europe Review*, <http://www.ce-review.org/kinoeye/kinoeye15old2.html> (last accessed 30 May 2015).
Kolodny, Annette (1975), *The Lay of the Land*, Chapel Hill: University of North Carolina Press.
Mazierska, Ewa (2010), *Masculinities in Polish, Czech and Slovak Cinema: Black Peters and Men of Marble*, London: Berghahn Books.

Moss, Kevin (2006a), 'Who's Renting These Boys? Wiktor Grodecki's Czech Hustler Documentaries', *Interalia: A Journal of Queer Studies*, 1, <http://www.interalia.org.pl/en/artykuly/homepage/05_whos_renting_these_boys.html> (last accessed 25 May 2015).

Moss, Kevin (2006b), 'Queer As Metaphor: Representations of LGBT People in Central and Eastern European Film', in Roman Kuhar and Judit Takásc (eds), *Beyond the Pink Curtain: Everyday Life of LGBT People in Eastern Europe*, Ljubljana: Peace Institute, pp. 249–67.

Oppermann, Martin (1998), 'Introduction', in Martin Oppermann, ed., *Sex Tourism and Prostitution: Aspects of Leisure, Recreation, and Work*, New York, Sydney and Tokyo: Cognizant Communication.

Pardo Bazán, Emilia, condesa de (1909), 'El talismán', in Linda M. Willem (ed.) (2010), *'Naufragos' y otros cuentos*, Newark, DE: Cervantes & Co., pp. 49–55.

Randolph, Charles Brewster (1905), 'The Mandragora of the Ancients in Folk-Lore and Medicine', *Proceedings of the American Academy of Arts and Sciences*, 40:12, 487–537.

Rubin, Gayle S. (1993), 'Thinking Sex: Notes for a Radical Theory of the Politics of Sexuality', in Enry Abelove, Michèle Aina Barale, and David M. Halperin (eds), *The Lesbian and Gay Studies Reader*, New York: Routledge.

Ryan, Chris and C. Michael Hall I (2001), *Sex Tourism: Marginal People and Liminalities*, New York: Routledge.

Said, Edward (1978), *Orientalism*, New York: Vintage.

Urry, John and Jonas Larson (2011), *The Tourist Gaze 3.0*, Los Angeles: Sage.

Volkman, Toby Alice (1990), 'Visions and Revisions: *Toraja* Culture and the Tourist Gaze', *American Ethnologist*, 17: 1, 91–110.

Williams, Bruce (2003), 'Julie Christie Down Argentine Way: Reading Repression Cross-Nationally in Bemberg's *Miss Mary*', *Journal of Film and Video*, 55:4, 15–29.

Williams, Linda (1989), *Hard Core: The Frenzy of the Visible*, Berkeley: University of California Press.

Wolff, Larry (1994), *Inventing Eastern Europe*, Stanford: Stanford University Press.

CHAPTER 8

A Mass Doubling of Heroes: Post-human Objects of Queer Desire in Vladimir Sorokin and Ilya Khrzhanovsky's *4*

Alexandar Mihailovic

In their 2004 film *4*, the contemporary Russian novelist and screenwriter Vladimir Sorokin and the young filmmaker Ilya Khrzhanovsky create a nightmare fantasy about the intersection of two seemingly unrelated processes of production. In Moscow, a new and deeply corrupt food industry processes chemically injected and possibly cloned pig meat; in the countryside, a community of elderly women craft a series of eerie toddler-sized dolls that they shape out of masticated bread dough. Both of these modes of production address anxieties about body boundaries being breached or invaded, with the national body becoming tainted or jammed up by what it ingests. Freud discovered that melancholic mourning is expressed by the mourner's introjection of the lost love object. Such mourning refuses to acknowledge the loss of its object of affection, and is caught up in the effort to hold onto it. In chewing bread and shaping it into idealised simulacra of rural types such as the farmer and the priest, the old women of the film try to hold onto a national past that is perhaps falsely remembered as idyllic. They find rich buyers from the cities for their products, even as it is made clear that these dolls and the environment where they are manufactured are truly sinister. Like the pig/human cohabitation and symbiosis that is at the forefront of other scenes in the film, the doll/human cohabitation suggests a moment of cultural anxiety about social reproduction. In the film, traumatic scenes of choking and stifling are visited upon a generation of men and women of prime reproductive age.

The Russia of Sorokin and Khrzhanovsky's film is incapable of reproducing itself in ways other than the symbolic and incorporeal; it is a country that is fertile only in its proliferation of politicised modalities and unsubtle ideological metaphors. As Lisa Ryoko Wakamiya points out in one of the few scholarly articles about the movie, Sorokin draws attention to the palpably experiential dimension of political metaphors, thereby blurring the line between the 'representation of the abject' and actual abjection and humiliation (Wakamiya

2013: 241). Yet the acerbic treatment of corrupt leadership and neoliberal production processes that we see in *4* is also bound up with a series of involute and knotted tropes about sexuality that seem to distract us from the political critique that Khrzhanovsky the filmmaker and Sorokin the screenwriter (and erstwhile novelist) are attempting to make. *4* is a film that makes us aware of our bodies as sites for modes of production that flourish to the exclusion of regeneration and procreation. Khrzhanovsky certainly pushes the stark motifs of Russian Necro-realist painting into a cinematic arena, evoking what two Russian art critics, in writing about the grim canvases of the artist Yufit, identify as the 'liminal states [concealed by] faux humanism': 'psychopathology, zoomorphism, [and] zombification' (Turkina and Mazin 2006: 2). Khrzhanovsky and Sorokin refract the faux- or pseudo-processes of production through the prism of gay male sexual practices, amplifying and transforming valid concerns about Russia's demographic future and economic decline through an unexpected linkage to non-reproductive gay sex. In the satirical political critique deployed by Sorokin and Khrzhanovsky, which at first appears to come from a liberal point of view, a homophobic message strong enough to please Russian far-right nationalists is encrypted under layers of anxiety about cloning, a tainted food supply, village poverty, and systemic government corruption. Cloning becomes a symbol of sterile or spurious reproduction. Moreover, buried historical trauma about cannibalism dating back to the siege of Leningrad in World War II is brought to the surface through a showing of humans cohabiting with pigs, whom they treat as children, but whom they also eat. In this context, gay male sex is coded as unclean and emasculating, since it may involve penetration from behind. The symbolic palette of *4* paints a picture of queer intimacy that knowingly embraces sterility. In Sorokin and Khrzhanovsky's film, this straight male fear of death through feminisation is projected onto society at large, which is undergoing economic changes in post-capitalism that wreak havoc with individual autonomy.

Among other things, *4* is as much a meditation on the varieties of rebirth as it is a portrayal of destructively repressive self-images. Sorokin and Khrzhanovsky remind us that losing an understanding of oneself, even if it was fundamentally informed by what Leo Bersani terms the 'proud subjectivity' of a repressive ego (Bersani 2010: 29), is never a trifling matter: it is certainly far easier to mourn than to celebrate the passing of a self-image, no matter how unhealthy and procrustean it has become. In a further complication of things, what character does our mourning take on – and what new self-image might we acquire – if we also have the opportunity to return our ancestors or recently dearly departed to the company of the living? The possibility of cloning would seem to call into question the viability of the elegiac mode. Writing in the burgeoning shadow of Vladimir Putin's headlong amalgamation of civic, religious and government institutions – arguably the most focused effort, since Leonid

Brezhnev's ousting of Nikita Khrushchev in 1964, at shoring up executive power on Russian soil – Sorokin contemplates this question in three works from different genres. In his 1999 novel *Goluboe salo* (*Blue Lard*), a quasi-monarchist Russia of the year 2068 struggles to maintain its superpower status against China, which has become its chief global rival. Much like the aggressive incursion of American business culture into the post-Soviet Russia of the 1990s (which Sorokin skilfully satirises here), a resurgent Ming-Dynasty-like China has injected a plethora of loan words into the Russian language. In the world of *Blue Lard*, this asymmetrical cultural interaction serves as one of many markers of a country under a non-violent siege. The weapons division of the Russian government creates clones of deceased Russian writers (among them, Tolstoy, Chekhov, Nabokov and Akhmatova) with the goal of harvesting from them a substance known as 'blue lard', which their bodies secrete. An ultra-nationalist group known as the Earth Fuckers [*Zemleyoby*] discovers the truth about 'blue lard', that it confers immortality on anyone who is injected with it. The Earth Fuckers – who imagine, among other things, that they gain strength through sexual contact with the soil of a meteor site in Siberia – steal vials of the 'blue lard' and dispatch them via time-travel to an alternative 1954, where Stalin and Khrushchev are lovers. The two men abscond with the blue lard to an undefeated Nazi Germany – in this timeline, Russia's closest ally. The novel ends with Stalin presumably becoming immortal, as a result of injecting himself through the eye with the 'blue lard'.

Much has been written about the Russian nationalist protest against the equation of Stalinism with Nazism in Sorokin's dystopian *Blue Lard*. In their 2002 protests against the novel, the Kremlin-sponsored youth group Russia Moving Together was particularly incensed by the representation of comity between a victorious Himmler and Hitler and the Soviet leadership of the 1950s, not to mention one elaborately detailed scene in which semen from a sexual encounter between Stalin and Khrushchev is ceremonially collected in a chalice. In *Blue Lard*, Sorokin contemplates the ramifications of what may be termed the anti-elegiac world-view of authoritarianism, distilled in the statement made by his Hitler that 'freedom comes and goes, but great leaders remain' (Sorokin 2002: 312). Men must become 'earth fuckers' to reinvigorate themselves for territorial conquest, needing government-ordered injections of blue lard harvested from clones of pre-eminent dead poets and composers. Together with *Blue Lard*, the screenplay for Ilya Khrzhanovsky's *4* and the libretto for Leonid Desiatnikov's opera *Deti Rozentalia* (*Rosenthal's Children*) represents a cycle of works by Sorokin that seems to reconsider the ideas of religious philosopher Nikolai Fyodorov about the literal resurrection of ancestors, as the ultimate synthesis within the Hegelian progress of human consciousness. In timing that seems deliberate, the making of the film coincided with the 2003 centenary of the Fyodorov's death. In her 1986 *The Body in Pain: The Making and Unmaking of the World*, Elaine Scarry argues that the official acknowledgements of collective tragedy such as a war often stand in direct opposition to mourning, by rhetorically re-enacting the outcome of a catastrophe 'through the process of memorialization' (Scarry 1987: 115). Alexander Etkind strikes a similar note about the ambiguities of memorialisation in his probing study about the centrality of representations of stymied or frustrated acts of mourning and elegiac reflection within the cultural space of post-Soviet Russia, writing that '[m]ourning has an unusual ability to deepen the contact with reality, but only when the reality has vanished' (Etkind 2013: 19). In *4*, Sorokin and Khrzhanovsky contemplate the practical impossibility of mourning in a world which relentlessly valorises a state-dictated notion of the new, or which insists that the past is ever-present.

Even the quotidian details of the collaborative engagement between Sorokin and the novice Khrzhanovsky – who at that time was primarily known for his family connections, as the son of the famous Soviet-era animator Andrei Khrzhanovsky – point to an understanding of the curious incommensurability within the experience of collective trauma among different human agents. In one interview, Khrzhanovsky takes particular note of the seemingly paradoxical fact that he needed to seek out people who were different from him in conviction and orientation, in order to make a film about clones ('Chetvertka s pliusami i minusami', 2005). In the end, many Russian viewers of Sorokin and Khrzhanovsky's film would be impressed by the thought that if *4* is indeed a tribute to the work of Nikolai Fyodorov, it can only be a prickly one, striking a note of bemused ambivalence reminiscent of a speech from a wake for a difficult friend. In one essay, Fyodorov describes the museum space as a prolonger of the catastrophic experiences of a necessarily patriarchal order. Rather than providing opportunities for muted reflections of the impact of the collective past upon the spirals and whorls of a visitor's particular biography, Fyodorov's museum space seeks to collapse all consciousness into an ideal of a seamless intergenerational continuum. Fyodorov writes that 'a person is distinguished from an animal only to the extent that he sees himself as a son', intent upon resurrecting his father and forefathers in the effort to continue the war against the enemies of his tribe or *gens* (Fyodorov 2015: 61). Certainly the film's portrayal of living copies and clones shows the theatre-of-cruelty-like reality of Fyodorov's conceit of political agency coming about only through the revivifying of multiple generations within the same space. Sorokin and Khrzhanovsky are intent upon turning Fyodorov's symbolic imaginary on its head: for them, the making of human copies does not result in a separation from the animal world, but rather in a devolution into it. The fact that these copies are made in the countryside only serves to throw into even sharper relief Sorokin and Khrzhanovsky's polemic with Fyodorov, who idiosyncratically described his sacral museum space as a 'transfer of the city into the village'

(Fyodorov 2015: 72). Whether they be in the form of piglets that are genetically engineered for the delectation of an affluent demographic, or of battalions of puppet-like soldiers mechanically trudging into the maw of a military personnel carrier, or of dolls that are (like the clones of *Blue Lard*) fortified by bodily secretions, in *4* copies and clones are unambiguously portrayed as the raw material – the source of sustenance – for a plutocratically reinvigorated Russian state.

In his attack on Fyodorov, Sorokin is engaging in a polemic that is, within the Russian context, arguably not only more controversial than his explicit portrayals of gay and hetero sexuality, but also considerably more pointed than any of his critiques of Stalinism and what he, in interviews and essays, has dubbed the 'cult of violence' in conceptions of the Russian state since the time of Ivan the Terrible. From the 1920s up until the 1960s, Fyodorov was the only philosopher from *fin de siècle* Russia who was deemed to be ideologically acceptable by both the Soviet academic establishment and religious philosophers within the émigré communities in Germany, Yugoslavia and France; in many ways, the tightly bundled congeries of his eccentric notions about corporate consciousness serve as the single most important bridge between the nativist conservatism of pre-revolutionary Slavophilism (which idealised the post-Emancipation commune) and Soviet-era adumbrations of the group or collective (*kollektiv*) as the most vital labour and administrative category within the state. Yet we also need to consider another aspect of collectivism in Sorokin and Khrzhanovsky's film, one that throws up a series of makeshift bridges within the conceptual archipelago of ritualistic violence, Fydorov's ideal commune of the living and the revived dead, and what Leo Bersani and Adam Phillips, in their 2008 book *Intimacies*, term the ego-shattering potentialities of the 'unlimited' or impersonal intimacy that is paradigmatically implicit in unprotected same-sex encounters (Bersani and Phillips 2008: 42–3). In *4*, copying and cloning are portrayed as forms of sublimated sexual intimacy, and are notionally configured as acts that are strange and queer, if not openly expressive of a queer sexuality. The question then becomes, what link can possibly exist between totalitarianism and same-sex desire, and does the idea of such an affiliation belie Sorokin's openness to the polymorphous possibilities within sexuality, which seem to be present in novels such as *Tridtsataia liubov' Mariny* (*Marina's Thirtieth Love*)?

In order to clarify these matters, we need to understand the theoretical framework that undergirds the film, and which has not been noted in any of the scholarship about Sorokin. The romance of cloning in *Blue Lard*, *4* and *Rosenthal's Children* has an important non-Russian source. In his screenplay for Khrzhanovsky's film, Sorokin draws a distinct parallel between the modernist trope of the authorial *doppelgänger* and the possibility of human cloning, regarding both ideas as paradigms for the production of political fictions that render subjects into what Jean Baudrillard terms 'industrial objects'. In his essay 'Clone Story', Baudrillard characterises cloning as a technology that eroticises mass production, rendering it into a kind of sublimated substitute for reproduction through sex:

> It is no longer even a question of being twins, since Gemini or Twins possess a specific property, a particular and sacred fascination of the Two, of what is two together, and never was one. Whereas cloning enshrines the reiteration of the same: 1 + 1 + 1 + 1, etc. Neither child, nor twin, nor narcissistic reflection, the clone is the materialization of the body by genetic means, that is to say the abolition of all alterity and of any imaginary. Which is combined with the economy of sexuality. Delirious apotheosis of a productive technology. (Baudrillard 1994: 97)

The fourfold repetition of the number one is especially significant as a structural model for the image of cloning in Sorokin's work. As Baudrillard puts it, mass duplication abolishes the 'subject's projection onto [an] ideal alter ego' (Baudrillard 1994: 96). Baudrillard's argument about the transformation of individual autonomy into a reproducible commodity was taken up by the theorists of Moscow Conceptualism, who emerged as a formative influence on Sorokin's early fiction and artwork. Shortly before the Soviet collapse, and clearly referencing the work of Baudrillard, Sorokin's friend Mikhail Ryklin (like Sorokin, an important theorist for Moscow Conceptualism in its heyday[1]) published an article entitled 'Consciousness and Power: The Soviet Model'. Ryklin argues that 'the model for the production of consciousness that we see in our society, like the model for the production of material comforts, "appalls" [*smushchaet*] us with the fact that it constitutes not a model of [political] representation, but rather of the nation' as a whole (Ryklin 1991: 34). Taking a cue from Ryklin as well as from Baudrillard, Khrzhanovsky and Sorokin document a crisis in the notion of what it means to be human. In *Rosenthal's Children*, cloned resurrections of Tchaikovsky, Wagner, Verdi and Mussorgsky speak identically in mind-numbing platitudes about the prophet-like status of the artist. In the film *4*, Khrzhanovsky explores in cinematic terms both the implications of, and possible alternatives to, this relentless multiplication of sameness. Baudrillard describes a world defined not so much by Sartre's over-cited notion of 'Hell [being] other people' as by the 'Hell of the same': in the realm of simulacra and simulation, a single idealised model is relentlessly duplicated and promulgated. In the film and the opera, Sorokin argues for a new kind of elegiac mood, one that is not so much a meditation on mortality as it is a contemplation of shared suffering. This new notion of the elegiac is more concerned with the experience of a life attenuated by Baudrillard's '[d]elirious apotheosis of a reproductive technology' than it is exercised by the fact of death. Genuine tragedy is represented by assimilation into an amorphous collective, by the victory of the herd.

Interestingly, one of the scenes in *4* that generated the most discussion is one of its least provocative. A mildly inebriated conversation in a Moscow bar unfolds between a piano tuner, a call girl and a buyer of wholesale meat. Vladimir, the piano tuner, relates to Marina and Oleg a far-fetched account about a Soviet project to develop generations of cloned citizens from the time of World War II, using technology developed by the Nazis. The meat buyer Oleg (who claims to be a supplier of mineral water to the Kremlin) in outrage responds 'How is that possible? It's prohibited. Not long ago there was some kind of international congress, and they outlawed the cloning of a human being.' The piano tuner, who tells a fib that he is a geneticist working in a lab that was formerly involved with the cloning project, replies, 'Well, gentlemen, have you forgotten about the kind of country we live in? What was prohibited to them, is permissible for us' (Sorokin 2005: 60). This encounter is the kind of cynical banter about politics that one still hears among educated Russians. With the possible exception of Andrei Zviaginstev's 2014 *Leviathan*, *4* is arguably the most controversial movie to appear in Russia since the collapse of the Soviet Union. *4* is notable for its openly jaundiced view of both the Soviet past – its contempt for political nostalgia – and the self-interested anti-ethics of contemporary Russia and its leadership. In a larger sense, 'what kind of a country do we live in?' is a question that both Sorokin and Khrzhanovsky pose to the audience of *4*. The fact that the piano tuner's name is Vladimir, like Sorokin's, points to a laboured insertion of authorial presence into the script. The character of Vladimir is the biggest creator of fiction in the scene, emerging as a natural double for the author himself. As Sorokin himself put it in a 2005 interview, his harassment by the crypto-fascist and nationalist youth group Russia Moving Together made him feel as if he had suddenly found himself 'within one of his own [literary] works'. Yet Sorokin does not see doubling and self-conscious autobiographical *mise-en-scène* as devices for shoring up the ruins of an authorial ego. Quite the contrary. In his script, the modernist trope of authorial *doppelgänger* is distinctly parallel to the cloning project: both are templates for the promulgation of political fictions that in fact rob us of human agency. We may regard the deliriously reproduced doubles and clones in Sorokin's work as the equivalent of puppets, corresponding to the idealised – and necessarily depersonalised – forms of being that Heinrich von Kleist described in his 1810 essay 'On the Marionette Theatre': 'Grace appears purest in that human form which either has no consciousness or an infinite one, that is, in a puppet or a god' (Kleist 1982: 244).

We will return later to Sorokin and Khrzhanovsky's treatment of copies and clones as relays on a power grid of collective identity. For the time being, we need to focus on this bar-room scene of quirky individuals who carry on like characters from a Beckett play, engaging in playful fibs – or, as the Russian expression has it, 'grating nonsense'. They are Vladimir, the meat buyer Oleg, and Marina, a call girl who enthusiastically tells the two men about her job selling a Japanese air-freshener guaranteed to lower the stress levels of office workspaces. The fourth person to round out this group is a dozing and somnambulist bartender. As Vladimir explains it, at the beginning of the Cold War cloning was equal in importance and secrecy to the development of the atom bomb in the Soviet Union. The somewhat euphemistic term 'doubling' [*dublirovanie*] was used at that time for the cloning project. Vladimir rhapsodises sardonically that '[t]he most incredible thing is, that the number four was never [regarded as] magic in the history of the world, and yet it turns out to be ideal!' (Sorokin 2005: 65). He goes on to relate that the first successful Soviet clone, developed by the Soviet academic Bronshtein, relied on a 'domino principle' of reproduction, allowing for the 'implanting of a double within the single cell of a donor'. In 1968, the geneticist Viktor Petrovich Golosov found a way of putting four complete chromosomes within a single cell, resulting in the lowest margin of error and 'the optimal percent of survival'. Vladimir goes on to embroider his story with an account of how he and a friend came across three hundred cloned quadruplets in an abandoned and dilapidated factory building while working in the Krasnoyar region. 'They were in tatters and dirty, dressed any which way' and grouped in rooms according to age and gender. The meat buyer Oleg cuts off Vladimir as he begins to tell a racist anecdote about a sexual encounter with girls in the room for underage female clones, and angrily exits from the bar. After he leaves, Marina says thoughtfully 'I have to say, what assholes [*kozly*] work in the president's office!'

Marina's use of the term *kozly* – which literally means 'goats' [sg. *kozyol*] – echoes an earlier statement of hers in the same scene. She comes into the bar upset because a car had just run over a dog on the street outside, saying that the city at three in the morning is deserted and yet the 'idiot' [*mudak*, roughly equivalent to 'dickhead'] driver didn't see the dog. 'People are such assholes [*kozly*]', she says, to which Vladimir crypto-syllogistically replies 'Dogs are assholes [or 'goats'] too', and Oleg chimes in with the opinion that a dog's life is 'extremely comfortable'. One of the conceits of the film is that the endless reproduction of a single human identity blurs the division between humanity and animals. The conversation takes an associative turn, following up on Marina's initial comment that all people are the same. If people are goats, and dogs are goats, then the distinct profile of humanity (in its supposed distinction from the animal world) becomes eroded to the point of vanishing. Yet this blurring of zoological distinctions also carries a strong sexualised component within the Russian speech of the scene, which Sorokin and Khrzhanovsky accentuate in a variety of ways. In addition to being an insult, *mudak* is a vulgar term for male genitalia (from *mudé*), and in some contexts is used paradoxically, to refer to an ineffective or weak man. The derogatory use of *kozyol*, or 'goat', originates in the subculture of organised crime networks that exerted *de facto* control over many wards within the gulag, and originally referred to the 'untouchables' of the prison system who were either passive homosexuals or the victims of rape. In the criminal argot, policemen can also be contemptuously referred to as *kozly*, as a way of rhetorically emasculating them and depriving them of compelling authority. Within the discussion at the bar, the collision of the car (genitalia) against a dog ('goat', passive homosexual) metaphorically plays out the act of same-sex prison rape. As Mark Lipovetsky points out in his review of *4*, later in the film the incarcerated Vladimir has probably become one of these untouchables, as suggested by his prison nickname of 'Filled with Holes' [*dyriavyi*] (Lipovetsky 2005). When Marina first sits at the bar and orders a curaçao, she and Oleg banter about the '[light] blue' colour of the drink, which will make them all gay. In a series of puns that is impossible to preserve in a word-for-word translation, Marina quips that the city is already 'full of them [gays] [*v zhopu*, lit., 'stuffed up through the ass']'. The equivalent of gay or 'lavender' in Russian is *goluboi*, or 'light blue', which is also the colour of the so-called 'lard' secreted beneath the skins (very much like the layer of fat between a pig's skin and its peritoneum) of resurrected Russian novelists and poets in Sorokin's *Blue Lard*. Between the novel and this scene in the film (which also, in a possible nod to *Blue Lard*, contains several statements by Marina and Oleg about China's rising geopolitical profile), Sorokin establishes a series of links between sexual alterity, foreignness (as represented by non-Russian provenance of curaçao), and the perpetuation of political, or at least Fyodorov-like, cults of personality.

In the bar scene, Vladimir makes a pass at Marina, who responds with interest but tells him to call her another day. She goes back to the apartment she shares with other call girls, and as he walks home Vladimir is arrested for no cogent reason by the police, whose car 'blocks his path' in an analogy to the dog hit by the car. Oleg, who skipped supper the previous evening after a nauseating visit to a beef warehouse with spoiled meat, decides after leaving the bar to go to a very upscale restaurant that serves round the clock. The sole customer in an enormous dining room, he asks for the restaurant's signature dish, which the obsequious waiter tells him is 'round piglet with apple-flavoured horseradish sauce'. Oleg snaps at him 'Look, friend, I've been buying meat for seven years, and I've never heard of 'round piglets' . . . How do they get that way? Do you stuff them with a pump?' The waiter indifferently replies that they are born that way, and offers to show them to him in the kitchen. There, with a theatrical flourish, a jaded chef removes a cheesecloth to reveal four unnaturally bloated piglets. Oleg stares at them with a stunned expression on his face. He leaves without eating, going home to a Spartan apartment maintained by his doddering and hygiene-obsessed father, who like the chef pompously removes a cheesecloth to reveal his food, consisting of steamed ground cutlets of an unspecified meat. Oleg explodes. 'I don't want – goddamn it! – to eat steamed cutlets anymore ... I've told you a million times. [It's been] seven months [like this] ... Just once, make me a normal steak. Just once! Is that so hard? Do you want things to get ugly?' Oleg's professional awareness of the murky provenance of meat makes him extremely wary of eating ground meat (a preparation that partially conceals low quality), and his borderline childish outburst to his father echoes an earlier scene, in which a shady seller of wholesale beef offers Oleg some ground beef. Oleg replies testily to him, 'I've told you a hundred times, I don't deal in ground meat.' Khrzhanovsky and Sorokin seem to suggest that one peculiarity of a newly market-driven economy is that it renders comestibles into prized commodities, and yet is unable produce them in sufficient quantities because it continues to rely on a ruined infrastructure that previously did not reward productivity. In an article about the marginalisation and foreclosure of small organic farms in Poland by the EU's highly bureaucratised standards for meat inspection and dairy production and promotion of genetically-altered grains, the British organic farmer Sir Julian Rose noted that '[t]he EU has adopted the same efficiency approach to food as it has to autos and microchips ... Those who can produce the most are favored' (Rosenthal 2008). In *4*, Khrzhanovsky and Sorokin portray the ascendancy of a shadow economy of food production, one in which the trafficking in nearly expired, or genetically enhanced, foodstuffs becomes a routine necessity.

The subsequent episodes of the film explore the moral implications of the production of food and the reaping of profit from its twofold consumption, in the act of ingestion as well as purchasing. The second half of the film is primarily devoted to Marina's visit to the village in which she grew up, where her sister Zoya recently passed away and which also serves as the location of the round piglet farm referred to earlier. As it turns out, Marina is one of identical quadruplets, and her two remaining sisters still live in the village. The death of the twenty-two-year-old Zoya was as grotesque as it was freakishly accidental. She was involved in the handicraft of making a very limited line of marionette-like dolls that were highly prized by collectors. Any Russian viewer of the film would recognise in the dolls' puffy and porcine bodies a distinct resemblance to the puppets on the television show *Kukly (Dolls)*, in which bloated caricatures of Russian political leaders, members of the Duma or Russian parliament, and pop stars would engage in confrontations that were more often Punch and Judy slapsticks than incisive political satires. The dolls in the village were made through a unique and repellent process. The bodies of the dolls were shaped from dried-out masticated bread, chewed over by old women in the village who hired themselves out in an effort to supplement their meagre pensions. The toothless gums of the old women were ideal for the making of such pulp, and Zoya, a sculptor, had a talent for moulding the dolls' faces. She had choked when she had attempted to produce a 'chewie' [*miagkish*, lit., 'soft clump'] herself, her death representing a catastrophe for the business because of her unique ability in sculpting the dolls. During the drunken wake after her funeral, Zoya's addle-pated husband Marat insists that he can duplicate her technique, and falls asleep on a table in the workshop embracing the last four dolls she had made. He awakes to find them devoured by a pack of starved feral dogs, and shortly thereafter commits suicide when he realises that she had taken the secret of her technique with her. Marina abandons the village for an uncertain fate, possibly as a younger version of the elderly women in the village, Vladimir is framed by the police for a crime he didn't commit and sent to serve as a soldier in Chechnya as a partial commutation of his sentence, and Oleg dies in an automobile accident as a result of speaking distractedly on his mobile to a customer as he swerves to avoid a dog crossing the road.

Khrzhanovsky and Sorokin suggest that the food economy of the new Russia is a reflection of grotesquely reconfigured human relations. The director and writer also seem to have in mind Vaclav Havel's famous moral dictum that a society that treats its animals badly is not likely to follow the golden rule in human relations. Certainly the spectre of cannibalism never seems to be far from the idea of cloning in the film. The satirical image of odious fellow humans as pigs, whose offensiveness can be redeemed through their slaughter and consumption, has been suggestively explored by Peter Stallybrass and Allon White in their study of Bakhtinian subversion, *The Politics and Poetics of Transgression*. Stallybrass and White argued that representations of porcine physiology in medieval and Renaissance folklore serve the purpose of providing symbols for states of 'displaced abjection'. The body of the pig is the site of mediation between urban centres and what Stallybrass and White evocatively term 'the dark corners of the land' (Stallybrass and White 1986: 53, 39). Certainly the resemblance of the dolls to the rounded piglets hints that the nearby pig farm serves as a point of inspiration for the design of the dolls, which in the banquet scene hang like pink carcasses from brackets over the dinner table. During the moonshine-soaked wake for Zoya, one of the old women begins to dance with the head of a pig, asking Marina, 'Well, my little one [*dochka*, lit. 'daughter'], do you think my Bor'ka [Boris] is tasty?', to which Marina replies, 'Very!' In the dialect of the Vyatka region, *dochka* or 'daughter' can also be used to refer to a sow (Dal' 1978: 487). The kinship and zoological terms of this dialogue suggest that cannibalism represents the ultimate expression of the mutual exploitation of one relative by another. Such language also points to the collapse of the extended family, that former mainstay of quotidian decency against the casual cruelty and multiple indignities of Soviet life. The intimations of same-sex desire among the elderly women in this scene – which has some of them stripping and fondling each other's breasts – serve to remind the viewer of the significance of Marina's earlier statement from the scene in the bar, where she takes note of what she feels to be the newly aggressive gay presence in the Russian capital. Here, as in *Blue Lard*, the symbolic figure of the pig serves as a conceptual space in which the parameters of normative or 'traditional' intimacy are traduced, if not erased. Expanding some of the terms of Stallybrass and White's analysis into our discussion of this film, we can understand the porcine body as a representation of a cloacal axiology within the cultural realm, of a body politic that simultaneously devours and copulates with others like it – and therefore, as Baudrillard would reason, itself as well. The perception of cannibalism as a form of excretion in reverse, signalled by a fascination with the ingestion of the lower bodily strata, is an *idée fixe* of much of the unofficial folklore of the gulag and the Leningrad blockade during the World War II. One pre-war children's song has a man 'carrying a corpse's arse [R. *zad*]' in a basket, until the time he can steal a baby from the neighbours' cradle (Reid 2011: 354). Sorokin and Khrzhanovsky blend the autoerotic aspect of the porcine body with an anxiety about the sterility and the absence of reproduction, together with the evocation of paedophilia (hinted at in the round, pink bodies of both the unfinished dolls and cloned piglets, as well as in the childless village of the old women) that is a *locus classicus* of homophobia. The association of the colour '[light] blue' with 'lard' also moves us to consider a link between same-sex desire and porcine physiology, which appears as a leitmotif within both the film and the novel. Pier Paolo Pasolini made use of the portrayal of polymorphous porcine sexuality as a sly metaphor for same-sex desire in his 1969 film *Porcile* (*Pigsty*), in a storyline where a young scion of a family fortune scorns his fiancée for intimacy with pigs on his family estate. Yet for Pasolini, this metaphor serves primarily as a critique of post-war bourgeois heteronormativity in Europe. In *4* and Sorokin's *Blue Lard*, we are confronted with the something entirely different: the possibility of same-sex intimacy not as a rejection of the values of state power, but rather an embrace of them. Are we in fact better off in our understanding of Sorokin's novel if we interpret *goluboe salo* as 'gay lard'?

Contemplating disparate scenes in the film and in Sorokin's prose, we would have to answer this question in the affirmative. One of the most vivid moments of Khrzhanovsky's film is Marina's discovery of Marat's hanging body. We initially see the body indirectly, from its reflection in a mirror, blocked from Marina's view. As viewers, we make the discovery of the corpse by entering into its vantage point. As Marina tenderly caresses Marat's unfinished and flawed dolls, the pendulous movement of the frame suggests that the cinematographer is intimately 'piggybacking' on Marat's swinging body. The inert body of Marat 'views' Marina obliquely, from her reflection in a cracked mirror.

The corpse evokes the multiple images elsewhere in the film of suspended carcasses in slaughterhouses, and the unfinished and 'naked' dolls that hang puppet-like, and in a suggestive line formation, over the table during the wake for Zoya.

Figure 8.1 Marina's caress of the dolls, seen from a rocking mirror (4)

Figure 8.2 Hanging dolls (4)

Those dolls, like the naked manikins in the window of the shop that serves as the backdrop for Vladimir's arrest, are bathed in an odd pale blue light. For a reader of Sorokin's prose, these tableaux resonate with scenes of depersonalised or sublimated same-sex sexuality in his 1985 novel *The Queue*, and with one scene in his 2006 dystopian novel *Day of the Oprichnik* where a group of state security insiders have sex with each other in a 'caterpillar' formation, 'entwined in brotherly embraces' and climaxing with the realisation that '[they] have the wherewithal to delight one another, as well as to punish Russia's enemies'. As the narrator of that novel describes his post-coital lassitude, 'the seed moves from the tail of the *caterpillar* to its head, which symbolizes the eternal cycle of life and the renewal of our brotherhood' (Sorokin 2006: 189, 173). In his 2008 afterward to *The Queue*, Sorokin writes about the Soviet-era queue in terms that are suggestively similar to this scene of sexual congress, as a 'fantastic, many-headed monster' characterised by 'stirring shouts', 'dramatic confrontations' and a 'joyous trembling of the person at the head of the line' (Sorokin 2008a: 254). The multiplication of the same lies behind this symbol of the caterpillar as a line formation of humanity, of intimacy as an impassioned assertion of ideological homogeneity (which, in *Day of the Oprichnik*, is distinctly Eurasian in character) and xenophobia. In *4*, Sorokin and Khrzhanovsky explore the implications of this relentless disenfranchisement of the moral self, made possible by the multiform abjection of human agents, and their subsequent descent into polymorphous sexuality. With the disappearance among us of any sense of agency, gendered difference and 'legitimate strangeness', animals, clones, dolls, and gay men and women blend into a composite mirror image of exploited humanity. What emerges most clearly from these representations of human blending through what Kleist terms the 'infinite' consciousness of the puppet is that Sorokin and Khrzhanovsky conceptualise the industrialised production of identity in the terms of what they apparently regard as a queer erotics.

Yet by representing collectives as variations on acts of animalistic congress among members of the same sex, Sorokin and Khrzhanovsky inevitably reinscribe homophobia even as they critique the unsavory and often violent homosocial old-boy networks that represented the political elite in both the Soviet Union and the post-Soviet Russian Federation. In 'Clone Story', Baudrillard notes that cloning requires a 'dissect[ion] of the body into organs and functions . . . [an] analytical decomposition of the body' (Baudrillard 1994: 98). In what is demonstrably an explicit link to Baudrillard's essay, in his 2008 afterword to *The Queue* Sorokin describes the queue as an institution that 'dissected the [collective] body into pieces', thereby 'pacif[ying] and disciplin[ing] it' (Sorokin 2008a: 257). In the post-Soviet Russia of the film, the purpose of cloning is no longer simply to guarantee ideological uniformity, but also to bolster demographically a society which is unable to feed itself through ethical means, and which is also hobbled by near-zero population growth. Taking a cue from Baudrillard, Khrzhanovsky and Sorokin document a crisis in the notion of what it means to be human, precipitated by the breakdown of heteronormative relations, as well as by disturbing images of the mammalian body's dismemberment. On a level of causality, what do the bleak, Tarkovskian scenes of post-industrial squalor that we see in *4* have to do with Marina's early observation in the film that Moscow is teeming with gays? In real terms, the answer is: nothing. Yet in this one instance in the film, Khrzhanovsky and Sorokin fail to make the necessary distinction between reality and one character's fantasmatic assertion about it.

Although Sorokin wrote the libretto for *Rosenthal's Children* a year after he finished his work for Khrzhanovsky's film, it represents in a condensed form many of the the ideas more fully developed in *4*. In contrast to *4*, homophobic motifs are entirely absent from *Rosenthal's Children*. Nevertheless, the representation of cloning as a form of debased being complements the treatment of 'queered' totemic copies in Khrzhanovsky's film, as metonyms for sterility and the divesting of personal identity. The figure of the German geneticist Rosenthal makes an actual appearance in the opera, and the details about his defection from Nazi Germany and his subsequent project are essentially the same as those told by the character of Vladimir in the film. The resurrected composers are by-products of a Stalinist project designed to bring about a 'mass doubling of the heroes of [the] country — a bridge to the communist future!'. Taking its cue from discredited Lysenkoist genetics, the project's goal was to pass on and multiply the invaluable and genetically tagged legacy of Stakhanovite labour onto subsequent generations, 'dividing and fragmenting into billions of the same' ('*delias' i drobias' na milliardy podobnykh*' [Sorokin 2005: 97, 99]). But Rosenthal turns his back on the prospect of a 'mass doubling' of heroes of socialist labour, deciding instead to clone, on a strictly one-time basis, personages from the pantheon of eighteenth- and nineteenth-century music such as Verdi, Wagner, Tchaikovsky, Mussorgsky and Mozart. As in the film, the Soviet state forgets about the 'doubles', effectively abandoning them. Two years after the Soviet collapse and a year after the death of Rosenthal, whom they regarded as their father, the composers are reduced to busking in Moscow railway stations, where Mozart falls in love with a prostitute named Tania. He takes her away from her enraged pimp, and the two get married. Mussorgsky proposes a send-off toast for Mozart and Tania before they set out on their honeymoon to Crimea. The cloned composers and Tania drink the toast from a bottle of vodka poisoned by the pimp. Days later, an emergency room doctor tells Mozart he is the only one who has survived, because of the immunity to poisoning he obtained from the mercury that Cosima Mozart and her lover mixed in his food during the time he composed his *Requiem*. The doctor explains that although Mozart succumbed to that poisoning, his genes retained a memory of it that resulted in an immunity in his 'second' life. The opera ends with a tableau of Mozart lying in his hospital bed, hearing the voices of Tania and the other composers from the other world, and 'attempt[ing] to play' a flute (Sorokin 2005: 134).

By alternately mocking and following the beliefs of Lysenkoist genetic theory, Sorokin in *Rosenthal's Children* presents a world where memory is encoded in somatic rather than cultural or social experiences. The principled and grand opposition in musical aesthetics that we think about whenever we hear the names of Tchaikovsky and Mussorgsky together is completely absent in the interaction between these two versions of the composers, and even when Wagner and Verdi speak their German and Italian, the statements fall into the same sump of melodramatic utterances. The final gesture of the opera, which has the bed-ridden Mozart picking up his flute after despairingly singing that 'you have all departed forever, and I am alone in this world', suggests that he, unlike Tamino in *Die Zauberflöte*, will not necessarily be able to use music as a talisman against spiritual and physical danger. Like all the cloned composers, Mozart retains only a murky memory of his cultural identity and music. His body, however, does retain a vivid memory of his former life, and resiliently 'learns' from an earlier failed attempt to save itself. In Khrzhanovsky's *4*, two requiem scenes become remarkable by their juxtaposition. The scenes of keening during Zoya's funeral and, later in the film, over the dog-mangled bodies of the last of her dolls are disturbingly similar, suggesting that the women are following the Russian Orthodox tradition of ritualised mourning in a manner that makes no distinction between the body of the deceased and badly damaged manufactured goods. We are made to understand that a nuanced memory of the past is essential for the elegiac mode, which these women conspicuously lack.

If an awareness of the stadial nature of that past is murky – if a cultural identity is dissolved, or if the destruction of artifacts is reflexively equated with actual deaths – then the traditional view of the elegiac becomes impossible. The new elegiac mode must then be located in what Baudrillard describes as the very generalised awareness that 'there is no possibility of return to an original being'; it must now become focused on the breakdown of the body rather than on the death of any particular, and presumably unique, individual. In *4*, the routinised spectacle of the mammalian body's dismemberment serves to enhance a sense of zoological continuum between humans and livestock. In *4*, the butcher is the new social engineer, aware of the possibilities in the reconfiguration of old bodies and the constitution of new and artificial ones; in Desiatnikov's opera, the geneticist is a similar kind of trafficker in what Baudrillard refers to as 'cuttings' of human beings, a facilitator of cultural amnesia who believes that genius can be resurrected thanks to bones having 'memory' (*'no kosti beregut/ Pamiat' svoiu'* [Sorokin 2005: 98]). In the Darwinist world of Putin's Russia that we see in much of Sorokin's work, immortality is achieved at the expense of individual autonomy, by rendering people into linked isomorphic units within a mass of humanity – by placing them, as Nikolai Fyodorov puts it, in a state of quasi-erotic closeness, if not inseparability, with both the living and the dead (Fyodorov 1982: 129).[2] In *Rosenthal's Children* and the screenplay for Khrzhanovsky's film, Sorokin conjoins Baudrillard's understanding of cloning – as an act that is predicated upon a cognitive dismantling of the self into its constituent elements of personal identity and belief, as a prerequisite for reproduction – with Fyodorov's curious notion about the prospect of the mass resurrection of the dead as a decisive blow to the egoism that is so characteristic of modernity. The manifestations of evacuated personal agency that we see in *Rosenthal's Children* are, in 4, cast in the form of failed heterosexual relations, in an erotics of sameness that is coded as homosexual.

To be sure, Khrzhanovsky and Sorokin do explore both the implications of and possible alternatives to this relentless multiplication of sameness, and at certain moments endeavour to see it outside of a homophobic frame of reference. Certainly the language of sexual desire in Sorokin's novels *Blue Lard* and *Marina's Thirtieth Love* (Sorokin 2008b) seems to project the sense of formulaic generalised eroticism that is highly representative of what Steven Marcus, in his study *The Other Victorians: A Study of Sexuality and Pornography in Mid-Nineteenth Century England*, terms 'pornotopia', a realm of compulsive routine and reductive identity (Marcus 1966). Sorokin's occasional portrayal of such repetition through the lens of same-sex desire is not always a gesture of homophobic *épatage*; at other times in his work, these motifs are not coterminous with desire itself, but rather with what Baudrillard terms the 'simulacra' of desire. In his 1983 novel *Marina's Thirtieth Love* (Sorokin 2008b), Sorokin portrays the eponymous heroine's exploration of her lesbian identity as a refuge from pressures to join an obnoxious Soviet elite. That novel ends with a prolix and self-important lecture delivered by another character about the moral necessity of an ideologically correct Andropov-era Soviet world-view, which shockingly drowns out Marina's distinctive voice in a way that deliberately evokes Tolstoy's displacement of his characters at the end of *War and Peace* by a tendentious essay about the philosophy of history. The last glimpse we have of Marina in this novel is of her proceeding into the deadening prospect of a heteronormative life, as she hews to the social conservatism and official ideology of a stagnation-era Soviet Union.

In the end, however, Sorokin and Khrzhanovsky cannot seem to help reproducing the homophobia that constitutes (as Lee Edelman points out in *No Future: Queer Theory and the Death Drive*) the basis of Baudrillard's anxious meditations about the death-drive implicit in non-reproductive sexuality, which purportedly leads to the end of legitimate strangeness within the social sphere (Edelman 2004: 61–6). Seen from the perspective of the homophobic subtext of some of Baudrillard's work, it is perhaps less than surprising that Vladimir, the one character in the film who enters into the realm of same-sex intimacy, marches off to his probable demise in a military conflict. Yet if this film has anything valuable to tell us, it is that the representation of political fictions does not, in itself, constitute an endorsement of them. As Leo Bersani and Adam Phillips put it in their discussion of Patrice Leconte's 2003 film *Confidences trop intimes*, we exist in two realms: ourselves and the stories that we tell about those selves (Bersani and Phillips 2008: 5–7). The possibilities for escaping the constriction of the bourgeois ego exist within the narrow space between those two realms. In the case of *4*, the stories that get told – whether they are the fairy tales that Oleg reads at home, or the dangerously unreflective quasi-religiosity of the women in the village – are copies that have lost what Walter Benjamin famously referred to as the 'aura of the original'. Much like the coy and unstable narratives that Vladimir, Marina and Oleg tell about themselves, the film's tropes about same-sex desire are not always congruent with desire itself, which has evacuated itself from the world of the film. In the storytelling scene at the bar, we find certain potentialities that struggle against the film's homophobic tropes. Let us not forget that the transformative 'blue' – or 'gay' – lard in Sorokin's novel of the same title comes from the bodies of resurrected Russian storytellers, or writers. As a form of queer – that is, alternative – intimacy, storytelling in *4* at certain times comes very close to what Leo Bersani, in one essay about new forms of same-sex intimacy, describes as a model of 'impersonal narcissism' that 'can break down the defensive formation of the self-congratulatory ego', leading to 'a fundamental restructuring of the social' (Bersani 2010: 34). The realm of the ego – what Russians call *sobstvennost'*, denoting both the habitus of the autonomous individuals and their overweening self-perception as entitled property holders – is, in a final analysis of Sorokin's and Khrzhanovsky's film, the realm of the unreal, or the copy. Like Bersani, the filmmaker and the novelist believe that the genuine self is entirely a matter of exploration, or 'grating nonsense'.

NOTES

1. See especially Ryklin's comments about Sorokin's early work, in the essay 'Ostorozhno, okrasheno!' (Ryklin 1992: 99–101). Ryklin places Sorokin's work in the context of the Moscow Conceptualists' desire to demystify the shibboleths of the Soviet experience, drawing particular attention to the 'traumatic depersonalization' (100) that often underlay it. Ryklin wrote the piece in 1988, during what was arguably the peak of the movement.
2. The statement is from the collection of Fyodorov's writings entitled *The Philosophy of the General Task* [*Filosofiia obshchego dela*], which was edited and published posthumously. The editors of this edition point out that this section of the collection was written in the late 1870s.

WORKS CITED

Baudrillard, Jean (1994), *Simulacra and Simulation*, Ann Arbor: University of Michigan Press.
Bersani, Leo (2010), *Is the Rectum a Grave? And Other Essays*, Chicago: University of Chicago Press.
Bersani, Leo and Adam Phillips (2008), *Intimacies*, Chicago: University of Chicago Press.

'Chetvertka s pliusami i minusami [A Group of Four with Plusses and Minuses]' (2005), *Novaya Gazeta*, 29 August, <http://www.novayagazeta.ru/arts/26467.html> (last accessed 27 January 2016).
Dal', Vladimir (1978), *Tolkovyi slovar' zhivogo velikorusskogo yazyka. Tom I*, Moscow: 'Russkii yazyk'.
Edelman, Lee (2004), *No Future: Queer Theory and the Death Drive*, Durham, NC: Duke University Press.
Etkind, Alexander (2013), *Warped Mourning: Stories of the Undead in the Land of the Unburied*, Stanford: Stanford University Press.
Fyodorov, Nikolai (1982), *Sochineniia*, ed. A. V. Gulyga, Moscow: 'Mysl'.
Fyodorov, Nikolai (2015), 'Muzei, ego smysl i naznachenie [The Museum: Its Sense and Meaning]', in: Boris Grois (ed.), *Russkii kosmizm. Antologiia*, Moscow: Ad Marginam, pp. 32–137.
Kleist, Heinrich von (1982), 'On the Marionette Theater', tr. Christian-Albrecht Gollub, in A. Leslie Willson (ed.), *German Romantic Criticism: Novalis, Schlegel, Schleiermacher and Others*, New York: Continuum, pp. 238–44.
Lipovetsky, Mark (2005), 'Of Clones and Crones', <http://www.kinokultura.com/reviews/R10-05chetyre-1.html> (last accessed 27 January 2016).
Marcus, Steven (1966), *The Other Victorians: A Study of Sexuality and Pornography in Mid-Nineteenth Century England*, New York: Basic Books.
Reid, Anna, *Leningrad* (2011), *The Epic Siege of World War II, 1941–1944*, New York: Walker & Co.
Rosenthal, Elisabeth (2008) 'Old Ways, New Pain for Farms in Poland', *New York Times* 14 April, <http://www.nytimes.com/2008/04/04/world/europe/04poland.html?pagewanted=print> (last accessed 27 January 2016).
Ryklin, Mikhail (1991), 'Soznanie i vlast': sovetskaia model'', in S. A. Korolev (ed.), *Biurokratiia i obshchestvo*, Moscow: Filosofskoe obshchestvo SSSR, pp. 28–59.
Ryklin, Mikhail (1992), 'Ostorozhno, okrasheno!' in Mikhail Ryklin, *Terrorologiki*, Moscow: 'Eidos', pp. 97–107.
Scarry, Elaine (1987), *The Body in Pain: The Making and Unmaking of the World*, Oxford: Oxford University Press.
Sorokin, Vladimir (2002), *Goluboe salo [Blue Lard]. Roman*, 6th edn, Moscow: Ad Marginem.
Sorokin, Vladimir (2005), *4*, Moscow: Zakharov.
Sorokin, Vladimir (2006), *Day of the Oprichnik*, tr. Jamey Gambrell, New York: Farrar, Straus & Giroux.
Sorokin, Vladimir (2008a), 'Afterword. Farewell to the Queue', tr. Jamey Gambrell, in *The Queue*, tr. Sally Baird, New York: NYRB Books, pp. 253–63.
Sorokin, Vladimir (2008b), *Tridtsataia liubov' Mariny [Marina's Thirtieth Love]*, Moscow: Astrel.
Stallybrass, Peter and Allon White (1986), *The Politics and Poetics of Transgression*, Ithaca: Cornell University Press.
Turkina, Olesya and Viktor Mazin (2006), 'Tikhomirov and Yufit: Energetic Men', tr. Thomas Campbell, in *Tikhomirov and Yufit: An Energetic Pair*, Moscow: Great Print, pp. 1–3.
Wakamiya, Lisa Ryoko (2013), 'Vladimir Sorokin's Abject Bodies: Clones and the Crisis of Subjecthood', in Tine Roesen and Dirk Uffelmann (eds), *Vladimir Sorokin's Languages*, Bergen: University of Bergen Press, pp. 230–44.

PART III

Carnal Histories

CHAPTER 9

The Touch of History: A Phenomenological Approach to 1960s Czech Cinema

David Sorfa

In this chapter, I trace the way in which certain ideas stemming from socialist realism were developed during the Czechoslovak New Wave by placing the human body at the intersection of historical necessity and individual freedom. I concentrate on three films from the mid-1960s by František Vláčil and Karel Kachyňa which exemplify an aesthetic tradition of *ostranenie* by highlighting the screen as itself an object of perception but also placing a moral weight on the representation of the human body. These films reflect a broader aesthetic style characterised by shallow focus, close-ups and symmetrical composition as well as a thematic preoccupation with touch and the surface of bodies and objects in Czechoslovak cinema of the 1960s. While the reasons for the emergence of such an aesthetic are difficult to isolate, clearly the importance of FAMU (the Prague Film Academy) as the central pedagogic institution for almost all filmmakers at this time, as well as the dominance of the Barrandov Film Studios in Prague, should not be overlooked (Szczepanik 2013). However, I wish here to concentrate on the importance of phenomenology as the 'dominant philosophical school' (Tucker 2000: 10) in Czechoslovakia, and in particular to consider the work on history and the body by the most influential Czech phenomenologist, Jan Patočka. I further examine the metaphorical use of 'touch' in film theory to move from its physical to emotional meaning, where images of touch are often said to result in spectators being emotionally 'touched'.[1] Kachyňa and Vláčil's films present touch in relation to Christianity, which figures prominently but ambiguously in the work of both directors. Religion functions as a form of resistance to totalitarianism while itself dictating oppressive norms of behaviour and thought. These Czechoslovak films explore individual freedom and human contact in the face of impersonal historical events.

Filmmaking in Czechoslovakia entered into a complex relationship with the Soviet conception of socialist realism, which saw literature and the arts as primarily instrumental in bringing about changes in ways of thinking but also as reflecting proletarian experience. Andrei Zhdanov exhorted the All-Union Congress of Soviet Writers in 1934 to 'Actively help to remold the mentality of people in the spirit of socialism' (1935: 24), and claimed that 'Never before has there been a literature which has based the subject matter of its works on the life of the working class and peasantry and their fight for socialism' (1935: 17). This socialist art was 'of one flesh and blood with socialist construction', and the 'engineers of human souls' would go on to 'remould the mentality of their readers' (1935: 23) with 'both feet firmly planted on the basis of real life' (1935: 21). This rhetoric of engineering and of flesh is strongly tied to an idea of the absolute reality of the body as the central figure in Soviet art and politics. However, as Peter Hames explains, this reality is one that does not exist in the world out there, but in the idealist space of Communist Party theory:

> Put at its simplest level, reality is defined by the Party. In practice, this gave rise to the 'theory of lack of conflict', in which 'positive' heroes must, at least morally, triumph over 'negative characters'. The enforcement of this requirement gave rise to a standardised plot in which an inevitable happy ending was preceded by nominal conflicts between 'negative' and 'positive' characters. (Hames 2005: 30)

Herbert Eagle argues, 'Characters represent their value systems clearly, and conflicts are seen in unambiguous terms . . . The official socialist realist system . . . encouraged the production of grossly distorted representations of actual life and actual history' (quoted in Hames 2005: 30). As a reaction to these 'distortions', it is clear that during the liberalisation of both politics and aesthetics in 1960s Czechoslovakia, filmmakers evinced a particular interest in the 'real', accompanied by a sense that the representation of reality or truth was not an easy or simple thing to achieve. In the films that I discuss here it is the individual human body that becomes the locus of each film's meaning and stands as an expression of a broader history, but also as a site of resistance to the totalising force of this history. The individual's body, and by extension their mind, is both a result and a refusal of history.

The three feature films I consider here are by directors from what Hames calls the first wave of Czech directors; that is, those who started making films in the 1950s and whose work achieved a certain maturity in the 1960s when the films of the better-known 'second' New Wave came to international attention.[2] I will examine František Vláčil's *Marketa Lazarová* (1967), voted the 'best Czech film ever made' by Czech film critics in 1998 (Hames 2009: 3), and two films by Karel Kachyňa, *Kočár do Vídně* (*Coach to Vienna*, 1966) and *Noc nevěsty* (*Night of the Bride* / *The Nun's Night*, 1967), with particular reference to the ways in which these films depict the body and its touch, and how the cinematography in these films emphasises the texture of the image itself. While these second wave films are also part of a haptic tendency in Czechoslovak cinema during the 1960s, I argue that this was not merely a youthful experimental quirk but rather a more general cinematic style which simultaneously spoke to and subverted the claims of socialist realism.

One of the effects of what we might call the haptic-phenomenological style is to foreground not only the supposed bodily reality of diegetic characters but also to bring attention to the actual process of viewing the film. It is important to avoid the easy politics of 'alienation' associated with Bertolt Brecht's *Verfremdungseffekt*, understood as a 'technique aimed at jolting the consciousness of his auditors and making them critically aware of contradiction in society' (Mitchell 1974: 74). It is now commonplace to designate any cinematic technique that highlights any conventions of representation, most often the 'breaking of the fourth wall' by the mannered look to camera, as somehow intrinsically politically progressive or subversive.[3] However, such self-reflexive techniques are very often used for comic effect or to instil in the viewer a sense of camaraderie and to therefore emotionally suture them more fully into the fictional world of the film. It seems more apposite to return to Viktor Shklovsky's prior term *ostranenie*,[4] literally a 'putting to the side', or more figuratively a 'making strange' (Mitchell 1974: 75). Shklovsky sees *ostranenie* in aesthetic rather than political terms, and writes:

> art exists that one may recover the sensation of life; it exists to make one feel things, to make the stone *stony*. The purpose of art is to impart the sensation of things as they are perceived and not as they are known. The technique of art is to make objects 'unfamiliar', to make forms difficult, to increase the difficulty and length of perception because the process of perception is an aesthetic end in itself and must be prolonged. *Art is a way of experiencing the artfulness of an object: the object is not important.* (Shklovsky 2004 [1917]: 16)

Thus the reflexive technique, rather than forcing its spectator to confront the ideological contradictions of their situation, allows that viewer to experience their own perception of the art object or film. It is this awareness of aesthetic experience that, for Shklovsky, is art. This is, in many ways, a quintessentially phenomenological position since phenomenology is a philosophy of experience as such, and it is experience that is the central concern of the films under discussion here. At the same time, I do not wish to deny the political content or intention of these same films, but I am hesitant about claiming that *ostranenie* as a technique is inevitably politically subversive.

The 1960s in Czechoslovakia ushered in a 'de-Stalinisation' of communist politics and culminated in Alexander Dubček's declaration of 'socialism with a human face' in April 1968 (Sayer 1998: 15; Golan 1971: 275–329). During this period cinema was invigorated both by new young directors such as Jan Švankmajer and Juraj Herz and by a more experienced generation, exemplified by Vláčil and Kachyňa, who both strove to represent a social reality beyond the orthodoxies of socialist realism. Vláčil and Kachyňa were able to make films that criticised certain forms of communist politics which would not have been possible in the 1950s, and I explore the way in which the politics of the time emerge through the cinematic stylistics of cinematic phenomenology.

PHENOMENOLOGY IN A CZECH CONTEXT

Philosophical phenomenology has an interesting history related to Czechoslovakia. Edmund Husserl (1859–1938), perhaps the central figure in the history and development of phenomenology, was himself born in Prossnitz in Moravia, then part of the Austrian Empire (the town is now called Prostějov in the east of the Czech Republic), and was mentored during part of his university education by T. G. Masaryk, who would go on to become the first president of Czechoslovakia on its establishment as a separate state in 1918 (Kohák 1989: 8–15). History is, of course, littered with such coincidences, but coincidence is central to Miroslav Petřiček's argument in 'The Meeting of Surrealism and Phenomenology in Magical Prague', (1996) in which he identifies the year 1935 as particularly important because of the 'objective chance' that brought both André Breton and Edmund Husserl to Prague to give lectures within a few months of each other. Petřiček singles out a number of other intellectual currents that seem to coalesce in Prague in 1935 and claims that 'at this moment, surrealism, phenomenology, logical positivism and structuralism, if not coincide, then at the very least touch [dotýkají] each other' (Petřiček 1996: 106: my translation). Here the metaphor of touch as communication and exchange explicitly connects art and philosophy. It is perhaps also an uncanny coincidence that one of Husserl's last students was from Czechoslovakia. Jan Patočka (1907–77) went on to become the most important phenomenological thinker in Czech philosophy, but was also one of the three main signatories of Charter 77, a critique of the communist regime's totalitarian tactics published in January 1977 during the radical foment of the late 1970s.[5] This act of defiance against a totalitarian regime resulted in Patočka's death when he died of a brain haemorrhage after extensive police interrogation on 13 March 1977 (Kohák 1989: 3; Tucker 2000: 87–8). The phenomenologist's brutal death is not separate from his philosophy, and it is the experience of violent touch that will be central in the argument to come.

Fundamentally, phenomenology is a philosophy of experience and 'consists to a large extent of an individual examination of consciousness' (Tucker 2000: 10). In his accessible introduction to what he calls 'experimental phenomenology', Don Ihde identifies four major stages in the phenomenological method: (1) the *epoché* (bracketing); (2) the identification of the immediate (or *apodictic*); (3) the equalisation of all immediate phenomena; and (4) the seeking out of structural or invariant features of the phenomena (Ihde 1986: 32–9). While it is not necessary to detail each of the steps here, we should note that to perform the *epoché* is 'to step back from our ordinary ways of looking, to set aside our usual assumptions regarding things' (Ihde 1986: 32). We could understand this as something like the formalist strategy of *ostranenie* – the making strange of the world, although for the formalists this was an inherent property of the object rather than an action on the part of the observer.

Patočka's phenomenological thinking was particularly concerned with the body of the perceiving subject, which he presented in a series of lectures in Prague in 1968–9 that survive through his students' notes and have been published as *Body, Community, Language, World* (1998). Patočka engages with the place of the body as the problematic core of subjectivity and objectivity in the history of philosophy and, following Heidegger, argues that we 'relate to ourselves by relating to the other, to more and more things and ultimately to the universe as such, so locating ourselves in the world' (Patočka 1998: 31). In essence, his argument is that the subject only ever exists in relation to the world, but that nevertheless, as Tucker points out, the phenomenological method of understanding such an existence 'embodies an individualist mentality, holding to one's personal convictions against enforced ideologies' (Tucker 2000: 10). Patočka argues for an existential humanism which, in the face of death, strives for an authentic truth beyond merely finding oneself in the world (he terms this 'acceptance'), or striving to make one's way through the world, particularly through labour ('defense') (Patočka 1998: 148). Without wanting to sacrifice the intricacy of Patočka's thinking, it may suffice to say here that it is in the authentic and individual experience of the world, both as a body and as mind, that Patočka sees the possibility of freedom.

TOUCH AND HAPTICS

I wish to highlight the use of the word 'touch' within phenomenology. Phenomenology is a way of explaining reality given the insight that this reality is available to us only through our experience of it (Husserl 1960: 12–13; Ihde 1986: 29–32; Sorfa 2014). It is through a bracketing and a 'reduction' that phenomenology attempts to focus on exactly what it is that we experience when we interact – or correlate – with the world. Phenomenology uses the idea of touch as a metaphor for direct communication between reality and ourselves. Touch is a symbol of true apprehension. In 'The "Natural World" and Phenomenology', Patočka writes that the 'main orientedness within the tactile region, however, is that which consists in the subjectivity of touch – that in it we feel both the thing and ourselves, our body' (1989a: 254; see also Barker 2009: 19). Patočka highlights the double nature of touch so that when we touch something or somebody we not only feel that which we touch, but also experience ourselves touching. This self-reflexive nature of experience is fundamental to phenomenology.

Writing in the 1960s, Susan Sontag identifies a 'new sensibility' in which 'Sensations, feelings, the abstract forms and styles of sensibility count' and argues that the 'basic unit for contemporary art is not the idea, but the analysis of and extension of sensations' (2001: 300). The idea of touch and understanding in film theory has been developed most notably by Vivian Sobchack in *The Address of the Eye: A Phenomenology of Film Experience* (1992) and Laura U. Marks in *The Skin of Film: Intercultural Cinema, Embodiment, and the Senses* (2000). The latter explains:

> Film is grasped not solely by an intellectual act but by the complex perception of the body as a whole. This view of perception implies an attitude towards the object, in this case a film, not as something that must be analysed and deciphered in order to deliver its meaning but as something that means in itself. (Marks 2000: 145)

It may not be entirely clear what Marks might mean here by 'means in itself', especially if we consider the importance of 'intentionality' for phenomenology; that is, Husserl's insistence that consciousness can only ever be a consciousness *of something* (Husserl in Welton 1999: 90). Nevertheless, it is important to note that it is the film itself as an object of perception, as well as a record of experience, that is foregrounded by this phenomenological approach. Jennifer M. Barker develops the work of Marks and Sobchack and sets out a haptic manifesto for film analysis:

> I will supplant traditional film theory's focus on such things as point-of-view shots, exchanged glances, and relationships as they are defined by a web of gazes with a feel for touch and movement, temperatures and textures, and the ways that materiality permeates the film experience. Rather than dwell in and on films' *visual and visible* patterns of difference and repetition, I attempt to put my finger on the *tactile and tangible* patterns and structures of significance. (Barker 2009: 25)

While this is a useful directing of our attention when viewing films, it does seem tendentious to argue that there is a way of accessing the 'tactile and tangible' in cinema *without* the 'visual and visible'. Tactility in cinematic experience surely must always reach us metaphorically – perhaps synaesthetically – through our sight. While Barker's sensitive and detailed analyses are often powerful, I am less convinced by a rather too easy move from physical, tactile 'touch' to the emotional state of 'being touched'. In a discussion of the image of skin in *Repulsion* (Roman Polanski, 1965), *Eraserhead* (David Lynch, 1977) and *Hiroshima mon amour* (Alain Resnais, 1959), Barker writes:

> the skin conceals and reveals, protects and exposes not only our innards but also our emotional states and our personal histories. It is the surface through which we experience and express feelings, of both physical and emotional varieties. Thus, when we're too easily insulted or hurt, we're said to be 'thin-skinned', and when nothing affects us at all we're called 'callous'. When the world has touched us too cruelly, we are said to be 'scarred' for life. It is the mingling of corporeality, emotion, and human history on the surface of the skin that concerns [Resnais's film]. (2009: 57)

Barker goes on to present a compelling reading of *Hiroshima mon amour*, but I want to highlight the explicit slippage between the physicality of the tactile and the emotional metaphors of 'being touched', in the sense of being touched in an emotional way. We must be careful not to allow metaphors such as this to do too much thinking for us. However, there remains the danger of taking the light patterns which resemble physical touch on-screen and reading these literally as emotional touches. It may, of course, be the case that some filmmakers may explicitly use techniques of extreme close-ups, shallow focus and a lingering on eyes, hands and the surface of the skin as metaphors for character emotions, but this does not imply that there is any natural move from seeing a representation of touch to feeling a corresponding emotion. Touch is not an automatic objective correlative of emotion. With these caveats around generalising too quickly in mind, I would like to move on to a discussion of the films that are our focus.

MARKETA LAZAROVÁ: AN ALLEGORY OF STATE, RELIGION AND FREEDOM

> Husserl became involved with the problem of the spirit of Europe, its roots, its present condition, and its future possibilities. He believed firmly in Europe's special, even privileged, mission in [*sic*] behalf of all humankind . . . What makes Europe special is . . . the fact that reason constitutes the central axis of its history. (Patočka 1989b: 223)

František Vláčil (1924–99) made a number of important Czech films, beginning with *Holubice* (*The White Dove*) in 1960 and ending with *Mág* (*The Magus*) in 1987. However, he is best known for his historical trilogy *Ďáblova past* (*The Devil's Trap*, 1961), *Marketa Lazarová* (1967) and *Údolí včel* (*Valley of the Bees*, 1967). The three films are 'deliberate attempts to resurrect the psychology of a past age and deal with the tragic outcomes of cultural and ideological conflict' (Hames 2000: 257) and all deal particularly with religious dogma and its impact on individual lives.

In *The Devil's Trap*, a sixteenth-century miller is accused of witchcraft, while in *Valley of the Bees* a young man dedicates himself to the crusading order of Teutonic Knights in the thirteenth century. It is, however, the 'visionary and barbaric qualities' (Hames 2000: 257) of *Marketa Lazarová*, also set in the 1200s, that have been particularly praised by critics. The film is adapted from Vladislav Vančura's 1931 novel and details the kidnap of Marketa (Magda Vášáryová) by the Lazar family's rival clan, the Kozlíks. This story is embedded in a complex network of other narratives, including the push to unify the Bohemian lands under the rule of a single monarch and a complex allegorical tale of incest and paganism, which echoes the movement from savagery to reason. However, *Marketa Lazarová* places its emphasis on 'psychological and economic realities' and depicts 'a world in which the dominant emotion was fear and in which pagan myths provided a potent source for "explanation"' (Hames 2004: 153). The film is overwhelming in its representation of historical reality, but that representation is heavily stylised and the spectator's position emphasised.

Vláčil's background in art history and aesthetics, unusual for any filmmakers in 1950s and 1960s Czechoslovakia, has him take a particular interest in the force of the visual. He says, in an interview at *Marketa Lazarová*'s 1969 Cannes debut:

> Film is primarily a visual thing. Even though painting and graphic art are something else, they are also concerned with composition, the arrangement of pictures. Films have to apply many of the same principles. The placement of a character in the picture, for instance, determines his position in the dramatic situation. In addition, in contrast to the kind of picture one hangs on the wall, films have a kinetic aspect. The ideal is – well, how to put it – let's say that a picture has a tremendous advantage compared to literature: it is internationally comprehensible. There is no need to translate or interpret it. So the ideal would be to make a film in such a way that one wouldn't have to dub it or supply subtitles. (Liehm 1974: 172)

Vláčil's claim is that the experience of the film itself should precede any particular concern with narrative or interpretation. This is an attitude that particularly inflects the phenomenological character of *Marketa Lazarová*. Vláčil's sense that the film should present an 'experience' of the past rather than merely a representation of it is crucial. He says:

> Whenever I watched a historical film, I always felt as if I were seeing contemporary people all dressed up in historical costumes. I wanted to understand them, see through the eyes of their lives, their feelings, their desires – in short, I wanted to drop back seven centuries. (Liehm 1974: 175)

Marketa Lazarová is an attempt to see 'through the eyes of their lives' and the film formally attempts to give the audience an experience rather than a representation, to show rather than tell.

Marketa has been promised to the Church, and the film's major conflict is between a prior paganism and an encroaching Christianity which is a harbinger both of civilisation and of stultification. Vláčil makes an explicit connection between the negative role of Christianity and the development of socialism in Czechoslovakia, a particularly forthright opinion to hold publicly in the year following the Warsaw Pact invasion of Prague in August 1968. He reflects:

> Doesn't it seem to you that the new social principles that they have been trying to assert for the past fifty years are based on dogmas and mysticism to those of Christianity? The similarity is striking. Recently I've come to feel that socialist thinking has in fact stopped developing, and turned into a religion, in which dogmas and principles are untouchable. If you take a poke at them, you are a heretic. The historical material in my films occasionally makes me realize that it is a much better way to disclose contemporary problems. (Interviewed in Liehm 1974: 175–6)

Marketa Lazarová is clearly, then, an explicit allegory of the contemporary Czech state. As in the mid-twelfth century, Christianity is the repressive force, so socialism becomes a similar agent of stable suffocation in the twentieth.

On a visual and aural level the film exemplifies some of the techniques of cinematic phenomenology. For a film about which so many claims for realism have been made, *Marketa* uses many cinematic strategies (close-ups, shallow focus and, especially, obscuring elements in shot foregrounds) and obviously metaphorical images that highlight the filmed nature of the action. This formalism throws us into the world of our experience of the film that works to embed us into the film world in a way that could not be achieved through standard continuity editing and conventional narrative filming. The film begins in darkness with Zdeněk Liška's abrasive choral soundtrack, which presents a sound ancient in its hymn-like nature but resolutely modernist in

Figure 9.1 *Marketa Lazarová*: the hawk through the branches

its repetitive atonality. We see a snow-covered landscape, empty until a pack of wolves comes hurtling across the screen.

The next shot is of a hawk seen through a tangle of branches, and this foregrounding of the subjectivity of the viewer becomes one of *Marketa*'s defining aesthetic traits. The viewer is offered a point of view that is embroiled in the diegetic world. We cannot see the hawk as clearly as we would like since the world is in our line of sight.

The title of the film appears across a toweringly blank snowscape, and the dual font used here – 'Marketa' in gothic lettering and 'LAZAROVÁ' in a contemporary san serif – reiterates the sense that we are entering two times simultaneously – the 1960s and the medieval age. The film explicitly doubles its historical place.

A group of travellers make their way along a rough track and our view is once again obscured by branches. Clearly there is someone waiting in ambush for them and the wolves and the hawk prefigure the Kozlík clan who attack the Saxon travellers. As the travellers are decimated, one of their group, Kristián (Vlastimil Harapes), runs into the snow and is pursued by Mikoláš (František Velecký) on horseback. Throughout this sequence, point-of-view shots, most markedly the view of the rider on the horse, work to metaphorically place the viewer in the action of the melée. The helpless Kristián is quickly captured, but on their return to the abandoned wagons the Kozlíls find that old Lazar (Michal Kožuch) is now picking over the spoils. Lazar cravenly begs for his life as the background behind Mikoláš becomes brighter and brighter and we see what might be his mystical vision of Lazar's daughter running in silhouette with the setting sun behind her.

The camera then cuts to a close-up of Marketa's exposed breasts as she cradles a wild dove in her hands. This unanchored vision of Marketa – it is unclear when or where or even whether this is taking place – foreshadows her kidnap by the Kozlíks and her eventual rape by Mikoláš. Marketa's body stands at the crossroads between pagan desire and Christian asceticism. The film presents the pagan world as a Hobbesian one in which personal inclination trumps social expectation, but with the concomitant loss of the rule of law, which means that life is cheap and violence and strength the only guarantee of safety. The Christian world provides a basic social contract but demands a strict morality which subsumes individual pleasure into collective order.

Throughout the film Marketa is presented as a dutiful innocent who wishes to enter the convent but who also falls in love with her rapist, marrying him on the battlefield as he dies. She is dismissed as a traitor when she returns to her father's household and cast out. On the way to find refuge at the convent, she encounters a magnificently horned stag in the forest. The stag is the final remnant of her pagan past and a reminder of the animistic world she will have to deny if she becomes a nun. The stag sequence features two odd idiosyncrasies. First, the image of the stag is frozen twice and the photographic nature of the film brought to the fore. These freeze-frames appear to be intentional, and it may therefore be legitimate to offer some sort of phenomenological interpretation of this technique. We could say that the freeze-frames emphasise a mythical view of the stag that stresses Marketa's choice and her inevitable destiny and fate. Second and more problematically, at one point we see the stag's handler, bequiffed and dressed in jeans and a tight-fitting shirt, nonchalantly waving a switch to persuade the stag to stay in the right place for the shot. It would be easy enough to dismiss this as a continuity error and deny that this figure has any significance in the film. However, regardless of intentions, this body from the 1960s *does* appear in the thirteenth century and so the film image here folds two historical moments – the time of its making and the time of its diegesis – together. The frozen body of the stag and the living body of the contemporary stag wrangler succinctly represent Marketa's position. She is caught between the anarchism of the past and the totalitarianism of the future, and the film hesitates and freezes the nostalgic past of myth but also includes a vision of contemporary youth and rebellion which, before August 1968, still offered a hope for a certain sort of freedom. This unknown young man's body, in a relationship with the stag at the far end of the image, neatly sums up the tensions at play in film and in history.

Finally reaching the convent, Marketa supplicates herself before a primitive wooden effigy of Christ as the nuns behind her pray for her salvation. This scene is intercut with Mikoláš's defeat by the king's men and a young boy comes to Marketa and leads her out of the convent and to Mikoláš as he lies dying and the two are married as he dies. Marketa's rejection of the Church – she says, 'Who can worship you from beyond the grave?' – is hallucinatory and as she leaves her dead husband's body she enters a phantasmagoric landscape filled with stag skeletons. Here she is found by the holy innocent Father Bernard (Vladimír Menšík), and as he follows, Marketa enigmatically walks off into the flat landscape and the ambiguous future. Vláčil's film ends without resolution, but Marketa is still alive and is handmaiden neither of the pagan or the Christian worlds. Marketa has achieved Patočka's third movement, that is, existence, which is a level of complete integration that is 'neither a matter of sinking roots in the world nor of the prolongation of being, but rather a task for all of life in its integrity' (1998: 151). For Patočka this is the phenomenological movement directed towards the future. Marketa has life and her body is her own in the world to come.

COACH TO VIENNA: TOUCH, GUILT AND REVENGE

Coach to Vienna begins in a mist-filled forest as the eponymous carriage, hijacked by two German soldiers towards the very end of World War II and driven by the peasant widow (Iva Janžurová), makes its way south out of Czechoslovakia towards the putative safety of Austria. Baroque organ music plays over the sepulchral wood as a staccato explanatory text appears:

> They hanged a rural woman's husband. He wasn't fighting against anyone. They killed him as an example, he had stolen a few bags of cement. They buried the dead man the same night, the frontline was approaching, who knows how long he would have had to wait [if they had not buried him]. Before cock-crow, two soldiers entered the house of mourning, they did not know what had happened. They ordered the widow to prepare the wagon, harness the horses and to ride with them.
> Yes, she said to herself, this is a sign from God as clear as daylight. She prayed that she would not waver and that she would have the strength to carry out justice. (my translation)

The invocation of God places the widow outside of the realm of 1960s communist rationalism and stresses the courage of Czech peasantry, which exists in a timeless, apolitical space and whose values are equally ageless and universal. The widow, even before she appears on-screen, is the harbinger of righteous retribution against the injustices of the Nazis, but also, by implication, against the communist regime's purges of the early 1950s (see Golan 1971: 9–10). In this opening sequence the camera has moved from facing forwards to looking backwards. We have now seen the past.

In the next shot, the camera now in the direction of the carriage's travel, we see the widow (Iva Janžurová) from behind dressed entirely in black with a shawl covering her head. Her isolation from the two soldiers is underscored not only by her nun-like garb but also by her silence and the fact that the soldiers only speak in German (the actors are Czech but their voices are dubbed by German speakers). The wounded older soldier (Luděk Munzar) lies uncomfortably on straw while his younger companion (Jaromír Hanzlík) walks ahead of the two huge dray horses and their impassive driver. Her point of view shows us the foolishly vulnerable soldier from behind and we are given access to the widow's thoughts as she glances down and the camera reveals an axe affixed to the bottom of the carriage.

The film alternates between shots of the widow driving the carriage and the reverse point-of-view shot of what she sees. Kachyňa infrequently deviates from this dynamic and there is a steady rhythm in this 180-degree oscillation which emphasises the proximity of the three protagonists while also highlighting the widow's captivity and the inexorable nature of her revenge. She is the hinge between the soldiers and their escape.

The young soldier begins to notice the woman's body beneath her shielding clothes. He stares as a blonde lock of her hair appears from beneath her headscarf, quickly turning away to his map and compass when she swivels to look at him. However, even as he begins to see the widow as a human being, or at least as a body, he is unable to discern her true intentions. He innocently believes that she is at worst neutral towards them. When he helps her to adjust the wheel of the carriage, the camera shows him from below with the cross-shaped axe centimetres from his hand as the widow looks down on him and the instrument of his possible death, painfully aware of the possibility of discovery.

The axe is the first of a number of significant objects in the film which foreshadow her intention to murder the two soldiers as she strips them of their defences. The second object is the wounded soldier's bayonet knife, which she manages to kick away when they stop to mend the wheel. The carriage disappears into the woods as the camera stays behind to highlight the knife.

Later, she does the same with the soldier's Luger and then the compass, and similar shots show these abandoned objects as the carriage moves away. After a while the soldier decides on a ten-minute break and washes himself in a stream, removing his shirt to reveal his naked torso. The widow looks at him from the carriage and the shot lingers on the soldier with out-of-focus twigs in the foreground emphasising both her and the audience's gaze. Her resolve to kill these men is being tested less by their sexualisation than by their presentation as being as helpless as her own husband in the face of inexorable violence. As they move through the forest, the men are stripped to what Giorgio

Figure 9.2 *Kočár do Vídně*: the vulnerable body

Agamben might call 'bare life' (1998) – a life beyond politics and culture, a life of only the body, life as such. It is in this vulnerability, emphasised once again by the obscuring foreground, which here resembles lashes on the soldier's back, that the widow begins to find empathy for these emblems of inhumanity since it is this position that she herself occupies.

As the film continues, the fog of the forest seems to get thicker until they hear bells that the soldier reads as announcing the end of the war and quickly removes identifying insignia from his uniform in case of challenge. He is now anonymous and unidentifiable.

The cinematography throughout the film uses a shallow depth of focus, and many of the images show figures or objects in medium close-up in fine detail while the background of forest and fog disappears into an increasingly blurred whiteness. While the soldiers seem terrified of what they cannot see, the widow is stoically at home amid this mesmeric topography. The young soldier tries to give her all his money and valuables and, as she struggles to prevent him from playfully placing these things into her leather satchel, his head rests in her lap. She grips the axe which she has managed to secrete next to her and is about to kill him, only to be interrupted by a German tank convoy which the soldier, now a deserter, is desperate to avoid. He leads the carriage off the path and it is soon stuck. He struggles to free the back wheel, until the widow exasperatedly comes down and helps him. She looks at him contemptuously and says, '*Posero . . .*' ['Loser'; lit. 'Shit'], which, as the first word she has spoken to him, he misunderstands as camaraderie and strokes the side of her face. She pulls away and they continue their journey.

Symbols of Christianity infuse the film with roadside votive crosses, and the figure of the wounded soldier presented both as a helpless baby in hay and a crucified sacrifice. Once the soldiers discover that the widow has disposed of the gun, bayonet and compass, the youngster threatens to shoot her and she crosses herself. Here Christianity is something pagan and primeval, like the forest, that protects the Czechs. The widow and the young soldier bury the now dead Hans and it is in this ritual that she acknowledges the soldier's humanity until they are discovered asleep, naked, in the back of the coach by the Czech militia. She is raped and he is shot.

The forest path is now in bright daylight, the fog is gone, and rays shine through the forest canopy. The widow, alone, drives the coach with her hair loose, facing grimly ahead. Once again, we cut to the axe, which is now back in its place under the carriage. We return to the familiar shot of the back of the wagon. This now contains her lover's corpse, his head covered with her black scarf. She opens the liminal gate out of the forest again and the final shot is from deep within the dark woods as the carriage returns to Czechoslovakia.

Coach to Vienna presents two people who are stripped down to their bodies in extreme close-ups and to their bare lives. It is only in their final touch that they not so much communicate as commune with each other, united by humanity in the face of the inhumane. The widow's husband and his friend are both dead and all she and the soldier have left is the fleeting comfort of each other's bodies.

NIGHT OF THE BRIDE: THE PROMISE OF COMMUNITY

Set just after the end of the Second World War and following the 1948 *putsch* – officially 'Victorious February' (*Vítězný únor*) – by the Communist Party of Czechoslovakia (KSČ: *Komunistická strana Československa*), *Night of the Bride*[6] tells the story, written by Kachyňa with long-time collaborator Jan Procházka, of a mentally unstable woman returning to a small farming village undergoing forced collectivisation. The film's critique of the KSČ, surprising even for the liberal 1960s, owes much to Procházka's eminent and protected position within the Party as a *de facto* poet laureate: 'What others would have been forbidden was permitted to him, what would have been unforgivable on the part of others was forgiven him' (Liehm 1974: 141). This favoured position 'held true until the film *Night of the Bride*, which, in showing the period of collectivisation of agriculture in a most unflattering light, initiated the open conflict between Procházka and the political establishment' (Liehm and Liehm 1977: 291). Thus *Night of the Bride* marks the beginning of the end of the laxity associated with socialism with a human face.

The film quickly establishes itself as somewhat experimental in form, as it begins with a montage of the insides of a ticking clock, a lacy black negligée, guns with burning candles in their barrels propped into a snowbank, various Christian emblems, and an out-of-focus figure loading a rifle and taking aim at the camera. This sequence prefigures the themes of time, violence and salvation that inform the film to come. We move almost immediately into a fantastical presentation of the dream of abundant socialism as the village overseer, Picin (Mnislav Hofman), prances through a fecund wheat field, grain rains out of the sky into the hands of the peasants, flocks of fat sheep run happily towards the abattoir, milk pours unceasingly and a beautifully modern crop-dusting aeroplane spreads its life-giving chemicals. This technological agrarian vision of plenty ironically echoes similar scenes in Sergei Eisenstein's *The General Line/ Old and New* (1929) and employs the Russian filmmaker's own theories of montage to juxtapose these imaginary scenes with the reality of the rain-sodden villagers as they stand mutely listening to Picin's bombastic panegyric to the benefits of collectivisation. A brass band plays as the farmers grudgingly parade their livestock and agricultural equipment before the village. Shots suddenly ring out and the militia break into a locked farmstead to find that one of the farmers has shot all his cattle and then himself. It is exactly at this moment that the farmer's daughter (Jana Brejchová) returns from her convent. The keening local women surround her, and as it begins to snow the Bride (the film does not give her a name) transforms into a young girl in a white spring-celebration dress. She is the saviour in the face of coming catastrophe. *Night of the Bride* operates in a quasi-magical realist mode where metaphors are literalised on-screen.

As winter sets in, the young and beautiful Bride is helped by the village man-child, Ambrož (Gustáv Valach). She in turn provides him with food, shelter and an intense intimacy tempered with cruelty. As she cuts his hair, his face intercut with a close-up of a statue of Christ, an extreme close-up shows his trembling fingers reaching out to touch her leg as it presses against him. She impassively deals out a harsh hand-whipping before he debases and purifies himself by immersing his naked body into a barrel of frozen water in front of a crucifix. His ritual repudiation of physical desire is echoed by the Bride's naked body as she changes into her nun's garb in preparation for celebrating Christmas Eve at the church – a practice forbidden, or at least strongly discouraged, by the communist powers. The village people rally around her as she travels to the church, forcing both Picin and the collaborativist priest to acquiesce to the celebratory rite. However, during the mass it becomes clear that the Bride is delusional and imagines herself to be the direct conduit of God's will. The priest casts her out of the church and the Bride's body is found dead in the snow. The final image is of her shapeless dark form in the landscape.

Like *Marketa Lazarová* and *Coach to Vienna*, *Night of the Bride* makes use of racked focus, stark compositions, foreground obstructions and images of touch to accentuate the texture of the cinematic image. This film also uses windows and doors to literally frame the camera's view. The subjectivity of character viewpoints is constantly underscored as figures look at each other with mistrust, adoration or lust. The Catholic imagery of the tortured body of Christ is repeated in the torment of various innocent bodies, but their ritualised punishment and sacrifice have no effect in the secular world of modern communism. The old superstitions have no more power under socialist rationalism.

Night of The Bride offers a bitter rumination on the delusions of rebellion and redemption. The Bride, supported in her misapprehension by the gullible villagers, imagines that she is an incarnation of Christ who will save the village, and by implication the nation, from communism. However, the film presents this as quixotic madness and pessimistically concludes that any rebellion will be savagely crushed. Folk superstition is no match for the destructive ideology of socialist politics. The Bride's body is offered as a sacrifice, but it is not one that has any efficacy in the brave new world that Kachyňa foresees. A year after this film was made, the Russian tanks roll into Prague and place Czechoslovakia under a blanket of silence for the next twenty years.

CONCLUSION

> What happens to the colors in a painting when they are no longer reflected in a look? They return to their notice status of things or ideas; they become chemical products or light vibrations and are no longer colors. They are colors only through and for whoever perceives them, and the painting is truly an aesthetic object only when it is contemplated. (Dufrenne 1973: 48)

I have tried here to highlight a certain aesthetic tendency in Czech cinema of the 1960s which seems to exaggerate the presentation of surface texture and to prominently highlight images of people touching each other, and their diegetic worlds. This thematic tactility is echoed in the construction of the cinematic image: there is an emphasis on extreme close-ups, on symmetrical composition within widescreen black and white, wide-angled shots and extreme long-shots emptied of depth through the use of zoom lenses. All these elements seem to add up to a phenomenological complication of the easy metaphor of touch, especially as it slides into the emotion of being touched. Writers like Barker and Marks sometimes overplay the 'touchiness' of touch by imagining too easily that images of touch allow us access to the real in a way that other images might not. My sense is that they lose sight of the metaphor.

There is also a certain phenomenological tendency in contemporary film criticism, perhaps influenced by the 'New Extremism' of contemporary French cinema, to highlight the body and its reality: for instance, Martine Beugnet and Elizabeth Ezra's 'Traces of the Modern: An Alternate History of French Cinema' (2010) and their 'A Portrait of the Twenty-First Century' (2009), in which they argue that in current film theory and filmmaking there has been a 'return to the corporeal and a concomitant reappraisal of film theory's abstract tendencies through a renewed focus on the material appearance and sensory impact of film and media images and sounds' (Beugnet and Ezra 2009: 77). The 1960s films I have discussed belie the historical progression implied here since they clearly reveal the (metaphorical) haptic quality of the cinema, but they also simultaneously complicate this apparently easy access to history, reality and emotion.

Zhdanov ends his speech to the All-Union Congress of Soviet Writers in 1934 with the rousing call:

> To be an engineer of human souls means standing with both feet firmly planted on the basis of real life. And this in its turn denotes a rupture with romanticism of the old type, which depicted a non-existent life and non-existent heroes, leading the reader away from the antagonisms and oppression of real life into a world of the impossible, into a world

of utopian dreams. Our literature, which stands with both feet firmly planted on a materialist basis, cannot be hostile to romanticism, but it must be a romanticism of a new type, revolutionary romanticism. (Zhdanov 1935: 21)

The utopian claim of 1960s Czech cinema was similarly interested in 'real life' but moved beyond the simplistic 'functional-stylistic' (Dobrenko 2008: 4) of socialist realism and into a phenomenological realism. The three films I have discussed here all foreground the image as a part of Czech society's contemporary reality and all employ discernible technical strategies (racked focus, obscuring foreground objects, careful composition) and give prominence to acts of touching and the vulnerability of the body. These elements encourage a phenomenological engagement not only with the films but with history itself. Following Patočka, we are asked to situate ourselves in relation to the historical and fictional worlds of the films.

NOTES

1. While this claim can sometimes seem far-fetched, it does appear to have some currency in contemporary cognitive science. See, for instance, Linden's *Touch: The Science of Hand, Heart and Mind* in which he places great importance on the linguistic congruence between emotions and metaphors of touch, claiming that 'touch metaphors really tell us something about the skin senses and their relationship to human cognition' (2015: 3).
2. The second New Wave is associated with the work of Miloš Forman, Vera Chytilová, Jiří Menzel and other students of the Prague film school, FAMU. See the excellent BBC documentary *Tales from Prague: Kids from FAMU* (Pawel Pawlikowski, 1990), <https://www.youtube.com/watch?v=Fbank_byZro> (last accessed 14 April 2016).
3. For a nuanced discussion of this tendency see Tom Brown's recent *Breaking the Fourth Wall: Direct Address in the Cinema* (2012).
4. Kristin Thompson presents a detailed consideration of Russian formalism and its significance for film analysis in *Breaking the Glass Armor: Neoformalist Film Analysis* (1988). She writes that 'Artworks achieve their renewing effects on our mental processes through an aesthetic play the Russian Formalists termed *defamiliarization*', and that our 'nonpractical perception allows us to see everything in the artwork differently from the way we should see it in reality, because it seems strange in its new context' (10). This then implies a value theory of art since 'works we single out as most original and that are taken to be the most valuable tend to be those that either defamiliarize reality more strongly or defamiliarize the conventions established by previous art works – or a combination of the two' (11). My claim is that these Czech films both break with previous conventions but also make strange the reality that they depict.
5. For a full discussion of Patočka's thought as it relates to his political activities, see Aviezer Tucker's *The Philosophy and Politics of Czech Dissidence from Patočka to Havel* (2000).
6. The title is often translated into English as *The Nun's Night*, but I follow Hames in using the literal version, *Night of the Bride*, since it better captures the nuance of the narrative beyond the focus on religious order.

WORKS CITED

Agamben, Giorgio 1998 [1995]), *Homo Sacer: Sovereign Power and Bare Life*, trans. Daniel Heller-Roazen, Stanford: Stanford University Press.
Barker, Jennifer M. (2009), *The Tactile Eye: Touch and the Cinematic Experience*, Berkeley, Los Angeles and London: University of California Press.
Beugnet, Martine and Elizabeth Ezra (2009), 'A Portrait of the Twenty-first Century', *Screen*, 50: 1, 77–86.
Beugnet, Martine and Elizabeth Ezra (2010), 'Traces of the Modern: An Alternative History of French Cinema', *Studies in French Cinema*, 10: 1, 11–38.
Brown, Tom (2012), *Breaking the Fourth Wall: Direct Address in the Cinema*, Edinburgh: Edinburgh University Press.
Dobrenko, Evgeny (2008), *Stalinist Cinema and the Production of History: Museum of the Revolution*, trans. Sarah Young, New Haven and London: Yale University Press.
Dufrenne, Mikel (1973 [1953]), *The Phenomenology of Aesthetic Experience*, trans. Edwards S. Casey, Albert A. Andersen, Willis Doimngo and Leon Jacobson, Evanston: Northwestern University Press.
Hames, Peter (2000), 'Vláčil, František', in Richard Taylor, Nancy Wood, Julian Graffy and Dina Iordanova (eds), *The BFI Companion to Eastern European and Russian Cinema*, London: British Film Institute, p. 257.
Golan, Galia (1971), *The Czechoslovak Reform Movement: Communism in Crisis 1962–1968*, Cambridge: Cambridge University Press.
Hames, P. (2004), '*Marketa Lazarová*', in P. Hames (ed.), *The Cinema of Central Europe*, London and New York: Wallflower Press, pp. 151–61.
Hames, P. (2005), *The Czechoslovak New Wave*, 2nd edn, London and New York: Wallflower Press.
Hames, P. (2009), *Czech and Slovak Cinema: Theme and Tradition*, Edinburgh: Edinburgh University Press.
Husserl, E. (1960), *Cartesian Meditations: An Introduction to Phenomenology*, trans. Dorion Cairns, The Hague: Martinus Nijhoff.
Ihde, D. (1986), *Experimental Phenomenology: An Introduction*, Albany: SUNY Press.
Kohák, E. (1989), 'Jan Patočka: A Philosophical Biography', in E. Kohák (ed.), *Jan Patočka: Philosophy and Selected Writings*, Chicago and London: University of Chicago Press, pp. 3–135.
Liehm, A. J. (1974), *Closely Watched Films: The Czechoslovak Film Experience*, New York: International Arts and Sciences Press.
Liehm, M. and A. J. Liehm (1977), *The Most Important Art: Soviet and East European Film After 1945*, Berkeley and London: University of California Press.
Linden, D. J. (2015), *Touch: The Science of Hand, Heart and Mind*, London: Penguin.
Marks, L. U. (2000), *The Skin of the Film: Intercultural Cinema, Embodiment, and the Senses*, Durham, NC and London: Duke University Press.
Mitchell, S. (1974), 'From Shklovsky to Brecht: Some Preliminary Remarks Towards a History of the Politicisation of Russian Formalism', *Screen*, 15: 2, 74–81.
Patočka, J. (1998), *Body, Community, Language, World*, ed. J. Dodd, trans. E. Kohák, Chicago and La Salle, IL: Open Court.
Patočka, J. (1989a [1967]), 'The "Natural World" and Phenomenology', in E. Kohák (ed. and trans.) (1989) *Jan Patočka: Philosophy and Selected Writings*, Chicago and London: University of Chicago Press, pp. 239–73.
Patočka, J. (1989b [1971]), 'Edmund Husserl's Philosophy of the Crisis of Science and His Conception of the "Life-World"', in E. Kohák (ed.), *Jan Patočka:*

Philosophy and Selected Writings, Chicago and London: University of Chicago Press, pp. 223–38.

Petříček, M. (1996), 'Setkání surrealismu s fenomenologií v magické Praze' [The Meeting of Surrealism and Phenomenology in Magical Prague], in L. Bydžovská and K. Srp (eds), *Český surrealismus 1929–1953*, Prague: Argo and City Gallery Prague, pp. 106–11.

Sayer, D. (1998), *The Coasts of Bohemia: A Czech History*, Princeton, NJ: Princeton University Press.

Shklovsky, V. (2004 [1917]), 'Art as Technique', in J. Rivkin and M. Ryan (eds), *Literary Theory: An Anthology*, 2nd edn, Malden, MA and Oxford: Blackwell, pp. 15–21.

Sobchack, V. (1992), *The Address of the Eye: A Phenomenology of Film Experience*, Princeton, NJ: Princeton University Press.

Sontag, S. (2001 [1965]), 'One Culture and the New Sensibility', in *Against Interpretation and Other Essays*, London: Picador, pp. 293–304.

Sorfa, D. (2014), 'Phenomenology and Film', in W. Buckland and E. Branigan (eds) *The Routledge Encyclopedia of Film Theory*, New York and London: Routledge, pp. 353–8.

Szczepanik, P. (2013), 'The State-socialist Mode of Production and the Political History of Production Culture', in P. Szczepanik and P. Vonderau (eds), *Behind the Screen: Inside European Production Cultures*, London: Palgrave Macmillan, pp. 113–33.

Thompson, Kristin (1988) *Breaking the Glass Armor: Neoformalist Film Analysis*, Princeton, NJ: Princeton University Press.

Tucker, Aviezer (2000) *The Philosophy and Politics of Czech Dissidence from Patočka to Havel*, Pittsburgh: University of Pittsburgh Press.

Welton, D. (ed.) (1999), *The Essential Husserl: Basic Writings in Transcendental Phenomenology*, Bloomington and Indianapolis: Indiana University Press.

Zhdanov, A. A. (1935), 'Soviet Literature – The Richest in Ideas, the Most Advanced Literature', in H. G. Scott (trans. and ed.), *Problems of Soviet Literature: Reports and Speeches at the First Soviet Writers' Congress*, London: Martin Lawrence, pp. 15–26.

CHAPTER 10

Corporeal Exploration in György Pálfi's *Taxidermia*

Małgorzata Bugaj

Few films provide such a vivid illustration of recent interest in the on-screen body and engage with such diverse theories on this subject as *Taxidermia* by Hungarian director György Pálfi. This 2006 family saga presents a grandfather, a father, and a son obsessed with their corporeal needs. The film plays in three distinctive parts: three generations, three political eras, three representations of the male body, and three aesthetic modes. Steven Shaviro has suggested that the 'conflict between visceral intensity and allegorical distance, or between vulgar bodily content and abstract, schematic form, is itself the whole point of *Taxidermia*' (2012: 11–12). In its allegorical dimension, the film portrays discourses of the body as representative of certain political eras. However, *Taxidermia* is also preoccupied with the actual physical nature of the human form, its exterior and interior. In its first part, the film concentrates on the surface of the body and recalls associations with changing temperatures and touch. Contrastingly, in its last segment it travels to visceral depths, while attempting to turn the aversion and fear ordinarily evoked by the inside of the body into aesthetic appreciation. Furthermore, while *Taxidermia* initially celebrates bodily life and abundant sensuous pleasures, it concludes with a corporeal form that, having rebuked biological needs, is reclassified as an aestheticised object on display.

With its exploration of the body as the major theme, *Taxidermia* lends itself to multiple readings. Inspired by the structure of the film, in this chapter I propose three different interpretations. The chapter begins with an investigation into how *Taxidermia* deals with bodies in relation to politics: here I refer to analyses by Steven Shaviro and Laszlo Strausz. The second section proceeds to discuss the film's exploration of both the surface of the body (examined in light of Laura Marks' haptic theories) and its interior (as subverting the conventions of horror cinema). Finally, the last part of my argument juxtaposes the film's references to the Bakhtinian carnivalesque and its depictions of grotesque corporealities celebrating their own biology (Bakhtin 1968), with Baudrillard's notion of the body in consumer society as a manufactured object that draws attention to its own cleansed surface (1998).

BODY AND POLITICS

Taxidermia depicts three generations of a Hungarian family inscribed into twentieth-century political contexts: a grandfather, a military private during World War II; a father, a sports champion during socialist times; and a son, a taxidermist in present-day capitalist society. Described by Strausz as 'the triptych of the body as a historical entity' (2011), the film investigates the corporeal forms of individuals as metaphors for political eras, a certain embodiment of national experience. According to Strausz, 'for three generations of the family, bodily performance becomes the main tool in defying the restrictions of the historical era or the given political system' (2014). While the succession of characters reflects socio-political changes in twentieth-century Hungary, the focus of the film – both literal and figurative – remains firmly on the biology of the human form.

The character central to the first part of *Taxidermia*, Vendel Morosgoványi (Csaba Czene), is a conscripted soldier stationed at a remote outpost during World War II. Both the period of war and Vendel's lower rank are indicated by the character's uniform; his life is regulated by military order and discipline represented here by his lieutenant. Vendel's superior acts as a restrictive force curbing the soldier's desires, particularly those connected with sexual pleasure. While performing as a servant to the lieutenant's family, Vendel escapes into a world of daydreaming and onanism. As Shaviro emphasises:

> Morosgoványi's phantasmic masturbation is the only form of action open to him in an entirely rigid social order. His every attempt to claim a bit of pleasure for himself is unavoidably transgressive; and he is eventually executed by the lieutenant in punishment for these transgressions. (2012:36)

Vendel's fantasies become indistinguishable from reality when the result of a (possibly only imagined) sexual encounter with his lieutenant's wife is her unexpected pregnancy.

The era of World War II in *Taxidermia* is associated with masturbation (Vendel's self-erotic compulsion) and murder (the character's death after he is shot by the lieutenant). It is an age of obsession and compulsion that marries Eros and Thanatos, procreation and death. With the state clearly represented by the lieutenant – the hand on the shoulder that says stop – military order and discipline are linked to sexual frustration. The political system is geared towards repression and restricts bodily desires and indulgences. Vendel's appearance (he is thin, uniformed and hare-lipped) comments further on the distortions created by fascism.

The second act of the film begins with a montage of socialist symbols: stars, red flags, anthems, young pioneers in uniform and cheering crowds. Kálmán Balatony (Gergely Trócsányi), the illegitimate son (supposedly) of Vendel, represents the second generation of the family and Hungarian socialism. The character is a competitive speed-eating champion – here a sport of international importance. After a romantic honeymoon with a top female speed-eater, Gizi Aczél (Adél Stanczel), he becomes a father.

Socialism, as presented in the film, is concerned with competition and the display of excess; here *Taxidermia* restages 'the official, self-celebratory culture of the system' (Strausz 2014). This is a spectacular display of over-indulgence, a celebration of the prowess of those privileged either through connections or special skill staged as 'a calculated figure for the excess, the bloated sense of importance, and the empty propagandistic displays that were characteristic of the culture of Eastern European socialist regimes' (Shaviro 2012: 34). With the competition between the nations (Kálmán is a representative of the national sports team) and the propagandistic demonstration of excess (similar to the space race or East German athletes), this part, centring on Kálmán's bloated body, is an allegory for the socialist state showing off in the international arena.

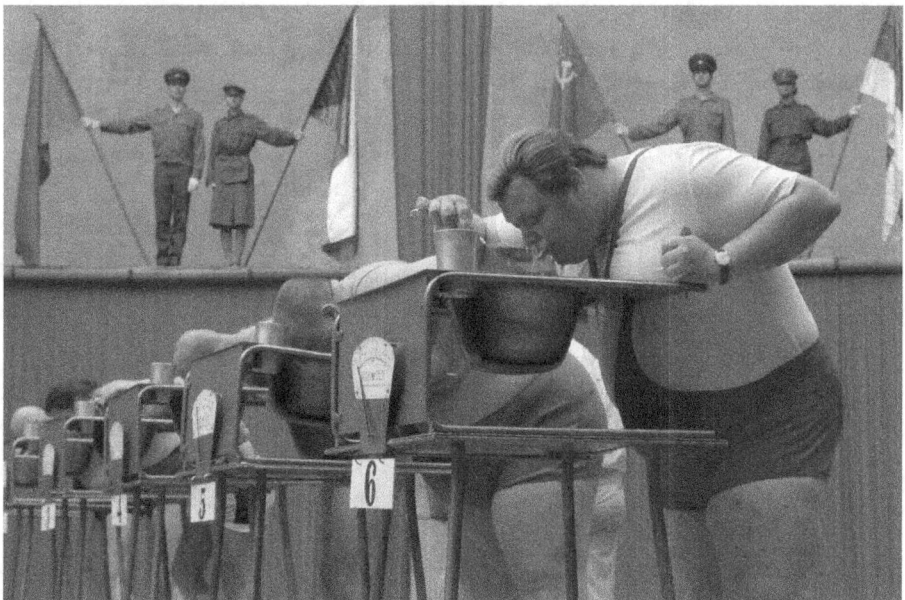

Figure 10.1 Györgi Pálfi's *Taxidermia*

The emblem of this system is the speed-eating coach who constantly pushes his athletes to eat more. In the subsequent political era, Kálmán's obese corporeality becomes grotesquely deformed as it reflects the transition of the old generation to the new capitalist era, and comments on the regime whose authority has been lost (Strausz 2014).

The final part of the film concentrates on Lajos Balatony (Marc Bischoff), a taxidermist in present-day capitalist Hungary. The era of the free-market economy is marked visually by identical blocks of flats and supermarket shelves stacked with an array of similarly packaged products. In contrast to his oversized parents (again, the parenthood is uncertain as Gizi embarked on an affair with another speed-eater), Lajos is a skinny and anaemic man. Dedicated to taxidermy, he also takes care of his father who is now of monstrous proportions and unable to move.

In the era of capitalist consumerism, the political system remains neutral with regard to its influence on the body; the individuals' bodily life is left unchecked and the state does not interfere (in contrast to the previous eras depicted in the film). However, freedom in this respect exists only in theory, as we see a larger system that has its own, more subtle, presence. Social and aesthetic norms that regulate the body are represented in the film by posters depicting Arnold Schwarzenegger and Michael Jackson.

In *Taxidermia*, the generations are (presumably) linked by blood ties but separated by their divergent preoccupations with the body. The film's depictions of corporeal forms and bodily urges constitute parodic comments on their respective political eras. Paradoxically, the periods characterised by strict control and austerity, namely the periods of war and socialism, are here distinguished by surplus. The grandfather and father are driven, respectively, by lust and gluttony, thus, by the over-indulgence of bodily desires. While acting as certain embodiments of political eras, the bodies of the first two protagonists are turned into sites of resistance against the oppressions of the regime. Strausz asserts that

> while for the grandfather resistance meant the creation of a sexual fantasy-world, a site for remembering and identity performance where the quotidian and the festival overlapped, the father revolted against the fakeness of 'existing socialism' via literally turning his body into a food container. (2011)

In contrast, capitalism is portrayed as an era of sharply defined rules and regimes pertaining to the corporeal form: the free will of the individual is confronted with an (un)achievable body image. If the previous characters represent enslavement to bodily needs, Lajos manages to break free from his urges. He transforms his corporeality into an object which defies its own materiality and mortality. The son takes the capitalist obsession with the surface to the ultimate extreme in his quest to achieve the ideal body of his era. Rather than rebelling against the system, Lajos acquiesces by responding to demands that consider biology excessive to body image. His final deed – suicide and the subsequent arrest of the decay of his corpse in an attempt to achieve a certain kind of immortality – marks an ultimate rejection of the organic nature of the body. Simultaneously, it is a renunciation of the obsessions of his father and grandfather (that is, their indulgence in bodily pleasures).

On the one hand, *Taxidermia* focuses on individuals: the grandfather, a sexually frustrated soldier; the father indulging in competitive gluttony, and the son rejecting biological needs in his search for an ideal corporeal form. On the other hand, their bodies are metaphorical incarnations of national experience in particular political regimes. The bodily forms present commentaries on fascism (escapist fantasies, solitary masturbation and violent death), state socialism (overindulgence in consumption linked with surface excess) and capitalism (almost impossible discipline towards the body and the rejection of its own biological nature). Crucially, while the film presents certain allegories, it is the body's materiality that remains at the centre.

SKIN AND VISCERA

Jennifer Barker suggests that 'both pleasure and horror arise from the skin's function as boundary – as something that keeps the carnality within us concealed and the carnality of the world at bay – but also as something that brings us into contact with the things in us and around us at the same time' (2009: 55). If in the first part of *Taxidermia* skin is perceived as a receptor of stimuli from the external world, in the last act it is a vessel for the inside of the body, disguising the carnal within. The aversion and fear ordinarily evoked by viscera are here turned into aesthetic appreciation; presented at a slow pace and in silence, the interior of the body becomes a poetic spectacle.

Taxidermia opens with two scenes that introduce its first protagonist, Vendel Morosgoványi, in contrasting settings. Immediately after the initial credits, he is presented in a candle-lit room, where the interior feels small and cosy. The film amplifies the confined nature of the space through the extensive use of close-ups. This device is also employed to imply an intimate proximity to the character. The camera explores different parts of Vendel's body in a series of quick close-ups imitating physical contact: his fingers holding a candle, his lips playing with the flame, his cheeks, his ear, bellybutton, nipples, eyes and toes illuminated by the flame. The heat provides pleasure but leads to pain when it becomes too intense. With a candle serving as a masturbatory prop (and imitating the warmth of another body), Vendel enjoys the activity, which is revealed as an act of solitary sex. The image of a candle evokes associations with the temperature felt by the character, while the sense of touch is alluded to in the moment when we observe Vendel's self-stimulation. Both sensations of skin are linked with the erotic. In this scene, *Taxidermia* appeals to our imagination by invoking senses other than vision and hearing, thus providing an illustration of Marks's notion of the haptic image which 'inspires an acute awareness that the thing seen evades vision and must be approached through other senses' (2000: 151).

Taxidermia explores skin not only as the site of sensuality, but also as a surface with its own unique texture. Vendel is portrayed through a succession of rapid close-ups, the camera quickly changing angles. The film meditates on the landscapes created by the exterior of the character's body illuminated by the candle: its fine lines, pores and hair. This particular fragment is an exploration of the translucent nature of skin and the play of the soft light of the candle reflected on the surface of the body. What is more, the light produced by the flame limits the close-up, resulting in a vignette effect and increasing off-screen space; the sense of focus on the physical exterior of the body is thus made even more intense.

Following the depiction of a warm and cosy interior, *Taxidermia* moves to a snowy landscape. After a few seconds of contemplating dense white fog, the film shows a silhouette in the distance: it is Vendel again, this time in a soldier's uniform. The character undresses in front of a water barrel, breaks the ice on top of it and washes. He is exposed to bright light and severe cold, in stark contrast to the darkness and warmth of the previous scene. The impenetrable whiteness of the fog, which makes perception difficult, creates an impression of expansiveness, again providing a counterpoint to the confined space of the preceding sequence. Additionally, the camera remains static and focused firmly on the silhouette of the character framed in middle shot, rather than the body fragmented in the close-ups. This shattered proximity introduces both emotional and spatial detachment. Vendel's activity is interrupted by his commanding officer, who orders him to recite his weekly schedule. The lieutenant first appears as a disembodied voice uttering Vendel's name. While listening to the description of the private's routine – presented to cinematic viewers as a succession of quickly flashing images – the lieutenant points to the measurements, times and order of things, indicating the precision and thoroughness of the oppressive timetable. The private's life is organised by those of a higher rank; his place within the hierarchy is the lowest one, with the power to command and punish being exercised over him.

From the lesson on discipline given to Vendel in the snow, *Taxidermia* moves again to a scene of bodily pleasure. The opening image is that of female buttocks: while two young women undress in preparation for a bath, Vendel, chopping wood under the supervision of the lieutenant, attempts to peek at the naked women. The bodies of the bathing women are explored in a succession of extreme close-ups reminiscent of the beginning of the film (Vendel playing with a candle): we are able to distinguish their nipples, necks and hips. This time, it is wet skin that is examined (as contrasted with the surface of the body reflecting the flame), and the water changes its texture. By employing close-ups, the camera mimics the gaze of the aroused character who occasionally manages to catch a glimpse of the bathing girls, seeking stimulation in order to elicit autoerotic capacities. His (and the spectator's) vision lingers on the surface of the female bodies – the gaze 'moves along the surface of the object' (Marks 2000: xiii), illustrating Marks' remark that 'the vision itself can be tactile, as though one were touching a film with one's eyes' (2000: xi).

The first part of *Taxidermia* investigates the surface of the body as the site of sensations; its final act, however, revisits corporeal depths. The film subverts the conventions of presenting viscera as repulsive and eliciting horror; instead, it emphasises the particular beauty of the inside of the body. In doing so, it recalls Cronenberg's comment on the allure of the inside of the body (the comment partially repeated in his *Dead Ringers* [1988]):

> It's not disgust. It's fascination, but it's also a willingness to look at what is really there without flinching, and to say *this* is what we're made of, as strange and as disgusting as it might seem at times. I'm really saying that the inside of the body must have a completely different aesthetics ... I could conceive of a beauty contest for the inside of the human body. (Billson 1989: 5)

It is the elaborate suicide of Lajos – the protagonist of the third part – that prompts the investigation of viscera. After discovering his father dead, Lajos, a taxidermist by trade, decides to preserve the corpse by turning it into a monument to his father's achievements as a speed-eater. Having achieved this, he arrests the biology of his own body through a complicated operation, ending his life and, ultimately, transforming himself into a lifeless, taxidermied form – the ideal body of his time.

The scene of Lajos' sophisticated suicide, which involves the removal of the viscera, comprises a series of extreme close-ups (a technique akin to that employed in the opening sequence of the film focusing on the skin of his grandfather and the bathing girls). In the sequences examining bodily exteriors in the first part of the film, the camera investigates the skin in a rapid succession of close-ups. These mimic the feverish gaze of the aroused character (Vendel) in an attempt to (re)produce his erotic experience. By contrast, the suicide scene beneath the skin is composed of a series of lingering close-ups. Such a measured pace of editing invites contemplation of the inside of the human body.

The scene begins with a slow tracking shot of a vast empty basement beneath the taxidermist's shop. The camera reveals a space submerged in semi-darkness; a spotlight is directed onto the naked body of Lajos trapped in a mysterious, terror-inspiring machine. Here *Taxidermia* bears the hallmarks of a torture horror film: the elements cueing the scene (the setting, darkness, the torture machine in the spotlight and threatening silence) conjure expectations of fright and graphic violence (as in *The Hills Have Eyes*, 1977; *Saw*, 2004; or *Hostel*, 2005). The clear suggestion of off-screen space strengthens the anticipation of a violent unknown – there may be something the implied victim does not know about. Furthermore, in order to accomplish the meticulously prepared suicide, Lajos employs a complex self-made machine (another of *Taxidermia*'s references to the genre of horror), which is revealed before the central scene depicting his death. The machine recalls a torture device, although it ultimately dismembers the body without inflicting pain (the operation is facilitated by sedatives and painkillers).

From the presentation of the underground space and the body in the suicide machine, the film moves to a close-up of a needle inserted into flesh. The syringe is followed by a scalpel that also cuts into the skin, while the camera begins an exploration of the inside of the body as it is subjected to a pseudo-medical operation. This scene comprises a series of extreme close-ups of body parts and medical instruments displayed against the background noises of bubbling fluids and beeping machines. For his operation, Lajos employs surgical tools: numerous syringes and tubes with various liquids, scalpels opening the skin and clamps stopping the flow of blood. Here the film comments on the ambiguous powers of medicine: healing and killing. Furthermore, medicine presents itself as opposed to taxidermy: they both concentrate on the physicality of the body, but while the goal of the first is to preserve life, the latter preserves only the lifelike exterior.

The expectations of terror are turned into an experience of beauty when the camera is placed intimately close to the body. As the sequence progresses, *Taxidermia* reveals the landscape of the body's interior: white flesh, coiled intestines, a membrane moving to and fro, and an empty tunnel formed by the ribs. The clean, sterile presentation of the viscera stands in contrast to their bloody mass during the actual opening of the body. The body's entrails are ordinarily perceived as terrifying and evoke disgust; their display is usually associated with dangerous and pathological situations implying a threat to life as their exposition usually occurs in violent accidents or in surgery. For Elkins, torn bodies in news coverage or fake wounds in horror films are 'marginal not only because they are painful to watch but also because the inside of the body is a powerful sign of death' (1999: 109). Our flesh is a reminder of our material basis and mortality; this is the part of a human being that is sure to be destroyed and turned into a lifeless form. In this sequence, however, the internal organs floating in liquid and the inside of the body seem intended to elicit aesthetic pleasure. Slow editing lets us meditate on viscera, as their textures and colours are placed in focus. This contemplation is facilitated by a lack of distracting sounds: the act is nearly silent, with only the quiet beeping of machinery and the bubbling of the pumped fluids.

Taxidermia's shift from the terrifying to the beautiful is made possible primarily through the defamiliarisation of the human form. In the suicide scene, we watch the body fragmented, both by cinematic techniques (close-ups) and in the literal sense (removal of organs and limbs). The camera focuses on disembodied organs with only an occasional glimpse of the figure of Lajos in his full dimension. While the violence inflicted on the body is graphically displayed, it is presented with a certain detachment brought about by the aestheticised context and clear medical references. In this way, the film inverts conventional depictions of viscera in horror films and produces a visually pleasing spectacle.

Pálfi remarks that 'in *Taxidermia*, the question was precisely this: what is beauty? Is the body ugly on the inside? No, it's beautiful, it's a whole universe of flesh and blood' (Kuzma 2013). The exploration of the sensuous in the first part is contrasted with the film's journey into viscera in the last segment. Abstracted and fragmented, the images of corporeal depths subvert their anticipated reception as terrifying and repulsive and, instead, present the inside of the body as cleansed and beautiful.

BAKHTIN'S GROTESQUE BODY AND BAUDRILLARD'S 'BODY AS A THREATENING DOUBLE'

With the characters of the first and second acts who immerse themselves, respectively, in the pleasures of lust and gluttony, *Taxidermia* resurrects the Bakhtinian concept of the carnival, centring on grotesque depictions of the body and bodily life. The film recalls further tropes particular to the carnivalesque: the subversion of official ideology, a distinctive sense of humour, the genres of the market-place and the central position of the pig (both literal and symbolic). If the first two parts of *Taxidermia* revive carnival conventions, the setting of the final part in the capitalist era provokes the replacement of a Bakhtinian grotesque corporeality with Baudrillard's notion of the body as a 'threatening double' (Baudrillard 1998: 131). Here, the legacy of bodily obsessions, passed from the grandfather through the father, is ultimately rejected by the son.

The carnivalesque – as discussed by Bakhtin in *Rabelais and his World* (1968) – celebrates fertility, feasting and death (linked with rebirth). A carnival element in *Taxidermia* is introduced through metaphorical comments on official ideologies and norms. The exaggerated images of the bodily forms – the caricatures of the dominant political systems – are both comic and repulsive. The film abounds in what Strausz calls 'tongue-in-cheek obscenities' which 'on [the] one hand . . . are supposed to gross out the viewer, but on the other hand it is hard not to notice the director's intentions to criticise the represented via the ironic, hyperrealistic mode of representation' (Strausz 2011). Contemporary political systems are here mocked through references to human biology.

A scene clearly recalling carnival genres and humour is that featuring the bathing girls (discussed above), in which the parallel editing juxtaposes the portrait of the naked girls presented in soft focus with the vulgar monologue of the lieutenant. The officer appreciates poetic descriptions of the female genitals as a lily, a rosebud, or a love chalice, and mentions the presence of such associations in poetry and song. He concludes, however, that 'what they really mean to say is "cunt"'. Correspondingly, the coarse language and the imagery of the fair and the market-place have formed the basis of the repertoire of carnivalesque genres excluded from official discourse, such as parodies, curses and profanities. These forms are based on the power of carnival laughter, which, as Bakhtin observes, 'liberates not only from external censorship but first of all from the great interior censorship; it liberates from the fear that developed in man during thousands of years: fear of the sacred, of prohibitions, of the past, of power' (Bakhtin 1968: 94). In the aforementioned scene in *Taxidermia*, such laughter collapses the dichotomies that can be the cause of anxiety (here gender difference) and engages with the prohibited (sexual pleasure).

Additionally, *Taxidermia* refers to carnival associations with the pig (the animal assuming the symbolic central position within the fair), which appears in the film both figuratively and literally. In the first and second act of *Taxidermia*, it stands as a metaphor for the abundant pleasures of excessive sex and eating that define the main characters. The pig also appears in the first part of the film in the flesh as it is entrusted to Vendel's care, only to be subsequently butchered and served during a festive feast. Later in this segment, Vendel wanders into a shed where meat is stored. Lit by a candle, a pig's carcass suggestively recalls female body parts (particularly genitals). Immediately, it reminds the private of the lieutenant's obese wife, Irma, or perhaps it *is* her lying on the remains of the animal. While Vendel passionately makes love to (an imagined?) Irma, the events of the day (the slaughter and the feast) merge with the character's sexual obsessions. Williams' 'meat shots' (1989: 83) – pornographic close-ups of penetration – are here literal: graphic depictions of joined bodies are juxtaposed with images showing a pig carcass. The sight of meat and the images of female bodies change before the eyes of the obsessed man, while ecstatic screams and the seductive voice of the woman are paired with the grunting of the pig. Correspondingly, the pig is evoked in the second act of *Taxidermia*. Its main character, Kálmán (born with a pig's tail, further emphasising the ambiguity of his father's coupling), is defined by gluttony. Just like Vendel, he is introduced through his greatest obsession; we meet him during a speed-eating competition. In this segment, the devouring of less than appealing dishes of food at great speed is portrayed as a sport of international importance. Vomiting is a part of the competition; we are also exposed to the sight of chewed food, which echoes Stallybrass and White's suggestion that the pig has been cherished and abused for its appetites (1986: 45).

Taxidermia evokes Bakhtinian carnival aesthetics celebrating the material nature of the body. The film offers exaggerated images of corporeal forms and their urges, with particular focus placed on the lower stratum: Vendel is associated with genitals and Kálmán with the belly and buttocks. Activities connected with the body here play a major role: sexual acts in the case of Vendel and eating in the case of Kálmán. Additionally, in the first and second act, the carnivalesque is resurrected through carnival humour and grotesque depictions of official ideologies along with references to the figure of the pig. In the third part, however, the carnival is subverted, as its joyful, down-to-earth festivity is replaced by the solemn, sterile atmosphere of an art gallery.

The final protagonist of *Taxidermia*, Lajos Balatony, is introduced as the camera enters the taxidermist's shop. Skinny and pale Lajos appears alongside his father, Kálmán, now a retired speed-eating champion immobilised in his flat by his monstrous obesity. Kálmán's grotesque figure resembles a statue, immortalising the gluttony that defines his story. The father and son are placed in stark contrast to one another, with regard not only to their appearance but also to their approach to bodily needs: the father overindulges, the son restrains.

Lajos is introduced at work mounting a bear; his profession is crucial to the third part of the film. The word 'taxidermy' is an umbrella term for various methods of creating lifelike representations of animals for study or as decorative hunting trophies. According to Eastoe, 'the technical definition of the word taxidermy means to arrange a skin. It derives from the Greek roots *taxis* meaning arrangement, and *derma*, meaning skin' (2012: 10). A taxidermist works with dead bodies, immortalising them in a simulation of life through a combination of craft skills and artistic talents. By freezing the biology of the body and turning it into a cleansed model, taxidermy allows a corpse to escape the process of decay. The internal organs are removed and the focus is solely on the surface, illustrating Desmond's observation that it is 'in the skin, in the "dermis" of taxidermy' that its 'authenticating ingredient' lies (2002: 161).

In its final section, *Taxidermia* moves to the 1980s–1990s, a time when, as Baudrillard asserts, the body is perceived as the finest of 'physically possessed, manipulated and consumed objects' (1998: 131). The French philosopher describes this era as marked by a consumer society in which visual representations (especially photography, film, and television) reproducing the body as a glossy smooth surface proliferate. This introduces a disparity between the hegemonic social construct (regulated mainly through images) and the biological body of an individual who attempts to live up to the requirements of society. The strict aesthetic norms centring on bodies regulated by diets, cosmetic surgery and bodybuilding dictate a split 'between the subject and the objectivised body as threatening double' (Baudrillard 1998: 131). The body as a physical thing, a 'threatening double', is in conflict with both the self (and the biology of the body) and the demands of the group.

The proliferation of images determining bodily norms is illustrated in *Taxidermia* by the presence of posters of pop culture icons: Arnold Schwarzenegger and Michael Jackson. In the gym, we encounter a poster of Schwarzenegger, the action film icon immortalised in his roles as a cyborg, a commando and a barbarian. As a body builder, Schwarzenegger operates within empty references; his strength is not projected outwards, his 'baroque muscles' are 'largely non-functional decoration' (Huxley 1988: 96). Meanwhile, in the taxidermy shop we find a poster of Michael Jackson. Jackson, as evoked in *Taxidermia*, represents a different kind of manufactured body, one that is carefully styled through diets, plastic surgery, chemical changes to skin colour and make-up (Brown 1984: 88). Bodybuilding and body styling are linked with training and discipline which can turn corporealities into 'self-created works of art, constantly worked over and redefined' (Tasker 1993: 9). Images of Schwarzenegger and Jackson are manifestations of both control and restraint with regard to the body (diet, exercise), as well as carefully directed excess (muscles). Constructed and manipulated, these bodies constitute an achievement in taming human biology.

The images of Michael Jackson and Arnold Schwarzenegger are placed in opposition to the grotesque bodies of the first and second segments (those of Vendel and Kálmán), that is, the bodies that celebrate their material nature. While in the previous acts of the film biology and bodily urges dominate the lives of the characters, in the last act of *Taxidermia* they are firmly placed under control, as signalled by the iconic bodies of the era. In posters, TV/cinema screens and photographs, the bodies of Jackson and Schwarzenegger seem frozen in time, their photographs displayed on walls as decorative items. The focus is solely on skin (with its texture obliterated in the image) and the shape of the body (with all its imperfections corrected), recalling Lajos's own art of taxidermy.

Taxidermia's references to Bakthin's and Baudrillard's discourses on the body are further emphasised in a scene in which the film moves from the underground of the taxidermist's shop (the site of Lajos's suicide) to an art gallery. After Lajos's death, his manipulated body is found by one of his customers, Dr Andor Regöczy (Géza Hegedüs). Interested in an unusual object (he returns to the shop to collect his order – a taxidermied foetus in a glass ball) and preoccupied with art, Dr Regõczy transfers the bodies of Lajos and his father to a gallery, where they assume the status of art objects.

In the gallery, the camera encounters the mounted figure of the father and then comes to rest on the torso of Lajos. His corpse is fixed in a pose that recalls a classical sculpture, the depiction of antique gods and heroes in a form known today from museums. Just as taxidermy developed conventional poses in which the specimens are presented, Lajos chooses classical art to model his masterpiece on. This echoes Menninghaus's statement that 'the classical body conforms both to the rules of today's dieticians and our own ideal of slenderness' (2003: 70–1); its proportions and symmetry correspond to contemporary perfect bodies. Crucially, the sculpture of Lajos recalls both the statues of the armless *Venus de Milo* and Michelangelo's *David*, the representations of generic ideals of, respectively, the feminine and the masculine. The classical body with its sealed surfaces is here opposed to the grotesque corporealities of the first and second parts.

For Ventura, 'Lajos' occupation (to strip once-living beings of their pith) and his final act (a mounting of his own corpse) represent rebukes of both the body and a legacy of enslavement to its needs. Pálfi posits that the end product of that abnegation is – or at least can be – art' (2012). While essentially rendered a corpse, the remains of the taxidermist are transformed into an object that defies its biological nature and is placed in an art gallery, a space 'suggesting longevity if not immortality' (Hannah 2004: 292). With the body emerging as a sculpture, Lajos has eternalised himself as both artist and object of art.

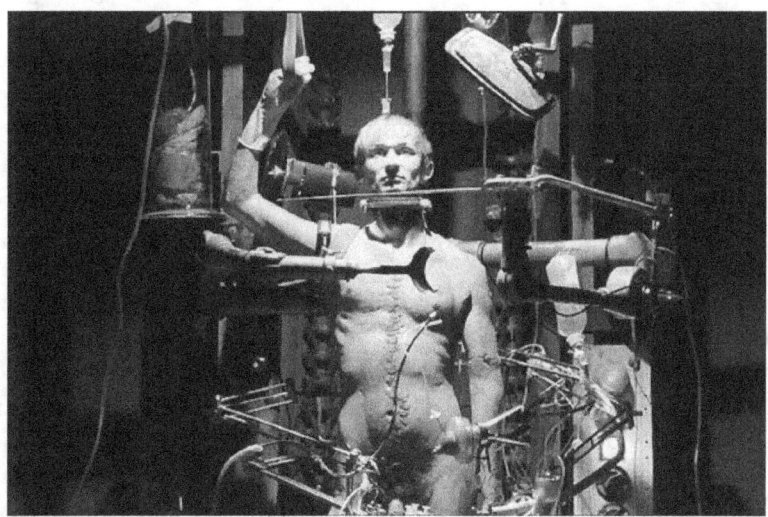

Figure 10.2 Györgi Pálfi's *Taxidermia*

In the last scenes of *Taxidermia* (the suicide scene and the sequence in the gallery), art disguises human biology and viscera which are ordinarily perceived as repulsive. The statues created by Lajos escape the process of decay and refer to the motif of eternally persistent corporeal remains. Frozen in time, cleansed and taxidermied, the bodies preserved in such an everlasting form succeed in placing biology under control, taming the 'threatening double'. By emerging as their own sculptures, they transcend the body and its needs celebrated by Bakhtin's carnivalesque. While the grotesque corporealities featured in the film make a spectacle of their own material nature and offer for view their depths and cavities, *Taxidermia* concludes with the focus on the 'closed, smooth and impenetrable surface of the body' (Bakhtin 1968: 318). Such a presentation of corporeality (illustrated by the pin-up posters of Arnold Schwarzenegger and Michael Jackson, as well as Kálmán and Lajos emerging as their own sculptures) makes the titular craft of taxidermy emblematic of the modern perception of the body with its focus on *dermis* (skin).

CONCLUSIONS

This chapter has suggested three possible readings of the film with regards to the representation of the body: that examining political regimes juxtaposed with biology, that investigating skin and viscera, and that referring to Bakhtin's and Baudrillard's discourses on the corporeal form. Fundamentally, *Taxidermia* engages directly with the body by investigating its exterior and interior. The film begins in intimate darkness with Vendel hidden from gaze and indulging in bodily pleasures, while it ends in sterile bright light with Lajos' body exhibited in front of a crowd in an art gallery. *Taxidermia* in its initial scenes centres on both the experience of the world through the surface of the body and the texture of skin. By contrast, its final scenes investigating the interior of the body mark the transition from an excess of stimuli to an absence of sensations, even those such as extreme pain (Lajos commits suicide with the use of sedatives). The film closes with an image of an abstracted and aestheticised bodily form.

On an allegorical level, *Taxidermia* investigates the intersection of the body with politics by considering human biology and bodily forms as representations of political and social ideas. The succession of contrasting corporeal forms acts as a metaphor for, or an ironic comment on, the historical circumstances the characters live in. Additionally, the film moves between the Bakhtinian interpretation of the body and that suggested by Baudrillard. If the first two parts of *Taxidermia* reference carnival convention and celebrate the material, the third part of the film describes an era that seeks abstract spiritual mastery over bodies and renounces its biological and physical nature.

WORKS CITED

Bakhtin, Mihail Mihajlovič (1968), *Rabelais and His World*, trans. Heléne Iswolsky, Cambridge, MA: MIT Press.
Barker, Jennifer M. (2009), *The Tactile Eye: Touch and the Cinematic Experience*, Berkeley: University of California Press.
Baudrillard, Jean (1998 [1970]), *The Consumer Society: Myths and Structures*, London: Sage.
Billson, Anne (1989), 'Cronenberg on Cronenberg: A Career in Stereo', *Monthly Film Bulletin*, 56: 660, 4–6.
Brown, Geoff (1984), *Michael Jackson, Body and Soul: An Illustrated Biography*, New York: Beaufort.
Desmond, Jane (2002), 'Displaying Death, Animating Life: Changing Fictions of "Liveness" from Taxidermy to Animatronics', in N. Rothfels (ed.), *Representing Animals*, Bloomington: Indiana University Press, pp. 159–79.
Eastoe, Jane (2012), *The Art of Taxidermy*, London: Pavilion.
Elkins, James (1999), *Pictures of the Body: Pain and Metamorphosis*, Stanford: Stanford University Press.
Hannah, Dorita (2004), 'Butcher's White: Where the Art Market Meets the Meat Market in New York City', in J. Horwitz and P. Singley (eds), *Eating Architecture*, London and Cambridge, MA: MIT Press, pp. 279–300.
Huxley, David (1988), 'Naked Aggression: American Comic Books and the Vietnam War', in A. Louvre and J. Walsch (eds), *Tell Me Lies About Vietnam: Cultural Battles of the War*, Milton Keynes: Open University Press, pp. 88–110.
Kuzma, Konstanty (2013), 'Interview with György Pálfi' in *East European Film Bulletin*, <http://eefb.org/archive/july-2013/interview-with-gyorgy-palfi> (last accessed 20 January 2015).
Marks, Laura U. (2000), *The Skin of the Film: Intercultural Cinema, Embodiment, and the Senses*, Durham, NC: Duke University Press.
Menninghaus, Winfried (2003), *Disgust: The Theory and History of a Strong Sensation*, Albany: SUNY Press.
Shaviro, Steven (2012), 'Body Horror and Post-Socialist Cinema: György Pálfi's *Taxidermia*', in A. Imre (ed.), *A Companion to Eastern European Cinemas*, Chichester: Wiley-Blackwell, pp. 25–40.
Stallybrass, Peter, and Allon White (1986), *The Politics and Poetics of Transgression*, Ithaca: Cornell University Press.
Strausz, Laszlo (2011), 'Archaeology of Flesh: History and Body-Memory in *Taxidermia*', *Jump Cut. A Review of Contemporary Media*, <http://www.ejumpcut.org/archive/jc53.2011/strauszTaxidermia> (last accessed 21 January 2014).
Strausz, Laszlo (2014), 'Back to the Past: Mnemonic Themes in Contemporary Hungarian Cinema', *East European Film Bulletin*, <http://eefb.org/essays/back-to the-past> (last accessed 21 January 2015).
Tasker, Yvonne (1993), *Spectacular Bodies: Gender, Genre, and the Action Cinema*, London: Routledge.
Ventura, Elbert (2012), 'Look Away', *Reverse Shot*, <http://reverseshot.org/reviews/entry/383/reverse_shot_taxidermia> (last accessed 21 January 2015).
Williams, Linda (1989), *Hard Core: Power, Pleasure, and the 'Frenzy of the Visible'*, Berkeley: University of California Press.

CHAPTER 11

Aerial Bodies in Polish Cinema

Dorota Ostrowska

Polish films about aviation belong to different genres and historical contexts. Many films feature the figure of an expert Polish pilot who belongs to the elite part of the Polish military and is involved in spectacular aviation shows. We find such representations in Józef Lejtes' 1933 *Pod Twoją Obronę* (*Sub Tuum Praesidium*) and also in a number of post-war films including *Sprawa pilota Maresza* (*The Case of Pilot Maresz*, Leonard Buczkowski, 1956), *Przeciwko bogom* (*Against Gods*, Hubert Drapella, 1961), *Zniszczyć pirata* (*To Destroy the Pirate*, Hubert Drapella, 1973), and *Na niebie i na ziemi* (*On the Earth and in the Sky*, Julian Dziedzina, 1974). In some Polish films flying is associated with terrifying plane crashes, which are devastating on the individual and collective level. We can include in this group Leonard Buczkowski's *Przerwany lot* (*Interrupted flight*, 1964), Krzysztof Kieślowski's *Przypadek* (*Blind Chance*, 1987), Anna Jadowska's *Generał: Zamach na Gibraltarze* (*General: Assassination in Gibraltar*, 2009) and a recent production of documentary films about the Smoleńsk plane crash (Przylipiak 2013: 217–37).[1] Collectively these films offer a good starting point to explore how the technology of flying impacts the representation of the body, in particular in the post-war context, when the majority of Polish films about flying were made. This chapter will specifically focus on the representation of the dynamics of the body in flight in selected Polish films from the period of state socialism including *The Case of Pilot Maresz*, *Against Gods*, *To Destroy the Pirate* and *On the Earth and in the Sky*.

The discussion of this chapter centres on the idea of 'socialist aerial bodies', which is informed by Paul Virilio's reflection about the relationship between the body and technologies developed for the most part during the Cold War, which coincided with the period of state socialism in Poland.[2] In Virilio's modern society, which he calls 'speed society', technology is one single and overriding factor transforming the body and its functions, social bonds and perceptions, beyond recognition. Virilio emphasises as important the political context of different wars, including the Cold War and, more recently, the post-Cold War conflicts. However, his arguments are not nuanced in a way that reflects the differences in the impact war technologies, such as flying, might have had in the socialist context as opposed to the non-socialist one with which he was much more familiar. This chapter is an attempt to fill this gap in Virilio's reflection on the aerial body by discussing the development of a specific representation of the body, referred to here as a 'socialist aerial body', which is impacted not only by the advancements in the technologies of flying, but also by ideological concerns – some of them unique to the socialist context.

As we will see in the first part of this chapter, 'The Cold War and Polish aviation films', which presents the historical context of this chapter's argument, the body-technology representation changes in each film because of the shifts in Polish politics. This fluid political context in turn impacted on the developments in civil and military aviation and modulated its renditions on the cinematic screen. The second section, 'Virilio's aerial bodies', which is the chapter's conceptual part, discusses Virilio's notions of the body and technology by focusing on questions of perception on the one hand, and human bonds on the other, which inform the ways in which the representation of the body is rendered in these films. It is the representation of human bonds shaped by the dynamics of the society under state socialism that characterises the socialist aerial bodies ignored by Virilio. The third part, 'Aerial bodies and human bonds', shows human bonds as a kind of affective technology, which shapes the socialist aerial body. Finally, the fourth part focuses on 'Disappearing and disabled aerial bodies' to explore another set of circumstances affecting the body and perception, one not discussed by Virilio. Namely, it analyses how the inability to fly owing to, for example, a physical disability affects the pilot's fields of perception by opening them into new areas, thus positioning memory, among other things, as a prosthesis of technology.

What the films discussed here collectively demonstrate is the way in which human bonds and physical disability work as a kind of prosthesis of flying technology in relation to the body. As a result, the body is uniquely shaped and transformed in the socialist context, allowing us to propose the existence of 'socialist aerial bodies'.

THE COLD WAR AND POLISH AVIATION FILMS

The Cold War period was never a time of actual military activity on Polish territory, but the atmosphere of impending conflict and confrontation left a mark on the films produced in this period. This was particularly the case with films about aviation, which almost always featured military personnel as key protagonists and were made with the help of various outfits of the Polish military, which always figure very prominently in the credits.³ Since the 1950s, and especially in the 1960s, the army was actively involved in the making of a great number of films, which Zwierzchowski refers to as the 'cinema of new memory'. Some three hundred films made in the 1960s and 1970s were films about World War II (Zwierzchowski 2013: 9). The army was involved not only for practical reasons, to film battle scenes and supply the necessary equipment, but also because it was interested in the positive representations of itself as it wished to appear as a legitimate guardian of the new political and social order.

Aviation films constituted a small fraction of these historical or contemporary films involving the military. The Polish air force was being restructured and rebuilt in a very ambitious way after World War II in much the same way as the army, and wanted to be accepted and appear legitimate like the army.⁴ Owing to the small number of films, it is rather difficult to talk about a tradition or a trend as such of aviation cinema in Poland. However, what is striking is that at every juncture in Polish film history, always affected by political ebbs and flows, at least one film about aviation was made, as though it were imperative to re-imagine flying anew each time round.⁵

The Case of Pilot Maresz, made in 1956, was a result of the political thaw in Poland following the death of Stalin. The film has a strong socialist realist flavour to it, but most importantly it can be read as a partly veiled, but nonetheless very readable to contemporary audiences, attempt to test and rehabilitate a former RAF pilot, Captain Maresz (Wieńczysław Gliński), who returned to Poland after World War II and became a domestic commercial pilot. A number of Polish pilots who fought in the RAF returned to Poland after World War II and re-entered the Polish air force under the condition that they accepted the new political regime (Przedpełski 1997: 272–3). With the onset of Stalinism many were accused of spying and imprisoned (Cynk 1972: 242). The life of one of the Polish RAF aces, Stanislaw Skalski, who was condemned to death by the Stalinist court in Poland and only released after the death of Stalin, was the subject of a documentary film, *Cyrk Skalskiego* (*Skalski's Circus*), made in 1986 by Jacek Bławut. Janusz Morgenstern's 1964 film *Życie raz jeszcze* (*Back to Life Again*) also featured a former RAF pilot as the main protagonist. The fact that the film was made later than *The Case of Pilot Maresz* is the most likely reason why the pilot's RAF past is directly referred to and is the source of the dramatic tension in the film.

Maresz's wartime past is not mentioned directly in *The Case of Pilot Maresz*, but British connections in his private life, as well as his entire demeanour, suggest his past in the RAF. While flying on one of the domestic routes his plane is hijacked by a man, Surowiec (Leon Niemczyk), who unsuccessfully tries to force the pilots to fly the machine to Denmark. The pilot Maresz, as well his co-pilots (Jerzy Michotek and Bogdan Niewinowski), manage to neutralise the hijacker, land the aeroplane safely and hand the culprit accused of spying over to the Polish police. The story of hijacking was a gesture towards the still lingering paranoia from Stalinist times, which found everywhere spies and saboteurs trying to undermine the new republic (Paczkowski 2003: 215).

The film navigates the muddy waters of Cold War reality in more than one way. Unlike most of the 1950s Polish productions it is made in colour, with careful attention paid to costume and interior design, evoking the sumptuous imagery of Douglas Sirk's melodramas. These striking stylistic choices are not accidental, but rather are an attempt to represent socialist reality through the glamorous lenses of civil aviation populated with handsome but righteous pilots, and their gorgeous sweethearts, all of them professional women who effortlessly manage the demands of their careers and private lives, which was a common feature of socialist realist films. The characters resolve their personal conflicts without much trouble; watching them the viewer may get the sense that post-war Poland might really be quite a good place in which to live and work. It is through these stylistic themes and gender representations rooted in socialist ideology that the film emerges as a propaganda weapon in the Cold War struggle owing much to socialist realist aesthetics. At the same time, through the introduction of new themes, especially those linked to the role of the RAF pilots, the film is also an early attempt to begin to divert Polish cinema away from socialist realist concerns (Lubelski 2009: 158).

Against Gods and *On the Earth and in the Sky* are set in military aviation bases. The events of World War II involving air battles against Germans are the source of tensions and conflicts among the same pilots, who remained in the active combat force in the decades after the war. The pilots discuss the past conflicts among themselves while remaining very conscious that they are being trained for a new kind of conflict. The representations of the military differ quite significantly in both films, and World War II conflict is represented with less intensity in the 1970s' *On the Earth and in the Sky* than in the 1960s' *Against Gods*. While *Against Gods* was made in the wake of the aforementioned efforts to rebuild and strengthen the Polish military, including the air force, the 1970s film features a modern and strong air force equipped with excellent machines and highly competent pilots. In many ways we could see the latter film as a coda to the process of beefing up the Polish military, which was the concern of the 1950s and 1960s Polish governments, but less so of the Gierek regime of the 1970s, which invested much more in industrial infrastructure and improvements in people's standard of living (Paczkowski 2003: 351–410). By the 1970s World War II was also losing its importance as the period that needed to be revisited and reinterpreted through cinema as the founding myth of the new republic. For Gierek, the here and now mattered much more, and this contemporary concern found its reflection in cinema, which featured World War II and the military much less frequently (Zwierzchowski 2013:

53–4). This is one of the reasons why *To Destroy the Pirate* is about civil rather than military aviation.[6]

To Destroy the Pirate does not feature a situation of direct war conflict either. Instead the film is focused on the tension associated with international glider competitions in which Poles participate. A glider, nicknamed 'The Pirate', constructed by Poles crashes during a test flight, killing one of the pilots and jeopardising the team's chances of entering one of the forthcoming competitions. The challenge of discerning the reasons behind the disaster is the premise for the entire film. The themes of nationalism in the context of international competition are a sublimation in sporting terms of the Cold War conflict, which persists in the 1970s but takes less militarised forms. The film is a reflection of this new political climate associated with Gierek. The fact that all these films are products of the socialist cinema is as important as the context of the Cold War. Centralisation, which characterised the film industry in socialist Poland, with its propaganda objectives, controls and censorship, could be justified as much by the threats of the Cold War as by the demands of new Polish regimes affected by Stalinism and then shaped by the leadership of Gomułka and Gierek. In these films, made primarily for the domestic market, the main target were Polish audiences, who were to be kept on standby because of the prospects of military confrontation with the West and who were in need of having their new Polish identity formed. The socialist aerial body responded to both of these demands.

VIRILIO'S AERIAL BODIES

The relationship between the body and the environment lies at the very centre of Virilio's philosophical preoccupations. How he sees the place of the body is informed by phenomenological concerns and is directly linked to questions of perception. What worries and fascinates Virilio is the fact that technologies of different kinds colonise the body, which is in danger of being transformed beyond recognition (James 2007: 23, 25). Flying is one such technology. Virilio writes about how the developments in flying technology transformed the bodies of pilots, affecting their senses and changing their vision and perception of reality. The fundamental issue is that of the merging of the body and the machine, which in the case of pilots is particularly pronounced owing to the speeds and interaction with space enabled by flying aircraft. As a result of this merger the body is dehumanised, as in the case of driving an armored car when 'an animal . . . disappears in the superpower of a metallic body able to annihilate time and space through its dynamic performances' (Virilio 2006: 84). Such a body grows ever more dependent on various control mechanisms such as 'speedometers, dashboards, remote tele-control' (Virilio

2006: 84). At the same time, the body of the pilot flying an aeroplane in a pressurised cabin is desensitised, as in the case of the pressurised cockpits of US Superfortress bombers used during World War II, which 'have become artificial synthesizers that shut out the world of the senses to a quite extraordinary degree' (Virilio 1989: 26). Flying them was an exhilarating and 'out of this world' experience (Virilio 2006: 84).

As the pilot becomes distant and disconnected from the ordinary world, new fields of experience are open and activated while his relationship with the ordinary world is being transformed. For Virilio the impact of this transformation affects, in the first place, perception, but it is also connected to the question of class and family relationships in a bourgeois society. This is because, as someone influenced by personalism,[7] he sees the body as central to the world and therefore the transformation of the body by technology must also affect the network of bonds and connections in which the body operates. What is postulated in this chapter is that a blind spot in Virilio's writings must be addressed. The argument of the chapter emphasises the difference in the way in which the body reacts to flying, and the way in which it is affected by flying which are not the same in the capitalist context, on which Virilio's writings focus, as in the state socialist one. The social and family bonds, the affective context in which the body is placed, are affected differently in state socialism and in capitalism. Before we discuss how the socialist context impacts on the affective web in which the body is caught we must first present briefly how Virilio understands such an impact in the context of capitalist bodies.

In his typology of pilots Virilio distinguishes between two sets of individuals – a dandy and a proletarian soldier. The first is a good-for-nothing aristocrat, or other such elite type, in search of thrills and excitement. Virilio explains how

> the exploitation of high speeds naturally becomes a sport reserved for dandy-warriors, a fantasy allowed to people who are otherwise useless, a new form of idleness permitted the well-to-do, which will make them regard movement itself as a life-style 'combining risk and comfort'. (Virilio 2009: 111–12)

The elites have always aimed at finding ways to 'transform [the war] from tedious work, where the elites were only servants to the weapons systems, into a more comfortable instrument, under the influence of the engineers, an indolence' (Virilio 2009: 111).

The other type of pilot is the opposite of this 'bellicose dandy seeking the rare sensations of the war' (Virilio 2006: 84). This other body enclosed in the flying machine or other type of war machine is that of a proletarian soldier, whom Virilio sees as 'doubly-unable' (Virilio 2006: 84). As a member of the proletariat he has always been deprived of his will, and 'he now requires physical assistance from a vehicular prosthesis to accomplish his historical mission' (Virilio 2006: 84). What must be considered next is the impact of the socialist context, in which the films discussed in this chapter are set, on these two types of pilots – a dandy and a proletarian soldier – both possible expressions of aerial bodies.

AERIAL BODIES AND HUMAN BONDS

The Case of Pilot Maresz: the socialist dandy in glamorous surroundings

The figure of the pilot Maresz combines the characteristics of both of Virilio's types. His elegant, laid-back, slightly arrogant and aloof manner, a comfortable lifestyle which involves a car and a British lover, Mary Godzicka (Lidia Wysocka), the leisurely pace of his days punctuated by coffees and lunches and culminating in dancing evenings, his tailored clothes, good looks and ability to hold a conversation on any topic, combined with his flying prowess, all point to the dandy type. The film constantly plays on Maresz's being a dandy and uses it to create dramatic tension. For example, we are not sure until the end of the film whether he is a loyal citizen of socialist Poland and will not elope the moment he gets clearance for flying on international routes. His two love interests – Mary, a mature British woman who is planning to return to Britain and an attractive young Polish doctor, Krystyna Flisakówna (Alicja Raciszówna) – are set against each other although they never meet. Maresz moves between the two throughout the film, not exactly hesitating over which one to choose, as he seems to be set on the young doctor, but nonetheless the possibility of rekindling the relationship with the British woman is always there, thus casting a shadow of doubt on Maresz all the way through.

Despite these enduring dramatic tensions, a dandy-like character could not possibly be an acceptable positive hero in socialist reality, and for this reason it does not come as a surprise that his allegiance to socialism must be tested before it is confirmed. This happens first when he agrees to fly rescue planes at weekends to spread a chemical substance to safeguard the forests, which are being marred by insects. He is completely rehabilitated when without hesitation he refuses to have any dealings with the hijacker-spy and flies the plane in such a way that allows his co-pilot to disarm the man. We thus see a different side of the pilot Maresz, who emerges as a conscientious member of socialist society – competent and loyal. The duality of his character shows that under state socialism there is a place and a task for everyone once one recognises and embraces one's duties and obligations and when one begins to employ the skills necessary to advance and help the socialist motherland. The post-Stalinist context moulded a hybrid aerial body that combined the characteristics of a dandy and a proletarian soldier. Such a fusion of the two was a feature of the socialist aerial body.

Against Gods: brother against brother – a generational struggle in the 1960s

Unlike in *The Case of Pilot Maresz*, the two later films *Against Gods* and *On the Earth and in the Sky* do not present different aerial types in one character, but rather contrast two generations of pilots and make them representatives of two different types of human beings depending on their past experiences. Both films take place in a military base and focus on military pilots rather than civil ones. The pilots, who have been in charge since the end of World War II in Poland, are in their fifties. They all share the experience of participating in the air battles of the war.[8] These officers are confronted with a new generation of pilots who are joining their squadrons but who have never participated in active combat. In *Against Gods* the heroism of the pilots during World War II, recounted often during social gatherings, sets a flying standard against which everyone is measured even many years after the war.

The centrepiece of the story is a conflict between two brothers, Karol Doroń (Stanisław Zaczyk) and Piotr Doroń (Mariusz Dmochowski), both of whom are pilots. Piotr lost his sight in combat during the war and can no longer fly. However, he is very much a part of the community of the pilots, spending his days at the airbase while he also shares a flat with Karol and his wife, Maria (Ewa Berger-Jankowska). His heroic behaviour during the flying accident makes him a highly respected member of the pilots' community, who are not just his colleagues but also friends. Karol continues flying until he is involved in a tragic accident, when the failure of his aeroplane results in his decision to abandon it in order to rescue himself. The plane crashes and for the rest of the film the big question is whether Karol had done absolutely everything to rescue the plane, while the suspicion looms that his act was cowardly.

Piotr, whose disability prevented him from ever flying the modern military jets, contrasts the experience of flying regular planes during the war with that of flying modern jets. He argues that the wartime planes made the pilots into a flying cavalry. Such flying was deeply emotional and something Piotr and his fellow pilots admitted to having loved. Flying supersonic jets, on the other hand, turns the pilot into an engineer who has to obey the machine without any emotion attached to the act. This juxtaposition of the emotional pilot in control of his machine with that of the pilot who is controlled by the machine echoes Virilio's contrast between the dandy elite pilot and the proletariat soldier. While the dandy officer welcomes the possibility of flying aeroplanes which he can control, for the proletariat soldier such a machine is a prosthesis, which only makes the disadvantages connected to his class more apparent.

Clearly, the contrast drawn by Virilio is not going to translate perfectly into the universe of the Polish films in question, for the simple reason that the narrative of these films is set not in the capitalist and bourgeois context, but rather that of state socialist reality. It is officers who are equals, and who are not divided by any class differences (and in some cases brothers sharing a flat, like Piotr and Karol), who are set against each other. In Poland of the early 1960s what matters is not class conflict but rather the tension that is connected to different experiences of World War II and the post-war period. The wartime pilot, Piotr, is recognised as a hero but also as someone who cannot understand what modern flying and contemporary warfare is about. In the best tradition of socialist ideology, the individual human decisions made by elite pilots fighting during World War II are replaced by the decisions made by the machine flown by Piotr and the commanding centre on the ground. Piotr's individual decisions, like that of Karol whose plane crashes, cause problems and uncertainty as to his individual judgement, which might have been motivated by fear. What makes the arguments raging throughout the film between the two brothers perverse is that it is Piotr who, motivated by jealousy or simply frustrated by his disability, is the first to cast the shadow of doubt over the motivations of his own brother whose life had been in grave danger. It takes another flight and another life-threatening accident for Karol to rehabilitate himself and to prove Piotr wrong.

The fraternal and generational conflicts reshape Virilio's aerial bodies when they are considered in the Polish historical context. It is this historical difference in the experience of World War II and its technologies present in Poland which forges the socialist aerial body into two different types – the dandy one associated with the wartime generation and the proletarian one associated with the generation of the post-war pilots.

On the Earth and in the Sky: forgetting World War II in Gierek's Poland

The contrast between the wartime generation of pilots and the younger generation is even more pronounced in *On the Earth and in the Sky*, probably because the film is a later production dating from the 1970s. There, the older generation is represented by a doctor, major Marcin Kosowicz (Gustaw Lutkiewicz), attached to the flying squad, who used to be a pilot himself during World War II. He was imprisoned and forbidden to fly after having refused to shoot down a foreign fighter jet that entered Polish airspace in the early 1950s. The doctor argued that the war was over and that he did not feel justified in shooting down the aeroplane, while his superior saw this as insubordination given that the Cold War had already started.

We learn quickly from the film that the doctor is reluctant to talk about his past, and we find out his story through a series of black-and-white flashbacks in an otherwise colour film. At one point in the film the doctor talks intimately with a new arrival at the airbase – a young officer, Major Janusz Horycki (Andrzej Chrzanowski), who becomes the second-in-command. He is an excellent pilot, handsome and loyal to his wife although awkward and distant when it comes to social interactions – which is noticed and commented on by the older generation. Quite provocatively the doctor asks him whether the younger colleague is not bored of only practising and exercising without being involved in active combat. In this way the doctor could be expressing not just the frustration he experiences as an unfairly dismissed pilot, but also frustration which could be felt collectively by the air force, which is preparing itself for the confrontation set up by the Cold War duality that never really comes. They experience the angst of Virilio's pure war. The emotional outpouring of the doctor contrasts with the cool and controlled reply of the younger officer, who says that he has no desire to engage in open combat or to kill anyone and that he is just content with doing what he does – flying every day and keeping at the top of his form. While his response has the aura of professionalism, it does not sound authentic or convincing. Importantly, it chimes with Virilio's conception of a pilot who becomes part of his machine, and his entire emotional life is that of the machine rather than his own emotions. He writes of how

> our existence as a metabolic vehicle can be summed up as a series of collisions, of traumatisms, some taking on the quality of slow but perceptible caresses . . . speed is the cause of death for which we're not responsible but of which we are also the creators and inventors. (Virilio 2009: 112)

What reinforces the younger pilots' identification with the machines is their age and physique. The male characters who dominate in the film are all of roughly the same age, height, weight and appearance, thus making them interchangeable with each other, but also a perfect fit with every jet available in the airbase for them to fly. Significantly, this uniformity also evokes the submersion of the individual under socialism in the collective, which strives to obliterate differences among the members of its collectivity.

The relationships that the military pilots in both films have with their wives further reinforce their identification with the machine and socialist collectivity. Family life as represented in both films is cold, joyless, stifling, and with hardly any hints of eroticism when compared to the excitement and rush that the men get out of flying. Any gestures which are attempts to bring the spouses together fail sooner or later because the underlying tensions connected to flying resurface and dominate. In both cases the wives are frustrated with being forced to live in small towns, but they do nothing to change their situation. There are no children in either family, and there is no talk about having any. Such representations of families, and more broadly human bonds and relations, which are weak (unless they are forged during flying among the male pilots), could be seen in light of the critique of bourgeois culture which Virilio sees in the speed society. Such a critique also chimes with the emphasis placed in socialism on collectivity as opposed to the nuclear family. For Virilio it is the experience of modern high-speed travelling that 'is literally the end of bourgeois culture; the reaction against exoticism and the lyricism of travel' associated with the nineteenth century (Virilio 2009: 111). What is left for the modern being is the experience of speed, in which we can lose ourselves because it 'allows us to think of nothing, to feel nothing, to attain indifference' (Virilio 2009: 111). Just as speed impacts on the experience of travel associated with the nineteenth century, it also disrupts or even obliterates human bonds.

In 1970s film production, the socialist aerial body, equivocal with the human bonds that tie together the aerial body, disappears with the experience of modern technology. Virilio's fear that the body will be annihilated with the encroachment of technology is thus realised in the socialist aerial body we encounter in *On the Earth and in the Sky*.

To Destroy the Pirate: a passion for flying versus family love

In *To Destroy the Pirate* human bonds are of a different kind, even though the test pilot's family is neither traditional nor complete. The wife of the pilot, Piotr Wilkosz (Tadeusz Borowski), is dead and he is raising his son, Paweł (Sergiusz Lach), on his own. This truncated family finds much support in the caring figures of a grandmother (Teofila Koronkiewicz) and a sister (Maria Rabczyńska); the latter also doubles as the medical doctor looking after all the test pilots. Family responsibilities are juxtaposed with the desire for flying. The test pilot interrupts camping holidays with his son in order to return to Warsaw to test-fly the glider. However, throughout his stay in Warsaw the son and the father remain in contact, ringing each other and sending each other telegrams that show that they have a close relationship. Out of concern for his son and sister he also conceals the fact that his flying mission carries a potential death risk. When his glider crash-lands in a controlled crash, allowing the pilot to parachute to safety, he makes sure the members of his family who hurry to the airfield do not see any debris, which is quickly removed from sight. That said, the gliders have the same pull and grip on the pilot as supersonic jets have on the military pilots. However, in comparison to the supersonic jets the gliders appear to be more sensuous, which is emphasised by the frequent shots of the glider landing on a soft grass airfield, sliding until it loses speed completely.

The socialist aerial body in this film possesses more human characteristics mostly because the technology with which it is associated is more tactile and closer to nature, dependent upon the elements, such as the wind. The community of the test pilots, who are also constructors, interestingly reinforces the existence of human bonds beyond family. These human bonds are forged through a much more caring and material contact with technology – as the pilots are also the creators of the aeroplanes which they fly and in which some of them end up dying. We can say that this socialist aerial body is thus both passionate and paradoxical, since the very technology that humanises is also the greatest potential threat to the body's survival.

Socialist aerial bodies represent a much greater range of variations or incarnations than Virilio's aerial bodies. They can be hybrid (dandy-like and proletarian), demarcated by generational and fraternal difference, annihilated by technology, and paradoxical. It is the network of human relations affecting the pilots that shape the aerial body in socialism – more so even than the technology of flying which is the primary force in Virilio's speed society. Just like human bonds, the inability to fly is an aspect of aerial bodies that is not examined by Virilio. The next part of this chapter presents an analysis of aerial bodies in relation to disability, explored in the socialist context, postulating disability as another feature of the socialist aerial bodies ignored in Virilio's discussions.

DISAPPEARING AND DISABLED AERIAL BODIES

Body and perception

Virilio argues that flying 'exploded the old homogeneity of vision and replaced it with the heterogeneity of perceptual fields' (Virilio 1989: 26). That is, aerial bodies have access to different fields of perception from those who only live on the ground and do not get a chance to fly aeroplanes. This heterogeneity of perceptual fields is represented in *Against Gods* and *On the Earth and in the Sky* but also in *To Destroy the Pirate* in a variety of ways. All these films feature sequences showing from the pilots' point of view the outcome of special-effects flying. This 'flying circus' demonstrates, just as Virilio noted, that 'in principle there was no longer an above or below, no longer any visual polarity. War pilots already had their special effect, which they called "looping", "falling-leaf roll", "figure of eight" and so on' (Virilio 1989: 24). The most bravura sequences in these films consist of shots representing sweeping bird's-eye views of the earth. This is a clear demonstration of the ways in which 'aviation was ceasing to be strictly a means of flying and breaking records ... it was becoming one way, or perhaps even the ultimate way, of *seeing*' (Virilio 1989: 22). As sight is one of the senses it is also an important element in any discussion about the body.

The sequences of flying in the films coincide with the moment when the body of the pilot is erased completely from the screen and the machine takes over, with the point of view alternating between the omniscient camera (comparable to the omniscient narrator), the point of view of the pilot, which merges human perception with the perspective of the machine, and the point of view of those observing the aeroplane from the ground. The process of the annihilation of the human body and the primacy gained by the machine, and the point of view it generates, is explained very eloquently by the narrator of *Against Gods* and is also captured in the experience of the disabled pilot – Piotr.

Against Gods: photographic memories of aerial bodies

In the opening of the film, the wide-open shots of skies and shifting clouds taken from the flying plane are layered over the male voice of the new commander of the airbase (Józef Kostecki). The commander is about to introduce himself, but then he changes his mind, which is a striking gesture that depersonalises his voice and experience and makes it universal for all those who fly. He explains how he was put in charge of a legendary World War II flying squad full of heroes and goes on to contrast everyday family life, which passes in a small town adjacent to the airbase where the pilots and their families live, with the thrill and excitement of flying. Spending time flying the supersonic military jets is in stark contrast with the leisurely life on the ground. What is paradoxical is that the pilots feel as if they are in a different world enclosed in their cabins while at the same time the speed of the plane means that if something goes wrong they will crash in a few seconds – their perceived distance from the ground annihilated the moment the machine breaks down. The words of the commander also make it clear that it is not the jets which are the potential enemy of the pilots but the earth itself, which in the case of an accident 'appears out of nowhere like the worst enemy. It is threatening and aggressive'.[9] The pilot's body fails him at this stage as though it were mimicking the failure of the machine: 'blood flows out of the brain. The eyes go black.' The commander concludes his monologue by saying that 'none of the pilots is frightened by any of these for this is their everyday life. To be fit, to be precise, knowledgeable and in control', all of which makes the pilot more like a machine than a human being.

For Virilio, flying obliterates human perception and supplements or even replaces it with a new kind of a perceptual field – which cinema supplies in much the way as photography initially did. Cinema and photography, both as loci of memory, are thus a type of perceptual prosthesis. The process of obliterating vision and its substitution are dramatised through one of the themes in *Against Gods*. Piotr, the hero pilot from World War II, literally loses his natural vision and is blinded as a result of flying. He still has photographs from his private archives, which he shares with his pilot colleagues, which serve as a kind of mnemonic prosthesis. The photographs capture something which – for the blind Piotr and his colleagues, especially the younger ones, who have no memory or experience of the battle – it is impossible to see. Therefore the photographs are themselves a powerful perceptive field. They have a dramatic effect as they become arguments in the 'battle of visions' which is at the heart of the film in more than one way. In order to humanise and sensitise this prosthetic vision, for a short moment in the film when the characters look at the photographs we hear sounds of the battle, which can only be the products of the imaginary perception of the characters viewing the images.

On the Earth and in the Sky: the ailing aerial body

The point in the narrative of *On the Earth and in the Sky* when a new perceptive field appears, that generated by the machine, is when the top pilot of the flying squad, Major Zygmunt Grela (Piotr Fronczewski), knows that this is his last flight for a long time because of his health problems. While we see him flying on numerous occasions, it is only when he becomes aware of his health condition that he decides to take his aeroplane for this thrilling spin. We see him in an exhilarated and euphoric state, as though this type of flying were synonymous for him with the ultimate exuberance flying could offer. As his body is ailing, the machine seems to compensate for its weakness in a truly spectacular way. Flying, like cinema, makes '"the unseen" visible, that is to say, a world-without-memory and of unstable dimensions' (Virilio 1989: 26). New types of unknown forms become visible, which can only be qualified as 'impossible, supernatural, marvelous' (Virilio 1989: 27). This obliteration of the ailing aerial body at the expense of the growing prowess of the aeroplane shows how the machine can take over the perceptive powers of the body and replace it, which is the threat that technology poses according to Virilio.

To Destroy the Pirate: the dead aerial body

In *To Destroy the Pirate*, the question of perception in the context of flying is presented as an ethical issue. A constructor who is also an experienced test pilot dies in a glider crash. His fellow constructors, who participated in the design and construction of the glider, try to find out what caused the tragic accident. They come up with a set of hypotheses, which can only be tested by attempting another flight on the same type of glider. The challenge lies in the fact that such a test flight has to involve a crash as well. For this reason a number of provisions are put in place which would allow the pilot to escape from the machine in time, although this does not change the fact that he is taking an extreme risk in flying the glider. The operation is successful and the hypothesis is proved to be correct. What is striking in the story is that it was not a construction error that could have been detected through a set of calculations. Rather, the accident had to happen for this construction error to become apparent. In this film the shift in the field of perception becomes an ethical issue when the aerial body is destroyed. Sacrifices involving innocent human lives and taking extreme risks with one's life are necessary to improve the construction, performance and, ultimately, the safety of the gliders, pointing to the greater importance of the machine over the human body and life. The perceptual field experienced by the pilot who died in the accident must be reconstructed and re-entered by another pilot in order to understand fully its dimensions and characteristics. His colleagues listen repeatedly to the recording of the crash, which is narrated step by step by the pilot who died. They are able to posit their hypothesis when they analyse the audio recording of the flight, taking into account the dead pilot's personality and how it would be possible for him to report one set of actions while doing the opposite. The pressure on the other test pilot is intense, not only because he puts his life at risk but also because understanding the origins of the problem will lead to improving the construction of the glider in such a way that this will enable it to represent Poland and compete internationally.

The existence of various types of disabled aerial bodies is not confined to films about aviation made under socialism. However, what this section has demonstrated is that the Polish context has created opportunities for a variety of dramatic situations involving the pilots and technology, which allowed for this aspect of the aerial body to be explored and represented. It is for this reason that the disabled body is also seen here as a possible expression of the socialist aerial body.

CONCLUSION

In conclusion it is important to note another characteristic of the socialist aerial body present in all the films discussed here – which is its connection to the earth. What all the films in question have in common is the fact that they are controlled by the command on the ground who guides the aeroplane, is aware of its whereabouts and grows anxious when contact with the aeroplane is disrupted or lost. This strict control is the expression of the attempt by those on the ground to harness and contain the fields of perception flying enables. The pilots are not supposed to fly too high or too low or out of the national borders of Poland unless instructed otherwise. If new fields of perception are activated pilots may end up taking decisions that go against the wishes of ground control. It is for this reason that the narrative of the films is punctuated with commands issued from the ground, juxtaposed with the bird's-eye views of the ground – which create an impression that the pilot has entered a different sphere where the link to the earth is in danger of becoming tenuous. Once in the air the pilots become aerial bodies subject to different laws and desires, and their bodies are something which needs to be contained – through the audio connection to ground command. The pressure to do so is greater in relation to the socialist aerial body because of the highly militarised, politicised and ideological context of the films in socialist Poland, versus other contexts where the aerial body operates. For in the Polish case the connection to ground control is not just about military discipline and the obligation on the soldiers to follow orders; the connection to the ground has a deep ideological dimension to it, which ultimately has to prevail and dominate the pilot's fields of perception. Anything different to that would be perceived as an error, as is the case in *To Destroy the Pirate* and *Against Gods*, or a possible challenge to ground command as is implied in *The Case of Pilot Maresz*.

NOTES

1. Przylipiak includes the following titles: *Solidarni 2010* (2010), *Krzyż* (2011), *Lista pasażerów* (2011) by Ewa Stankiewicz and Jan Pospieszalski; *10.04.10*, *Anatomia upadku*, *Anatomia upadku (Part II)* directed by Anita Gargas; *Mgła* (2010) by Joanna Lichocka and Maria Dłużewska; *Letter from Poland* (2010) by Mariusz Pilis; *Smoleński lot* (2011) by Monika Sieradzka; *W milczeniu* (2011) and *Tragedy in Smoleńsk* (2011) by Ewa Ewart.
2. Virilio acknowledged World War II as the formative experience for his intellectual identity, which developed further in the period of the Cold War, which he referred to as 'pure war' – the continuous preparation of a conflict that was always delayed (Virilio and Lotringer 2008: 176).
3. *The Case of Pilot Maresz* was made with the support of LOT Polish Airlines and Liga Przyjaciół Żołnierza/Soldier's Friendship League; *Against Gods* with that of Dowództwa Wojsk Lotniczych/AirForce Command and OPLOK – System Obrony Przeciwlotniczej Obszaru Kraju/The Air Defense System of the Country's Territory; *On the Earth and in the Sky* – Wojsk Lotniczych OPK (System Obrony Powietrznej Kraju)/Air Force belonging to the Air Defense System of the Country. The exception here is the latest film considered in this chapter, *To Destroy the Pirate*, which was about a community of glider constructors and test pilots whose production was supported by a non-military gliding society – Aeroklub Polskiej Rzeczpospolitaj Ludowej/The AirClub of the Polish People's Republic.
4. As Przedpełski notes, the development of civil aviation was another way in which the air force sought to be legitimised (1997: 276). *The Case of the Pilot Maresz* is in part the reflection of such efforts.
5. It is interesting to note that Polish cinema was not the only one featuring films about aviation in the Cold War period. According to Paris, '[a]viation films located in the events of the cold war and glorifying patriotic endeavor and technical achievement, formed an important element of American cinema from 1953 through to the mid-1960s' (1995: 195).

6. Unlike other films it is also a film production meant for TV – another institution that went from strength to strength in the 1970s.
7. Ian James argues that 'they [Virilio's politics] should, rather, be understood in relation to the personalist movement in France and the thinking of personalism developed during 1930s by Emmanuel Mounier who founded the influential Catholic review *Esprit* in 1932. Personalism was a political doctrine which set itself squarely against what it would call "bourgeois liberalism", individualism and industrial capitalism . . . it sought to promote the notion of a community organised according to the value of the person, that is a community in which persons and personal relations would form the key reference point' (2007: 117–18).
8. The dialogues of the film suggest that these pilots were active in the Polish Air Force formed in the Soviet Union rather than in the RAF, unlike in *The Case of Pilot Maresz*.
9. All translations from the Polish are mine unless otherwise indicated.

WORKS CITED

Cynk, Jerzy B. (1972), *History of the Polish Airforce. 1918–1968*, Reading: Osprey.
James, Ian (2007), *Paul Virilio*, London: Routledge.
Lubelski, Tadeusz (2009), *Historia kina polskiego. Twórcy, filmy, konteksty*, Katowice: Videograph 2.
Paczkowski, Andrzej (2003), *The Spring Will Be Ours. Poland and the Poles from Occupation to Freedom*, trans. Jane Cave, University Park, PA: The Pennsylvania State University Press.
Paris, Michael (1995), *From the Wright Brothers to Top Gun: Aviation, nationalism and popular cinema*, Manchester and New York: Manchester University Press.
Przedpełski, Andrzej (1997), *Lotnictwo Wojska Polskiego. Zarys Historii 1918–1996*, Warszawa: Wydawnictwo Bellona.
Przylipiak, Mirosław (2013), 'Memory, National Identity, and the Cross: Polish Documentary Film about the Smolensk Plane Crash', in L. Berezhnaya and C. Schmitt (eds), *Iconic Turns: Nation and Religion in Eastern European Cinema since 1989*, Leiden: Brill, pp. 217–37.
Virilio, Paul (1989), *War and Cinema: The Logistics of Perception*, trans. Patrick Camiller, London: Verso.
Virilio, Paul (2006), *Speed and politics*, trans. Marc Polizzotti, Boston: MIT Press.
Virilio, Paul (2009), *The Aesthetics of Disappearance*, trans. Philip Beitchman, Los Angeles: Semiotext(e).
Virilio, Paul and Sylvère Lotringer (2008), *Pure War*, trans. Mark Polizzotti, Los Angeles: Semiotext(e).
Zwierzchowski, Piotr (2013), *Kino polskie wczoraj i dziś. Kino nowej pamięci obraz II wojny światowej w kinie polskim lat 60*, Bydgoszcz: Wydawnictwo Uniwersytetu Kazimierza Wielkiego.

CHAPTER 12

The 'Chemistry' of Art(ifice) and Life: Embodied Paintings in East European Cinema

Ágnes Pethő

> It would seem that things and senses are no longer in conflict with one another but have struck an alliance thanks to which the most detached abstraction and the most unrestrained excitement are almost inseparable.
> Mario Perniola (2004: 1)

BODIES OBJECTIFIED AS PAINTINGS

Steering away from all the mainstream 'new waves' which emerged in post-communist cinemas – and which are in some ways loosely connected to the tradition defined by the cinematic poetry of Andrei Tarkovsky, the ornamentalism of Sergei Paradjanov and the bizarre surrealism of Wojciech Has – we can distinguish a persistent undercurrent in recent East European cinema consisting of films that favour a painterly style, foregrounding the sensual and conceptual charge of the cinematic image. This is a tendency that is perhaps most palpable in the manifold revitalisation of the trope of the *tableau vivant*, of bodies posed in compositions resembling paintings, and in an aesthetics that shifts the focus from narrative to the compelling visual attraction of carefully crafted, autonomous frames. While the critical and theoretical reception of contemporary East European cinema repeatedly focuses on issues of time, space and identity, reflecting the complex changes brought about by the fall of communism, the disintegration of borders, and the growing tendencies of globalisation,[1] these 'undercurrents' may challenge us to shift our points of view and observe in them an intense fixation on the language of moving images itself, a search for new forms of cinematic pictorialism which go beyond the conventional rhetoric of picturesque images enhancing the emotional impact of a narration and emphasise a complex relationship between the photographic image of the film and the art of painting. We may find, however, that this perspective does not just redirect our attention towards matters of style and mediality or intermediality in general, but may also reveal different ways in which these films manage to dissolve the cultural boundaries between East and West by connecting to particular, universally-known references to Western art, as well as through their affinity with more widespread trends in arthouse cinema, while maintaining their distinctively local, historical reference frames, thus operating a new, complex system of 'liminalities'.

This shift of focus from narrative to visuals, and the excessive emphasis on pictorial effects, is a poetic strategy that is by no means specific to East European or even to contemporary world cinema. Painterly compositions in a broad sense (descriptive, *tableau*-like shots achieved with minimum movement), or re-creations of specific paintings in cinema (i.e. *tableaux vivants* in a narrower, theatrical sense), can be seen as intermedial figures that are present in different ways throughout film history. The *tableaux* compositions of early cinema, for example, were used instead of a more elaborate narrative structure unfolding in time, in order to condense multiple figures and the whole action into one image resembling a painting or a carefully devised theatrical scene. In some of the genre films of classical Hollywood (westerns, musicals), or so-called historical 'heritage' films, we see a more decorative, rhetorical, or even ideological use of *tableau*-like images producing moments of aesthetic detachment. In modern and postmodern cinema, the *tableau vivant* became a mode of self-reflexivity and deliberate subversion of the classical narrative style. Jean-Luc Godard's 1982 film *Passion*, for example, uses the re-enactment of a series of famous paintings as a platform for an explicit critique of Hollywood-style storytelling. Peter Greenaway elaborated a so-called database aesthetic based on lists, permutations and a series of theatrical and painterly *tableaux* as an alternative to classical narrative forms. In contemporary cinema, the reconceptualisation of the cinematic *tableau* (both in its wider and narrower sense) often occurs in the context of what has been described as 'picto-films',[2] 'contemplative/slow cinema'[3] bordering on minimalist, experimental 'stasis films',[4] a type of cinema that may already be discussed as an individual paradigm, one that has arguably advanced from being associated with cinemas of the 'periphery' (i.e. working outside canonical forms of Hollywood-type storytelling and outside powerful centres of the film industry) to dominating a major slice of the repertoires of film festivals. Moreover, digital media (with its gifs, cinemagraphs, parallax scrolling websites, large-scale video loops, and so on) have revitalised various forms of the *tableau* as typical post-cinematic images permeating all layers of contemporary visual culture, connecting the still 'photographic' and the moving 'cinematic' experience. The examples from East European cinema discussed below can clearly be situated within such a broad context, in which both the borders between East

European and global art cinema and the borders between traditional 'high' art and new media have become increasingly porous within the so-called post-postmodern and post-media era.

In her book *The Material Image: Art and the Real in Film*, Brigitte Peucker reminds us that in addition to fashionable parlour games of the eighteenth and nineteenth centuries, the *tableau vivant* also has its origins in pornographic staging of sexually enticing bodies, and considers that it is exactly 'in its manifestation of embodied painting' (2007: 30), often 'as or through the female body', and essentially through the presence of the illusion of palpable flesh, that the *tableau vivant* 'figures the introduction of the real into the image – the living body into painting – thus attempting to collapse the distance between signifier and signified' (2007: 31). There is, however, the possibility of conceiving the *tableau vivant* as a reversal of this process, in which embodiment is not erotic in nature (as we see, for example, in all of Greenaway's films) or, at least, not in its conventional sense, but can be related to what the Italian philosopher Mario Perniola has described as 'the sex appeal of the inorganic' (2004), resulting in a fascination with the image itself: not with painting viewed in the form of 'real', living, breathing (eroticised) bodies but with bodies objectified as paintings. Accordingly, the *tableau vivant* does not always attempt to merge representation with the real and to collapse the distance between signifier and signified, but in certain cases emerges as a site for cultivating their distance in the opposition of sensuous form and abstract meaning, moving image and static painting, live bodies in action and objects contemplated as a visual display, framing their intricate plays of in-betweenness. I have found that, in some of the films I have analysed, the *tableaux vivants* proper (i.e. images imitating a particular painting or sculpture) together with other, similar techniques in cinema (static, *tableau*-like shots, inserts of photographs and photographic reproductions of paintings) not only reflect on the connections between the visual arts, but, perhaps even more importantly, enclose almost irreconcilable extremes: from a sensation of corporeality in pictures coming alive as embodied paintings to the distanciating effect generated by conspicuous artificiality and stylisation.

CADAVEROUS *TABLEAUX VIVANTS*

The quintessential image framing such antithetical extremes of 'things' and 'senses' (as perhaps the most puzzling instances of the rhetoric of pictoriality in East European cinema) can be identified in the type of *tableau vivant* that is, paradoxically, closely connected to the idea of death (the imminence of death, the sight of a disfigured, ailing body), in which a live body is displayed as a corpse, or the other way round: a corpse is presented as an embodied picture, or an object of art made of flesh. The striking still compositions that can be associated with paintings, painterly styles, pictorial photographs, or art installations incorporated by cinema have the rhetorical function of highlighting the grave undertones of a narrative which always leans towards the construction of a more or less overt allegory, in the mood of tragicomedy and the grotesque, of gritty family drama, or of a more abstract or lyrical meditation with biblical or philosophical connotations. In each case, the *tableau* form confers on the filmic discourse a degree of constructedness and aestheticism that often emerges in a tense interplay with unsettling subject matters, or, in certain cases, even a repulsive naturalism of scenes.

The most extreme example that offers an emblematic image for a typical East European mixture between artificiality and 'life', conceptualisation and corporeality embodied in a *tableau vivant* (and also a kind of literal presentation of the desire, described by Perniola, to become an object), can be found in the ending of György Pálfi's *Taxidermia* (2006). The film is constructed in the form of a triptych of three satirical episodes, centred on the lives of three consecutive generations (or rather, as the critic Peter Bradshaw (2007) called it, 'degenerations') of men made representative of three distinct historical periods in Hungary. The first part takes us to the generation of World War II, the second part revisits the period of Soviet domination, and the story concludes in the present, in a Hungary stripped of any distinctive features, in the clinically sterile environment of an art gallery. Each of these parts can also be seen as a bizarre tale of survival. The survival of social humiliation in a hierarchical society and of the ordeals of war leads to an instinct towards animalistic procreation and bizarre sexual proclivities. The survival in (what used to be considered by some) 'the merriest barrack' of the Eastern bloc under Soviet rule, in what has come to be known as 'goulash communism', takes the form of insane consumerism practised as popular, national sport. Finally, a 'survival' of the fall of communism is achieved by reinventing the same degenerate family as an exhibit in a macabre panopticon of stuffed bodies that can be presented as 'art', moving the characters out of 'the communist barrack' directly into an aestheticised freak show displayed for the entertainment of Western art consumers. Each of these constitutes a grotesque caricature of an era by focusing on different activities connected to the body and presented as a kind of performance: magical-realist sex, a twisted gargantuan gorging of food in a speed-eating competition, and, finally, hyperrealist taxidermy (the last progeniture preserves the family 'heritage', i.e. their own bodies, by mounting them for an installation). In the grandiose finale, we are shown, in a harrowingly long sequence of close-ups, how the protagonist's body is eviscerated, stuffed, stitched up and eventually transformed into an artwork (a body sculpture or body installation), and exhibited in a well-known pose for Western art in a trendy, contemporary art gallery (reminiscent at the same time of paintings

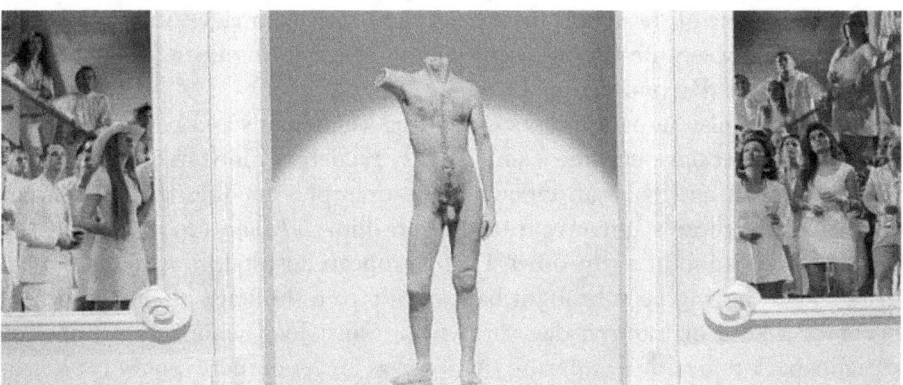

Figure 12.1 György Pálfi: *Taxidermia* (2006)

depicting the martyrdom of Saint Sebastian and of Hellenistic torsos) in front of an audience also posing motionless as a *tableau vivant*.

Steven Shaviro called the film 'viscerally charged and icily allegorical' (2012: 33), and as a whole Pálfi's film is an uncanny combination of social satire and concept art, with shocking, gut-wrenching images of flesh. The imagery has its source in the provocative meat-sculptures of the Hungarian installation artist Géza Szőllősi,[5] who served as an art director for the film, and whose shocking artworks grouped in his 'Project Flesh' use raw meat to create hyperrealist sculptures of truncated human bodies. Pálfi's film can be seen as an extension of such a visceral concept art of the flesh, initiating in his cinema a direct dialogue with contemporary art.

Leaving aside the unique combination of the disgusting with the decorative in *Taxidermia*, on a more abstract level, the *tableau vivant* displaying a corpse captures the potentially cadaverous nature of all *tableaux vivants*. As Aura Satz pointed out,

> the living picture lacks articulation (vocal, physical, and narrative), it has ossified into rigor mortis, and if and when it slackens, this is only so as to shift into the next pose, the next statue, or to snap out of it and back to normal fluid life. The *tableau vivant* is in fact a temporary cadaver, a presence which has petrified into object. (Satz 2009: 163)

Moreover, we can add, quoting Caitlin Baucom's (2014) interpretation of Satz, that the *tableau* can be conceived as 'a cadaver of a cadaver because it hardens into something already dead, referring always to a body image outside of its own'.[6] The taxidermied corpses at the end of Pálfi's film perform this morbidification of dead bodies into other bodies becoming art exhibits, and are highly symptomatic of the almost inhuman detachment, if not always irony, with which some of these films construct their stylised images building on the opposition between life and art, sensual and abstract, fossilising their human figures into 'dead' iconographic forms.

We see this also in paraphrases of Andrea Mantegna's and Hans Holbein's dead Christ that have become a surprisingly recurrent motif in contemporary East European and Russian cinema. The examples include the Hungarian Kornél Mundruczó's unconventional opera-film *Johanna* (2005), set in the depressing location of a run-down East European hospital, in which a female drug addict, having been brought back to life from the stage of clinical death, becomes a kind of modern-day, provincial Saint Joan who nurses hopeless patients back to health by offering them sex as an act of mercy, only for her to be killed and discarded from the medical facility like trash. The film contrasts the dismal artificial world of the hospital where people are strapped to beds and connected to machines with the supposed naturalness of the sexual act, the abject sight of the sickly bodies with the rendering of dialogues as opera arias or recitatives, with the stylised colour palette of the images enhanced by sequences presenting the listless, prone bodies as paraphrases of the Dead Christ or showing Johanna resembling Vermeer's painting of *The Girl with the Pearl Earring*. All of this results in a mixture of aestheticism, absurdity and pathos which the viewer may find just as disturbing as Pálfi's combination of nauseating sarcasm and stunning visuals.

Mundruczó reprises the allegorical contrast between the unnatural and natural, cultural and instinctive in his next film, *Delta* (2008), in which the male protagonist (played by the renowned world music violinist and composer Félix Lajkó[7]), returning home after a long time away, engages in an incestuous affair with his sister (who has a telling name, Fauna) with tragic consequences amid the 'primitive' and harsh realities of a colony of fishermen, and in which again, we find a paraphrase of Mantegna's famous painting. This time, the elements of the painting and of the Biblical situation are reversed: it is not the Virgin Mary leaning over the body of Christ overcome by grief that we see, but the frail body of the innocent young woman lying feverishly on a bed in the small cabin that the siblings have built on the water. After she has been raped by her stepfather it is her Christ-like brother who takes care of her, wraps her in a damp cloth (arranging her in the reclining position we have come to know from Mantegna's famous canvas), and sits by her side. The tone here is more elegiac than socially critical; the beautiful shots of the Danube Delta paint a mythical backdrop, a kind of lethal paradise, where the unravelling tragedy is subdued by the gorgeous cinematography. The image reminiscent of Mantegna's Christ is prepared slowly as the male protagonist carefully arranges the sheet around the woman's body, and the *tableau* emerges seamlessly from the flow of other picturesque compositions. There is no shock value in its appearance, the association is subtle, and the image becomes like a fading palimpsest, the familiar pose and composition barely resurfacing within the cinematic *mise-en-scène*.

A similar melancholic mood prevails in Béla Tarr's last film *A torinói ló* (*The Turin Horse*, 2011), which also unfolds an allegorical story, staging through a slow, minimalist narrative and a series of photographic *tableaux*, how – in a reversal of Genesis – the world comes to an end. Death acquires cosmic and philosophical proportions and is prefigured by presenting the protagonist as the embodiment of both Mantegna's and Holbein's dead Christ. These paraphrases not only constitute in their austere simplicity a sublime figuration of lamentation for the end of mankind but also underscore Tarr's extraordinary attention to how each frame is constructed. The elements are simple, the film is constructed using only a few building blocks (an old man, a daughter, a horse, a house, a tree); each scene is like a slowly moving photograph within a video installation, there is nothing left to chance. And while we have a heightened sensation of photographic realism in the details (e.g. we see the fine grain of the wooden table, the rough texture of the plain clothes, etc.), everything is stylised and far from lifelike. Instead of a story with characters revealing psychological depths there is only a sequence of repetitive actions, and bodies framed and reframed as images, and, ultimately, images fading away.[8]

Benedek Fliegauf's *Dealer*[9] (2004), presenting the last day in the life of an unnamed drug dealer, conceives the cinematic image in the same vein as Tarr. The mostly uneventful narrative is slowly paced, with static images of cold and eerie beauty, and deals primarily with feelings of loss and emptiness. The dialogue is scarce; the protagonist moves in spaces that are either cluttered with junk or seem vacuous and sterile, accompanied by metallic, trance-like non-diegetic music. The film concludes with a long sequence in which the protagonist takes an overdose of drugs in a fitness salon and climbs into a tanning bed as if it were a coffin. As he lies down, his stretched-out body, seen through the narrow opening of the machine, is reminiscent of Holbein's elongated corpse of the dead Christ, resulting in a powerful image crossing modern technology with classical iconography, an ironic view of the cult of the body and a melancholic awareness of the hopeless isolation and transience of the body. The sequence is prolonged and the image of the tanning bed moved further and further away from the viewer against a dark background, until it disappears like a spaceship within the infinite black universe, or is reduced to a dot on the screen before its final blackout as the film itself shuts down like a machine. Death appears at the same time as mechanical (as a final disconnection from the world), grotesque (self-destruction in a fitness salon), and transcendental. The cold, artificial light cast over the body of the protagonist in this pose retroactively sheds a different light over the whole story, elevating it both from its realistic portrayal of contemporary urban ennui or desolation, and from a mere exercise of style, by capturing the moment of death as an enigmatic *tableau vivant* eliciting multiple associations among which the famously humanised depiction of the dead Christ is also one, though not an exclusive, possibility.

Perhaps the most complex use of the reproduction of Mantegna's painting can be found in Andrei Zvyagintsev's debut film, *Vozvrashcheniye* (*The Return*, 2003), where it not only becomes a clearly marked vantage point that doubles the reference frame of the otherwise realistic narrative, suggesting the possibility of an allegorical reading, but also makes the viewer prepared for further, less obvious biblical motifs or cinematic quotations, and initiates an intricate play between images and media.

The film is about two teenage boys whose father returns after a long and unexplained absence.[10] One day, coming home after playing with their friends, out of the blue, their mother tells them that their father is home and asleep; they go into the house and find him in the bedroom in the posture that we know from Mantegna's painting. The sons contemplate his appearance in awe standing in the doorway of the room where his foreshortened body is lying on the bed, like a strange exhibit in a glass cage.

The viewer immediately sees the resemblance to the painting in the details of the *mise-en-scène*, but is also struck by the incongruities: instead of Mantegna's sculptural and massive corpse lying on a marble slab with the Virgin Mary weeping at his side, we behold the inert body of a man very much alive, covered with shiny silk bed sheets during an afternoon nap, with a cool breeze flowing through the open window and birds chirping outside. The cold bluish-green colours that blend together the elements of the scene, filtering the image like a thin veil, separating the viewer and the body on display, cannot erase the palpable impression of the mild sweat over the skin, of the spiky stubble on the man's chin, or the hairs over his chest moving slowly as he breathes deeply, sunk into the oblivion of sleep. The scene captures the

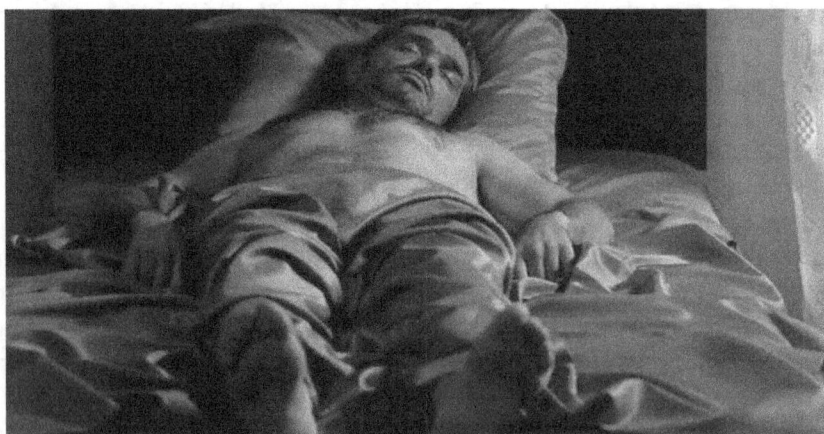

Figure 12.2 Andrei Zvyagintsev: *The Return* (2003)

essence of the cinematic *tableau vivant*, which is not simply a reproduction, a re-enactment of a scene, a pose recorded by a camera, but a 'performance' laying bare what cinema does best: suspending the image of the body in the in-between zone of life and death, rendering it at the same time aestheticised and plainly corporeal, distanciating and intimate, familiar yet disturbingly strange.[11]

As the boys do not remember the man, they run off to compare the photo they have of him with the image appearing to them in the bedroom. The father, who has until now existed for the boys only as a figure in a photograph (tucked away in the attic in an album illustrating biblical scenes, placed in the category of symbolic images), materialises in this way in an uncanny form duplicating a painting, as a body, an image, an idea – also, perhaps, as an incarnation of the myth of the Father as the embodiment of virility and of Russia itself.[12] When he awakes, he appears to be distant, unsympathetic, eager to assert his paternal authority and enigmatic. He sits down to a final meal together with the two women (mother and grandmother, who have both been left outside the frame reproducing the painting earlier) and his children, in a shot reminiscent of Leonardo da Vinci's *Last Supper*. Then he sets out on a mysterious voyage, a fishing trip with his sons. The story unfolds within a mythical time frame (beginning with Sunday, when the father-creator rests and ending with Friday, when the Christ-like father dies), along clearly symbolic axes: horizontally (undertaking a symbolic voyage of initiation, as the father takes the boys on a road trip) and vertically – the acts of ascent, descent, rise and fall. The film is framed by the image of a tower: at the beginning we see the younger son being too afraid to dive into a lake from it; at the end, being angry with his father, the same boy climbs another tower threatening to jump down, and as he attempts to go after him the father accidentally plunges to his death. At which point his sons are faced with the difficult task of acting as grown-ups dealing with the lifeless body of their father and driving home on their own.

The title of the film, *The Return*, may be interpreted both literally, referring to the father who returns to see his two teenage sons, and symbolically, given that the film introduces the sleeping father as the replica of the dead Christ and presents events leading up to his actual death. The death of the father can, in this way, be seen as a return to this initial state (the parallelism is striking: the corpse of the man lying in the boat is shown from the same angle as that from which we saw him lying on the bed imitating the Mantegna painting, and the boys are left with a similar, if even more horrified, look on their faces as the boat suddenly begins to sink). So it is actually the loss of the father that returns. But while the body of the father disappears in the murky water of the lake, and the impression of Mantegna's painting is washed away by the photogenic layer of the waves within the cinematic frame, the power of the 'image' itself is reinstated and reinforced. What has been lost in painting is now regained in photography. The film ends with a series of photographs, in which – except for the very last frame – the father is absent, yet we are now aware of his existence either 'off space' (as we remember the scenes when the photos were taken) or behind the camera (in the old photos that we presume he took of his wife and infant sons). These final photographs, used as a substitute for the diary of the boys, contrast the performativity of the instantaneous, personal snapshots (being singular, subjective, incidental) and imprints of bodies in motion with the constructedness, stasis and symbolic weight of pictorial iconography manifest in the explicit *tableau vivant* scene, as well as with the sensuous elements of the moving image in the carefully-framed photographic shots or in the recurring landscape *tableaux* of the film. Thus the film rounds up different possibilities of people becoming images and images moving from one medium onto another. From the art-historical 'aura' and symbolism of the Mantegna painting, and the enigmatic cinematic embodiment as a *tableau vivant*, the image of the father is carried to other associations with drawings illustrating the Bible, to frames of pictorialist cinematography (which delight the eye but only enhance the enigmatic character of the father, whose aestheticised images do not compensate for the fact that his actions remain unexplained), and finally to the intimacy of the family photographs. In this way, by foregrounding both the symbolic value of images and their performativity in our lives (how we are affected by them, how we interpret the world through them, how their signification may puzzle us, or how we may affirm ourselves through their various palpable forms), the allegory is as much about our indissoluble, intimate relationship to images, accordingly, about the relationship between image, body and differences in medium (painting, film and photography), as it is about oedipal rites of passage standing in for contemporary traumas in a post-communist society.

Zvyagintsev's next feature film, *Izgnanie* (*The Banishment*, 2007), expands the theme of the loss of the father into the disintegration of the traditional family, the loss of the mother, the loss of 'faith',[13] the banishment from 'paradise', and makes this meta-referential layer even more complex with frames composed like paintings, with biblical symbolism, and with photographs counterpointing both filmic images and paintings in a dreamlike narrative. Among the many references to paintings, there are a couple of examples which seem most relevant for this line of thought. The first is a kind of *mise en abyme*: in one of the most powerful sequences of the film, just before the protagonist's wife undergoes an abortion, we see how a group of children are working on a jigsaw puzzle, fitting together pieces reproducing Leonardo da Vinci's *Annunciation*. The picture is dismembered and spread out on the floor, and as the camera films them from above the children are not only made part of the ensemble, but are incorporated within the pattern, overlaid as images over images. The quotation is explicit; it is not a cinematic *tableau vivant* reproduction. The picture alludes, however, to the crucial element in the plot (the possible birth of a child whose father is unknown), emphasising the possibility of a symbolic reading, and reflects a salient feature of the visual style directing our attention to the recurring static frames which constitute jigsaw-puzzle-like *tableaux* in the film, or in which different kinds of images are laid on top of each other. Mantegna's image of the dead Christ, which was so accurately reproduced and placed at the gravity centre of *The Return*, seems to haunt this film as well, as elements of the painting resurface in two scenes. In both cases, the bodies we see are not dead but in extreme shock: in a reversal of the position of the body we see the father (played by the same actor, Konstantin Lavronenko) stricken with grief, as he collapses after the death of his wife with his face down; in the flashback sequence we see the wife in a similar position as Christ in the painting with her feet towards the viewer after her attempted suicide. Focusing this time more on the figure of the woman, who is depicted through a dense mesh of pictorial references, the film draws a similar circular trajectory from filmic presence and painterly stylisation to the photograph as a recording of the moment and object of memory (and back) to the trajectory seen in *The Return*, offering a synthesis in the photo of Vera and her two young children captured in the pose paraphrasing Da Vinci's *Virgin and Child with St Anne and John the Baptist* (1499–1500). As such, if Pálfi's use of conceptual 'body horror' (Shaviro 2012) in *Taxidermia* can be positioned at the extreme of morbid satire (and a narrative literalisation of contemporary art's fetishising of bodies exhibited as objects), Zvyagintsev's films, gracefully weaving together painting, cinema and photography, may be placed on the opposite pole, as examples of a poetic use of 'embodied images' as 'embodied ideas'.

NOSTALGIA FOR 'THE BIG PICTURE'

Perhaps the most important question regarding these films, which give such prominence to references to paintings and *tableau vivant*-like images, is how we should interpret this highly rhetoricised/allegorical mode of expression. Is it an excessive repetition of the modernist models of abstraction that critics usually associate with such films?[14] Should we attribute the phenomenon to Eastern Europe's peripheral status against Western Europe and global capitalism (taking into account Jameson's highly controversial assertion about the connection between the allegorical mode of expression and 'third-worldish'-ness[15]) and to the perpetuation of frustrations caused by social and political crises that pushes artists towards an abstract, fragmented style and the construction of parables (see Xavier 2007)? In another chapter included in this collection, Hajnal Király speaks of the sublimation of crisis through beauty in recent Hungarian cinema corresponding to the extended concept of *anamorphosis* as a complex symptom of *melancholia*, and also as a form of cinematic mannerism. Or we may find, in this emphasis on aesthetic stylisation of individual images, and in these repeated allusions to masterpieces of European art, the gesture of offering to Western audiences tales told in the manner they expect from these cinemas, which, following the heritage of 'various post-war national new waves', in the words of Randall Halle (2010: 303), have become 'associated with high cultural film art'. In this context, 'universal' themes and imagery derived from (primarily Western) art history can be expected signs of sophistication. Moreover, these easily recognisable references can facilitate connections to a wider cultural and artistic heritage, and we may wonder if as such they can also be interpreted as manifestations of a persistent self-colonising instinct seeking to reaffirm connections between the cultures of Eastern and Western Europe.

Then again, we may note that the recurrence of paraphrases of famous paintings alongside secularisations of religious iconography which can engage with a multinational audience, and the penchant for *tableau* constructions (and even for triptych formats), also corresponds with an established practice in video and new media art (see for example some of Bill Viola's controversial video installations), so, at least in part, this may prove just as strongly a genuine affinity with what is happening in the field of contemporary art and 'expanded cinema'. What seems also plausible, therefore, is that this extraordinary preoccupation with form and allegorical layers of mediation is somehow not just a displacement, a means of avoiding addressing issues in a more direct way, but can be regarded in connection with experimentation and authorship. As opposed to in times of dictatorship, the author in contemporary Eastern Europe no longer needs to adopt the stance of a political dissident forced to speak in arthouse-style parables. However, facing the deficiencies of institutional backgrounds in filmmaking (and a total lack of demand for East European genre films on global markets), authorship has become the default mode of creativity, with style offering the possibility of exercising absolute control and, in certain cases, of deliberately solidifying the 'art' component in the 'art film' that may guarantee (with the rise of the festival circuit) a global appeal for these films. Accordingly, the carefully crafted single image, the *tableau* form in its expanded sense, has been turned into an agent for asserting creative authorship[16] and authority, for implementing order against chaos.

Despite all their elements of excess and neo-baroque emphasis on visual language and form, therefore, these films in East European cinema are neither eccentric nor isolated examples of recycled imagery, exhausting a pre-existent set of poetic devices and well-known cultural references in ironic language games. On the one hand, I suggest, this inclination towards artificiality in the image, the challenging of the tactile and the embodied aspect of the cinematic medium in the name of visual objectification, and in the form of the shot we can isolate as an autonomous entity resembling a painting, may be linked, on a most general level, to what Mario Perniola considers – in the book leading up to his already-quoted idea about the 'sex appeal of the inorganic' – 'the Egyptian moment in art' (1995). In the opinion of the Italian philosopher, we live in an age of the civilisation of 'things' and of the 'look'; while technology seems to take over the human role in the perception of events, and thus to assume organic properties, humans deliberately treat themselves as objects. Perniola finds that in the history of humanity 'the Egyptian mummy alone evokes such a radical will to become a thing' (1995: 52), and that people today are engaged in various processes of self-mummification. He also remarks that

> *tableaux vivants*, which appear, alongside dance, to have been one of the ancient Egyptians' favourite forms of spectacle, conveyed just this form of *bewilderment and estrangement* . . . This is a more general feature of ancient Egyptian art, which rather than striving to mimic nature, seeks to create things that are independent of it, endowed with equal *dignity and autonomy*, that are as things among things. (Perniola 1995: 45–6; emphasis mine)

Accordingly, the *tableau* sequences in these films appear not only like *anamorphic* details emerging within the cinematic frame, but, as such 'things among things', to unfold from a sensuous, corporeal world as images endowed with mysterious 'dignity and autonomy'. Just think of the way Zvyagintsev's boys look at their father, trying to identify the body presented to them in the bedroom with the picture they have of him, the photograph in the attic, a look representing the perplexity of the spectators themselves comparing the cinematic shot with Mantegna's *Dead Christ*.

On the other hand, when humans are treated as pictures in these films, and flesh acquires the quality of painted texture or sculptural mass, and live bodies are objectified as static images, recalling familiar elements of famous paintings, there is also another process taking place. The fluidity of the moving image imitating the 'flow of life' becomes visibly contained within a certain aesthetic order and structure; chance movements are replaced by the predetermined spatial organisation of a particular picture frame, and by the universality of symbol and the endurance of myth. We may connect this feature of these *tableaux vivants* to what Lyotard, in his short essay 'Acinéma', called the 'figure of return', that is, 'the folding back of diversity upon an identical unity', 'the repetition and propagation of sameness' (Lyotard 1978: 55). Lyotard speaks of the structure of classical narrative films, which, despite their movements of diversity, tend to return to identical patterns or rhythms shaping films as 'productive, consumable objects' (1978: 54), as opposed to what he defines as the uncontained movement of '*jouissance*' seen as pure, 'unproductive' 'fireworks', and '*détournement*' in experimental, avant-garde art. In the references to well-known paintings we may also find a similar movement of '*rétournement*' to a fixed, familiar pattern, repeatedly 'absorbing diversity into unity', where this movement is one that folds cinema, as representation, not back onto the world (as in the case of classical narratives), but back onto the interpretive frame of visual arts, channelling cinematic diversity back to recognisable sameness in painting (thus restructuring, reproducing the cinematic image as a 'consumable object' for art connoisseur audiences). Paradoxically, at the same time this may also mean, in a way, a reversal of Lyotard's postmodern principle of replacing grand, universal narratives with small, local narratives: constituting attempts to open up these small, local, often minimalist narratives through the insertion of the 'grand image' towards equally grand (biblical, archetypal, mythical) narratives. This movement of 'return', symptomatic of nostalgia for belonging or for tradition, is characteristic of what literary theory has been describing for some time as post-postmodern art.[17]

The repeated reconnection with a universal cultural heritage of 'grand images' (of Western European painting) harnesses their power to coagulate (equally well-known, allegorical) narratives around them, and instead of acting as a disruption, a pause within the flow of narration, the *tableau vivant* becomes the prototype of other repetitions and the focal point of circular movements not so much constructing a unique linear narrative as offering a blueprint for a 'big picture', a comprehensive and suggestive vision of the world (reinforced by the recurring mythological themes of the genesis or end of the world, the loss of Paradise, archetypal stories of the act of sacrifice, and so on). All of Pálfi's idiosyncrasies and *jouissant* 'fireworks' in *Taxidermia* 'return' to order and to what Lyotard calls 'good form' in the symmetry of the timeless triptych structure (where each historical part constructs a grotesque model for the world, birth and creation being at the core of each of them) and in the final display of the body as archaic torso. Zvyagintsev's *The Return* constructs a circular metanarrative, ritualising the passage from image to body, and back to image, while in the case of *The Banishment* – from which Zvyagintsev deliberately removed any sign of particular place and time – not only do most of the *tableau*-like sequences present grids delimiting pictures within pictures, thus unfolding from parts assembled as a puzzle, but the whole film is presented as an enigma where the viewer should labour on the reconstruction of the whole, big picture, just like the children who reassemble pieces of the reproduction of Da Vinci's painting.

While the narratives present the failure of their characters to become heroes of mythical proportion, the films themselves can be viewed as metafictional allegories of this very urge for reconstruction, reinstatement, and re-embodiment of myths. By repeatedly showing us bodies dying into art, and ideas reified as images, these films present us with uncanny rituals of 'becoming an image', with a yearning for a reintegration into something universal and lasting, surrendering to the 'sex appeal of the inorganic'. At the same time, however, along with this movement towards objectification, circular structures and stasis, the *tableau vivant* in these films also performs, paradoxically, a movement of '*détournement*' by consistently counterpointing the inherent aestheticism of the *tableau* constructions with a subversive emphasis on bodies and senses,[18] establishing – in Perniola's words, as mentioned in the motto (2004: 1) – a fragile alliance between 'the most detached abstraction and the most unrestrained excitement'.

This work was supported by a grant from the Romanian Ministry of National Education, CNCS – UEFISCDI, project number PN-II-ID-PCE-2012-4-0573.

NOTES

1. Here are some of the volumes which contain analyses focusing on such topics: *East European Cinemas* (2005) and *A Companion to Eastern European Cinemas* (2012), both edited by Anikó Imre; Rosalind Galt, *The New European Cinema: Redrawing the Map* (2006); Luisa Rivi, *European Cinema after 1989: Cultural Identity and Transnational Production* (2007); Ewa Mazierska, *European Cinema and Intertextuality: History, Memory and Politics* (2011); Aga Skrodzka, *Magic Realist Cinema in East Central Europe* (2012); *Postcolonial Approaches to Eastern European Cinema: Portraying Neighbours on Screen* (2014), edited by Ewa Mazierska, Lars Kristensen, and Eva Näripea; *European Cinema after the Wall: Screening East–West Mobility* (2014) edited by Leen Engelen and Kris Van Heuckelom; *East, West and Centre: Reframing post-1989 European Cinema* (2015), edited by Michael Gott, Todd Herzog et al.
2. The term was coined by François Jost (1990), who, in his eponymous essay, outlined different ways in which, in certain films, the screen can be used in a similar way to the canvas of a painter, and cinematic reconstructions of paintings can be incorporated.
3. Films labelled by this pair of terms have generated a series of heated debates over the last decades. See a comprehensive overview of related publications in the blog Film Studies For Free, managed by Catherine Grant: <http://filmstudiesforfree.blogspot.ro/2013/04/a-long-hard-look-at-slow-cinema-studies.html> (last accessed 10 May 2015).
4. See a recent focus on such experimental films which operate with pictures that barely move in Justin Remes' book *Motion(less) Pictures: The Cinema of Stasis* (2015).
5. Pálfi even incorporated some of Szöllősi's creations directly in the final art gallery scene.
6. See <http://incidentmag.com/issue-1/critical-essays/performative-models/> (last accessed 10 May 2015). We can also note here the long tradition in theorising the image connected to the idea of death and the dead body: from Régis Debray's (1992) idea of the image as a 'domesticated terror' (the prototype of which is the Egyptian mummification of the body, an opposition to the decomposition of the body in death through its recomposition as an image), to Barthes's or Bazin's views of photography as death mask.
7. Félix Lajkó brings a set of complex associations to the role (being an artist whose art constantly moves from ethnic specificity towards universally recognisable patterns). A former child prodigy, he has become known as a world music virtuoso with an air of mysticism and an intensive style of playing the violin and the zither. His repertoire includes a mixture of almost anything, from folk music to rock, classical music and jazz improvisations.

8. See a more detailed examination of Tarr's photofilmic gesture of freezing live figures into images in my chapter 'Figurations of the Photofilmic: Stillness versus Motion – Stillness in Motion', in the volume *Photofilmic Images in Contemporary Art and Visual Culture* (2015).
9. The English term (and spelling) used as the title of the Hungarian film already suggests a more universal and detached view of the subject.
10. Spectators can merely speculate as to whether he has been in jail, has fought as a soldier in the Afghan war, or has just neglected his family for several years.
11. Ten years after Zvyagintsev made this film, Mantegna's original painting itself underwent a much debated, 'cinematic' reframing: the Pinacoteca di Brera in Milan, which owns Mantegna's masterpiece, commissioned the Italian film director Ermanno Olmi to devise a new display for the painting. Through the removal of the original frame and the placing of the painting in a light box embedded in a black wall, hung low at about the level of a visitor's waist, *The Lamentation over the Dead Christ* became part of an art installation emphasising both the theatricality of the scene within a screening-room-like space, and the translucent, photographic qualities of the monochrome picture. Compared to a more traditional museum setting, Zvyagintsev's *tableau vivant* sequence appears in an even more meaningful relationship to this particular display, which already seems to transform Mantegna's painting into a photographic *tableau*, and puzzles viewers, who can no longer tell whether they are in the company of an original or a high-resolution digital reproduction.
12. Accordingly, Zvyagintsev's film can be interpreted as a parable of post-Soviet Russia, which, having lost its great historical father figures of undisputed authority, has to cope both with their loss and with the 'return' of such figures in different forms, only to repeatedly experience their inadequacy and unreliability.
13. As many reviewers have noted, this is emphasised by the fact that the woman is called Vera (the word 'vera' meaning 'faith' in Russian).
14. Jancsó's stylised parables and highly artificial visual style are usually invoked in connection with these Hungarian directors' preference for the allegorical mode, and Tarkovsky or Bergman are usually cited as precursors of Zvyagintsev (who himself notes the even more determining influence of Antonioni instead).
15. 'All third-world texts are necessarily . . . allegorical, and in a very specific way: they are to be read as what I will call national allegories', he contends, abolishing 'the radical split between the private and the public, between the poetic and the political . . . The story of the private individual destiny is always an allegory of the embattled situation of the public third-world culture and society' (Jameson 1986: 69).
16. The paraphrases and reproductions of well-known paintings prove to be just the right 'double edged sword' in the hands of these authors: they appear in a unique and original form through their corporeal and contextual appearance, while they also strongly anchor the cinematic image within a familiar body of Christian imagery.
17. See a good summary of these ideas in the foreword to the volume *Postmodernism and After: Visions and Revisions* (Rudaitytė, 2008), and also in *Literature after Postmodernism* (Huber, 2014).
18. In an earlier version of this text published in *Acta Universitatis Sapientiae: Film and Media Studies*, 9 (2015), with the title 'The Tableau Vivant as a "Figure of Return" in Contemporary East European Cinema', I have argued that the choice of art-historical references (to pre-modern rather than modernist, abstract artworks) is also relevant in foregrounding the sensual, disquieting aspects of these *tableaux*.

WORKS CITED

Baucom, Caitlin (2014), 'Performative Models', <http://incidentmag.com/issue-1/critical-essays/performative-models/> (last accessed 15 January 2015).
Bradshaw, Peter (2007), 'Taxidermia', *The Guardian*, 13 July, <http://www.theguardian.com/film/2007/jul/13/comedy.drama> (last accessed 15 January 2015).
Debray, Régis (1992), *Vie et mort de l'image, une histoire du regard en Occident*, Paris: Bibliothèque des Idées, Gallimard.
Engelen, Leen, and Kris Van Heuckelom (eds) (2014), *European Cinema after the Wall: Screening East–West Mobility*, Lanham, MD: Rowman & Littlefield.
Galt, Rosalind (2006), *The New European Cinema: Redrawing the Map*, New York: Columbia University Press.
Gott, Michael, Todd Herzog (eds) (2015), *East, West and Centre: Reframing post-1989 European Cinema*, Edinburgh: Edinburgh University Press.
Halle, Randall (2010), 'Offering Tales They Want to Hear: Transnational European Film Funding as Neo-Orientalism', in Rosalind Galt and Karl Schoonover (eds), *Global Art Cinema: New Theories and Histories*, Oxford: Oxford University Press, pp. 303–20.
Huber, Irmtraud (2014), *Literature after Postmodernism*, London: Palgrave Macmillan.
Imre, Anikó (ed.) (2005), *East European Cinemas*, New York: Routledge.
Imre, Anikó (ed.) (2012), *A Companion to Eastern European Cinemas*, Chichester: Wiley-Blackwell.
Jameson, Frederic (1986), 'Third-World Literature in the Era of Multinational Capitalism', *Social Text*, 15, 65–88.
Jost, François (1990), 'Le Picto-film', in Raymond Bellour (ed.), *Cinéma et peinture*, Paris: PUF, pp. 109–22.
Lyotard, Jean-François (1978), 'Acinéma', *Wide Angle* 2, 52–9.
Mazierska, Ewa (2011), *European Cinema and Intertextuality: History, Memory and Politics*, New York and London: Palgrave Macmillan.
Mazierska, Ewa, Lars Kristensen, and Eva Näripea (eds) (2014), *Postcolonial Approaches to Eastern European Cinema: Portraying Neighbours on Screen*, New York: I. B. Tauris.
Perniola, Mario (1995), *Enigmas: The Egyptian Moment in Society and Art*, London: Verso.
Perniola, Mario (2004), *The Sex Appeal of the Inorganic: Philosophies of Desire in the Modern World*, London and New York: Bloomsbury.
Pethő, Ágnes (2015), 'Figurations of the Photofilmic: Stillness versus Motion – Stillness in Motion', in Alexander Streitberger and Brianne Caitlin Cohen (eds), *Photofilmic Images in Contemporary Art and Visual Culture*, Leuven: Leuven University Press, pp. 221–43.
Peucker, Brigitte (2007), *The Material Image: Art and the Real in Film*, Stanford: Stanford University Press.
Remes Justin (2015), *Motion(less) Pictures: The Cinema of Stasis*, New York: Columbia University Press.
Rivi, Luisa (2007), *European Cinema after 1989: Cultural Identity and Transnational Production*, New York: Palgrave Macmillan.
Rudaitytė, Regina (ed.) (2008), *Postmodernism and After: Visions and Revisions*, Newcastle upon Tyne, Cambridge Scholars Publishing.
Satz, Aura (2009), 'Tableaux Vivants: Inside the Statue', in Aura Satz and Jon Wood (eds), *Articulate Objects: Voice, Sculpture and Performance*, Oxford and New York: Peter Lang, pp. 157–83.

Shaviro, Steven (2012), 'Body Horror and Post-Socialist Cinema: György Pálfi's *Taxidermia*', in Anikó Imre (ed.), *A Companion to Eastern European Cinemas*, Chichester: Wiley-Blackwell, pp. 25–41.
Skrodzka, Aga (2012), *Magic Realist Cinema in East Central Europe*, Edinburgh: Edinburgh University Press.
Xavier, Ismail (2007), 'Historical Allegory', in Toby Miller and Robert Stam (eds), *A Companion to Film Theory*, Oxford: Blackwell, pp. 333–62.

Index

4, 19, 166–83

Adorno, Theodor, 130n
Adrienn Pál, 70, 77–81
Afrić, Vjekoslav, 139, 140
Against Gods (Przeciw Bogom), 222, 225, 229–30, 231–2, 233–5, 237
Agamben, Giorgio, 69, 77, 200
Aleksandrov, Grigorii, 91
Alive (Zhivoi), 95
Allen, D. C., 160
And Woman . . . Was Created (Et Dieu . . . créa la femme), 118
Angelopoulos, Theo, 67, 68, 86n
Ashes and Diamonds (Popiół i diament) 32, 36–8, 40, 41, 42, 44, 45–6
Astronauts, The (Les Astronautes), 118

Babel, Isaak, 96
Bach, Johann Sebastian, 154, 164n
Backman Rogers, Anna, 7
Back to Life Again (Życie raz jeszcze), 224
Bacon, Frances, 47–8n, 79, 82, 85
Badiou, Alain, 118
Bakhtin Mikhail, 9, 17, 89–90, 215–20
Balabanov, Aleksei, 94
Balázs, Béla, 7, 22n
Balsom, Erika, 57
Banach, Andrzej, 129–30
Banishment, The (Izgnanie), 248–9, 252
Bardot, Brigitte, 117
Barefoot, Guy, 114, 130
Barker, Jennifer M., 14, 192–3, 203, 211
Barthes, Roland, 73, 83, 253n
Bataille, Georges, 127

Baudrillard, Jean, 20, 171–2, 177, 179, 181–2, 183, 208, 215–20
Beast, The (La bête), 116–17, 122–9
Bede, 154
Behind the Convent Walls (Interno di un convento), 113, 117, 123, 126–8
Beksiński, Zdzisław, 129
Belle noiseuse, La, 119
Bellour, Raymond, 72, 73
Bemberg, María Luisa, 150
Bencze, Ferenc, 53
Benjamin, Walter, 114, 183
Berling, Peter, 54–5
Berry, Ellen, 8
Bersani, Leo, 167, 170, 182, 183
Bieńczyk, Marek, 35
Bíró, Yvette, 68, 69, 81
Blanche, 113, 115, 122, 124, 126–7
Blind Chance (Przypadek), 222
Body without Soul (Tělo bez duše), 146, 151, 153, 156–8
Bondarchuk, Fedor, 95
Borowczyk's Dr Jekyll, 114
Borowczyk, Walerian 10, 18, 113–31
Bourdieu, Pierre, 4–5
Bradley, J. F. N., 147
Brando, Marlon, 32
Branice, Ligia, 118, 125
Bresson, Robert, 58, 67
Bridge on the River Kwai, The, 138
Bunzl, Matti, 149, 151
Butler, Judith, 6, 98

Caes, Christopher, 43
Čap, František, 133
Cargo 200 (Gruz 200), 94

Case of Pilot Maresz, The (Sprawa Pilota Maresza), 222, 224–5, 228–9, 237
Céline and Julie Go Boating (Céline et Julie vont en bateau), 119
Chabrol, Claude, 118
Charcot, Jean-Martin, 33, 40
Chiaureli, Mikheil, 92
Chion, Michel, 57–8
Circus (Tsirk), 91
Clark, Kenneth, 89–90
Clark, Larry, 153
Clifford, James, 149, 152
Coach to Vienna (Kočár do Vídně), 198–201
Coates, Paul, 42
Collins, Daniel, 83
Colombetti, Giovanna, 46
Courtine, Jean-Jacques, 11
Cranes Are Flying, The (Letiat zhuravli), 93
Cronenberg, David, 327
Cybulski, Zbigniew, 32, 36–8, 44

Da Vinci, Leonardo, 247, 248, 249
Damned Roads (Baza ludzi umarłych), 117
de Lauretis, Teresa, 7
de Mandiargues, André Pieyre, 118
de Villiers, Nicholas, 146, 151–5, 157
Dealer, 69, 77, 84, 245
Dean, James, 32
del Toro, Guillermo, 160–1
Deleuze, Gilles, 11, 16, 54, 65, 79, 82, 84, 85
Delta, 69, 75, 81, 244
Demon, The, 100–4
Didi-Huberman, Georges, 40, 43
Długołęcka, Grażyna, 115
'Dolgushov's Death', 96
Donne, John, 160
Douglas, Mary, 59, 62
Duras, Marguerite, 73, 80
Dworkin, Andrea, 121, 131
Dyer, Peter John, 32
Dyer, Richard, 139
Dykhovichnyi, Ivan, 99

Easthope, Antony, 89, 90–1, 94, 95, 96, 97
Edelman, Lee, 182, 184
Eden and after (L'Eden et après), 148
Eisenstein, Sergei, 7, 12, 22n, 42–3, 201
Emmanuelle 2, 130
Emmanuelle 5, 113, 116, 122–3
Etkind, Alexander, 3, 169
Etkind, Efim, 169, 184

Fall of Berlin, The (Padenie Berlina), 92, 99
Fisher, Jaimey, 32–3

Flanagan, Matthew, 67, 68
Fliegauf, Benedek, 67–8, 69, 74, 76, 77, 82, 84, 245
Forefathers' Eve (Dziady), 35
Foucault, Michel, 4, 9, 78, 133
Freud, Sigmund, 4, 16, 33–4, 35, 37, 40, 91, 166
Fyodorov, Nikolai, 168, 169, 170, 174, 181–4

Gavrin, Gustav, 134–41
General: Assassination in Gibraltar (Generał: Zamach na Gibraltarze), 222
Generation, A (Pokolenie), 32, 40–1, 42, 44, 45–6
German, Aleksei, 93
Gierek, Edward, 225–6, 230
Giotto, 123
Godard, Jean-Luc, 118–20, 129–30, 158, 240
Gomułka, Władysław, 116–17, 226
Goto, Island of Love (Goto, l'île d'amour), 115, 117, 119, 122, 126–7
Greer, Germaine, 5
Griffiths, Robin, 11, 151–2
Grodecki, Wiktor, 11, 18–19, 146–65
Grosz, Elizabeth, 3, 4, 5

Hajdu, Szabolcs, 67
Hammer and Sickle (Serp i molot), 96–100, 104–5
Hanich, Julian, 45
Haraway, Donna, 6
Hendricks, Barbara, 154
Herzog, Werner, 54
Holbein the Younger, Hans, 70, 72–5, 80–1, 83–5, 244, 245
Holland, Agnieszka, 10
Horton, Andrew J., 146

Iankovskii, Filipp, 97, 100–4
Ibroscheva, Elza, 10–11
Immoral Tales (Contes immoraux), 122
Immoral Women (Les héroïnes du mal), 117, 119, 122–3, 126, 128
Immortal Youth (Besmrtna mladost), 140
Imre, Anikó, 13, 15
Interrupted Flight (Przerwany lot), 222
Intimate Strangers (Confidences trop intimes), 182

Jagielski, Sebastian, 13
Jancsó, Miklós, 120
Janion, Maria, 31
Jazz Singer, The, 138
Jetée, la, 118

INDEX

Jędrusik, Kalina, 117
Johanna, 69, 77–81, 244
Just the Wind (Csak a szél), 69, 76–7

Kachyňa, Karel, 20, 199
Kalatozov, Mikhail, 91–2, 93
Kałużyński, Zygmunt, 116, 131
Kanal (Kanał) 32, 44, 45–6
Khrustalev, the Car! (Khrustalev, mashinu!), 93
Khrzhanovsky, Ilya, 19, 166–83
Kitliński, Tomek, 34–5
Kleist, Heinrich von, 172, 179, 184
Kocsis, Ágnes, 67–8, 77, 80, 82
Kolodny, Annette, 149
Kordian, 35
Kovács, András Bálint, 54, 57, 64, 70–1, 73
Krasiński, Zygmunt, 35
Krasznahorkai, László, 59
Kristeva, Julia, 17, 70, 73–6, 78–80, 82–5
Król, Marcin, 32
Kurz, Iwona, 36, 117

Lacan, Jacques, 39, 83, 92
Larsen, Jonas, 149, 165
Leconte, Patrice, 182
Lenica, Jan, 115–16
Lermontov, Mikhail, 101
Leszkowicz, Paweł, 34–5
Leviathan (Leviafan), 172
Life is Ours – The People from the Railway (Život je naš – Ljudi s pruge), 134–7, 143
Lipovetsky, Mark, 174, 184
Livnev, Sergei, 96–100, 104–5
'Love Letter', 22
Love Meetings, 153
Love Rites (Cérémonie d'amour), 119, 123–4, 129
Lubelski, Tadeusz, 38
Lulu, 122–3
Lyotard, Jean-François, 22, 68, 69, 70, 72, 84, 85, 251–2

Macbeth (1982), 53
Majmurek, Jakub, 128
Makavejev, Dušan, 10, 12, 22n, 115
Malczewski, Jacek, 129
Mandragora, 146, 151–2, 157, 159–61
Mantegna, Andrea, 17, 21, 70, 72, 75, 79, 81, 83–5, 244–9, 251, 254n
Marcus, Steven, 182, 184
Margherita, 123
Margin, The (La Marge/Streetwalker), 113, 118

Marker, Chris, 118, 120
Marketa Lazarová, 193–8
Marković, Mile, 134–5, 137
Markowski, Andrzej, 114
Markowski, Michał Paweł, 35, 38
Marks, Laura U., 8, 14, 15, 43, 192, 203, 207, 212, 213
Marx, Karl, 2–3, 8
Mazierska, Ewa, 116, 131, 147–8, 163–5
Mészáros, Márta, 78
Metz, Christian, 123
Mickiewicz, Adam, 31, 35, 39
Miéville, Anne-Marie, 129–30
Miller, Henry, 121–2
Miss Mary, 150, 151
Mitchell, Julia, 33, 42, 46
Monk Brne's Pupil (Bakonja fra Brne), 141–3
Moscow Parade (Prorva), 99
Moss, Kevin, 146–7, 149, 151–2, 154–5, 160–3, 165
Mozart, Wolfgang Amadeus, 147–8, 154, 164n, 180–1
Mroz, Matilda, 7, 43
Mulvey, Laura, 7, 16, 73
Mundruczó, Kornél, 67–8, 74, 79, 244
Munk, Andrzej, 117
My Life to Live (Vivre sa vie), 119, 158
My Stepbrother Frankenstein (Moi svodnyi brat Frankenshtein), 94–5

N. Rolled the Dice (N. a pris les dés), 148
Nevzorov, Aleksandr, 95–6
Night of the Bride (Noc nevěsty/The Nun's Night), 201–2
Not Angels but Angels (Anděle nejsou anděle), 146, 151, 153–4, 156–7

On the Earth and in the Sky (Na Niebie i Na Ziemi), 222, 225, 229–32, 233, 235
Oppermann, Martin, 150, 165
Orbach, Susie, 6
Oshima, Nagisa, 120
Ostrowska, Elżbieta, 14
Owen, Jonathan, 118, 131

Pálfi, György, 14, 15, 20–1, 207–21, 242–4, 249, 252
Pan's Labyrinth (Laberinto del fauno, El), 160–1
Parisi, Luciana, 6
Pasolini, Pier Paolo, 120, 153, 177
Patočka, Jan, 20, 190–1, 197–8, 204
Perniola, Mario, 239, 241, 242, 251, 253
Petelski, Czesław, 117

Pethő, Ágnes, 14, 74, 77, 126
Petőfi, Sándor, 66n
Petrović, Aleksandar, 130
Peucker, Brigitte, 241, 255
Phillips, Adam, 170, 182, 183
Pierro, Marina, 125
Pigsty (Il Porcile), 177
Pod Twoją Obronę (Sub Tuum Praesidium), 222
Pogačić, Vladimir, 134, 139
Polanski, Roman, 10, 130n
Polevoi, Boris, 92, 105
Price, Janet, 1, 5, 6
Prisoner of the Mountains (Kavkazskii plennik), 93
Proshkin, Aleksandr, 93
Proust, Marcel, 123
Ptushko, Aleksandr, 91
Purgatory (Chistilishche), 95–6
Putin, Vladimir, 105, 167, 181

Quinlivan, Davina, 57

Rancière, Jacques, 16, 54, 60, 65, 69, 76
Raphael, 123–4, 126
Red Flower, The (Crveni cvet), 137–41, 143
Reich, Wilhelm, 114, 127, 131
Return, The (Vozvrashcheniye), 74, 246–8, 249, 252
Richardson, Michael, 113
Rivette, Jacques, 118–20
Robbe-Grillet, Alain, 148
Rodowick, David, 69, 70, 72, 73, 78, 84, 85
Rogin, Michael, 138
Rohmer, Eric, 118–19
Rou, Aleksandr, 91
Rubin, Gayle S., 154, 165
Russian Revolt (Russkii bunt), 93
Ryklin, Mikhail, 171, 183, 184

Said, Edward, 149, 165
Sakwa, Richard, 11
Sátántangó, 16, 53–66
Sedgwick, Eve Kosofsky, 135
Scarry, Elaine, 169, 184
Shaviro, Steven 14, 15, 68, 86n, 207, 208, 209, 243, 249
Shildrick, Margrit, 1, 5, 6
Shilling, Chris, 4
Skalski, Stanislaw, 224
Skalski's Circus (Cyrk Skalskiego), 224
Slattery, Dennis, 46
Slavica, 139
Słowacki, Juliusz, 35, 39

Sobchack, Vivian 7, 8, 192
Sontag, Susan, 7–8, 121–2, 130n, 192
Sorokin, Vladimir, 19, 166–83
Sowa, Jan, 39
Stalin, Josef, 90, 91, 92, 98, 99, 105, 108n, 168, 224
Stallybrass, Peter, 176, 177, 184
Starowieyski, Franciszek, 129
Stein, Edith, 46
Stevenson, Robert Louis, 114, 123
Stolper, Aleksandr, 95
Story about a Real Man (Povest' o nastoiashchem cheloveke), 92, 105
Story of Sin, The (Dzieje grzechu), 113, 119–20, 123–8
Strange Case of Dr. Jekyll and Miss Osbourne, The (Jekyll et les femmes), 114, 119, 123–4, 129
Strausz, Laszlo, 15, 70, 207, 208, 209, 210, 216
Streetwalker (La Marge/ The Margin), 113, 118
Švankmajer, Jan, 12, 15, 190
Sword Bearer (Mechenosets), 97, 100–4

Tarkovsky, Andrei, 14, 239
Tarr, Béla, 13, 16, 17, 53–66, 67–74, 81–2, 245
Taxidermia, 14, 15, 20–1, 207–21, 242–3, 249, 252
Thief, The (Vor), 93
Third Part of the Night, The (Trzecia część nocy), 120
To Destroy the Pirate (Zniszczyć Pirata), 222, 226, 232–3, 235–7
Todorovskii, Valerii, 94–5
Tropic of Cancer, 121
Turin Horse, The (A torinói ló), 53, 59–60, 67, 69–74, 81, 245
Two or Three Things I Know about Her (Deux ou trois choses que je sais d'elle), 119

Uncle Žvane (Barba Žvane), 140
Under the Volcano, 65
Urry, John, 149, 165

Vadim, Roger, 118
Valerii Chkalov, 91–2
Veledinskii, Aleksandr, 95
Vermeer, Johannes, 81, 124, 244
Vidal, Belén, 72, 82, 84, 85
Villa-Lobos, Heitor, 154, 164n
Virilio, Paul 21, 222–3, 226–35, 237n, 238n
Vláčil, František, 20, 193–4

Volkman, Toby Alice, 149–50, 152
von Trier, Lars, 77

Wajda, Andrzej, 15–16, 31–3, 36–8, 40–7, 117–18
Wakamiya, Lisa Ryoko, 166–7, 184
Warhol, Andy, 153
Werckmeister Harmonies (Werckmeister harmóniák), 62
White, Allon, 176, 177, 184
Widdis, Emma, 14
Williams, Bruce, 150, 165
Williams, Linda, 7, 121, 130–1, 158, 165

Wojtkiewicz, Witold, 129
Wolff, Larry, 147, 165
Wyatt, Justin, 136, 137

Zanussi, Krzysztof, 118
Zaraï, Rika, 148
Żeromski, Stefan, 120, 122
Zhdanov, Andrei, 188, 203–4
Žižek, Slavoj, 38–9
Żuławski, Andrzej, 120
Zvyagintsev, Andrei, 74, 172, 246–9, 252
Zwierzchowski, Piotr, 224

EU representative:
Easy Access System Europe
Mustamäe tee 50, 10621 Tallinn, Estonia
Gpsr.requests@easproject.com

www.ingramcontent.com/pod-product-compliance
Lightning Source LLC
Chambersburg PA
CBHW062125300426
44115CB00012BA/1810